FOR MARCY

HANG ON TO THIS
BOOK - IT WILL BE
A FAMILY HEIRLOOM
ONE DAY,

BEST WISHES

Albut S Shul
11/01/06

DEAR MARCY & FAMILY
HOPE YOU ENJOY THIS BOOK
ESPECIALLY PAGE - 34. 38 -

LOVE.

GRANDPA BOB

The Troopers Are Coming II

New York State Troopers
1943-1985

by

Albert S. Kurek - NYSP Retired

Bloomington, IN  Milton Keynes, UK

authorHOUSE®

AuthorHouse™
1663 Liberty Drive, Suite 200
Bloomington, IN 47403
www.authorhouse.com
Phone: 1-800-839-8640

AuthorHouse™ UK Ltd.
500 Avebury Boulevard
Central Milton Keynes, MK9 2BE
www.authorhouse.co.uk
Phone: 08001974150

First published by AuthorHouse 10/3/2006

ISBN: 1-4259-5674-2 (sc)

Library of Congress Control Number: 2006908296

Printed in the United States of America
Bloomington, Indiana

This book is printed on acid-free paper.

TABLE OF CONTENTS

INTRODUCTION

The outbreak of World War II resulted in a serious drain of Division manpower with 305 of its 1000 members placed on military leave. Six members were killed while on duty with the armed forces. Troopers were asked to do more with less and they rose to the occasion. Thanks to the war and Divisions role, many technological improvements were made.

Communication links via teletype with the FBI, War and Navy Departments were installed. A mobile radio transmitting station was put into service and the first two-way radios were placed in Division cars and installations on Long Island. The State Police Laboratory acquired a portable X-ray machine to facilitate bomb detection. These services were utilized to their fullest.

When the war came to an end in 1945, only 110 men of the 305 who left for military duty returned to the Division for duty.

Fuel rationing and travel restrictions placed limitations on motor vehicle traffic with only necessary travel allowed. At wars end, the unrestricted traffic increase brought new problems to highway safety and was the primary concern to the State Police. Traffic congestion on summer weekends had reached the saturation point. The era of commuter travel came into play. More and better highways along with increased traffic enforcement were a priority. 1957 brought proof that a nationwide network of organized crime existed when troopers uncovered a conference of organized crime leaders in Apalachin, New York. This led to another area of selective law enforcement.

The 1950s brought a hint of the illegal use of drugs. In 1955, Division for the first time conducted a cooperative investigation with Federal law enforcement agents that resulted in the arrests of 17 "pushers" in Suffolk County and four distributors in New York City.

The 1960s brought social unrest with "baby boomers" openly rebelling against society and those who represented its authority. Police at the same time had to deal with an increase in violent crimes. The widespread acceptance of recreational drugs were in high demand bringing untold profits to organized crime.

In 1965, troopers entered the computer age. Computers made rapid communications a reality saving countless hours in time and manpower.

The use of radar for speed enforcement increased throughout the decade. In 1962, radar accounted for 57.4% of all speeding arrests. In 1968, the first VASCAR units were placed in service to enhance the Division's speed enforcement capabilities.

Drunk driving increased dramatically during the 1960s, as did the Division's efforts to identify and apprehend drivers operating motor vehicles under the influence of alcohol. The use of Breathalyzers was expanded.

The 1970s proved to be one of the most turbulent periods in United States History. The social unrest that began in the 1960s peaked in the 1970s. Terrorism, both domestic and international was rampant. Terrorists and even national governments adopted hostage taking as a preferred tool for pressing their causes with criminals also adopting this tactic for their own purposes. Inflation and unemployment resulted in a drastic increase in criminal activity.

The 1980s dawned with international attention focused on the New York State Police as the Division provided security and traffic control for the 1980 Winter Olympics in Lake Placid. Thanks to extensive preparation and training, the performance of the State Police was nearly flawless.

One of the greatest challenges in the 1980s was the increased illegal drug use and trafficking, particularly in cocaine and crack. A new threat now appeared with criminal cartels controlling the cocaine trade.

Hopefully, the reader will come away with a better understanding of the New York State Police and the manner in which Division adjusted to the continued new threats that came with social change and technology.

The contents of this book are as historically accurate, as could be determined through my several years of research. My intent is to provide the reader with a more detailed and different view of the troopers and their history. The events described are incidents that actually occurred, however, in many instances, case dispositions could not be determined due to poor or inadequate record keeping, lost files, destroyed or misfiled documents and human error. This publication covers the years 1943 to 1985 with empahsis on occurrences and events that took place in Western New York State.

Unless otherwise indicated, the majority of articles in this publication were found in archived Batavia Daily Newspapers located at the Genesee County, New York History Department, Batavia, New York.

This book would not have been possible without the assistance of the many men and women who provided access to library records, court records, vital statistics, scrapbooks, newspaper files and personal interviews. My heartfelt thanks to my wife Anne for her patience, support, and understanding. Many thanks to John Sikora, Editor, Batavia, N.Y. and Keith Hammond, Technical Advisor, Pembroke Enterprises, Corfu, N.Y. for their many hours of personal assistance and guidance.

BOOK I — ADMINISTRATIVE

MANUALS AND GUIDES

RULES AND REGULATIONS

The first handbook of Rules and Regulations prescribing the conduct of all troopers was submitted and approved by the Governor in 1945 with copies issued to all members. The document covered every thing from the wearing of the uniform to rules of conduct both on and off duty.

EVIDENCE GUIDE

A Troopers Evidence Guide was prepared and distributed to all members during 1945. The guide outlined the facilities of the State Police Laboratory and the manner in which evidence should be safeguarded and forwarded for examination and analysis. Copies were sent to police agencies throughout the state. The Evidence Guide was received with such interest that a second edition was printed in 1946. The US Army, responsible for training police in South Korea, was given permission to reprint the guide in the Korean language.

SUMMONS BOOK

A new traffic summons and summons book were placed in use during 1945. It was made of a heavy black plastic that was durable enough, that a summons could be written without first removing it from the holder. It replaced the double snap leather summons holder.

TROOPERS MANUAL

The trooper's manual last printed in 1930 was reprinted in1947. In 1964, the updated 1500 page trooper's manual designed to provide guidelines for all persons associated with the state police were distributed. It contained techniques, policy, instructions, procedures and rules and regulations of the Division. It was considered the most comprehensive publication of its type in the world.

TROOPER MAGAZINE

In May 1963, the first issue of "The Trooper" brought to reality a personnel publication for all employees of the division. It was felt that an internal magazine would serve to better acquaint division members with informal news, individual activity and bring everyone greater knowledge of the Division and its people. It was by and about members. The magazine was published monthly from articles sent by members in the various stations and offices. The Chief Editor from its inception until 1969 was Louis B. Van Dyck Jr. He resigned to take a position with the NYS Education Department. His successor was Kurt Wachenheim, a member of the staff from the Albany Knickerbocker News.

The cost of printing the Trooper magazine for the fiscal year 1972-73 was $6,365.00. 6500 copies were printed monthly at a cost of less than nine cents a copy. In addition to active and former members, a copy was distributed to judges and media around the state.

Due to budgetary constraints, the magazine was printed six times a year rather than monthly effective with the March-April 1976 issue.

NEW YORK STATE
TROOPERS VEHICLE
WEIGHING MANUAL

New York State Troopers

RADAR MANUAL

STATE OF NEW YORK

THIS IS NOT A CHECK

EMPLOYEE'S STATEMENT OF SALARY AND DEDUCTIONS

LINE NUMBER	GROSS SALARY	RETIREMENT ARREARS	BONDS	STATE HEALTH INS.	SOC. SEC. TAX	DUES	GARNISHEE
533	174 04			4 38	4 35	25	2 68
INS.	105 98	24 35	10 08	30 60			21 97
	NET AMOUNT	RETIREMENT NORMAL	LOANS	MAINT.	INS.	DUES	FEDERAL TAX

MO.	DAY	YR.
6	03	59

FOR PAY PERIOD ENDED

DETACH BEFORE CASHING AND RETAIN AS EVIDENCE OF YOUR SALARY AND DEDUCTIONS

ARTHUR LEVITT, STATE COMPTROLLER

HOURS OF DUTY

The troopers are a quasi-military group recognized as an outstanding, fearless, efficient and unbiased law enforcement agency. Officers always expected more of their men than would be required elsewhere. Troopers worked anywhere from 109 to 126 hours a week. They were required to remain at their duty station in a standby reserve status in the event they were needed. There was no overtime.

A day off was from 3:00PM one day until 10:00 AM the next day. This hardly gave troopers any time with their families, unless they lived near the station. Shifts were twelve-hours with two nights off a week, but you were required to live at the barracks in case of an emergency.

Hours of continuous duty on investigations pushed troopers beyond their abilities. Lack of sleep resulted in accidents, as troopers fell asleep at the wheel or motorcycle. In many cases, this resulted in death. No one would admit falling asleep for fear of having his job terminated. During the period 1921 to 1954, twenty-five troopers were killed in automobile accidents.

60 - HOUR WORK WEEK

Division headquarters recognizing that their scheduling requirements were not in line with a changing pattern of society took action to alter the troopers work schedule. Effective June 28, 1958, Troopers started a five-day workweek. (12 hours a day with the remaining 12 hours in an "on call" status.) It called for two 24-hour passes a week in lieu of the current 21-hour pass per week. The average workweek was 68 hours allowing for holiday time. In addition the per diem rate was increased from $4.50 to $5.25. Under normal circumstances, troopers would not be on the road for more than 8 hours of the 12-hour tour. Although on call, troopers were allowed to go home as long as their location was known and they could return to duty within 30 minutes. Still, no overtime.

In 1960, a trooper's probationary status was changed from six months to one year.

42 1/2 - HOUR WORK WEEK

Thanks to the initiative and streamlining of the State Police by Superintendent Arthur Cornelius, the first 42 1/2-hour workweek began on May 1, 1963. The previous 60-hour workweek consisted of duty shifts from 8:00 to 8:00 with two days off weekly. Until 1962, troopers were required to stay at the various stations. The change resulted in three basic tours covering periods of 11:00PM – 7:30AM (A Shift), 7 AM to 3:30PM (B Shift) and 3:00PM to 11:30PM (C Shift). The basic workweek was designed to be five days a week, 8-½ hour elapsed hours with ½ hour for meals. Communication personnel worked a straight eight-hour day with meals taken while working. Division Headquarters personnel worked from 8:30AM to 5:30AM with an hour for a mid-day meal. BCI members worked basically the B or C shifts. Field members were given one additional day off in every 29-day period in lieu of legal holidays. There was no overtime until 1964. Troopers were required to take compensatory time, usually at a time designated by the station sergeant.

One of the champions for a forty-hour workweek was 85-year-old George Fletcher Chandler. He also advocated a 12 Troop Plan that would mean smaller areas of patrol for the same number of men. He advocated the closing of stations that required a deskman who could be put on patrol. He also suggested that the term of Superintendent be a fixed five-year term. He felt it would take appointments out of the political arena.

TROOPER SYMBOL
During 1966, a head & shoulders sketch of a trooper was first used as an identifiable State Police symbol. It was first used on Division printing and in telephone directories to aid in locating State Police phone numbers.

STATE PENSION CHANGED
During 1969, the state police pension plan was revised by legislative action that implemented a negotiated agreement between the state Office of Employee Relations and Police Benevolent Association. Changes called for a mandatory retirement age fixed at 55 with goal's to be reached by 1974. It also permitted retirement at half pay after twenty years of service instead of twenty-five years and provided for additional benefits for each year of service between the 20th and 30th years. Previously, no benefits accrued after 25 years.

The move toward the 55-year retirement began in 1969 with those who reached age 60 or were over that age. Each year thereafter, the retirement was mandatory one year earlier. Among those reaching first year mandatory retirement were Deputy Superintendent Albin S. Johnson, Major Harold T. Muller and Deputy Chief Inspector John J. Quinn.

MINORITIES

RECRUITMENT – 1979
During the 1970s, efforts were made to recruit qualified minorities to apply for positions with the state police. In 1973, the first female troopers were accepted as recruits. Despite the division's efforts, the Federal Court in 1979 ordered specific percentages of minorities and women to be hired until the workforce composition reflected the State's racial composition. Hiring began in 1979 with each academy class being composed of 50% white males, 40% minority males and 10% females.

FIRST AFRICAN AMERICAN TROOPERS
Prior to the mid 1950s, the New York State Police force was not a welcome place for African Americans. Segregation was still practiced with African Americans treated as second-class citizens. My research found that the first African American to serve in Troop "A" was Charles E. Baugh who enlisted in October 1955 and resigned on February 21, 1956 for marital reasons. He was not however the first African American to serve in the state police. According to Lieutenant Pamela Shelton Sharpe, Division Headquarters, that distinction went to Frederick Robinson who enlisted at Troop "C" in 1953. He was the trailblazer that cracked the ice for those who followed.

The second trooper to serve in Troop "A" was Louis Mentis who enlisted on May 22, 1958 at Batavia, N.Y. He was re-assigned to Troop "D" Oneida, N.Y. in January 1959 where he served until January 25, 1966, when he resigned. Investigator Karl Limner recalled an incident involving Mentis while at Batavia. Trooper Mentis was instructed to dress in civilian clothing and was given an assignment to follow a Buffalo bookmaker who came to Batavia on a regular basis. Mentis followed the man diligently for an entire day noting every location the man stopped. Eventually, the bookie returned to Buffalo, N.Y. twenty-five miles away where he entered a tavern. Undaunted, Trooper Mentis also went into the all white tavern. He was confronted by the bartender who told him he would not be served and told him to leave. Mentis displayed his trooper badge that the bartender kept while he called Buffalo Police. Mentis waited patiently. When the police arrived, Mentis was arrested, for impersonating a police officer. Because he was a black man, no one believed that he was a trooper.

He was jailed until the following morning, when Investigator Robert Powell traveled to the Buffalo City Lock Up to verify his position as a trooper and have him released.

The first African American Trooper from Genesee County was Louis P. Steverson of Leroy, N.Y. He enlisted in 1960 serving until 1989, when he retired to taking a position with the New York State Ethics Commission. He rose to the rank of Investigator and was assigned to Troop "E" Canandaigua and Division Headquarters, Albany, N.Y.

The first African America female trooper in the state was Pamela T. Shelton of Buffalo, N.Y. She enlisted on February 20, 1978 and after completing basic training, was assigned to SP Batavia patrol. In 1984, she accepted a transfer to Albany where she researched and wrote the first official version of the New York State Police History. Assigned at Division Headquarters, she was promoted to Technical Lieutenant, a rank she still holds today. She recalled that the most difficult thing for her as a trooper was the difficulty she encountered trying to balance a career and family life. She was divorced with sole custody of her only child, Eric. Another problem encountered was the attitude from fellow troopers and the public in accepting females in what was perceived as a position for males only. She sensed that a feeling existed that a woman was not capable of doing what had always been a mans work.

WOMAN TROOPERS - 1973
For the first time in it's history, the New York State Police admitted female officers to their ranks. 9000 applicants including 459 women took the March 1973 competitive examination. Five women were selected from the final female pool of 145.

In August 1973, Superintendent William E. Kirwan notified the five females of their appointments. They were Carol A. Desell, age 22, Watervliet, N.Y., Maureen P. Gordinier, 24, Rochester, N.Y., Regina M. Roberts, 22, Syracuse, N.Y., Pamela Bowers, 24, Bloomington, N.Y. and Carole J. Johnston, Geneva, N.Y. Kirwan explained that the troopers were able to become co-ed as the result of a federal directive banning sex-discrimination and legislative approval to fill 230 vacancies. (Not following federal guidelines would have resulted in the federal government withholding funds for various state projects.) They were sworn in on September 6, 1973 at the State Police Academy prior to the commencement of 16 weeks training. Kirwan stated that their training would be the same as their male recruit counterparts. All except Bowers graduated from the Academy. Commencement exercises took place on January 11, 1974. Starting salary at the time was $10,000.00 per annum.

The appointment was delayed briefly when Thomas Button, age 21, an Albion, N.Y. Village Policeman filed suit in Supreme Court stating he was the victim of reverse discrimination and was bumped off the appointment list although he had earned a higher score on the examination than did the four women. The suit was dismissed. Button was appointed to the State Police on September 14, 1973 as the result of another recruit dropping out creating a vacancy.

On patrol, the female troopers wore trooper gray slacks and jackets during winter months and skirts and jackets during summer months.

They were treated as any male trooper. Initial skepticism greeted the four women. Many male troopers felt female troopers could not measure up physically because of the nature of the job. As in any business, job or profession, the lady troopers eventually proved their worth and in many instances, did the job much better than many of their male counterparts.

In July 1979, Regina M. Robbins was the first female promoted to the rank of Sergeant and on July 17,1980, was appointed station commander at SP Pulaski.

Carol J. Johnston was the first female trooper appointed to the Bureau of Criminal Investigation on July 17, 1980.

CHARLES E. BAUGH - 1955

BUILDINGS
In May 1964, Division Headquarters was moved from Downtown Albany to its new permanent quarters in the Public Security Building on the State Campus, Washington Avenue, Albany, N.Y. The Pistol Permit Bureau and Scientific Laboratory were also re-located there.

CLOSING OF MESS FACILITIES
In a cost effective meeting held with Division of Budget, it was determined that the mess facilities at Batavia Headquarters would be closed no later than July 1, 1957. Only necessary food purchases were permitted and arrangements made to find suitable employment for those whose jobs would be terminated.

In a memorandum from Captain J.P. Ronan, the Batavia Kitchen was officially closed on June 13, 1959. The Kitchen help, with the exception of Mrs. Beatrice M. O'Grady were carried on vacation until July 1, 1959. Mrs. O'Grady continued her employment at Troop Headquarters, as janitress. The closing affected the following employees:

William J. Rodgers, 7 Summit St., Leroy, N.Y. – Cook – since January 30, 1956

Beatrice M. O'Grady, 132 Harvester Avenue, Batavia, N.Y. – Assistant Cook since May 24, 1942

Gladys A. Peio, 105 Ellsworth Ave., Batavia, N.Y. – Kitchen Helper since April 1, 1946

Agnes A. Ray, 130 Bank Street, Batavia, N.Y. – Kitchen Helper since August 1, 1947

TROOP "E", CANANDAIGUA, N.Y. - 1967
The new Troop "E" became operational in July 1967. Headquartered in a new facility near Canandaigua, N.Y., it served the Counties of Monroe, Livingston, Steuben that had been a part of Troop "A" and Wayne, Ontario, Seneca, Yates & Cayuga that had been a part of Troop "D".

TROOP "F", MIDDLETOWN, N.Y. - 1968
The new Troop "F" was activated on August 12, 1968. A new troop Headquarters was located at Middletown, N.Y. and served Sullivan, Rockland, Orange, Ulster and Green County. As a result, all of Troop "K" was now located on the east side of the Hudson River.

NEW TROOP "A' BARRACKS
On March 30, 1976, the troopers relocated to their new modern barracks on West Saile Drive just North of the City of Batavia. It was a sprawling one floor plan building shaped like an H with office's, a reception area and communications center in the front. The center housed the patrol office, lunchroom, sleeping quarters and classroom with the rear portion containing a garage and storage area. It replaced the original three-story building located on East Main Street at the Batavia City line. The building is no longer in existence; only the original garage gives silent testament of time gone by.

SP MANHATTAN

SP Manhattan was opened in 1976 serving New York City. A BCI Captain was in charge of 15 Investigators who conducted criminal investigations and 4 troopers who served as a warrant squad. Today, it is known as Troop "NYC".

SATELLITE OFFICES

Due to a national fuel shortage in 1977, the Division initiated a satellite office program. It was a measure that kept troopers closely assigned to their posts while saving on fuel costs. 34 offices were initially established statewide growing to 60 during the next two years. In Troop "A", offices were established at Leroy, Gowanda, Fillmore, Delevan, Grand Island, East Aurora, Newstead, Holland, Ellicottville and Alden.

PARKWAY POLICE ASSIMILATED

Troop "L" was created on December 31, 1979, when NYS Parkways on Long Island were assimilated along with 193 Parkway Officers who opted to join the State Police. Also coming under the State Police jurisdiction were the Palisades Parkway, Niagara Frontier Parkway and the Lake Ontario State Parkway. The new troop was under the command of Major James A. Kaljian and was headquartered at Islip Terrace with stations at Valley Stream, Bethpage, Lake Success and Riverhead.

New Hq. State Police - Albany
11 May 1964

TROOP "A" HQ. - 1921 TO 1976

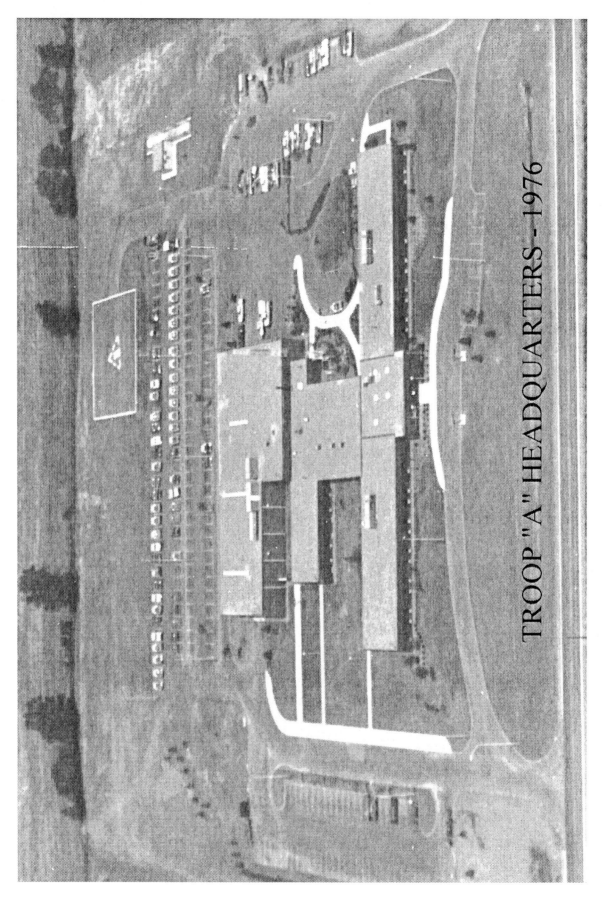

TROOP "A" HEADQUARTERS - 1976

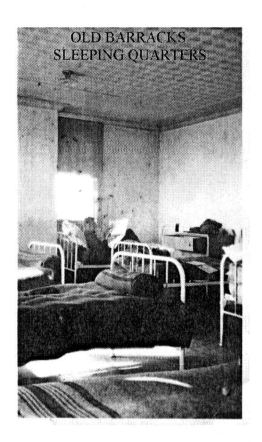

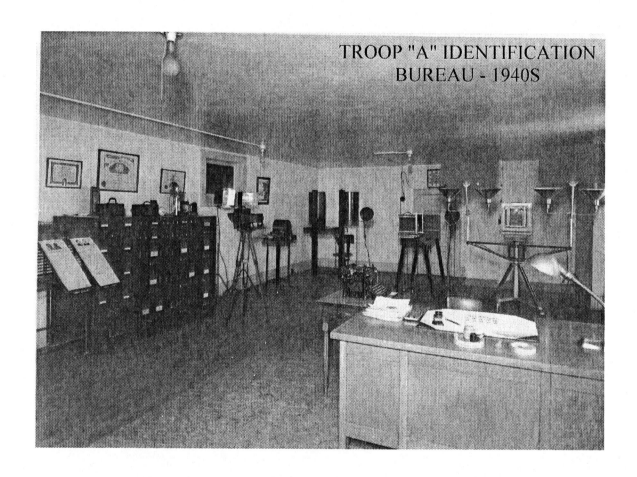

TROOP "A" IDENTIFICATION
BUREAU - 1940S

1980 BATAVIA PATROL
FRONT- T.TUCKER-R.BARRETT- M.SCHRADER
D.ROSE- R.LATHAN- M.ROTH- W.URBANSKI
D.OCCONNOR   REAR - G.WILKERSON- T.ASKEY
P.GALLIVAN-C.MAHONEY- J.BRADLEY- M.WUINLAN
F.WALSH- M.DEMBROW- F.HANNIGAN

NEW PROGRAMS

EDUCATION
In 1970, members were encouraged to continue their formal education through a Division Tuition Assistance Program. There also was a federal government program known as the Law Enforcement Assistance Program (LEAP). This program required that each recipient earn a degree related to Law Enforcement or Social Sciences and spend one year in law enforcement after graduation for each year of educational assistance received. In addition, those members that had served in the military were eligible for educational benefits under the GI Bill. The amount of aide received was determined by length of service and whether you were a full or part time students. New York State also encouraged higher education by providing a Tuition Assistance Program (TAP). Five members earned Masters Degrees while many others earning Bachelor Degrees. Jerome O'Grady, Socrates Lecakes, Edmond Culhane, Francis DeFrancesco and Thomas Constantine earned master degrees. Troopers William Gethoefer and Albert Kurek were the first troopers to earn an Associates Degree in Police Science from Genesee Community College, Batavia, N.Y. Both continued their education at Buffalo State Teachers College, Buffalo, N.Y. earning a Bachelor of Science degree in Criminal Justice.

INSPECTION TEAM
An inspection team was formed in 1961 with the responsibility of conducting troop and headquarters' inspections to insure that proper procedures were being followed and to recommend revisions and changes of operations, when necessary. Inspections were conducted of each troop once a year.

MOUNTED PATROL
During 1983, the mounted horse patrol was re-activated. A six-week school was conducted at the fairgrounds. The unit was made up of six horses permanently stabled at the Syracuse Fairgrounds from where they could be dispatched throughout the state in SP horse vans. The horses and troopers were trained in mounted skills that included crowd and traffic control, search techniques, escort procedures and other activities. The unit was exposed to the public at ceremonial events, parades and fairs.

Troop "A" had several horses owned by or available to troopers for many years prior to the official horse patrol activation. Troopers Louis P. Macri, Philip Attea, Robert Dossinger, James Wilson and Arthur Buczkowski appeared regularly at county fairs, parades and field searches.

NEW YORK'S 12 MOST WANTED PROGRAM
On May 9, 1984, widespread media attention was given to the 12 most wanted criminals in New York State. The program dubbed "The Dirty Dozen" with published bulletins providing a photo and description of the wanted persons was given banner headlines. It gave a toll free number to call and pleaded for public assistance. In the first year, 9 of the 12 most wanted were arrested. An additional 1,150 arrests resulted because of the publicity from the flyers.

STATE POLICE SUMMER PROGRAM
In 1976, the state police initiated a program that brought 100 under privileged boys to the academy during August for a learning vacation. The youngsters varying in age from 9 to 12 came in groups of 25 for one-week stays with emphasis on sports, physical activities, tours and classroom sessions. The programs intent was to promote friendship and understanding between troopers and boys leading to

constructive relationships. State police selected boys equally from the eight troops with funding and responsibility falling on the State Police with support from the State Division for Youth.

The program coordinator was Lieutenant Jerome O'Grady assisted by a sergeant and six trooper counselors. Each boy was picked up and dropped off at their homes in a marked troop car.

PRINT A KID
A joint effort of the State Police and Division Of Criminal Justice Services initiated a statewide program during 1984 to provide parents with fingerprint records of their children. It was felt that the program would help in the event that a child should become missing. Local Burger King restaurants sponsored the inaugural program by providing 500,000 fingerprint cards.

ACADEMY
The first New York State Police School was opened in 1921. Officers from any police agency within the state were eligible to attend the school. From 1921 to the end of 1960, 3,698 troopers and 864 members of municipal police departments had graduated from the State Police School.

The New York State Police School was closed from 1941 until the end of WW II. Of the 305 troopers who left for military service, only 110 returned to the ranks after the war. The returnees had to be re-trained with the school re-opened in August 1945. In addition, all veteran troopers that had not attended basic school in the previous 5 years were required to participate in a two-week refresher course. It is known today as "In Service" School. The basic school for recruits was re-instituted and the course extended to six weeks.

1955 STATE POLICE SCHOOL STAFF
Director- Inspector Everett C. Updike
Assistant Director - Inspector Martin F. Dillon
Executive Officer - Lieutenant George W. Ashley
Training Officer – Lieutenant Melvin Handville
Firearms Instructor - Sergeant A. B. Jackman

NAME CHANGED
In February 1961, the New York State School for Police was changed to the New York State Police Academy. The graduation of the sixty-sixth session of the school ended classes held at Troy, N.Y. Temporary classes were held at Troop "G" barracks where classrooms and facilities were provided for 50 men. The State University at Oneonta accommodated two classes of 50 men each during the summer months.

RECRUITS
Until 1961, newly hired troopers were first assigned to a station where they were required to do menial maintenance duties, wash cars and did generally everything except police work until a school session was started. Classes at the Troopers Police School were held during winter months so several months would pass in some instances before they were sent to the school.

Retired Trooper Leonard Bochynski recalled that on one occasion, as a recruit at Batavia in 1955, a call came in reporting the finding of a body at a local trash dump. With no patrol available, Sergeant C.Z. McDonald instructed Bochynski to take the station pickup truck and investigate the report. Unfamiliar with investigative procedures, he returned to the barracks with the body loaded in the back of the truck. The sergeant ordered him to immediately return the body to its original location and stay with it until a coroner and mortician arrived. That was the extent of Bochynski' police work until graduation from the police school.

RECRUIT TRAINING CURRICULM

The recruit basic course required 640 hours of classroom work. During the 16-week training program, the new troopers received instruction in the Penal Law and Criminal Code of Procedure. They were trained how to make arrests, investigate crimes, how to use firearms safely, how to investigate accidents, how to drive and render first aid. They were taught how to write reports, testify in court, handle radio transmissions and interact with people. Daily physical exercise was required. A counselor who helped and advised in the event of a problem supervised each recruit. After graduation, the recruit trooper was assigned to work with an experienced trooper for several months until his supervisor felt he was capable of working alone.

FIRST SCHOOL COUNSELORS

Trooper George Mills, Troop "A" recalled that in 1961, Superintendent Cornelius had the academy curriculum reviewed by an outside consultant that resulted in new training procedures. Mills and Trooper Hugh McElheny of Troop "B" were selected as the first Academy counselors. Mills recalled that housing for staff and recruits was the Henry Hudson Hotel with classes held at the Masons Lodge at Troy, N.Y. The last half of the recruit training was conducted at Troop G, Loudonville Barracks. The counselors were required to type out a weekly progress report for each recruit and submit it to the Superintendent for his personal review. This was no easy task, as errors weren't acceptable and the old typewriter with carbon paper wasn't very forgiving.

NEW PENAL LAW

On September 1, 1967, extensive changes were made, when the state legislature enacted a new Penal Law. As a result eight sergeants and investigators from each troop were designated to become instructors in the new law and to teach the 3000 troopers of the division. Each troop member attended a three-day session.

1968

1968 marked the eighth-year the facilities at State University at Oneonta were utilized during summer months to house and train recruits. The first eight weeks of training were held at Camp Smith, Peekskill, N.Y.

POLICE SCHOOL COURSES

1945 – Refresher course – 2weeks
1921 - 1946 – Basic school – 4 weeks
1947 – Basic school – 6 weeks
1949 – Instructors Course – 2 weeks
1950 – Auxiliary Police Classes started
1957 – NCO Refresher course – 2 weeks
1958 – Basic school - 8 weeks
1962 – Basic school -12 weeks
1964 – Basic school increased from 12 to 16 weeks

A two-week non-commissioned officers course was established in 1964. The purpose was to provide a good foundation in principles and supervision as well as the duties of a Sergeant. 148 received training the first year.

TROOPERS ACADEMY

A period of expansion commenced with the hiring of new Superintendent Arthur Cornelius. A huge increase in patrol troopers required facilities to teach and train them. In-service training was conducted at the Loudonville barracks. Basic training for recruits required housing and other facilities as well as classroom space. Recruit training was held at Oneonta University during summer recess, as well as Syracuse University, the state fairgrounds, a Catskill resort hotel and Camp Smith. Training had to be scheduled when facilities could be obtained, rather than for the convenience of the division.

The 1966 legislature authorized $3.6 million for the construction of a State Police Academy building. Contracts for its construction and a groundbreaking took place on May 15, 1968. The site selected was adjacent to Division Headquarters on the State Campus. Plans called for a main building for instruction and administrative offices with two three-story dormitories capable of accommodating 100 persons each.

The main building was 330 by 310 feet in dimension featuring an auditorium with a 304 seating capacity, a gymnasium, library, and a cafeteria-style dining room with kitchen. A 10 position firing range was located in the basement. The two classrooms had tiered seating able to seat 100 persons.

The dormitory rooms were connected to the main building. Each room was designed for double occupancy with a connecting bath

In May 1970, the State Police Academy was completed with the first class of 98 recruits admitted. Highly skilled instructors have continued to provide the most current and accurate information available. The motto "Excellence Through Knowledge" was adopted by the Academy.

The academy gradually increased its curriculum and length of the recruit classes. By 1984, the Basic Training School was 22 weeks long. Recruits were exposed to a highly structured semi-military environment that tested their learning abilities, physical limitations and their ability to handle stressful situations.

Over 900 hours of instruction are provided in Criminal Procedure, Vehicle and Traffic and Penal Law, First aid, Radar and Breathalyzer operation and firearms training. Veteran troopers are assigned as counselors with demands made on them, just as the recruits. They are required to maintain the same hours, sleep at the academy and participate in the training program. They are always available to assist the recruit. Upon graduation, each graduate is armed with the basic knowledge to perform his or her duties as a New York State Trooper.

DISTINGUISHED SERVICE AWARDS

NEW YORK DAILY NEWS AWARD FOR VALOR

TROOPER JOHN G. CHVATAL – 1942

On December 25, 1942, Trooper John G. Chvatal while assigned at Herkimer, single handedly captured three soldiers being sought for armed robbery. The soldiers armed with a Thompson sub-machine gun and three handguns hijacked a taxicab near Watertown, N.Y. They forced the taxi driver to take them to Manlius where he was robbed and left stranded with the assailants driving off in the cab. He immediately reported the crime to local police who sent out an alert via teletype message. Trooper Chvatal reading the alert took a position on Route 20 near Cherry Valley and was soon rewarded when the taxicab passed. He took up a pursuit position and forced the stolen car to a stop at gunpoint. All three men were taken into custody without a shot being fired.

The New York Daily News recognized trooper Chvatal for his bravery. A citizen's committee felt he displayed exceptional bravery and performed a distinguished and valorous service at the risk of his life that was beyond the call of common duty.

Governor Thomas E. Dewey awarded the Daily News 1942 Medal of Valor to Trooper Chvatal in a ceremony held at the State Capitol on February 24, 1943.

TROOPER KENNETH J. TROIDL - 1968

On December 26,1967 at 10:20 AM, a frantic call for help was received at the Lewiston barracks by Trooper Patrick Petrie. A distraught mother reported her daughter had been swept into an underground tunnel by rushing water. Lynn Atchison, age 7, along with her cousins James 11, & Janice Atchison, age 10 were playing on the ice & snow covered Fish Creek near the mouth of a 1,700 foot long underground tunnel that ends approximately 100 feet above the Niagara River gorge. Lynn was sitting near the tunnel opening when an ice dam containing about 5 feet of water broke, washing her under the gate into the tunnel mouth. James heard his cousin's frantic cries for help, then silence. He immediately ran for help.

Troopers Kenneth J. Troidl and Thomas Campbell along with Sergeant William Peterson and Investigator Reginald Perry responded immediately to the Niagara Falls Country Club where the tunnel was located. Trooper Troidl volunteered to go into the tunnel in an attempt to locate the girl. Sergeant Peterson tied two 50-foot lengths of rope together tying one end around Troidl and the other to himself. As they proceeded deeper into the tunnel, it became increasingly slippery with Troidl losing his footing. This created enough pressure to loosen the rope's knot. Troidl fell face down, feet first into the icy water. Unable to recover, he started to descend with ever increasing momentum until the conduit level changed from a gradual incline to a 46-degree downward rush. As more & more water entered from sub-conduits, the speed of his downward travel increased. Sergeant Peterson now in a panic had Trooper Campbell who was joined by Lewiston DPW employee Robert Blolinski go to the exit of the conduit while he returned to the station to report on the events to his superiors. Troidl managed to slow his descent somewhat by pressing his knees and elbows into the cement bed of the tunnel. As he neared the tunnel's outlet, he was able to slow his progress and eventually stop by grabbing some teeth like objects located on the floor. He had no idea how long he lay in the conduit before he saw and heard the friendly voice of Blolinski looking down at him through an opening. Still tied to a section of the rope, he was able to throw it up and was pulled to safety. He was wrapped in a blanket and taken to St. Mary's Hospital by Trooper Campbell who called on the radio to advise that Troidl was safe. Shaking and in shock with a body temperature of 94 degrees, Troidl was treated by Doctor Alphonse L. Bax for shock, an injury to his shoulder and hyper-thermia and was admitted. Trooper Campbell returned to the vicinity of the conduit outlet to search for the missing girl. The US Coast Guard was notified and conducted a search of the river to no avail. On the second day with the temperature at 14 degrees and water temperature at 35 degrees, a boat and scuba detail consisting of Troopers Michael O'Rourke, Thomas Bowman, Donald Vogt and William Reynolds searched the riverbanks and area where the conduit emptied into the Niagara River without success. The Ross Steel Erecting Company volunteered and provided a crane with 2000 feet of cable to aid in the search. Troopers Don Vogt and Walt Hornberger were harnessed to the cable and lowered into the conduit to search for the girl. The entire length was scanned without success. Although tragedy had escaped Trooper Troidl, the same could not be said for 7-year-old Lynn Atchison. Searches along the river were conducted for several weeks after the accident; the body of the girl was never recovered. May she rest in peace.

On May 21, 1968, Trooper Troidl was recognized for his harrowing rescue attempt. He was awarded The New York Daily News Distinguished Service Award. The action he took was above and beyond the call of duty and with immediate risk to his own life. His wife Lorine, Superintendent William Kirwan and Major John P. Nohlen were part of the ceremonies held at the Daily News Building. He was awarded an engraved plaque and .357 Smith and Wesson combat magnum. This was the last time the Daily News Award was awarded a member of the New York State Police, as the Brummer Award took its place in 1968.

BRUMMER AWARD

The Brummer Award was a trust fund established in March 1968 by Wall Street financier Bertram F. Brummer and his wife Susie. $12,000.00 in US Treasury bonds was placed on deposit to be used as an annual award to recognize a New York State Trooper who distinguished himself by conspicuous bravery in the performance of duty. It consists of a written citation describing the occurrence, a small monetary gift and special service ribbon worn by the recipient on the uniform. Brummer died on January 31, 1976. His appreciation for the State Police was demonstrated many times through his continued increasing of the trust fund.

INVESTIGATOR PETER W. MANN – 1ST BRUMMER WINNER

On January 17, 1969, Bertram Bummer presented Investigator Peter W. Mann the award before members of the SP Academy at Camp Smith. Mann had been undercover for 10 months during 1968 conducting sensitive investigations. He had endured threats of bodily harm and great mental pressures with constant exposure to a dangerous criminal element.

TROOPERS FROM WESTERN NEW YORK AWARDED THE PRESTIGIOUS BRUMMER AWARD

TROOPER LOUIS J. LANG – 1978
TROOPER SCOTT C. SAUNDERS

On November 28, 1977, Troopers Louis J. Lang and Scott C. Saunders of the Batavia patrol were traveling to a rifle range for training, when they overheard a Channel 9 CB radio transmission of a serious accident near the Pembroke Thruway interchange. Upon arrival, they began to attempt to free the lone occupant of the car, 25-year-old Joanne Kelsch whose leg was pinned under the crushed dashboard and brake pedal. Hampered by smoldering flames and heavy smoke inside the car, they physically removed the front seat and part of the door and were able to free the trapped woman. They removed her from the car and administered first aid until arrival of an ambulance. Truckers on the scene used fire extinguishers from their rigs to keep the flames down until the fire department arrived. Both troopers were given oxygen by the Indian Falls Fire Department to combat illness from smoke inhalation. The woman suffered a head laceration requiring 60 stitches to close, a broken leg, a shattered ankle, internal injuries and loss of a large amount of blood.

Upon her release from Genesee Memorial Hospital, Batavia, N.Y. 28 days later, she met the troopers she credits with saving her life. Hugs, kisses and tears were part of the re-union, as well as her deep, sincere thanks.

The accident occurred when Kelsch lost control on the snow covered highway sliding across the median into the path of an oncoming vehicle. A graduate of Nazareth College in Rochester, N.Y. she was returning to Purdue University to continue graduate studies, when the mishap occurred.

The CB radio with the troopers monitoring channel 9 was one of ten that had been donated to the Batavia State Police by the Batavia Kiwanis Club. It saved a life.

An honor board consisting of Deputy Superintendent George L. Infante, Chief Inspector Daniel A. Dakin and Deputy Chief Inspector Francis P. Stainkamp selected Troopers Lang and Saunders to be recipients of the Annual Brummer Award. They were the first troopers from Troop "A" to be so honored. The honor board citation read: "Working in a heavy pall of smoke and with a complete disregard for their own safety, the troopers freed the trapped driver to the amazement of many onlookers who described the scene as one of horror, convinced that the young woman would be burned to death

INVESTIGATOR ROBERT L. VAN HALL – 1980
INVESTIGATOR WILLIAM G. GORENFLO

On December 4, 1980, Investigators Robert Van Hall, age 35 and William Gorenflo were members of the Troop E drug task force working in the Corning, N.Y. area. While observing drug activity at the Market Street Car Wash, they stopped a car in the nearby parking lot. Witnesses said that as they pulled alongside the suspect vehicle, the occupants opened fire with a double-barreled shotgun. Gorenflo was able to get off three shots, as the vehicle fled. Van Hall, the passenger, was mortally wounded. He suffered gun shot wounds to the face, chest and back. Gorenflo was admitted to Corning Hospital with head and shoulder wounds. Gorenflo was able to send out a distress signal with Trooper G.P. Granger responding to the scene.

Granger arrested Joseph W. Comfort, age 33 who was still holding the shotgun. Also arrested was Larry J. Comfort, age 30 both of First Street, Corning, N.Y. They were charged with first-degree murder, narcotics possession and weapons possession.

TROOPER GARY E. KUBASIAK – 1982
INVESTIGATOR TIMOTHY HOWARD
SERGEANT GEORGE R. BERGER

On August 30, 1982, Trooper Gary Kubasiak, age 32 was dead on arrival at Tri-County Hospital, Gowanda, N.Y. following a shoot-out, when responding to a domestic dispute. Charged with the killing was 33-year-old James J. Swan, Route 62, Dayton, N.Y., an ex-mental patient at Gowanda State Hospital. Troopers answered the call of a domestic dispute with Investigator Timothy Howard, a nearby resident responding. Kubasiak and his dog Donivan were also summoned to the scene from his nearby residence. Swan was known to and knew both officers and it was felt the personal contact was needed to handle the situation. Kubasiak along with "Donivan" entered the home through a rear kitchen door identifying himself and was immediately shot three times with a .30-.30 rifle. The shots struck Kubasiak in the abdomen, chest and hand killing him instantly. Investigator Howard had climbed into the house through a window and confronted Swan almost immediately after hearing the rifle fire. Swan holding the rifle was ordered to drop the weapon. Instead, he whirled pointing the rifle at Howard. Howard fired three rapid-fire shots with one shot striking Swan in the chest. Howard seeing Kubasiak wounded on the floor went immediately to his side rendering first aid. In the meantime, Swan not seriously wounded barricaded himself in a side bedroom. Sergeant George Berger entering the residence and not seeing Swan conducted a room-to-room search. Opening a bedroom door, he was confronted by Swan holding a shotgun pointed at him. Swan pulled the trigger but the gun misfired. A few minutes later, Swan surrendered without further incident. Investigator Gerald Forster recalled that District Attorney Larry Himelein was able to prove that Swan was legally sane at the time. He was convicted of Murder and sentenced to a term of 35 years to life imprisonment.

An honor board made of Deputy Superintendent Donald G. Brandon, Chief Inspector Nicholas G. Lecakes and Deputy Chief Inspector Frederick D. Thumhart selected Trooper Kubasiak, Investigator Howard and Sergeant Berger to be recipients of the Brummer Award.

INVESTIGATOR WALTER DELAP - 1984

On January 8, 1984, Investigator Walter M. DeLap along with his dog "Dillon" were called to assist the Elmira, N.Y. Police Department Swat Team. Two armed fugitives were barricaded in an apartment complex. The dog was sent into the complex to determine the fugitive's location. As the SWAT officers moved into position in the apartment, the fugitives emerged from a back room rapidly firing shotgun blasts pinning down the detail for 15 minutes. Delap, under fire and in the dark, was able to find a window, which allowed the SWAT team to exit. Still under gunfire, Delap returned to assist and remove critically wounded Elmira Police Sergeant John Hawley to safety and recall Dillon. The lengthy siege ended when one fugitive killed the other, then took his own life.

An honor board made up of Deputy Superintendent Thomas A. Constantine, Chief Inspector Joseph J. Strojnowski and Assistant Deputy Superintendent Frederick D. Thumhart selected Delap for the Brummer Award citing his "Initiative and courage while under fire and his fortitude and unselfish actions"

UNIFORM

The trooper's uniform has always been provided by the state to insure uniformity.
The most obvious uniform changes were made during the 1950s. The troopers appearance was changed to a more practical, comfortable uniform and troop car colors and markings changed for easier recognition by the public.

SHEEPSKIN COATS
In the fall of 1944, new cloth overcoats were introduced replacing the heavy fourteen- pound sheepskin coats that had been previously issued to all troopers. These older coats were satisfactory for the days of horse patrol and open car travel, but were found to be too cumbersome while in a patrol car. The heavier coat could still be worn at the trooper's option.

SHOULDER EMBLEM – FIRST DIPLAYED IN 1954
Superintendent Albin S. Johnson (1953 to 1955) oversaw the development of the modern NYSP uniform. With the demise of the horse, the original dark gray woolen 1917-era cavalry-style tunic, riding breeches, leather puttees and spurs were replaced with a lightweight Class A blouse and straight legged trousers in a lighter gray color. A .38 Special Colt Official Police revolver carried in a swivel holster was worn on the side of the shooting hand. It replaced the cross draw .45 caliber revolver. For the first time, the uniform shirt and jacket sported a distinctive patch displaying the New York State seal and legend New York State Police. The shoulder patch motto "Excelsior" translated means "Ever Upward". The uniform weighed four-pounds less then its predecessor and was cheaper to manufacture. Each trooper was clothed and equipped for about $113.00. The uniform was introduced publicly in July 1954, when a detail of troopers provided security at the U.S. Governors' Conference in Lake George, N.Y. The breeches were retained until 1957 for motorcycle details. They were worn by all troopers during winter months until the existing supply was depleted. The spurs were retired in 1955. Shoes worn were an above the ankle laced work shoe for patrol and field duty while a low cut laced shoe was worn while on barracks assignment.

SCUBA DIVING EMBLEM - JUNE 1965
Several years prior to 1965, the Division approved a shoulder patch designed by Trooper D.R. George, Troop K, Monroe, N.Y. The symbolic patch is worn on the fatigue uniform of the SCUBA divers. Its striking appearance of an octopus with encircling tentacles indicates the denizens of the deep.

SHORT SLEEVED SHIRTS
During the summer 1973, the first lightweight short-sleeved shirts were issued much to the troopers delight. A necktie was initially required, but soon done away with. The short-sleeved shirts were worn during summer months only. A new type footwear was also introduced. The black shoe's issued to all troopers was an above the ankle dress-work shoe with a single strap and buckle. They are still worn today. The heavy felt Stetson hat continues to be the headwear of choice.

MISCELLANEOUS WEAR
WINTER GLOVES – The early gloves were mittens made of leather lined with sheep's wool. They had a large cuff that extended over the wrist and were ideal for horse and motorcycle patrol. They were eventually replaced with a wool fingered glove with leather handgrip sewn on. These tended to separate after getting wet. The newer gloves were actually two pair of gloves. A woolen glove was worn that fit into a second leather glove that proved to be comfortable and durable.

WINTER HEADWEAR – Troopers were issued sealskin winter caps with flaps tied by a string. When needed, the flaps were lowered to cover the ears and forehead. These were replaced with a similar type cloth cap with fur ear piece's and a snap buckle strap.

SOCKS – Trooper socks are gray in color. During the 1940s and 1950s, the toe of the sock was made of a white knit material. The purpose was to prevent athlete's foot problems. Every trooper was issued six (6) pair of socks a year.

DRY CLEANING

Troopers are expected to be neat and clean at all times. The uniforms are dry cleaned as needed. The state pays for the dry cleaning through open bidding by local vendors. Alterations are at the trooper's expense.

NEW ISSUE UNIFORMS – 1954

1/1/55 - GOVERNOR HARRIMAN INAUGURATION
STICKNEY-DENNIS-SLADE-BYRNE-FITZWATER
NOHLEN-HENDERSON-SCHUSLER-STEINMETZ
RUSSELL-TUMULTY

OLD BATAVIA RECORDS ROOM - 1964
D.SEAMANS- M.ZON- L.SANDO- A.DIRIENZ
H.MONAHAN- N.NEWTON

CONGRATULATIONS AND SO LONG - - Lt. H.D. Smith, now in charge of the Vestal Zone of Troop C, was honored by office employees at Troop A as he was about to leave the first sergeant post there. Surrounding the new Lieutenant are from left, first row, Cheryl Jimerson, Linda Sando, Linda McCabe, Mary Zon, Hazel Monaghan, Sharllann Walker, Jeanne Stefaniak; second row, Nancy Pfaff, Toni Tabone, Faye Pridmore, Veronica Chilano, Dorothy Manahan, Dorothy Chase, Muriel Willard and Bernetta McDonald.

1964 TROOP "A" OFFICERS
J.SAGE- C.BUKOWSKI-C.COBB- K.WEIDENBORNER
C.BAILEY- J.NOHLEN- A.WRIGHT- M.VANSKIVER
J.MOOCHLER- H.SMITH

LEO WATKINS - BOB BARRUS - DICK OLMA -
1954

J. Long. W. Schenke. L. Bochynski. D. Burt. W. Terryberry. J. Lenihan. E. Gilbert -- 1959

BOOK II — TROOPERS AT WORK

TROOPER AIRCRAFT DIVISION

FIXED WING

The New York State Police initiated the use of aircraft in July 1931 with the purchase of a 125 horsepower "Model 8 Fleet" airplane built by Consolidated Aircraft Inc., Buffalo, N.Y. The Chief Pilot was Lieutenant Tremaine Hughes, a skilled & experienced flyer. The air division was short lived, when on January 15,1932, Hughes crashed during inclement weather near Cazenovia, N.Y. The plane was totally destroyed and Hughes along with passenger Theopholis Gaines were instantly killed. Albany Headquarters deemed flying to be too dangerous even by skilled pilots and terminated the program. It took forty-four years to resurrect the air division of State Police.

PLANE TO CAR

Word that aircraft working with patrol cars soon will police the New York State Thruway should serve as a warning to heedless motorists. More than ever, they will be unable to disregard speed and safety regulations confident they will be able to detect the watchful eye of the trooper before he sees them.

Motorists used to complain about unmarked cars and radar, but both seem to have been accepted. Some drivers using electronic devices are able to avoid detection. The hovering aircraft will be even harder to detect. Reasonable traffic laws are created to protect all motorists including the reckless with the careful. If drivers respect the law at all times, they wouldn't have to worry about being summoned and we would all be safer for it.
(Newburgh Evening News September 13, 1966)

FIRST USE OF AIRCRAFT BY THE THRUWAY

During the summer of 1966, Troop "T" experimented with the use of aircraft in the enforcement of speed limit regulation. Markings were painted across the highway at ¼ mile measured distances. The small aircraft then flew at an altitude of 800 feet. When a speeding car was observed, the trooper observer in the plane, using a stopwatch, would time the vehicle between the highway markings. These highway markings were painted one foot wide across the entire width of the roadway. Using a conversion chart, the observer would convert the time into speed. A car traveling a quarter mile in less than 13.8 seconds was speeding, because the mathematics works out to the 65 MPH speed limit allowed. The pilot would then radio a patrol vehicle below, give a description of the vehicle and keep the violator in sight until apprehended.

The program got into full gear on September 1, 1967 with a purpose of increased law enforcement and service to the public. Troopers flew a plane owned by the NYS Thruway Authority. It was a four passenger Cessna Skyhawk painted in Thruway blue and white with registration # N8231-L assigned. The plane cost $13,500.00 before installation of radios and equipment. (The same plane today sells for $200,000.00) The normal cruising speed was 120 MPH at an altitude of 800 feet, but was capable of slowing to 80 MPH. During the first four months, the plane was in the air 350 hours. Speeding arrests totaled 194 with motorist's assists accounting for 176 distress observations. Members of the unit were Chief Pilot John F. Ryan, Andrew J. Liddle, Kenneth R. Earle and Robert C. Stoddart. The pilots were designated with the rank of Technical Sergeants.

Effective April 1, 1969, the Division purchased the fixed wing Cessna Sky Hawk from the Thruway Authority. The Thruway on a rental basis made arrangements for partial use of the plane.

T/SGT. ROBERT C. STODDART – PILOT

Trooper Stoddart related the following about his career with the NYS Police. He enlisted on June 26, 1961 being assigned at Waverly, West Winfield, Henrietta and Wellsville. He replied to a State Police announcement-seeking candidates for the position of trooper pilots. During the summer of 1967, fifty (50) applications were processed and a written examination given. Successful candidates were given a flight test by an FAA examiner on general aviation knowledge. Four candidates were selected with Stoddart being one of them. He and his flying partner, Trooper Kenneth Earle of Cattaraugus, N.Y. possessed commercial licenses with instrument rating and had at least 500 hours flying time. Bob learned to fly in 1956 at the Buffalo Airpark, West Seneca, N.Y. The plane was based primarily at the Schenectady County Airport. The work schedule consisted of a five-day workweek. Flights were alternated with the plane manned in teams of two. Flying time would average approximately 4 hours daily. If not flying, the pilots would travel to the courts that serviced the Thruway explaining the use of aircraft in speeder apprehension.

Watching for speeders and dangerous situations were part of the duties. When the plane went into service for the day, the pilot would check in with the Thruway Authority and the local patrol cars. The cars had large orange numbers on the roofs and were radioed the identity of the violator car that was kept in sight until stopped. First use was on the Berkshire spur and later, the main line between Utica and Syracuse. On September 15, 1967, T/Sergeant Robert Stoddart, as an observer, was the first trooper to call out a speeding violation to a marked car on patrol.

Stoddart left the State Police on January 1, 1968. The Thruway Authority was non-committal on the status and future of the aviation branch. His wife residing in Elma, N.Y. had just given birth to their son. He had recently taken and passed an examination for a position, as Warrant Agent with the New York State Tax Department. He accepted the position because this would keep him near home with his family. Although he loved the troopers and flying, it was a matter of looking after family first. Stoddart continued his relationship with the Buffalo Air Park where he gave flying lessons to a countless number of young pilots until 1996.

His partner, Trooper Kenneth R. Earle was killed in an off duty motorcycle accident on July 17, 1976 at Chazy, New York.

BERGEN SWAMP – MISSING CHILD AND GRANDMOTHER

On April 7, 1969, 65-year-old Rose Patri visiting her 5-year-old grand daughter, Ann Marie McCahera decided to take a casual walk with the child. The family resided near that 2000 acre Bergen swamp known for its prehistoric age heavy foliage infested with rattle snakes. Failing to return home, troopers were notified and a massive search organized. Several hours into the night, the search was called off until daylight. Arrangements were made to have the newly acquired division aircraft available at first light. At about 8:15 AM, two volunteer firemen found Ann Marie. Hearing the airplane overhead, she stood to get a better look and was seen by the observer who directed her rescue. Unfortunately, Mrs. Patri's body was found lying in a stream where she had slipped and drowned in three feet of water.

WRECKED PLANE FOUND

On February 22, 1972, a twin engine Piper Aztec directed to the Albany, N.Y. airport from Burlington, Vermont was reported missing. The pilot had earlier reported heavy icing and turbulence. An immediate intensive search was initiated without success. Heavy snow and high winds held search efforts to a minimum. The search continued for several months. On May 23, 1972, Trooper pilot A. J. Warjas and observer T.J. Forster spotted the plane wreckage fifty feet below the peak of Mother Myreck Mountain eight miles east of the New York State border. Lieutenant Foster Corliss of the

Vermont Mountain Search and Rescue Team was notified and flown to the scene. His team reached the wreckage finding the two occupants still strapped in their seats.

HELICOPTER

The New York State Police air patrol by helicopter officially began on July 23, 1968. The helicopter purchased was manufactured by the Bell Helicopter Company of Fort Worth, Texas and was based at Page Airways, Albany, N.Y. It had commercial, as well as state police radios installed and was fitted with pontoons to permit landings on lakes and waterways. It had three seats and traveled at a maximum speed of 105 miles per hour with a cruising speed of between 84 and 91 miles per hour. It could remain aloft without refueling from four to five hours depending on its load. A blue-tinted plexi-glass bubble provided high optical quality and maximum vision range. The helicopter operated at a normal patrol height of 500 feet.

The helicopter was used to transport medical aid to the scene of accidents, cover wide areas during searches for missing and wanted persons and was used in surveillance of buildings and bridges during presidential campaigns.

ROBERT L. TILLMAN

Senior Investigator Robert L. Tillman, a trooper since 1947 was designated Chief Pilot. His experience included 3000 flying hours as a US Navy fighter pilot during World War II & the Korean Conflict and 1300 hours as a helicopter pilot while commanding a Naval Reserve Helicopter Squadron. Technical Sergeants John F. Ryan and Andrew J. Liddle were selected as helicopter trainees and served as co-pilots. Tillman died unexpectedly on November 22, 1974 from a heart attack while hunting with fellow troopers in Allegany County. He was 53 years old.

The first division helicopter pilots received their training at Prior Aviation, Buffalo, N.Y.

Stanley Roberts filled the vacancy created by Tillman's death. He enlisted in the State Police on September 2, 1962. He earned his fixed wing pilots license in 1957 and held a rating of airline transport pilot. Roberts joined the air division in 1968. He was trained as a helicopter pilot at Prior Aviation, Buffalo, N.Y. in 1969. In 1970, he was certified to instruct helicopter pilots and was designated the unit commander in Lieutenant Tillman's absence.

HELICOPTER RESCUE

In December 1971, a cabin cruiser traveling from Nova Scotia to Florida capsized in the Hudson River throwing two men into the icy water. One man drowned while the other made it safely to the boat that was being held against the spillway by the backwash near the center of the river. Alerted by nearby residents, Z/Sgt Russell A. Guard and a volunteer went his aide in a small aluminum boat, but also capsized. A second boat with two men aboard arrived at the scene only to capsize, now leaving five men stranded on the larger craft. T/Sergeant Stanley Roberts and A.J. Warjas arrived in the Division helicopter and hovered over the scene. A rope was lowered and each man was pulled to shallower water, then lifted aboard the helicopter. Roberts and Warjas were presented the Army's Medal of Valor for their efforts.

NEW HELICOPTERS

During June 1970, the Division Air-wing became fully operational. A federal grant of $690,000 covered the cost of three new helicopters and paid for training expenses and equipment maintenance for the first year. The new Bell Model 206A Jet Rangers had a maximum speed of 150 MPH with a cruising speed of 130 MPH. They had a range of 400 miles without refueling. The grant also paid for two mechanics. John L. Hurst and Durwood Berryman both experienced mechanics were hired to maintain the fleet.

Personnel in the Aviation unit were T/Lieutenant R.L. Tillman and T/Sergeants J.F. Ryan, G.E. Preston, W.C. Murray, K.R. Earle and Troopers W.J. Bendo Jr., J.E. Cuneo, T.J. Forster, S.R. Thomas and T.E. Dixon

The helicopters were based at three locations within the state.

A new 206A Bell Jet Ranger was stationed at Timbello's Helicopter Service, East Syracuse, N.Y. and would service Troops A, D & E.

A 206A Bell Jet Ranger and a Bell 47-G helicopter were stationed at Stewart Airport, Newburgh, N.Y and would service Troops C, F and K.

A 206A Bell Jet Ranger and a fixed-wing Cessna Skyhawk were stationed at Page Airways, Albany, N.Y. and would service Troops B & G. Chief Pilot Robert Tillman was assigned here along with a stand ready helicopter mechanic.

HUEY
During the spring of 1978, the air wing was increased with the addition of a UH-1B helicopter, a Huey. It was obtained through federal surplus channels and picked up from the National Guard in Colorado. The helicopter was in excellent condition and was flown back by Lieutenant Roberts, T/Sergeant A.F. Peters and Trooper J.A. Radley.

MEDIVAC
The Division started emergency medical flights in 1978. During the year 1982, over 100 rescue missions were flown.

FLEET UPGRADING - 1984
During March 1984, the Division helicopter fleet was upgraded by the acquisition of three new helicopters fully equipped to handle all police missions and emergency medical emergencies. In total, five of six helicopters were replace. A lease purchase agreement was in place that would save money because the state police no longer did the mandatory maintenance. The contract would be paid for from the sale of five Division helicopters, two of which were over twenty years old. Two of the seven seat Bell 206-L1 machines with a speed of 150 MPH were received in March with a price tag of $900.000.00

In 1984, the Division air-wing consisted of 15 pilots each with up to 7000 hours of flight experience headed by Captain Stanley Richard Thomas.

KEN EARLE - LT. ALEX GALLION - BOB STODDARD

DIVISION AIRCRAFT - 1967

GARY PRESTON - SUPERINTENDENT
CHESWORTH
1984

BOB TILLMAN - RON BUTTERFIELD - NICK
GIANGUALANO

BUREAU OF CRIMINAL INVESTIGATION

The BCI was initially started in 1936 with the appointment of men from the within the ranks. These troopers would perform their normal every day duties until a major crime was reported requiring further investigation. They were then assigned to work the case until a successful conclusion was reached. The eleven Troop "A" BCI men were assigned to duties at Batavia because of its central location in the troop area. In 1943, Lieutenant Eugene F. Hoyt assigned BCI men to various stations within the troop. This was an effort to save money on war time restricted gasoline and tires by driving less miles and responding to crime scenes almost immediately.

In January 1955, the BCI of Troop "A" was compromised of 22 troopers, corporals and sergeants. They were located at Batavia and the 12 substations of the troop. Assignments were made from members of the uniform force who had some years of experience in police activity and who had exhibited aptitude and initiative in investigation of crime. An extra sum of $350.00 was added to the yearly pay in lieu of uniform and clothing allowance. When additional BCI investigators were needed, the District Inspector or Captain submitted a recommendation to the Chief Inspector and appointments made accordingly.

When a serious crime was reported, a uniform trooper was assigned the initial investigation and determined if the BCI unit was needed. If so, a BCI investigator responded to the scene and took over the investigation until it was resolved.

As criminals became more sophisticated, special units within the Bureau were created. There was a Gambling Unit, Narcotics Unit, Polygraph Unit, Auto-Theft Unit, Major Crimes Unit and Identification Unit.

In 1985, the BCI was credited with dealing a blow to the Columbo crime family when 25 members were indicted under Federal RICO laws and drug conspiracy.

Seventeen other arrests ended a lucrative counterfeit credit card operation.

125 Hells Angels were arrested on multiple charges bringing public awareness to their ruthless, criminal involvement with drug trafficking.

The first important case handled by Troop "A" was in November 1937, when several young couples reported having been beaten and robbed while parked at a Hamburg, N.Y. lover's lane. The culprits on three occasions had bound, gagged and robbed the male escort and then attacked the female. The BCI men laid a carefully planned trap. They selected the locations where the crimes had taken place, then parked at these locations with one of the troopers dressed in female attire. The plan worked, as five men were taken into custody at gunpoint and placed under arrest. Four others were later charged. All served time in prison for the crimes.

1962 – there were 353 BCI men in the state.
1964 – 24,631 cases.
1968 – 37,156 cases.

CANINES

BLOODHOUNDS

The New York State Police obtained and have utilized "Bloodhounds" for the purpose of trailing the scent of human beings since 1934.

Troop "A" acquired three bloodhounds named "Olga", "Bess" and "Molly" in 1937. Trooper Albert Perry volunteered as trainer and handler. Perry handled the dogs for several years, however no information regarding them could be found from WW II until 1964. Bloodhounds had been continually assigned at Hawthorne and Malone. Trooper William Horton and the "K" Troop dogs responded to any requests from Troop "A".

In 1963, a kennel was established at Troop "D" Oneida to serve Central and Western N.Y.

In 1964, a kennel was re-established at Troop "A" Batavia. The Batavia dogs were successfully used in eight criminal and seven lost persons searches that year. Trooper David Schwartz was the assigned handler.

The bloodhound is lamblike in its gentleness although he does look sad eyed and ferocious. They are taught not to bay when following a scent, because it could frighten a small child or give a trailed criminal notice of the approach. While tracking, the dogs are held by a leash and seldom are more that two used on the same case. They follow body scent and if conditions allow, can follow a trail four or five days old. There is no smoking when on a trail, because a few whiffs would dull the dog's senses. The scent of a human is stronger than any animal with no two people having the exact same scent. Human scent does not come from a person's shoes, but actually rises from the top of your body and falls to the ground. A bloodhound could be 20 to 30feet off of the actual trail due to blowing wind.

BLOODHOUND TRAINING

The dogs start to learn their trade, when they are 18 months old. Until then, they enjoy a normal puppy-hood. Training starts when a dog is taken out into a sizeable field and allowed to sniff a piece of liver in an assistant trainers hand. This gives the dog the idea that the assistant is a good man to keep his eye on during proceedings. The assistant runs about 50 feet while the dog strains at the leash thinking about the liver. He is then allowed to run to the assistant who gives him the meat. This procedure is repeated and distance lengthened at every try. A garment owned by the trainer is used to teach the dog to follow a given scent. He strains at the leash until he finds the assistant. Since the wind may blow the scent to one side of the actual trail, the dog is not expected to follow the actual trail, only go in the right direction. The assistant leaves a paper trail to show the trainer the actual trail. The dog is now learning to track with the assistant completely out of sight. No fooling around is allowed. The dog soon learns not to mix business with pleasure. When the dog finds the assistant, a big fuss is made over the dog and he is rewarded with a piece of liver. This type of training usually takes six months before a dog is placed into duty.

Several basic rules are in place prior to using a bloodhound in a field search. Since a dog picks up the human scent from an article of clothing known to have been worn by the person to be trailed, it is absolutely imperative that any article of clothing known to be worn by the person, "NOT BE TOUCHED" except by the dog handler. Keep the area clear of large groups of people. Bloodhounds usually work best when the trail is less than 24 hours old.

FILLMORE, NEW YORK - 1964

Bob the Batavia bloodhound became a hero of a trouser hunt, when a Fillmore, N.Y. resident reported his home entered and his trousers containing a wallet and $40.00 stolen.

Bob led troopers to the home of a neighbor where the trousers, wallet and money were found. The neighbor was arrested for burglary. The following appeared in a local newspaper.

BOB THE BLOODHOUND

August 20, 1964

"Bob" the bloodhound, sniffed around
And then took off across the ground
He found his prey not far away
So, Jones' pants are back today

Bloodhounds Dan & Bob joined Troop "A" in June 1964.

Bloodhound "Bob", age 8 died during the fall of 1966. In January 1967, 14-month old "Guy of Empire" was transferred to Batavia from Malone.

HANDLER LEON DYWINSKI

Trooper Leon Dywinski, the Troop "A" dog handler from 1965 to 1978 recalled a few memorable cases he was involved with. On April 17, 1974, the State Police in Erie, Pennsylvania requested assistance in the search for a missing 18-month old child. The child missing for a day had been playing outdoors with his siblings. The temperature during the night was a frigid 30 degrees. A civilian bloodhound handler attempted to track the child without success. Bloodhound "Guy" who was recovering from surgery a few days earlier was started on piece of the child's clothing, but was unable to work the scent away from the house. Bloodhound "Dutchess of York" was started on another piece of clothing further away from the house. She crossed a busy highway and proceeded to track the infant. The Pennsylvania trooper accompanying Dywinski was certain the dog was wrong in it's tracking. A short time later, "Dutchess" led them to the lifeless body of the child. He was found lying in a farm field a short distance from his home. He had died from exposure. Dywinski commented that this was one of the hardest finds emotionally, that he had ever made.

KIDNAPPING

During February 1966, a fourteen-year old girl walking to school was kidnapped and assaulted by a man who forced her into his car. He threatened to shoot her if she resisted. He then drove two miles to a dirt road where he twice assaulted her. He then returned her to an area near the school and released her. She provided a description of the car that was found abandoned a short time later. The Troop "A" bloodhounds arrived and followed a scent to a nearby home. The male occupant readily admitted to the crime.

In 1969, bloodhounds were kenneled at Batavia, Malone, Oneida and Hawthorne and responded to more than 100 calls for assistance during the year.

JAMESTOWN, N.Y. BANK ROBBERY

During the summer of 1970, a lone bandit robbed the Marine Midland Bank of $619.00 and was last seen on foot running into a dump and swampy area behind the bank. A handgun was displayed making the robber dangerous. Responding were Trooper Peter Roughead and four Jamestown Police Officers who quickly sealed off the area. Trooper Leon Dywinski with bloodhound "Guy" responded spending 2 ½ hours crisscrossing the swampy area. Guy led searchers to a beach bag used to conceal the gun and plastic bag that held the money. A short time later, Guy led police to the suspect who was secreted in a clump of bushes. Four hours had elapsed from the robbery alarm to the arrest. Dywinski and Guy thoroughly soaked and covered with swamp slime were never deterred from their assignment.

ERIE COUNTY PENITENTIARY ESCAPEES

Three escaped prisoners from the Erie County Penitentiary at Alden, N.Y. were captured after two days of freedom. A house burglary several miles away led to the capture. One of the burglars had cut himself on a window during the burglary. Trooper Leon Dywinski and bloodhound "Guy" went to the burglary scene and picked up a trail. Accompanied by Troopers Bill Loft and Robert Hummel, a trail through heavy grass led to a heavily wooded area where a blanket, wallet and gloves taken during the burglary were found. A few minutes later, Guy flushed the trio from hiding and a foot chase ensued for more than a mile. The three were taken into custody while trying to hide in tall grass.

LOST BOY

A young boy was lost at a campsite in Wyoming County. Trooper Dywinski got to the scene after dark with "GUY" who was started on a piece of the boy's clothing. He began tracking in and around the various tents and trailers, went up a hill and became very excited near a pile of rocks. Nothing found. He then tracked to a very large tree. Again nothing. He would go back and forth between the rocks and the tree. This went on for about 20 minutes until the boy was found hiding behind the big tree. Afraid of a scolding, he would change his location every time he saw the flashlights approaching.

1981 – Bloodhounds were kept at Troops A, B, D, G, & K.

TROOP "A" DOG HANDLERS

Albert Perry	1934
David Schwarz	1964 – 1965
Leon Dywinski	1965 – 1978
Louis J. Lang	1978 - 1982
Scott C. Saunders	1982 - 1984
Michael Quinlan	1984 - 1986
Donald Martineck	1986

OTHER TROOP "A" BLOODHOUNDS

Merlin – DOB 6/28/81. Obtained from Troop "B" in September 1981. Poor tracker. Given to Neville Spring, Basom, N.Y. on 8/6/86.

Dudley Do Right – DOB 7/7/82. Poor tracker. Given to Henry Keicher, Cowlesville, N.Y. on 11/7/85

Duke - DOB 3/18/85. Obtained from Gerald Strong, Buffalo, N.Y. on 5/6/86. Poor tracker. Given to Erin Considine, Corfu, N.Y. on 11/17/86.

Angie – Acquired on 3/28/85. Donated by Dr. Robert Early, Williamsville, N.Y. Replaced Merlin

BIO SENSOR GERMAN SHEPHERDS

In 1975, the Division acquired three "bio-sensor" German Shepherds from the US Army for the sum of $10,000.00. They were named Crow, Miss Jicky and Baretta. They were trained in the detection of explosives in preparation for the 1980 Winter Olympics in Lake Placid, N.Y. Also purchased was a Labrador named Pearl.

TRAINING

Because it possessed one of the largest canine units in the country, the Baltimore Police Department was chosen1 as the training agency. The prevalent training method was to have aggressive dogs kenneled when not in use. The "Baltimore Method" required the dogs be sociable, allowed to be in and around the general public and reside at the handler's residence.

In 1978, the division initiated its own canine training program utilizing the Baltimore Method. Technical Sergeant John Curry was appointed to administer the canine program. The first training location was the State Police Academy. It was moved to Sidney, N.Y. in 1979 where it remained until 1987. The unit relocated to the Great Meadow Correctional Facility grounds at Comstock, N.Y. until 2000, when a permanent home was found in Cooperstown, N.Y. A 2000 acre countryside estate was donated by the Jane Forbes Clark foundation to be used as a training facility. Canines are now trained in narcotics detection, cadaver recovery and explosives detection.

The course consists of a twenty-week training period that teams a dog and handler that are instructed in obedience, agility, handler protection, explosive or narcotic detection, tracking, building searches, veterinary first aid and a map and compass course for land navigation. All training aspects must be passed for the team to be certified. Handlers are re-certified bi-annually.

On November 1, 1983, 13 one-year old dogs were graduated as trackers, sniffers and protectors. Each dog had completed 1000 hours of training. Seven were added to the state police roster and for the first time, six were trained for other agencies. Each trooper dog was named after a state police member that had been killed in the line of duty. Among them was Gary E. Kubasiak, the first dog handler killed.

MAX - FIRST TROOP "A" GERMAN SHEPHERD

In about 1974 - 75, Troop "A" Commander Albert Bardossi was seeking a canine to detect drugs. He was told that a bloodhound could be used, but they were not aggressive enough for that type of search. As luck would have it, Troop "A" dog handler Leon Dywinski was given a German shepherd that he personally trained. The brother of a trooper from Dresden, N.Y. who was relocating and could not keep him had donated the dog named "Max". Dywinski would take the dogs out for training almost daily. Max was also trained to find people, guns and marijuana. One of the first finds for Max was locating a shotgun that had been used in a crime. The weapon was found in less than 30 minutes in a heavily wooded area. On another occasion, Max assisted the Watkins Glen Police in the search for an escaped felon. Finding no scent material available, the dog started a field scent search locating the escapee hiding in tall grass in less than five minutes. Sometime around 1980, Max had to be put to sleep because of a hip displatia.

During winter months, Trooper Dywinski played an important role in public relations and child safety. He did demonstrations with the dogs and safety talks to children at schools throughout the troop area. For several years, he did a weekly guest appearance on the popular children's television show "Commander Tom" hosted by Tom Jolls on Channel 7 in Buffalo, New York. He did one live show monthly and while at the studio, taped three other shows for presentation at a later time. In 1980, Dywinski was told that due to a manpower shortage, he could no longer appear on the show, as there were more pressing duties. Thus ended the most highly educational and child safety programs ever presented in Western New York by a trooper.

LEON DYWINSKI - DOG HANDLER

1945 - TROOPER HORTON - K
TROOP

1965

LOCAL PUBLICITY - - "Bob" was the center of attention when Tony Zerbo of the Dunkirk Evening Observer arrived on the scene of a recent training detail. Also present with the dog were Tprs. N.L. Gumhalter and D.J. Swarts.

Leon Dywinski with Bloodhound pups – C. 1968

COMMUNICATIONS

Until 1931, the only source of communicating with troopers was by word of mouth, mail or telephone.

TELETYPE

The first communication improvement in the State Police occurred on September 15, 1931 when the first teletype system was placed into use. The system was perfected and improved upon through the years becoming one of the most efficient and expedient ways to relay information. The system was also improved with the installation of automatic sending and receiving teletype machines at the central control point, Division Headquarters. Teletype points were added at the Glens Falls Police Department and Henrietta State Police substation. There were now 110 teletypewriter points and 145 teletypewriter instruments within in the state.

In 1953, a teletype message would report that a 14 state alarm message was dispatched after a serious crime was committed. This was accomplished through the New York State Police communication system. The communication system at the Batavia Barracks supervised by Technical Sergeant John M. Long was the central point for the dissemination of alarms for Western New York. As an example, Buffalo Police would send a teletype message requesting a 14 state alarm to Batavia. It was immediately forwarded to Oneida and Albany. From Albany, the message was sent to all New York State police departments, barracks and stations equipped with a teletype machine. It was also sent to law enforcement agencies in Connecticut, Delaware, Maryland, Massachusetts, New Hampshire, New Jersey, Ohio, Pennsylvania, Rhode Island, Virginia, Vermont, North Carolina and Washington D.C. In addition to the teletype, Troop A was in direct communications by radio with all substations and trooper cars in the troop area. It is also connected with a statewide system with Albany the focal point for making the connections. Troop "A" also monitored short wave radio communications of the Rochester and Buffalo Police Departments and sheriff's departments in the 11 county area.

The National Police Teletypewriter Network was activated on December 25, 1955 opening direct communications between New York and 34 other states. It was anticipated that the system would put to rest jurisdictional problems and afford a written record of warrant requests from one agency to another. The speed of the system would also offset the advantage of escaping criminals from one jurisdiction to another.

During 1960, the teletype system was expanded with the addition of 17 states, 39 municipalities and 11 sheriff's offices.

RADIO

1943 - A site near the Attica State Prison was selected to install a new state police, 300-foot tall radio-transmitting tower. Extensive tests showed this to be the best-suited area to service stations and patrol cars in the 11 County Western New York area.

One-way radio communications were first installed in 1933 at Troop G Headquarters, but it took until 1944 for this advancement to reach Troop "A". The installation of radio station WBTC operating on a frequency of 1658 kilocycles at the Batavia State Police Barracks completed the network. The addition of 1000-watt radio transmitters at Troops A, D and C Headquarters completed coverage of the state by short wave radio. Fourteen division members attended a four month long communications school and were licensed as second-class radio operators by the Federal Communications Commission.

Sergeant Charles Z. McDonald was in charge of the Batavia Communications Section. Radio operators were required to have a Class 2 radio license in order to operate the radio and send broadcast information. Three secretaries working at the barracks also obtained radio licenses. They were Winifred Miner, Viola Schwingle and Mabel Keister. The station was manned 24 hours daily with a station announcement and time check given every half hour. Prior to the system installation, all state police cars in the area were tuned onto the Buffalo Police radio transmitting station.

In 1945, an emergency telephone service was initiated throughout the state. Telephone books all carried the legend: In an emergency, call or dial an operator and say "I WANT A STATE TROOPER". The telephone operator would then complete the call contacting the nearest State Police Station without delay or charge.

A new radio system was installed by the New York Telephone Company in 1946. It was a three-way frequency modulated radio system that in effect, would cover every inch of the state. The initial installation cost was $735,000.00 with a yearly maintenance cost estimated at about $300,000.00. The key transmitter unit for Western New York was located at Batavia, New York. Troop cars in the near vicinity could now talk to one another. There were 73 radio transmitters and receivers installed at troop headquarters, zone stations and twenty four-hour substations across the state. Precincts where only a few troopers were assigned had radio receivers only. Two way radios were placed in the departments 382 automobiles and one motorboat used for patrol purposes. In addition, 16 sets of portable radio equipment powered by gasoline motors were provided for use at disasters or serious crimes. Forty-two military style walkie-talkies were also provided with 7 assigned to each Troop Headquarters. Two-way communications were now available between stations and patrol cars as well as emergency sites and between patrol cars. The entire communication system was changed from AM to FM with the last installation completed on August 29, 1947.

Two-way radios were installed in all motorcycles in 1954.

By the end of 1961, the Division had two boats, twenty motorcycles and 715 patrol cars equipped with radios.

Walkie-talkie field unit radios weighing 15 pounds were replaced in May 1965. A new General Electric Handi-Talkie radio was distributed to the various troops. The unit weighed less than 4 pounds with a usable field battery life of up to 80- hours between charges. They were weatherproof, had a leather carrying case with a shoulder strap or belt hooks, and had external speakers with batteries chargeable on a 110-volt current charger. The effective range was from three to five miles.

In 1966, the New York State Police were chosen by the FBI to be the states link to the FBI's National Crime Information Center (NCIC).

A high band radio system was initiated in 1970 to alleviate interference problems. Hand held radios were used for the first time making it possible to communicate while away from the vehicle.

A statewide channel was added to the radio system in 1976 making it possible to have inter-troop communication.

CB RADIOS

A Citizen Band craze took place during 1976. Everyone seemed to have one or needed one. A fifteen-month program was initiated to determine the value of the CB in police work. The US Department of Transportation awarded a $75,000 grant to evaluate their use in a highway environment. A $50,000 Traffic Safety Committee grant allowed the installation of CB radios in 150 State Police cars and 15 stations in the Troop "D" area. The test period realized 30,000 requests for assistance. Emergency response time was reduced, unsafe driving conditions and traffic violations were reported as well as criminal acts.

Citizen band (CB) radios installed in troop cars were assigned call letters KNY0911 by the Federal Communications Commission. The Batavia Kiwanis Club donated ten (10) CB radios to Troop "A" for use in patrol cars.

In 1977, new radios were installed in Thruway vehicle's making it possible for Thruway cars to communicate with local patrols directly.

A twenty-four foot mobile communications command vehicle was purchased through a Governors Traffic Safety Committee grant in 1981. It was environmentally controlled and able to function as a command center and communication center.

COMPUTER

On March 1, 1966, the first electronic computer was utilized at division headquarters. It had the capacity to perform numerous police functions, but was initially used to speed up teletype transmissions between Division installations and make information available to the road trooper almost instantly.

The computer was an electronic communications message switching and inquiry system installed by UNIVAC Division of Sperry Rand at a cost of $330,200.00. It was designed to reduce time for delivery of messages from an average of 40 minutes to five minutes or less. It had a memory component that was used to store registration plate data on stolen cars & plates and have the information available to the road trooper within five seconds.

Under the old system, messages were sent to a relay point when a circuit was open and it would be forwarded to division communications in Albany. Albany would then forward the message to another relay point and so on until it reached its destination. The new system eliminated the relays system. All stations had a two-letter designation code assigned. A teletype message would be sent directly to the computer in Albany where the computer would search and forward the message directly to the coded designation. The effect of the new system created a direct line of communications between any of the 78 teletype equipped state police stations and 68 municipal and sheriff's departments that were on the system.

In 1970, a new mainframe computer was installed, upgrading information management and expanding services to local police departments. As a result, the New York Statewide Police Information Network (NYSPIN) began functioning in 1971. 1972 saw the input of data on lost, stolen and recovered guns. Users also interfaced with the New York State Identification and Intelligence System (NYSIIS) that maintained a database on persons missing or wanted in New York State. NYSIIS was replaced by DCJS, (Department of Criminal Justice Services) at the end of 1972. During 1973, the Department of Motor Vehicles database was added providing driver and vehicle registration information almost instantly to the trooper on road. The computers were also utilized to maintain personnel records, statistical data and activity time reports.

High speed video terminals were installed statewide that provided on screen message formats with the ability for high-speed transmission. These terminals were known as "Dataspeed 40 Video Display/ Printers" and consisted of three parts, a typewriter like keyboard on which messages were tapped out, a television screen that displayed the message and a recorder on which messages were printed. Installation was started in 1974 with 310 units installed by mid 1975. The new terminals were capable of transmitting and receiving at a rate of 1200 words a minute compared to the rate of 75 per minute with the older terminals. Another advantage was the ability to call up a message format, fill in the blanks and make instant corrections without starting from the beginning. Seven different message originators would respond to a normal inquiry in less than seven seconds.

911 EMERGENCY TELEPHONE SERVICE

The first telephone call was a call for help. On March 10, 1876, Alexander Graham Bell and Thomas A. Watson, in different rooms, were about to try a new transmitter. Watson heard Bell's voice saying, "Mr. Watson, come here. I want you!" Bell had upset the acid of a battery over his clothes. The first telephone call became a part of history.

The idea of being able to dial a single (universal) number to report emergencies was first utilized in Great Britain in 1937. Citizens could dial the digits "9-9-9" and reach a central operator who would in turn dispatch law enforcement, fire, or ambulance as needed.

INTRODUCTION IN THE UNITED STATES

It took more than thirty years to be introduced in the United States. The idea of a three-digit emergency number in the United States was the result of the urging of some concerned citizens and the Presidential Commission on Law Enforcement in 1967. It was introduced to Congress and committees were formed to decide how to make the concept a reality.

First, the telephone companies had to find a three-digit number that was not being used anywhere in the United States or Canada as a central office exchange or an area code. Other considerations were that it should be easy to find on the telephone dial or easily dialed in the dark. The telephone industry decided on the digits "9-1-1".

The first 9-1-1-telephone call was placed on February 16, 1968 in Haleyville, Alabama.

At first, basic 9-1-1 could only provide a voice connection to a predetermined emergency response agency. Callers knew that a call to 9-1-1 would connect them to the right people for emergency help, but the emergency responders did not have any information other than what was provided by the caller. Still, basic 9-1-1 was a big improvement in emergency services.

Later enhanced 9-1-1 provided the caller's location information and telephone number via special computers and display screens. Enhanced 9-1-1 also provides features for selective routing and selective transfer of 9-1-1 calls to multiple emergency response jurisdictions.

Selective routing is really the essence of enhanced 9-1-1. A master street address guide was developed that lists street number ranges within an emergency service zone. The appropriate Police, Sheriff, Fire and Emergency Medical Service for each zone are identified and a unique emergency service number assigned. All 9-1-1 calls within that geographic area are sent to a pre-defined public safety answering point responsible for handling calls in that area.

SERGEANT JOSEPH (FRED) JOHNS

Technical Sergeant Joseph (Fred) Johns who spent his entire law enforcement career as the State Police Communications expert retired on December 19, 1969. This ended a career that started June 1, 1929. Johns was assigned to learn teletypes from the ground up although at the time, there were no trooper teletypes. It was anticipated there soon would be so Johns practiced many dry runs, as well as radio broadcasting. He supervised the installation of one way broadcasting to troop cars before the two way messaging was developed. In 1931, he became the "Voice of the Troopers" when he broadcast a 15 minute nightly broadcast from Division Headquarters in the Capitol. It was aired originally over station WOKO in Albany, New York. It was the Empire State Network that is now defunct. His familiar radio sign off was "This is Trooper Fred Johns of the New York State Police wishing you a good night."

On September 15, 1931, Sgt. Johns dispatched the first of five teletype messages to inaugurate an era of rapid information transmission. Governor Franklin D. Roosevelt was at his side and also poked out a message.

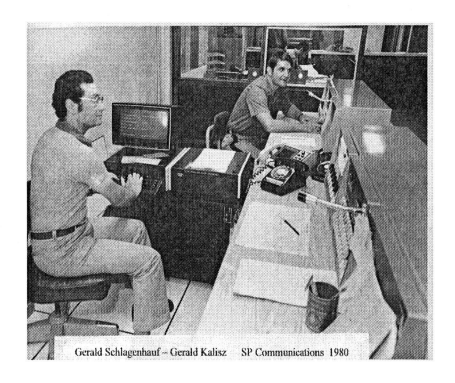

Gerald Schlagenhauf – Gerald Kalisz   SP Communications 1980

NY STATE FAIR

HISTORY

1810 - The Berkshire Agricultural Society at Pittsfield, Massachusetts, held the first recorded actual permanent state fair in 1810.

1851 - The first International Exposition was held at the especially built Crystal Palace, London, England in 1851.

1819 - The New York State Fair was actually organized in 1819. The New York State Legislature appropriated $20,000.00 for distribution among the states agricultural societies. Onondaga County was eligible for $300.00 provided the citizens raised an equal amount and organized an agricultural society for holding of a fair. A society was formed with the first fair held on November 2, 1819. Fairs were held annually for five or six years, then, discontinued for lack of interest.

1838 - The Legislature passed an act re-organizing the Onondaga County Agricultural Society.

1841 - An amount of $180.00 was provided by the state and the New York State Fair was held for the first time in Syracuse, N.Y. under the auspices of the New York State Agricultural Society. 15,000 persons attended the four-day event that recorded expenses of $100,000.00 with receipts of $2,000.00.

During the early years, the State Fair was held at various locations through out the state.

1899 – The New York State Fair Commission was formed and permanent fairgrounds established at Syracuse, N.Y. because of its central location and accessibility.

1900s - During the early 1900s, less attention was paid to agricultural exhibits with entertainment featured to attract higher attendance. Horse racing was an amateur hobby at the time, but thanks to the fairs, developed into a highly professional sport. High profits were realized by breeders, but little to agriculture. Soon, the time for holding of fairs was determined more for the convenience of the racing circuit than the needs of the agricultural societies.

1910 – 1911 - Attending the fair became an institution for the farmer. They would come to see animals exhibited by breeders and the horse shows. Huge crowds came to watch the horse races, airplane demonstrations, auto races and midway attractions. The automobile races were held on the last day of the fair in 1910 & 1911. During the 1911 races, one of the cars crashed through the fence killing eleven spectators. Auto races were suspended, but resumed in1919 after concrete crash walls had been built.

1920 - This was a year to remember. Horse racing featured the great horse "Peter Manning" winning the $10,000 race classic. Automobile races featured Ralph DePalma, Gaton and Louis Chevrolet. An airplane propeller in view of thousands of spectators fatally slashed stunt pilot Tex McLaughlin.

1938 – The title of the New York State Fair was changed to the "New York State Agricultural and Industrial Exposition"

STATE POLICE

1917 – The State Police have policed the state fair since their formation in 1917 with the exception of those war years, when no fair was conducted. Members of the Division were invited to participate in horse show exhibitions and demonstrations. Each troop had crack riding teams that participated in trick riding demonstrations.

1956 – The fair was eight days long with one hundred twenty-five troopers and seven BCI men assigned. They were housed in a dormitory on the fair grounds. Fair goers showed an increased interest in the activities of the state police. Their opportunity to observe troopers was limited to observing traffic direction, general activities and a modest exhibit. During 1956, a fully detailed exhibit was presented showing a full picture of the trooper's activity. Ten troopers were assigned the display explaining various functions supported by displays and photographs. 68,500 persons visited the display. 9000 children signed a Junior Citizen Safety Pledge and were given a certificate. Entrants were also eligible to get a German shepherd puppy during a public drawing. The lucky winners were David Dopp of Manlius and Linda Robson of Waterloo, N.Y.

1957 – Retired First Sergeant Vernon Clayson recalled his first fair assignment. Troopers stayed in a tin building with one shower at the end of the room for the entire 100-man detail. We didn't have individual beds, when you got up, the next shift laid down and usually in the same bedding for the entire nine days. The building was next to the Native American Indian display and they beat their drums and chanted all day long. On one occasion, I was driven to a location a mile away to direct traffic and was soon forgotten. I stayed there for twelve hours before hiking back, because I was angry and hungry. No one cared or said anything. We had to eat on the grounds as no other provisions were made for meals. Most of the members freeloaded their food from local vendors. I refused to take a free meal and paid for what I ate. On the last day of the fair, I was assigned the 12-hour day shift at the main gate, and then assigned to patrol for twelve hours on the night shift while everyone else partied. At fairs end, the casual observer would see dozens of teddy bears and stuffed animals in the back seat of Troop cars leaving the fair grounds, both Troopers and Sergeants taking their cheap loot to their children. I vowed never to go back and didn't. Howard Smith assigned me to go again the next year, but I related my feeling to Lieutenant Keeley and was replaced by Gerry Kitchen who never forgave me.

1958 – 497,134 visitors were attracted to the nine day fair.

1964 – 1975 – First Sergeant Howard Smith made member assignments to the State Fair detail with a trooper from each station assigned. We stayed in a two story open bay barracks on the fairgrounds adjacent to the Indian Village. There was no air conditioning with late August being very hot. I recall Trooper Walter Linden always being assigned barracks desk duty and Danny DeJohn, a former US Marine bringing in a duffel bag full of thick telephone books that he would tear in half with his bare hands. I usually volunteered because we were guaranteed at least two-days overtime pay that was dearly needed because of our low salaries. I don't recall exactly what year, but arrangements were made to house the fair detail at the Northway Motel a few miles from the fair grounds. What luxury! There were two of us to a room with our own bathroom. Our room had three occupants. My roommate seemed to shuffle a girl friend in and out between visits from his wife. Many of the troopers would have a wife or girlfriend come visit while at the fair. I can recall my family visiting for the day and being driven around the fairgrounds in a troop car. Parking was no problem. Legally parked cars were towed to make nearby parking available for family members. A trooper's family was always taken care of by the uniformed troopers on duty. That's the way things were done back then, doing for one another. I don't think Sergeant Clayton Snook who was in charge at the time would have approved, but then there wasn't too much he did approve of.

1969 – The State Police Exhibit had been improved upon to the point it was a major attraction at the fair. It was anticipated that during the seven-day exhibition, 600,000 spectators would be in attendance. Under the supervision of Sergeant Joe Christian, 4000 square feet of exhibit area allocated three years earlier was completely re-furbished.

Sergeant Tom Sackel and Bob Miazga designed a hippie pad with psychedelic décor to recount the perils of drug use and abuse. A breathalyzer booth provided demonstrations to impress viewers of the hazards of drunken driving.

Troopers Walt Hornberger and Bill Truesdale raised the level of the diving tank making it easier for spectators to view.

During the fair, Bill Truesdale and Trooper Gene Griffin could be found outside the exhibit astride Morgan horses hoisting youngsters into the saddle for photos and displaying their horsemanship.

Sergeant Tom Scanlon was in charge of a 10-man detail conducting a popular bicycle skill contest introduced in 1968.

Other displays included shooting demonstrations, bloodhounds, a radar demonstration and laboratory exhibit.

The seven-day fair detail was made up of 174 uniform troopers, 11 BCI men and 34 members assigned to the exhibit.

Troopers continue to police the fair grounds and maintain a display area within the State Exhibit Building that is one of the more popular on the grounds.

(BCI Bulletin, 1957 – VOL 22 NO 2) (BCI Bulletin, 1958 – VOL 23 NO 3)
(Trooper Magazine, August 1969)

DIVING OPERATIONS

Man has dived below the surface of the water for hundreds of years to provide food or financial gain through the gathering of sponges and pearls. Only mans lung capacity determined the length of the dive. The first snorkel in recorded history was a hollow reed.

In 1934, the State Police purchased a single Morse Shallow Water Diving Apparatus that made it possible for a diver to descend to a depth of 50 feet.

World War II provided the background for the development of self contained underwater breathing apparatus (SCUBA) by the French Navy. It was the British & Italian naval frogmen who proved its worth during special diving assignments.

Divers are called out in all types of weather and conditions to search for a victim of drowning or evidence from a crime. More often than not, diving operations are conducted under adverse conditions. Visibility and low temperatures create the largest impediment as well as underwater hazards and polluted water. All underwater dives are in two man teams and the divers remain within sight of one another.

TRAINING

The first Division Diving School was conducted on September 17, 1956 at Lake Lauderdale, Cambridge, N.Y. Twenty (20) trooper volunteer divers with military experience passed a rigid physical examination and began training. They were trained and qualified in skin diving and use of deep-diving gear. Captain George W. Ashley, Sgt. Robert E. Lund and Corporal H.T. Smetana gave instruction.

Members that attended & successfully completed the course were:

TROOP

A - Cpl. R.E. Powers	Tpr. R.E. Minekheim	Tpr. D.P. Studd	
B – Cpl. J.W. Kelly	Tpr. R.J. Trombly	Tpr. R.A. Buell	
C – Tpr. M.C. Capozzi	Tpr. J.F. Franke	Tpr. F.W. Leibe	
D – Tpr. E.W. Singleton	Tpr. R.E. Parrow	Tpr. H.G. Stewart	
G – Tpr. W.J. Ennis	Tpr. W.E. Draghi	Tpr. C.A. Judkins	Tpr. D.J. Guiry
K – Tpr. P.F. Paquet	Tpr. D.M. Bender	Tpr. D.D. Deviney	

"A" TROOP SKIN DIVERS – 1958

Several state troopers from Troop "A" received underwater training at the US Navy School in New Jersey and upon returning provided training to others in the Troop. They were: George Zink, Daniel O'Halloran, Robert Minekheim, Raymond Meyering and Donald Studd, James Moochler, John Braisington and Thomas Salvameni. The men were equipped with full-face masks and carried a 35-pound compressed air tank with lung equipment and could descend to a depth of 125 feet.

WBTA RADIO – BATAVIA, N.Y. AUGUST 24, 1958
RADIO EDITORIAL

Skin diving training for six members of Troop "A" will materially increase the effectiveness of the troop's water search and rescue service. Working in teams of two, the State Police skin divers will be able to operate at depths up to 70 feet. Troopers are called on frequently to search for drowning victims and underwater hunts for evidence in criminal cases are not uncommon.

Having Troop "A" at our door for forty years, Batavians need to be reminded now and then that the gray clad officers of the law are a big factor in the community's low crime rate. Such crimes of violence as bank hold-ups are fairly common in Western New York, but Batavia has never experienced a bank stick-up. Crime doesn't pay in the home of Troop A.

ADVANCED TRAINING

In 1960, three - two week classes were given to 38 members in Advanced Underwater Diving. It was intended to acquaint divers with the latest phases of scuba and aqua lung-equipment, underwater investigation and search techniques. The curriculum consisted of one week training and classroom instruction at the Y.M.C.A. at Troy, N.Y. and a second week of actual diving at Lake George and Sacandaga Reservoir.

During April 1965, twenty-three troopers reported to Sergeant Theodore Smetana at the gymnasium of State University College at Oneonta, N.Y. where they started their training. The first phase was classroom instruction in care and use of scuba equipment, medical aspects of diving and various techniques used. They practiced their skills in the college pool where they learned how to snorkel and use their fins and mask properly. During underwater training, they learned mask clearing, ditch and don procedures, station-to-station breathing and underwater search with blacked out facemasks simulating turbid water conditions.

The second phase was at Lake George with ½ mile swims done before breakfast. Training involved practicing under conditions that would be faced in future diving assignments and instruction from Army demolition experts in the use of mine detecting equipment that could be used to locate medal objects.

Instructors included Troopers Walter Hornberger, Delbert George, Robert McDowell and Gerry Zappolo.

The new drivers were:

Troop A - Thomas Bowman, Robert Burns, Michael O'Rourke and William Reynolds.

Troop B – James Gayton, William F. Myers, Wayne Bailey and John Stafford.

Troop C – Brian O'Connor and Richard Beauman

Troop D – Mathew Homes

Troop G - Martin Cech and Warren Curtis

Troop K – John Ryan, Jerry Storch, Arthur Krug and John Schmidt.

In 1966, the state police had thirty-four qualified scuba divers.

UNDERWATER COMMUNICATION SYSTEM
In the spring of 1966, the New York State Police put a new submersible version of the walkie-talkie in service. It is called the Aqua Sonics Hydra Phone and had an effective range of 6000 feet. It was powered by a cylindrical battery about two inches wide and two feet long, which was strapped to the compressed air tank. A microphone was placed in the diver's mouthpiece and small receiver fit into the hood. They were connected to a small aerial projecting from the hood. The Hydra Phone enabled divers to talk to one another or to a surface unit. Prior communications was done through hand signals, if the water was clear enough or by tapping on the air tank or tugging on a rope or cord. Two advantages of the system were the safety factor provided in case of equipment failure and relieving the diver's feeling of isolation.

THREE YOUTHS DROWN – SKANEATELES – APRIL 1966
Between April 11 and 18, 1966, 1,800 man hours were accounted for by a joint troop diving detail to recover the bodies of three youth that had drowned in Skaneateles Lake. Two 14-year-old boys, Russell Cayer and Donald Cain along with 13-year-old Betsy Loftus were lost, when their canoe overturned. The first report of the mishap was received at 6:45 PM. The massive search lasted one week with fourteen divers, twenty-eight additional state police members, five volunteer fire departments and the Conservation Department Helicopter utilized during the search and recovery operation.

The diving detail started out facing the difficulty of a lake with a depth of up to 165 and icy cold water. Aided by two professional divers, approximately 250,000 square yards of lake bottom was covered by divers and draggers. On April 15, the body of the girl was recovered in 60 feet of water. The bodies of the two boys were recovered two days later. It was noted that the "duck" crews provided by the

Owasco, Cayuga, Union Springs and Aurora Fire Departments were invaluable. Logistics provided by the Skaneateles Police and Fire Departments provided outstanding logistics with the Conservation Department helicopter observing from above and being available in case decompression was needed for a diver.

TROOP "E" – FIRST DIVING DETAIL
In 1968, the Troop "E" diving team was formed made up of Troopers F.A. Moochler, M.W. Holmes, W.F. Myers and Sgt. T.R. Reese.

EARLY 1970s

Dave O'Brien and some other SCUBA guys had the boat out during some flooding in the Silver Creek area but it was needed elsewhere. They kept coming up with excuses for delaying the assignment before admitting they had swamped it by neglecting to put the drain plug in before floating the boat.

Trooper Donald Vogt was assigned to the Troop Headquarters desk duty because he was a member of the SCUBA team and would readily available if needed. He was happy to oblige, because he didn't really want to be involved in any police work. When he resigned, there was no lead diver to inspect and maintain the SCUBA equipment so Dave O'Brien was designated. He explained how the SCUBA gear should be stored and maintained and did so with great care realizing that this equipment and apparatus was vital for life support when submerged.

STOLEN CARS RECOVERED – 1972
During the summer of 1972, the Troop "A" diving team assisted the Buffalo Police Department along the Buffalo waterfront of Lake Erie and the Niagara River. The diving operation required two weeks resulting in the recovery of fifteen stolen late model cars that had been stripped for parts, a rifle and two safes. The dive was particularly difficult because of fast currents, murky water and the volume of debris on the lake floor.

LOST SHIP LOCATED - 1981
During a practice dive in the Niagara River, Troop "A" divers came upon a sunken 40- foot sloop in 35 feet of water. The ship had been lost during a violent storm in 1940. Over the years, divers had searched for the wreck without success. Its location was marked and the US Coast Guard notified for further investigation and possible recovery.

1963 DIVING SCHOOL
FRONT - P.PAQUET- R.VAN ALSTYNE- T.BRENNAN
R.MINEKHEIM-N.GALIZIA-N.KILFOYLE
BACK - V.MARTINEZ- D.MERGENTHALER- E.RITZMAN
W.GARRITY- D.GEORGE- C.GRECO- J.COTTER
J.MOOCHLER

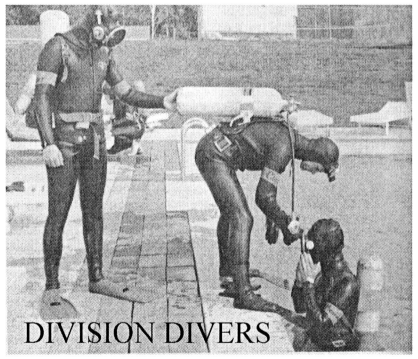

DIVISION DIVERS

M.WRIGHT - W. ERNST - T. PALUCH
1980 TROOP "A" DIVERS

STATE POLICE PATROL BOATS
VIGILANT AND SYREN II

The Division, as the needed utilized canvas inflatable boats and small fourteen-foot aluminum crafts. Many were borrowed from local fire departments for search and rescue missions, rather than wait for a boat to be sent from troop headquarters.

During the spring of 1945, the Division acquired a sleek high powered motorboat for patrol on the St. Lawrence River. It was named SYREN II and was kept at Alexandria Bay where it was available for duty twenty-four hours a day.

A second patrol boat, VIGILANT was acquired in 1948 and placed in service patrolling the entire length of Lake Champlain. These boats were utilized until 1963, when they were taken out of service.

The boat patrols were responsible for making the waterways safe for use by recreational boaters, as well as for commercial traffic.

ST. LAWRENCE DISASTER

On September 24, 1947, the 664-ton tanker "Translake" was struck by the heavily laden 1094-ton Collier "Milverton" while headed upstream in the St.Lawrence River. Oil from the "Translake"gushed onto the "Milverton" creating a terrific explosion and fire. Surrounding water became an inferno with the "Translake" running aground on the Canadian shore. The "Milverton" drifted downstream three-miles until grounding itself on a shoal near the American shore. Syren II rushed to scene rescuing crew members that had jumped or were blown into the water by the explosion. They were transported to shore for treatment at local hospitals. The oil fires burned atop the water and on "Milverton" throughout the day and night with hundreds of curiosity seekers arriving for a glimce. The "Milverton" advised that if the fires reached the boiler room, there was the possibility of another explosion occurring. Safety measures were taken with resident's in the immediate area evacuated, highway traffic restricted and other vessels stopped from using the river locks. On September 26th , the scene was brought under control with troopers boarding the Milverton where they found and removed five bodies and the remains of a sixth. Other bodies were later recovered from the river.

LAKE CHAMPLAIN RESCUE

On May 25, 1953, the Vigilant was called to an area near Plattsburg, N.Y. where cries for help were heard through a heavy fog. Due to heavy seas and poor visibilty, a trooper located himself where he could barely see objects in the water and gave instructions to the Vigilan by radio until it reached a capsized boat with three people clinging to it. Two men and a woman were safely pulled from the water and taken to shore for transport to a local hospital. The Vigilant then returned to the scene retreiving the capsized boat.

During the early 1960s, Division purchased several "Boston Whaler" watercraft replacing the original boats that proved cumbersome by comparison. They measured 16 feet, 7 inches and were equipped with a 90 HP motor. The craft could cruise at 45 MPH and was selected for its stability during use on diving details.

TROOPER PATROL BOAT

TROOPER PATROL BOAT
VIGILANT

FIREARMS

EARLY TROOPER FIREARMS

In 1917, Colonel Chandler selected the Winchester Model 1894 carbine to supplement the .45 Colt Revolver. The carbine was chambered for the .30 Winchester Center Fire cartridge and when fully loaded held seven rounds. The cartridge had a 170-grain metal case bullet, 30 grains of smokeless powder and a muzzle velocity of about 2,220 feet per second. The barrel length was 20 inches with an overall length of 38 inches and weighed about 6 ½ pounds. The carbine was commonly referred to as the "Winchester .30 - .30". The rifle was carried in a scabbard attached to the saddle in the early days. Fearing loss or larceny when the trooper was away from his horse, it was determined that the carbine was to be kept at the stations and made available in case of an emergency. It was used until 1965.

The Colt "New Service" Revolver was the standard firearm of the trooper. It was a double-action revolver and chambered a .45 long Colt cartridge. The arm had a five & one half inch barrel, weighed 39 ounces and had a lanyard loop affixed to the butt. The backstrap was stamped "N.Y.S.T."

The .45 Colt was replaced in 1954 by the lighter Colt "Official Police" revolver. It had a six-inch barrel, weighed 34 ounces and used a .38 caliber special cartridge.

The Colt "Official Police" model was introduced in 1962. It was a.38 caliber revolver with a four-inch barrel and was used until 1974, when troopers went to the Smith & Wesson Model 28, .357 Magnum. It was more powerful than the .38 caliber revolver. The change was made after Trooper Ray Dodge was killed during a shootout. He had shot and hit the perpetrator twice, but the .38 bullet was not enough to stop his assailant who continued to shoot resulting in the trooper's death.

During recruit firearms training in November 1978, it was discovered that the ejector rod and ratchet assembly on the Smith and Wesson .357 Magnum became separated during sustained firing using .357 ammunition. Until the problem was being resolved, 38+P ammunition was issued.

OTHER WEAPONS

In 1938, the troopers obtained a number of 1917 Enfield rifles with slings. They used a 30.06 cartridge and were intended for long-range use. They were discontinued in1965.

The trooper armament at one time included a 1928 model Thompson Submachine-Gun that was obtained in 1940. It used a .45 caliber cartridge and was equipped with either a box or a drum magazine having a capacity of 20 and 50 cartridges. It would fire at a rate of 700 to 725 shots per minute. Deemed too dangerous for police work, its use was discontinued in 1962.

The 12-guage Ithaca Model 37 "Featherweight" pump action was the next weapon of choice. Received in 1963, it had a 20-inch barrel with the rifle slug & "00" buckshot the only authorized ammunition to be used.

The Winchester Model 70 was used from 1965 to 1988. It was a .270caliber, bolt-action rifle with a 21-¾ inch barrel. It was equipped with a sling and telescopic sight with detachable mounts for accurate shooting at long ranges.

The special purpose tear gas gun is part of the division arsenal. It has a 1-1/2 inch bore and is capable of firing projectiles from its 10 inch barrel at ranges from 225 to 325yards or using pyrotechnic flares.

FIREARMS TRAINING – 1950

Recognizing the importance of a trooper carrying a handgun for the purpose of protecting life and property, Division policy required that every member be qualified on an annual basis. Each autumn, the 250 troopers of Troop "A" took part in marksmanship drills using the shotgun, rifle and machine guns. During the spring, they qualified with their service revolvers at an indoor range. Training was done at the New York National Guard site at Camp Owen in Wethersfield, N.Y. Every member of the troop was required to take the marksmanship test and failure meant added instruction until minimum qualifications were met. Although the use of rifles and shotguns was rare, troopers were trained to be ready for any eventuality.

1961 brought about changes in the firearms training program. The Practical Pistol Course, a combat type course was incorporated into the state police- training program. Twenty-six troopers attended an FBI "Instructors' Course" conducted at Camp Smith.

These trained firearms instructors then conducted training in the new course to all field personnel.

Retired Trooper Peter C. Detoy recalled that in mid 1960s, the following were range instructors from Troop "A". Sergeant's William Mulryan and Jim McDermott, Troopers Jack Arnet, Nicholas Gumhalter, Donald Pettit, R.F. Manna, John Kulikowski, Robert Harlock, Paul Stephens, Frederick Porcello, Lawrence Austin, Harold Hatch, George Hyder, Leon Dywinski and Donald Girven. There were others, but he could not recall their names. Troopers were required to qualify twice yearly. During the summer months, the Camp Owen, Wethersfield, N.Y. range was used with defensive tactics part of the training. During winter months, training was conducted at the indoor range at the NYS Armory on State Street, Batavia, N.Y. or at the NYS Armory at Lockport, N.Y.

The combat course was:

7 yd line - 12 rounds 25 seconds hip level

15 yd line - 12 rounds point shoulder

25 yd line - 18 rounds - 6 kneeling/ 6 strong hand barricade/ 6 weak hand barricade

50 yd line - 24 rounds - 6 sitting/ 6 prone/ 6 strong hand barricade/ 6 weak hand barricade.

5 rounds of 00 buckshot was fired from a 12-gauge shotgun.

In 1965, troopers were required to re-qualify three times yearly. Instructions were also given in civil disturbance and crowd control formations.

During the 1970s, qualifications were reduced to once yearly.

PISTOL TEAM

Firearms competitions had been held annually to determine the best shooters in each troop who then competed against one another to determine the best qualified in the division. This inter-troop firearms competition had ceased in 1935 because of increased traffic duties during summer months, the second- world war and re-organization after the war.

The New York State Police Division Revolver Team was revived in June 1955. Members of the Pistol Team were chosen after competing in a Division statewide elimination match held at West Point. Troopers with the highest scores in each troop were selected for a competitive shoot-off. The top ten scorers were then selected to represent the Division. The team competed in six (6) matches with Trooper H. J. Uranitis scoring a perfect 300 at the Lower Merion, Pa. meet.

In 1956, the Troop "A" team was made up of R.G. Dennis, J.G. McDonald, J.C. Moochler, P.H. Beck, M.J. Fiordo, E.J. Gluch, R.D. Koenig, C.L. McCartney, H.I. Moose and C.A. Salmon. None qualified for the Division Pistol Team.

During 1957, the Division Pistol Team entered 11 tournaments winning 11 trophies.

In 1958, the Division Pistol Team rolled up a record of eight victories, three seconds and two third place finishes in thirteen matches against elite competition. During a match at Springfield, Massachusetts, Trooper E. F. Griebsch of Troop B shot a perfect 300 score. 4000 entries participated in the Daily Mirror-Colt 26th Annual International Police Tournament held at Hempstead, N.Y. The Division Pistol Team set a new record for the match scoring 1,197 out of a possible 1200.

During May 1960, the Division Pistol Team under the direction of Lieutenant J.C. Miller set a new world record in the four man team competition at the Police Pistol Matches in Fairlawn, N.J. The team made up of Uranitis, Griebsch, Janssen and Paquet shot 1198 out of a possible 1200.

In 1964, the Division Pistol Team established an all-time indoor combat record. The team was made up of P.F. Paquet "K", 589: W.F. Mulryan "A", 590: Steve Kurpil "C", 586 and B.L. Cutten "K", 577.

HAZARDOUS DEVICES

Until 1972, State Police explosive device training consisted of several hours of training by the US Army in recognizing bombs and explosive devices. Troopers were instructed to recognize a devise as dangerous, secure the area and call a US Army Demolition Unit.

In 1972, a growing number of bomb threats led to the training of nineteen volunteers, two from each troop to be equipped with the skills needed to handle such complaints. They attended a one-week training course at the State Police Academy and were later trained at the Hazardous Devices School at Red Stone Arsenal in Alabama. In the first year, the unit was called upon to investigate 32 explosive devices, 11 incendiary devices, 21 found explosives and 115 bomb threats.

M-80 DEMOLITION MISCUE– APRIL 28, 1978

Retired Trooper Eric Hammerschmidt relates this serious story that became humorous and is referred to as the **M–80 Caper** in the re-telling. Investigator Joe Sarnowski had received information that one Edward R. Chmielesky of Lancaster, N.Y. had several cases of the powerful M-80 "Cherry Bomb" firecrackers stored in his garage. Investigation by Senior Investigator Gene Fechter, SP Clarence led to the arrest of Chmielesky for Unlawful Possession of Fireworks. Fifty-seven cases of the fireworks were confiscated and stored initially at the Clarence sub-station before being transported to the Troop Headquarters at Batavia. The following day, Lancaster Town Justice Edward Dwan signed an order of destruction giving the State Police the authority to destroy the fireworks under a section of law permitting dangerous material destruction before trial.

The Troop "A" firearms instructor, Trooper George Hyder trained in explosive demolition was assigned to destroy the fireworks. After consulting with demolition experts at Albany Headquarters, it was determined the best course of action would be to pile eight-cases of firecrackers on top of one another below ground level, cover them with railroad ties and explosion proof heavy mesh, soak it all with gasoline and ignite it with a highway flare. The eight cases contained 11,000 powerful cherry bombs. The location was a shooting range owned by Hyder on the Scotland Road adjacent to the US Gypsum plant just east of Akron, N.Y.

Hyder having thrown a burning flare onto the pile had walked about 50 feet, when the fireworks ignited creating a tremendous explosion. The troopers and others present were surprised and horror struck when the exploding fireworks propelled the railroad ties several hundred feet into the air before reducing them to mere pieces of kindling. The force of the blast blew the windows out of Fechter's troop car and a Town of Newstead fire truck parked several hundred feet away. The roof lights and brake lines from the Troop "A" supply truck were also blown off, as well as windows shattered in the nearby range building. Investigator Fechter and Civilian Stanley Sochalec, the Troop "A" quartermaster were standing near the quartermaster truck and were knocked to the ground from the blast. Fechter recalled seeing dirt and debris flying through the air. Sochalec had a cigarette blown from his hand with only the filter left intact. A small aircraft flying at the nearby Akron airport was thrown off course from the shock waves. The blast was felt twelve miles away having traveled below ground through the gypsum mine shafts. Dishes were knocked from shelves and slight water leaks occurred in many residences. Residents actually believed an earthquake had taken place. It was wisely determined that no other fireworks would be destroyed at that time.

Several claims of broken windows and foundation damage were investigated by New York State Engineers and in some cases, compensation paid.

Sochalec while returning to Batavia only then realized that he had no brakes, when he was unable to stop at an intersection. He turned off the ignition and excitedly walked to a nearby home for assistance. Having been deafened by the explosion and in a highly nervous condition, he was unable to communicate with the female resident who locked the door and called for police help. Unwittingly on her part, that is what Sochalec wanted.

Fechter recalled that a large crater resulted from the blast. Only bits and pieces of the mesh and railroad ties were found. According to Fechter, Trooper Hyder was instructed to place a few cases of fireworks below ground level and cover them with railroad ties. This would force the impact of the explosion to go downward into the ground. Hyder selected an area with only a slight dip in the ground as opposed to a deep pit that was obviously not deep enough.

State Police Lieutenant Edward Cass said the blast was larger than expected. Those involved knew the M-80s were dangerous, but underestimated the force of the fireworks. Fireworks are manufactured in New York State, but are illegal for sale or use in the state and few had experience with fireworks of this magnitude.

The remaining forty-nine cases were stored in a local facility licensed to meet storage requirements. They were eventually turned over to a US Army Explosive Ordinance Unit for disposal. According to retired Trooper Charles (Skip) Scroger, they were taken to Fort Drum where they were placed in a heavily fortified concrete bunker and ignited. The resulting explosion totally destroyed the bunker leaving only stone size bits of concrete.

Up until 1966, large firecrackers such as M-80s and cherry bombs were legal in the United States, and anyone could buy them and shoot them off. If you look through old fireworks catalogs from the 1930s, 40s and 50s, you will see these and even larger firecrackers advertised, all of them perfectly legal at that time. But it all ended in 1966. The Child Protection Act, passed by the U.S. Congress in 1966, specifically banned these devices. In 1976, the federal regulations were rewritten specifying a limit of 50 milligrams of pyrotechnic composition for any firecracker sold to the public in the United

States, and that limit is still in effect today. It doesn't matter what they look like or what they are shaped like - ground firecrackers can only contain 50 milligrams of pyrotechnic content per cracker. (Aerial "reports," which are contained within aerial devices such as rockets and shells, can contain up to 129.6 milligrams of composition per report.)

VERNON CLAYSON'S RECOLLECTION

Captain Robert Kilfeather was involved in a situation involving the storing and demolition of some confiscated fireworks that might have caused more serious consequences than it actually did. We were in the new building at the time and for no particular reason I looked into the furnace room and was amazed to find that someone had stacked cases and cases of cherry bomb fire crackers in the room, I believe there were sixty cases of them. Cherry bombs are approximately the equivalent of a quarter stick of dynamite and I could envision them leveling our 50,000 square foot building. I told Bardossi, he was still troop commander, and Kilfeather was also in the office at the time, that some dummy had placed sixty cases of cherry bombs in the furnace room. Kilfeather mumbled around the subject, giving me the impression that he was probably the dummy who had approved it. He said he would check with division they being the all-knowing entity to him. He came back and said "they" had told him the fireworks were innocuous, however, having heard the Ozella fireworks plant on the Eldred-Portville Road blow up twice, once in about 1950, long before I was a trooper, and once about 1965 while passing by in a troop car, I had a very good idea what black powder could do. Both times it had left bits and pieces of the proprietors, the Ozellas, all over the landscape. Anyway, I had them put in the quartermaster truck and parked far away from the building. I did not want pieces of myself spread over Genesee County. They were logged in as evidence and photographed. We received permission to destroy them and this is where the fun began. George Hyder was one of the troop's explosive and demolition experts. Jack Cornell was the other. George was a headquarters desk man and therefore closest so he was selected to rid us of this dangerous material and along with Stanley Poquadeck. They drove them to a gravel pit near Akron somewhere, I don't recall exactly where. George knew he didn't want to blow them up all at once so he limited himself to three or four cases as a test. He placed them in a shallow pit and covered them with chicken wire and some boards then set fire to one of the boxes and withdrew about fifty feet to see the results. The results were spectacular, to say the least, the explosion knocked them off their feet, broke windows in buildings a mile away and caused waves in former trooper Jim Mohn's pool six miles away. That was part of the bad news; the good news is that it didn't cause a secondary explosion of the fireworks still on the truck. It didn't, but unknown to Sochalec, it had damaged the brake lines on the truck. Hyder realized he was in over his head and called US Army Ordinance. The remainder was returned troop headquarters. Sochalec, already unnerved, started back with the truck and soon found he had no brakes. He managed to coast to a stop without running over anyone or anything and walked to a nearby house to use their telephone. His disheveled appearance, covered with dust and his nerves on edge, frightened the lady of the house who called police. Stan was able to call the barracks and in a hysterical voice, advise us of his predicament. Sochalec was one of the tensest individuals I've ever known and was wound tight most of the time. Despite this, he was good to have around

BODY ARMOR

VEST SAVES TROOPER - 1979

Trooper K.W. (Skip) Beijen of Troop "C" was the first New York State Trooper to escape serious injury or possibly death because of a protective vest that he wore on patrol. He and his night patrol partner had stopped a suspicious looking car and were questioning two occupants, when the driver fled the scene on foot. Beijen's partner caught him a short distance away. A struggle ensued with the runner getting control of the trooper's revolver and firing a shot striking Beijen in the chest. Beijen drew his weapon, but did not shoot, as the shooter dropped the pistol. The bullet did not penetrate the body, because Beijen was wearing a personally owned bulletproof vest. He was hospitalized for observation with the only injuries being chest bruises and contusions.

On November 13, 1980, two men driving a stolen car fired shots at Trooper Peter Casella with three shots finding their mark. The protective bulletproof vest that he wore deflected one shot and stopped a second. The third shot did not cause serious injury. He fully recovered after hospital treatment.

ISSUED EQUIPMENT
On November 20, 1980, the legislature and Governor Carey appropriated $600,000.00 for the purchase of Division-issue soft body armor for all members. The protective body armor would be provided to each of the Divisions 3,400 members at a cost of approximately $150 to $175 per unit. Troopers are now issued body armor as part of the uniform and are required to wear it while on patrol.

FIREARMS QUALIFICATION

READY, AIM, FIRE -- On the firing range at Camp Owen in the Town of Weathersfield in Wyoming Co. are this trio of Troopers from left, D.M. Pettit (Castile), Range Chief R.F. Manna (Clarence) and Instructor John Arnet (Falconer). Every year more than 450 state troopers must pass qualifying tests on this range. (Rochester Times Union photo by Fred Fagan)

Bob Szymanski . Louis Macri . Bill Sobolewski – 1965

Brenda McCoy . F/Sgt. Vernon Clayson atBatavia Hq. - 1977

SCIENTIFIC LABORATORY

1944

The New York State Police Scientific Laboratory was created in 1935 under the direction of Dr. Bradley H. Kirschberg until his passing in 1941. William E. Kirwan, a trooper lab assistant was appointed to the vacant position serving as Director until 1961. He was promoted to Deputy Superintendent and later retired as the Superintendent. Lieutenant John N. Cesaro replaced Kirwan in the lab.

The purpose of a laboratory is primarily the examination of evidence in the course of a criminal investigation. It can furnish the investigator definite information concerning the evidence assisting him in uncovering all known facts of the crime. The lab services are available to all law enforcement agencies, courts, prosecutors, coroners and military forces.

In early 1944, the Scientific Laboratory was moved from its original Schenectady location to 545 Broadway, Albany, N.Y. New, modern equipment was purchased making it one of the finest labs in the country.

During 1944, 305 cases requiring analysis of 4000 pieces of evidence were investigated. No charge was made for lab services and the highly skilled technicians were available for testimony and explanation of the examinations. The lab also conducted 35 Pathometric examinations (lie detector cases)

LAUNDRY MARK FILE
During the mid 1940s, a BCI investigator was assigned to catalog marks that laundry and dry cleaning services placed on clothing. The file was maintained at Troop K, Hawthorne, N.Y. and put to use in 1947, when it was 95% complete. The markings aided in the solving of fatal accidents where no victim identity was available, the identity of victims of burglaries whose valued clothing was stolen and identity of perpetrators. The files were transferred to the Laboratory in Albany, N.Y. where it was phased out in the late 1960s. Laundries were now using alternate means to identify customers clothing.

AUTOPSY FILM
In 1947, the Laboratory developed and produced a widely acclaimed 16 mm film called the " Medico-Legal Autopsy". The film illustrated the proper procedure for performing a thorough and accurate autopsy including the proper collection of evidence from a dead body and the proper packaging and preservation of such evidence.

LABORATORY MOVED
On April 1, 1953, the Scientific Lab was moved to 8 Nolan Road, Town of Colonie, N.Y. Due to the increased demand of lab services, a larger facility and increase in manpower were necessary. It was designed strictly for lab purposes and consisted of 7500 square feet of floor space. A trooper chemist was added to the staff to handle chemical analysis.

In 1964, the laboratory was relocated to the third and fourth floors of the Public Security Building on the new State Campus, Washington Avenue, Albany, N.Y. with the following members and staff assigned:

Director –	Lieutenant J.N. Cesaro
Chemistry –	Sr. Investigators O.M. Rinaldi/Robert McKinley
	Roy Cornell/Frank Madrazo
Firearms -	Sr. Investigator Andy B. Hart/T/Sgt. K.I. Gleason
Photography –	Frank Marshall
Handwriting –	Sr. Investigator J.F. McCarthy
	Roger Bechard/Thomas Sackel
Pistol Permit Bureau –	Sr. Investigator William Brefka/Trooper Russell Shibley
	Karen Mink/Ann Pritchard/Lillian Rosenberger
	Schulyer Westervelt
Senior Physical Chemist –	Charles W. Rankin
Laundry Marks –	Sr. Investigator D.N. Hardy
Clerical Staff –	Trooper Thomas Kemmy/Alma Rehling/Pat Bevan

In 1964, the lab conducted 4,479 examinations.

In 1965, the lab was able to conduct the following examinations and analysis:

Chemical Examinations – organic and inorganic substances found near a crime scene

Toxicological Analyses - body fluids, organs, poisons, food, blood

Micro-Chemical – spot test for identity of tiny samples, scrapings, ink etc.

Blood Identification – liquid or dried to determine origin & classification

Seminal Stains – determine presence of spermatozoa in sex crimes

Explosives and Bombs – portable x-ray, maintains a file on explosive materials

Firearm Identification – identify bullets and casings as to manufacturer

Powder Patterns – examine clothing & bodies to determine distance, when shot

Serial Number Restoration – restore serial numbers from obliterated or destroyed items

Pistol Permit Bureau – depository for all pistol permits in the state (450,000)

Glass Fractures – examination to determine direction of force

Spectrographic Analyses – material analyzed to determine metal content

Tool Marks – identify tools marks left at a crime scene

Lie Detection – Pathometer in 1938/Polygraph in 1954

Microscopy – examination of hairs, fibers, powders and minerals

Document Examination – handwriting comparison, document authenticity

Photography – photographic documentation of evidence

Research – research scientific problems associated with a crime

Field Examination – provide experts, as needed

Laundry and Dry Cleaner Marks Bureau – complete file on all in the state

Breath Testing Instruments

In 1968, the lab examined 9,628 pieces of evidence.

1973
The Division was awarded a Federal Grant that allowed for the hiring of fourteen scientists to help in the analysis of ever increasing drug arrests. In 1974,the laboratory for the first time utilized two work shifts to close a severe backlog of drug related cases.
A gas chromatograph-mass spectrometer was purchased that could indisputably identify drugs and other chemical substances.

DNA
The deoxyribonucleic acid (DNA) molecule is the genetic blueprint for each cell and ultimately the blueprint that determines every characteristic of a living organism.

Francis Crick, James Watson, and Maurice Wilkins using X-ray diffraction discovered the DNA molecule in 1951. In 1953 Crick described the structure of the DNA molecule as a double helix, somewhat like a spiral staircase with many individual steps. In 1962 Crick, Watson, and Wilkins received the Nobel Prize for their pioneering work on the structure of the DNA molecule.

Deoxyribonucleic Acid (DNA) is genetic material of all cellular organisms and most viruses. DNA carries the information needed to direct protein synthesis and replication. Protein synthesis is the production of the proteins needed by the cell or virus for its activities and development. Replication is the process by which DNA copies itself for each descendant cell or virus, passing on the information needed for protein synthesis. In most cellular organisms, DNA is organized on chromosomes located in the nucleus of the cell.

Forensic science uses techniques developed in DNA research to identify individuals and identify suspects who have committed crimes. DNA from semen, skin, or blood taken from a crime scene can be compared with the DNA of a victim or suspect, and the results can be used in court as evidence.

KEY DATES IN DNA PROFILING
1953 - James Watson and Francis Crick publish landmark paper identifying the structure of DNA.

1980 - American geneticists discover a region of DNA that does not hold any genetic information and which is extremely variable between individuals.

1984 - Alec Jaffrey's discovers a method of identifying individuals from DNA - Restriction Fragment Length Polymorphism (RFLP). He dubs it 'DNA Fingerprinting'.

1985 - Police in the UK first use forensic DNA profiling.

1987 - In the UK, police use DNA profiling in the celebrated Pitchfork case to clear a seventeen-year-old suspect of two rape-murders. Police collect blood samples from over 5,000 local men to identify the perpetrator, Colin Pitchfork.

1987 - Also in the UK, Robert Melias is convicted of rape. He becomes the first person to be convicted of a crime on the basis of DNA evidence.

1989 - In the USA, Gary Dotson becomes the first person to have a conviction overturned on the basis of DNA evidence. Dotson had served 8 years of a 25 - 50 year sentence for Rape.

THE LIE DETECTOR

HISTORY

1895 - Cesare Lombroso conducted experiments on criminals to determine their innocence or guilt by recording changes in their blood pressure or pulse.

1908 - English heart specialist Sir James Mackenzie invented the "ink polarograph". It was a heart recorder that became the forerunner of the lie detector.

1914 - Vittorio Benussi succeeded in using changes in respiration as an index of deception with persons being questioned.

1915 - William Marston was successful in using changes in blood pressure as an indication of guilt or innocence.

1921 – John A. Larson devised an instrument that was capable of continuously recording blood pressure, pulse and respiration.

1930s – Reverend W.G. Summers, Dr. Joseph Kubis and Dr. Fabian Rouke at Fordham University, New York developed an instrument known as the Pathometer. It recorded electro dermal changes that occur in the body.

All lie detectors's basically record and interpret a person's involuntary physiological reaction. It is widely used in criminal investigations, but its use is not generally accepted as direct evidence by the courts.

Early detectors recorded blood pressure, pulse and respiration changes with later developments including muscle movements and galvanic skin reaction. These involuntary changes are measured by electrodes and transferred to pen recorders onto moving graph paper. A permanent record is now in hand.

The examinations are carried out in a private room free from noise and interruption. The persons present are the examiner and the subject. The emotion that a lie detector examiner seeks to isolate is that of fear, "the fear of getting caught in a lie".\

A polygraph instrument is a combination of devices that are used to monitor changes occurring in the body. As a person is questioned the person's heart rate, blood pressure, respiratory rate, and electro-dermal activity (sweatiness) are recorded.

Polygraph exams are most often associated with criminal investigations. Polygraph examinations are designed to look for involuntary responses going on in a person's body when that person is subjected to stress, such as the stress associated with deception.

POLYGRAPH INSTRUMENT

The polygraph instrument has undergone a dramatic change in the last decade. For many years, polygraphs were those instruments that you saw with little needles scribbling lines on a single strip of scrolling paper. Those were called analog polygraphs. Today, most polygraph tests are administered with digital equipment. The scrolling paper has been replaced with sophisticated algorithms and computer monitors. When you sit down in the chair for a polygraph exam, several tubes and wires are connected to your body in specific locations to monitor your physiological activities. The examiner is looking for the amount of fluctuation in certain physiological activities.

POLYGRAPH EXAMINERES

There are only two people in the room during a polygraph exam are the person conducting the exam and the subject being tested.

The examiner performs several tasks in performing a polygraph exam:

- Setting up the polygraph and preparing the subject being tested

- Asking questions

- Profiling the test subject

- Analyzing and evaluating test data

How the question is presented can greatly affect the results of a polygraph exam. There are several variables that an FP has to take into consideration, such as cultural and religious beliefs. Some topics may, by their mere mention, cause a specific reaction in the test subject that could be misconstrued as deceptive behavior. The design of the question affects the way the person processes the information and how he or she responds.

(BCI Bulletin, 1957- VOL – 22- NO.1)
(The Crime Busters – Verdict Press, 1976)
(Partially Edited version of an article written by Michael E. Tamres, Auburn Citizen-Advertiser)

PISTOL PERMIT BUREAU

Chapter 792 of the Laws of 1931 provided that a copy of all applications to carry or possess revolvers and pistols must be filed with the Division of State Police. The Pistol Permit Bureau was established and started functioning in 1932 with a total of 85,000 applications. It maintains records of every legal handgun transaction that takes place in the State. It is a repository for records that accompany sales by gun dealers or between private citizens.

Licensees were card indexed and all licesnsed revolvers classified under a numerical filing system. This system allowed for every licensed revolver by serial number to be classified under a three digit indexing system. Today, entries are made into a master database.Documents are filed by county and type of transaction. Current ownership of the weapon and the legality of a person's possession of the weapon can be quickly determined. In less than 24 hours information can be provided to police investigators with information pertaining to handguns that may have been involved in the commission of a crime.

1944 – 126,000 pistol permit applications were on file

1962 – 431,012 pistol permit applications were on file

1976 – 594,506 pistol permit applications were on file. Total records on file totaled 3,024,145. All existing firearm registrations were automated during 1976.

1983 – 829,659 pistol permit applications were on file

BOOK III —TRAFFIC ENFORCEMENT

TROOP TRAFFIC BUREAUS

The establishment of troop traffic bureaus in 1937 brought many new duties to that office. Among them were:

1   Conduct investigations for the NYS Traffic Commission

2. Maintain an accident spot map and accident location file

3. Supervise all military traffic and maintain all pertinent records

4. Review all accident reports

5. Compile and analyze accident and arrest statistics

6. Supervise motorcycle and traffic patrols based on high traffic volume and accident incidence from their analysis

During the early 1940s, enforcement of the speed laws required the "clocking" or following of a potential speeder for a distance of 1/4 mile prior to making an arrest. As speed zones were established to restrict the speed of vehicles in specified areas, the ¼ mile rule was waived. It was declared that speed zone limits were absolute and to exceed the posted limit violated the law. In 1942, the state police policy declared that a tolerance of not less than 5 MPH or more than 10 MPH be permitted with arrests made on this basis.

Highway safety was a primary concern during the early 1950s. Highway congestion on roadways leading to beaches from nearby cities brought traffic to a virtual standstill. Highways weren't built to accommodate the high traffic volume. In 1954, sections of the NYS Thruway were opened to the motoring public helping alleviate much of the congestion.

In 1954, in an effort to prevent accidents, surveys of high accident areas were made and files maintained at each Troop Headquarters. This determined the number and peak times of the accidents resulting in "Selective Enforcement". Patrols were assigned to these high accident areas and strict enforcement of accident causing violations made. Public information bulletins in conjunction with holidays and special events were made through use of the media bringing attention of the public of increased and stricter enforcement.

NEW COMBINED SUMMONS

During 1945, a new type of combined summons and arrest record was adopted. It reduced the amount of time required in compiling reports and provided more time for patrol duty.

Formerly, after the issuance of a summons for a traffic law violation and upon the case being disposed of by the court, it was necessary for the arresting trooper to type a report in quadruplicate. A great deal of time was thus consumed.

The new combined summons and arrest record came in sets of five, with pre-inserted carbon paper, and in one operation, the summons to the violator and four copies are made at the same time. The road troopers and courts favorably accepted it with plans being put in motion to adopt them in all the troops. They definitely were a time saver.

SUMMONS HOLDERS

In 1945, Division introduced a new summons book holder. The one used during 1939 and I assume was in use until 1945 measured 4"x 9" and appears to be made of leather with a double snap button on a slight overlapping lid to secure it.

Retired Z/Sergeant Pete Taylor relates that in 1955, he was issued a summons book that had a hard cardboard base covered with black canvas glued to the cardboard. It was also about 3"x 9" and the top was just a flat board hinged at the bottom. (3"end) When you opened it, the second layer was a clipboard with a clasp at the top to hold the summons. It was hinged at top with canvas straps. There was a third section, the bottom, with 3/4" high sides that served as a storage compartment. Generally, the fellows used a rubber band cut from an old inter tube to hold it closed. The one Taylor was first issued had Troop "A" F/Sergeant McDonald's name in it and he said that it served him well, when he was on the road.

Retiree F.G. Dirschka related his experience with the summons book of the 1950's. I can't specifically recall the black material the summons book was made of in 1950 but whatever it was it was very sturdy stuff. I had issued a summons to a fellow at the speed zone in Chester on Route 17, which was two lanes with a big bump dividing the lanes, when passing it was a bit like an ATV Whoop-T-doo. After writing the summons on the trunk of my troop car, I got back in the cruiser and drove off forgetting the summons book was on the trunk. I didn't miss it until pulling over another city dweller trying to escape the heat of New York City for the mountains of Sullivan County. Golly! No summons book! Oh Sh-t, only a few months on the job and screwed up already thinking the book was history with the amount of traffic on Route 17. I drove back to the scene of the disaster easily locating it by a path of summonses strewn all along the highway. I easily located by summons book, which was in great shape. It was made of good stuff for the summonses, due to the carbons, clearly showed the imprints of the tires that had run over the book. I was disturbed over a couple of missing summonses that I never found, but no one ever questioned their absence and be sure I never brought them up.

Retiree Robert McDowell similarly described the summons book he was issued on April 1, 1953. I would venture that although there may have been newer summons books in existence, the old retreads were issued to recruits for use until exhausted.

When I started in 1962, the summons holder was made of a black plastic material that constantly cracked at the flap. Retired Investigator Doug Paulsen described it as a piece of junk. These were taken out of service and according to Retiree Dan Scribner, were replaced by an all aluminum holder in 1966. These proved to be most durable and were still in use, when I retired in 1985. The holder was hinged on the long side and when opened, displayed a flat sheet of metal for writing the summons. When flipped up, the summonses (usually issued in packs of 25) were exposed in the second level where they were kept held in place by a snap clip The bottom tray area was where the officer's copy of the ticket was secured.

WEIGHT LAW MANUAL - 1951

During the year 1951, a Vehicle Weighing Manual was prepared and published. The manual explained the weight laws and proper procedure for weighing vehicles to bring uniformity throughout the state. A copy was distributed to all members and was made available as a public service to persons or corporations engaged in the trucking business, public officials and other police departments. Sketches of various types of vehicles were included together with an explanation of the applicable weight laws of each type. It received instant approval.

Form 22. 9-13-34-25,000 (LD-1896)

STATE OF NEW YORK

DIVISION OF STATE POLICE

SUMMONS 7425

To _____

You are hereby summoned to appear before _____ at his office

Justice of the Peace of the Town of _____

_____ Street, in the Village of _____

of _____ 193___ at _____ M, to answer a charge made against you for violation

of Section _____ Paragraph _____ Article _____ of the _____ Law

of the State of New York, committed at _____ and upon your failure

to appear a warrant will be issued for your arrest. Dated at _____ N. Y.,

this _____ day of _____ 193___

_____

_____ Troop _____ Division of State Police

Rank

7425

Date _____ 193___ Time _____ M.

Name _____

Address _____ St.

Vehicle License No. _____

Chauffeur } License No. _____

Operator

Owner of Vehicle _____ St.

Returnable at _____ M.

_____ 193___

Before Justice _____

Address _____ St.

Issued by _____

Write description of vehicle and violation on
reverse side of this stub.

GENL. 4

UNIFORM TRAFFIC TICKET
NEW YORK STATE POLICE
TROOP A - BATAVIA

A

TO:
Defendant _GUSTAFSON EDWARD BY_

Last   Middle   First

Street _61 BARKLE_

City _JAMESTOWN_   State _N.Y._

Dr. Lic. No. _7347743_ State _N.Y._ Date of Birth _4-4-34_ Sex _M_

Employer _JAMESTOWN LUMBER_

Address _JAMESTOWN, N.Y._

80039

YOU ARE HEREBY NOTIFIED TO APPEAR IN THE

Court _J.P. CAMPBEL_

TOWN OF CARROL

On the _18_ Day of _SEPT,_ 19_57_ at _8 P._ M

TO ANSWER A CHARGE OF

☐ SPEEDING over limit:	m. p. h. in	m. p. h. zone	
☐ Improper LEFT TURN:	☐ No signal	☐ Cut corner	☐ From wrong lane
☐ Improper RIGHT TURN:	☐ No signal	☐ Into wrong lane	☐ From wrong lane
Disobeyed TRAFFIC SIGNAL ☐ (when light turned red)	Past middle ☐ Intersection	Middle of ☐ Intersection	Not reached ☐ Intersection
☐ Disobeyed STOP SIGN:	☐ Wrong place	☐ Walk Speed	☐ Faster
☐ Improper PASSING	☐ At Intersection	☐ Cut in	Wrong side ☐ of pavement
AND	☐ Between Traffic	☐ On right	☐ on hill
LANE USAGE	☐ Lane straddling	☐ Wrong lane	☐ on curve

OTHER CHARGES: _FAILED TO KEEP_
RIGHT

IN VIOLATION OF

Section _1132_ Subdiv. _A_ of the _V.T._ Ord. Law

Committed on the _18_ Day of _SEPT_ 19_57_ at _11:40 A._ M

at _CORD. 310_ _CHAU_ County

Owner, If other than Defendant _AXEL GUSTAFSON_

Address _JAMESTOWN_

Reg. No. _147253_ State _N.Y._ Yr. of Mfr. _55_ Make & Type _PIERC_

Officer _R.C. REILLY_ Shield No. or Rank _771_

A plea of guilty to this charge is equivalent to a conviction after trial. If you are convicted, not only will you be liable to a penalty, but in addition your license to drive a motor vehicle or motor cycle, and your certificate of registration, if any, are subject to suspension and revocation as prescribed by law.

YOUR FAILURE TO APPEAR MAY RESULT IN A WARRANT FOR YOUR ARREST

| N. Y. STATE POLICE | | UNIFORM TRAFFIC TICKET | | NO. | 1765 |

NAME TO: DEFENDANT:

LAST | FIRST | MIDDLE (INIT.)

YOU ARE HEREBY NOTIFIED TO APPEAR IN THE _____ COURT

OF _____

ADDRESS

DATE OF BIRTH | SEX

REG. PLATE NO.

COURT ADDRESS _____

CITY | STATE

OP | CH | JR | LEARN PERMIT | INTERIM PERMIT

PLATE YEAR | STATE

ON _____ 19 ___

LICENSE OR IDENT. NO.
STATE

YEAR & MAKE OF VEH.

AT _____ M.

DATE ISSUED | DATE EXPIRES

BODY TYPE

PRINT ALL ENTRIES

A PLEA OF GUILTY TO THIS CHARGE IS EQUIVALENT TO A CONVICTION AFTER TRIAL. IF YOU ARE CONVICTED, NOT ONLY WILL YOU BE LIABLE TO A PENALTY, BUT IN ADDITION YOUR LICENSE TO DRIVE A MOTOR VEHICLE OR MOTOR CYCLE, AND YOUR CERTIFICATE OF REGISTRATION, IF ANY, ARE SUBJECT TO SUSPENSION AND REVOCATION AS PRESCRIBED BY LAW.

TO ANSWER A CHARGE OF THE

FOLLOWING VIOLATION COMMITTED ON THE _____ DAY OF _____ 19 ___

AT TIME _____ PLACE _____

IN VIOLATION OF SEC. _____ OF _____ COUNTY _____ (LAW, ORDINANCE OR REGULATION) OF _____

CHARGE (IF NOT SPECIFIED BELOW) _____

☐ SPEEDING OVER LIMIT: _____ M.P.H. IN _____ M.P.H. ZONE

DISOBEYED TRAFFIC CONTROL DEVICE | SIGNAL STOP SIGN | YIELD SIGN PAVEMENT MARKING

18—5 YOUR FAILURE TO APPEAR MAY RESULT IN A WARRANT FOR YOUR ARREST.

☐ IMPROPER PASSING & LANE USAGE | ☐ IMPROPER TURN

OFFICER'S SIGNATURE _____ | SHIELD OR RANK _____

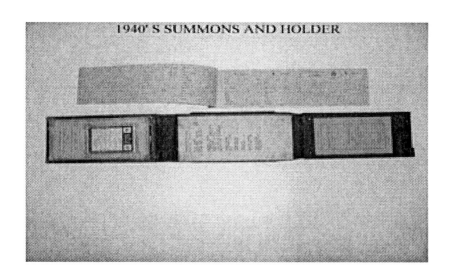

1940' S SUMMONS AND HOLDER

87

PORTABLE WEIGHING STATIONS

A portable weighing station was purchased and assigned to Troop "A" during 1953. It consisted of a special trailer frame and a platform with wells to hold four loadometers. By pushing a lever, the ramp and scales were lowered to the pavement and ready for operation. The unit was towed by a patrol car. They were needed due to a heavy volume of truck violations that were going unchecked by using alternate routes to avoid the fixed scales. Former Trooper George Mills recalled working these scales with Trooper Fred Hoffman and found them to be heavy and cumbersome. They did prove to be very satisfactory in weight enforcement. Weigh stations at Silver Creek and Alexander required a large number of trooper man-hours to operate. With the completion of the NYS Thruway, this fixed scale site was closed, as it was now more expeditious for the trucking industry to use the new super highway.

During 1957, two Gledhill Portable Truck Weighing Units used for several years were replaced with three newly improved units. Each of the three units was operated by two troops alternately for fifteen-day periods every month. Greater coverage for overloaded trucks was provided in this manner. These scales were referred to as the Goose Necks and weighed in the vicinity of 70 pounds each.

In 1969, loadometer details checked 101,769 vehicles, weighed 29,007 of which 9518 were found overloaded.

ELDEC
In early 1978, the US Department of Transportation censured New York State for inadequate weight enforcement. The loss of $340 million in federal highway project funding was averted with the purchase of the new electronic scales to curb overweight truck trafficking. The loadometer detail was also increased from 44 to 84 trained in using the new equipment. The Eldec scales were loaded onto a trailer and taken to a site where they were laid on a level surface. Suspected overweight vehicles simply drove across the scales with weights electronically recorded. This method required approximately 90 seconds to complete the weighing of a truck. More than 100,000 trucks were weighed the first year. During the year 1980, 86 troopers assigned to weigh and measure trucks made 16,278 overload arrests and 2,964 for oversize vehicle.

DRIVING WHILE INTOXICATED - (DWI)

DWI LAW - 1941
The 1941 NYS Legislature at the recommendation of the American Medical Association enacted evidentiary legislation for Drunk Driving. The law stated that a person who operated a motor vehicle in an intoxicated condition was guilty of a misdemeanor. If previously convicted, it was a felony punishable by imprisonment of from 60 days to 2 years and or a fine of from $200 to $2000. Prima facie evidence required for intoxication was fifteen hundredths (.15%) of one per centum by weight of alcohol in the blood.

DWI TESTING
The New York State Legislature enacted a new section to the Vehicle and Traffic Law effective July 1, 1953 permitting police officers to secure specimens of blood, urine, breath or saliva to be used for chemical analysis to determine blood alcohol content. The evidence obtained could be used in the prosecution of driving a Motor Vehicle while intoxicated. The State Police Laboratory distributed specially prepared test kits to safe guard blood and urine samples that were made available to all division members.

Prior to the enactment of this law, there was no legal mechanism to secure specimens.

It was strictly voluntary on the defendant's part. In 1941, the State Attorney General ruled that the extracting of urine, saliva or blood from an unwilling person would constitute a legal assault. Needless to say, there were very few arrests with conviction.

ALCOHOL IN THE BODY
When an alcoholic beverage is consumed, it is not digested; rather it remains alcohol and is absorbed at once directly into the blood stream primarily through the small intestine and stomach. Being absorbed, it travels throughout every body part that contains water. Immediately after absorption, the liver starts to burn the alcohol. Approximately one third of a fluid ounce is burned per hour. The unburned alcohol continues to circulate the body through the blood system. All blood flows through the lungs where breath comes into contact with the blood capillaries. If there is alcohol present, some will enter the breath via the lungs.

ALCOHOL MEASURING DEVICES

HARGER DRUNKOMETER
The first "Drunkometer" was designed and built in 1931. An improved version was introduced in 1936 and was first used by the Indiana State Police. Dr. Rolla N. Harger, a professor on the medical staff at Indiana University designed the machine. It was the result of his research and study of the effects of alcohol consumed and the subsequent behavior of humans that included tests for intoxication. The Drunkometer simply analyzed the breath to determine whether alcohol was present and how much.

The amount is governed by Henry's Law discovered in 1803 and states simply that if alcohol is present in a water solution, in a container, with equal volumes of water and air, there is a definite ratio between the alcohol in the air and the alcohol in the water. As the temperature rises, the ratio increases.

To operate the Drunkometer, a sample of the person's breath is gathered in an unused balloon immediately before the analysis. The balloon was then attached to a glass inlet tube that allowed the breath to enter a reaction tube containing a mixture of potassium permanganate, sulfuric acid and distilled water. As the breath passes through the solution, alcohol present changes the color of the purple solution depending on the amount. The color is compared to a comparison tube that contained the same solution. This was known as the end point used in analytical chemistry. The color change would determine the degree of intoxication.

The same basic principle to detect alcohol in the breath was used in all testing equipment.

During early 1954, two troopers from Batavia attended a one-week course receiving instructions in "Breath Testing" given by the State Police Lab. On July 2, 1954, a Harger Drunkometer was assigned to Troop "A".

During 1955, 547 DWI arrests were made throughout the Division. Troop "A" accounted for 116 of them. 518 blood tests were given with 29 urine tests accounting for the rest.

INTOXIMETER
The Intoximeter was a compact portable instrument that tested breath for alcohol content through first, preliminary color, then actual content in the sample. It was available during 1954 – 1955 through the Intoximeter Association, 334 Buffalo Avenue, Niagara Falls, N.Y. This instrument was the first type of alcohol screening devise. It consisted of a balloon for the collection of a breath sample, a

small glass vile filled with potassium permanganate and sulphuric acid used as a preliminary color test, a vial filled with magnesium perchlorate that absorbed the alcohol in the breath and a tube filled with ascarite to absorb the carbon dioxide.

The subject would blow into the balloon inflating it to an 8-inch length. The breath was then passed through the sulphuric-permanganate solution destroying the color, if alcohol was present. There was a 90 second time limit ending the test, if no color change took place. If the color was changed, then further testing was administered.

PHOTOELECTRIC INTOXIMETER
The Photo-Electric Intoximeter was developed by Dr. Glenn C. Forrester in 1959 and was also available through a Niagara Falls, N.Y. manufacturer. The instrument provided for an optional double analysis of breath alcohol; Euphoric-chromic acid oxidation with direct reading of results and capturing of a breath sample for additional lab testing. It weighed 34 pounds and was housed in a steel cabinet.

ALCOMETER
The Alcometer was the invention of Dr. Leon A. Greenberg and Frederick W. Keator of Yale University. The Frederick Keyes Company of Cambridge, Massachusetts, distributed it. It was built into a portable metal case that required 110 volt AC current to operate. It was designed to give accurate and automatic determination of alcohol in the blood. There were three principles used in the testing. The collection of a measured volume of expired air without loss of alcohol through condensation; reaction of alcohol with iodine pentoxide, yielding a quantitive production of free iodine; photoelectric measurement of the intensity of color produced by the liberated iodine in a fixed volume of starch & potassium iodine solution.

BREATHALYZER
The breathalyzer was defined as an accurate scientific instrument which directly tests the breath of a person to indirectly determine the percentage of alcohol in the blood of that individual.

In 1954, Robert F. Borkenstein applied the 2100:1 Blood/Breath Alcohol ratio and invented the Breathalyzer. It measured 1/40th of the 2100:1 ratio, making for a workably sized instrument.

Breathalyzer Description

A. Sample Chamber Thermometer Proper operating temperature is 50 degrees centigrade + or − 3 degrees.

B. Sample Chamber Control Knob - 3 positions

   Take - Allows breath sample to be taken

   Analyze - allows breath sample to pass through the test ampoule.

   Off Position - only at conclusion of the test.

C. Piston - forces the breath sample through the test Ampoule

D. Sample Chamber - holds the piston

E. Ampoule - contains 3 ml of solution comprised of: .025 Potassium Dichromate 50% by volume Sulphuric Acid Catalyst of silver nitrate.

The defendant must be given the test within two hours of arrest. The breathalyzer operator was trained and certified in its use. He makes sure the temperature is correct and that each ampoule has the same lot # and the correct equal amounts of solution. The defendant then blows into a tube (deep lung air is alveolar air) for several seconds. The breath passes through the solution, which changes color depending on the amount of alcohol in the breath. This change is reflected in visual meter that reflects the amount of alcohol.

A new Breathalyzer instrument was carefully studied from July 1956 through December 1957. It was a lightweight compact devise for breath alcohol determination developed by Lieutenant Robert F. Borkenstein, Director of the Indiana State Police Laboratory. Several of the machines were purchased. The machine basically is a scientific instrument that quickly shows how much alcohol a person has in his system. At about the same time, the Medical Societies of several NYS counties adopted a resolution that they would not be a party to the withdrawal of blood for alcohol determination at the request of a trooper. This resulted in the expediting of training of troopers in the use of the Breathalyzer.

In order to have continued DWI enforcement, the SP Lab conducted extensive training in the use of the Breathalyzer. The following instruction was provided: Classes in:

Alcohol enforcement problems

Necessary proof in DWI cases

Demonstration and explanation of the Breathalyzer

The Physiology and psychology of alcohol

Practice on the Breathalyzer

Actual testing of an intoxicated person

In 1959, the Vehicle and Traffic Law provided that a blood alcohol level of more than 0.05% and less than 0.15% was relevant evidence and a blood alcohol level of 0.15% or more could be admitted as prima facie evidence that a person was in an intoxicated condition. Submission to a test for alcohol by persons arrested for drunken driving was not mandatory but if a driver refused a test, his operator's license is revoked.

At the beginning of 1969, there were 28 Breathalyzers in service throughout the Division.

During the summer of 1969, a program was initiated to train 438 troopers in the operation of breath testing equipment with the purchase of 73 new Breathalyzer machines through a $75,051.00 federal grant. Every station in the state was assigned a Breathalyzer.

Effective September 1, 1969, the SPENO Law went into effect. It was a new on the spot balloon test to determine alcohol use. Under the new law, a driver suspected of drinking could be requested to take a roadside test that measured the presence of alcohol in the blood. Each device consisted of a chemical measuring tube through which the suspect's breath is forced and a clear plastic bag that indicated a sufficient amount is exhaled for a proper test. An arrest was not needed to ask the driver to take the test. Those who refused could be arrested for refusal to submit to a test and for drunk driving.

In 1971, the NYS Court of Appeals upheld the validity of the breathalyzer for determining blood alcohol content. This judicial recognition eliminated the need to have scientists from the laboratory testify at drunk driving trials.

DRUNK DRIVING ARRESTS

1955 -	1,228
1964 -	1,840
1965 -	2,912
1972 -	10,000
1980 -	14,583
1985 -	15,050

MOTOR VEHICLE INSPECTION PROGRAM

The 1954 New York State Legislature enacted a law requiring a compulsory Motor Vehicle Inspection (MVI) program. The law called for semi-annual inspection of all vehicles starting in 1955. Inspection certificates were printed and issued for the year 1955-56 but due to a lack of inspection stations and amendments to the original bill did not become a reality until 1957. One amendment read that only vehicles over four years old and those vehicles less than four years old upon resale or transfer be inspected.

The Department of Motor Vehicles was assigned the responsibility of administering the program and selecting licensed official inspection stations with the State Police delegated the enforcement authority. As years passed, regulations were improved. In 1965, regulations required mandatory written tests for mechanic inspectors and record keepers.

The greatest changes came in 1966 with the passage of a law mandating annual inspections of all vehicles registered in the state regardless of age. As a result of the new inspection law, annual inspections went from 3.1 million per year to 8.5 million per year.

The first trooper detail was comprised of 15 troopers originally assigned in October 1956. The detail was gradually increased with 68 troopers including 5 technical sergeants assigned in 1967 with Technical Sergeant Edward J. Gilbert designated the MVI supervisor at Division Headquarters. An MVI training school was established at the State Police Academy in 1965. Troopers assigned were required to have knowledge of automobiles, trucks, trailers and the many types of inspection equipment used and were instructed in regulations, as well as updated regulation changes and inspection procedures.

1954 – Inspection mandatory to all cars four or more years old.

1957 - The MVI Detail was increased to 35 troopers who conducted 22,462 inspections and reviews and investigated 499 complaints against inspection stations.

1958 – The MVI Detail conducted 30,491 garage inspections.

1964 – 557 concealed inspections were conducted resulting in 256 arrests and 82 warning letters being sent for minor violations.

1965 – Troopers began a new program of written tests to determine the knowledge of inspectors about their job. 16,310 were given by the end of the year with 4,071 failures. Those who failed were no longer permitted to conduct inspections.

1966 – Legislation passed requiring inspection of all cars.

1967 - Detail members conducted 55,018 routine inspections, 1,168 concealed inspections and 1,166 complaint investigations resulting in 4,985 enforcement actions.

1969 – Conducted 57,328 MVI inspections. 1,124 concealed identity resulting in 557 arrests and citations.

1970 – In 1970, an inspection fee was $3.00. Seven million cars were registered in NYS.

11,052 garages and service stations were licensed to make inspections collecting $20 million in inspection fees.

1974 – MVI detail uncovered fraud-involving hundreds of thousands of dollars in the sale of new and used cars by turning back odometers. Twenty-five felony indictments resulted in 400 charges. Some odometers were turned back as much as 10,000 miles. Charges included grand larceny, forgery, falsifying business records and offering false instruments for filing.

A garage desiring an inspection license first sent in a fee of $25.00 to the Department of Motor Vehicles. Troopers were then detailed to check the applicant to see if there was sufficient space and proper equipment to conduct inspections. Those who would be involved in the inspection were required to pass a background investigation and a written test administered by the trooper. The test questions only tested a person's knowledge of inspection regulations, not his mechanical skills.

Trained trooper inspectors had knowledge of inspection regulations and the proper manner in which inspections were to be conducted. In order to assure compliance, a concealed identity inspection program was initiated. Troopers in plain clothes driving unmarked vehicles systematically conducted inspections of licensed facilities. In this manner, the deterrent necessary to insure proper inspections was maintained. Troopers were responsible for the review of inspection records, insuring that proper testing equipment was in good working order and that only licensed inspectors conducted the inspections. They investigated all complaints in order to substantiate allegations of improper inspection, over-charging, and unnecessary or unauthorized work being performed.   (Edited version of an article written by T/Sgt. Edward J. Gilbert in 1967)

Trooper William F. Schencke (54-76) assigned to the MVI program for several years said the inspection program was concluded on December 24, 1975, when it was turned over to the Department of Motor Vehicles. There was no opposition from the State Police officials who determined there was a greater need for troopers to perform other traffic related duties.

Trooper William F. Sobolewski, an MVI trained trooper recalled one investigation that resulted in several arrests. Trooper Thomas J. Fulton reported observing a Sunoco Service station in the City of Lockport, N.Y. conducting what he believed to be an unusually high amount of vehicle inspections. As luck would have it, an unoccupied house was listed for sale next to the service station. Trooper Sobolewski obtained keys to the house and for an entire day, observed inspection sticker after inspection sticker being placed on cars without benefit of an inspection. He carefully documented his observations before issuing a summons to the mechanic at the service station and KIPO Motors whose cars were being inspected. Both the service station and used car dealership had their licenses suspended for thirty days. Jack Kirschberger and Edward Poole owned KIPO Motors and were friends to many troopers in the area.

THE TRACK-TEST FIFTH WHEEL SPEEDOMETER - 1955

During 1955, the fifth wheel, a highly accurate device to check the accuracy of a speedometer was put in use by the division. The fifth wheel (the size of a bicycle tire) was attached to the rear bumper of the car being checked and was connected electrically to a calibrated Weston Meter on which the actual road speed of the vehicle was measured. By comparing the speeds shown by the speedometer and the meter, the degree of accuracy of the speedometer was established and any variance recorded. State police cars were checked in this manner every 60 days.

Speedometers had previously been checked by comparing their registered speeds with the reading of a master speedometer running simultaneously from the same activator. This method checked only the accuracy of the speedometer head, but did not reveal variances.

During the test, the car was not to be driven in reverse and only on dry pavement. Tire pressure was to be maintained at 25 PSI. A speedometer deviation record was kept with the vehicle tested and a copy maintained at Troop Traffic Bureaus.

Troop "A" Traffic Supervisor T/Sergeant David Miller reports that the fifth wheel was taken out of service several years ago with trooper cars now being certified twice yearly through radar verification.

DRIVER EDUCATION SCHOOL – 1956

In order to make troopers better drivers and reduce troop car accidents, the New York State Police Driver Education School was opened in January 1956 at Albany State Teachers College. 560 troopers attended the two and one half day sessions during the year. They were given classroom and field study instruction involving lectures and driver attitude films, physical laws, emergency driving, road tests, tests of driving skills and a series of psychophysical tests.

One qualified member of each Troop conducted road tests and gave each new recruit instruction in safety and police vehicle operation.

New and experienced motorcycle riders were also instructed and tested in the proper and safe operation of the motorcycle.

The schools were increased to five-day training sessions during 1960.

In 1979, the one week long Emergency Vehicle Operator's Course (EVOC) was introduced to improve members driving skills.

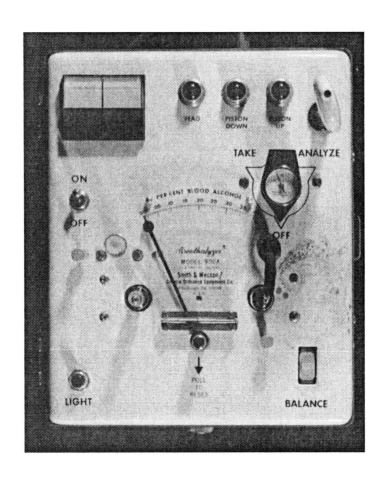

AL KUREK - 1980 HAZMAT DETAIL

RADAR UNIT - 1963

Ron Spink – Harry Jones   Loadometer Detail – 1963

RADAR

Radar was developed for military purposes during the 1940s. Police first used it for traffic speed-measuring purposes in the 1950's, although its use was relatively infrequent until the early 1970's. The very early traffic radar devices were large, cumbersome, and suitable only for stationary use, i.e., the speed-measuring device had to be stationery itself to obtain an accurate indication of the speed of oncoming vehicles. A radar detail required a radar operator and a pick up man. The operator would select the location and place the antenna unit on a tripod with a cable providing power from the car. A second cable was attached to a speed chart-printing machine that used red ink to indicate the speed of every car that went through the radar. Before use, striking certified tuning forks and placing them in front of the antenna unit for a reading checked the unit. Tuning forks were calibrated to equal speeds of 40, 50 & 60 MPH. The pick up man then drove his car through the radar at a pre-set speed to verify the unit's accuracy. The operation was now ready for use. The pick up man could either chase a violator down or would be located several hundred feet down the road with a description of the violator car radioed to him. He would then step out and direct the violator to pull over. The vehicles registration plate number was then radioed to the operator who wrote it down on the graph paper next to the speed of the violator.

In the early 1970's the use of radar speed-measuring devices increased rapidly. An antenna that could be placed on the inside or outside of the rear car window with the speed indicated and held for several seconds on a visual meter replaced the graph style unit. Troopers were assigned to a radar detail as a team, particularly on the NYS Thruway. The radar operation utilized a pick up man until 1987, when Trooper Alvin Kurdys was killed while standing along the highway attempting to stop a violator. He was struck and killed instantly. This method of radar enforcement was immediately terminated.

Traffic radar devices operate in a doppler mode, meaning that they use the doppler effect of a frequency shift in the signal reflected from a moving target vehicle to detect the speed of the vehicle. As doppler radars, these devices emit what is known as "continuous-wave," or CW, radiation. CW radiation is emitted in a continuous, rather than pulsed or intermittent manner. All of the devices emit less than 100 milliwatts of microwave power, an amount considered to be rather low. Most radar units emit power in the range of 15 to 50 milliwatts. The emitted power of traffic radar devices is lower than or comparable to other microwave or radio frequency radiation-emitting devices used in close proximity to persons in the general public, such as garage door openers, cellular telephones, and infant monitors.

Traffic radar units have been produced in two basic types, a one-piece unit designed for hand-held use, and a two-piece unit designed for a fixed mount. Hand-held units were first introduced in the late 1970's. The two-piece units consist of an antenna and a separate electronics component that contains the controls and the display panel. The antenna can be mounted in various locations, and has been used with mounts on the front dashboard, the rear dashboard (at the rear windshield behind the seat), or with a bracket on one of the side windows, which can hold the antenna inside or outside, facing forward or back. In some cases, two antennas are used in the same vehicle (usually one front and one back dashboard mount) with a switch provided to choose one or the other antenna at a given time.

In the 1970's, radar units became available that could operate in either a stationary mode or a moving mode. Stationary mode radars had to be used by an officer in a fixed position, but moving mode radars could correctly adjust for the motion of the patrol vehicle while determining the speed of the target vehicles coming toward the patrol. The determination of which mode to use was entirely a matter of choice of the officer.

In late 1957, the Division purchased six Radar Speedometers assigning one to each troop. The Traffic Supervisor and three troopers from each troop were trained in its use and general theory. They were also schooled in proper presentation of such cases and problems that might be encountered. They were placed in service during January 1958 used at locations primarily where speed zones had been established by the State Traffic Commission.

Division Headquarters Traffic Bureau prepared and published in booklet form the "New York State Troopers Radar Manual" in 1958. It described methods and procedures for using Radar Speed Meters to enforce speed limits established by the State Traffic Commission.

MOVING RADAR
During 1975, new radar units were purchased that were known as the "moving radar". The new unit had the ability to determine the speed of oncoming traffic while traveling in an opposite direction. It had a range of 2500 feet; about five times that of a stationary radar. It also had a feature where a predetermined speed could be set and when an approaching car exceeded that speed, a warning signal was emitted with the car's speed shown on visual screen.

VASCAR
In 1958, Arthur N. Marshall of Richmond, Virginia recognized the need for a speed-checking device. He had observed a trooper turn around to pursue an obviously speeding car. The car seeing the trooper turn slowed to within the legal limit avoiding apprehension through the clocking method.

Marshall began a series of experimentations with algebraic equations and charts with the end result of his work a product that he called VASCAR, Visual Average Speed Computer and Recorder. It was based on the simple accepted principle that speed can be calculated providing quantities of distance and time are known.

The New York State Police adopted this new approach to accident reduction in cases where speed was a major factor. It was tested and put in service during 1968. VASCAR was a newly developed electronically operated mechanical self-contained machine no bigger than a cigar box. The unit measured quantities of distance and time simply and accurately and computed the resultant speed. It was a one-man operation and could be used to measure speed of vehicles traveling in going or coming directions. The machine measured the time and distance required to move between two points and computed it to an average speed traveled.

VASCAR PASSES COURT TEST – 1969
On December 15, 1968, Trooper William Gorenflo arrested Alan R. Persons, an attorney for speeding 74.5 MPH in 60 MPH Zone using VASCAR. A trial was held before Perinton Justice Thomas E. Goldman who ruled "the machine accurate and proper for detecting a speeding violation" It is believed this test case was the first in the nation.

In his decision, Judge Goldman noted, "there was reasonable proof concerning extensive training and testing of VASCAR operators. He noted that the real issue was whether the trooper had operated the machine accurately. Trooper Gorenflo had successfully completed the requisite training and his test results showed a maximum error of four-tenths of a mile per hour. His testimony concerning the testing of the machine was sufficient and convincing and his testimony concerning his clocking of the defendant was clear and exact. Guilty

THE SPEED COMPUTER
BY SGT. FRANK SMITH
DIVISION HEADQUARTERS – 1970

YOU TEAR DOWN THE ROAD, YOU WEAVE AND PASS
YOUR ONLY THOUGHT IS "GIVE IT MORE GAS"
WHEN ALL OF A SUDDEN, FROM OUT OF THE BLUE
COMES A SIREN! A TROOPER IS MOTIONING TO YOU
COMING OR GOING, IT MATTERS NOT WHICH
HE KNOWS WHAT YOU DID BY THE FLICK OF A SWITCH
ACCUSED OF SPEEDING - - IT CAN'T BE DISPUTED
YOU'VE HAD IT! YOUR SPEED WAS ELECTRONICALLY COMPUTED.

STATEWIDE SPEEDING ARRESTS
1950 – 24,117
1955 – 45,374
1960 – 80,701
1965 – 207,555
1970 – 212,989
1975 – 265,999
1980 – 262,029
1985 – 294,115

MOTORCYCLE
OLD DAYS

During the early days, every trooper was trained to ride a motorcycle. Most were Harley's with a sidecar with a few Indians also in service. Corporal Howard Blanding (1939 – 1946) recalled that when he joined the troopers, all the motorcycles were Harley's with Corporal Richard "Trixie' Lemay instructing in their use in the old corral area behind the Batavia Barracks. In 1940, he recalled that the only bike riders in the troop were the following:

Harvey Gregg	John Fennell	Devillo Chamberlain	Judson Peck	
William Welch	Kenneth Hemmer	Ingwald Hicker	Richard Brecht	
John Chambers	Stanley Smith	Lyman Fortner	Kenneth Wiedenborner	
Ed Broughton	Howard Blanding	Harold Moose	Ralph Gibson	William Rimmer

Blanding was experienced having owned his own motorcycle before becoming a trooper. He rode to Florida on his bike and while traveling through Georgia, hit a cow. Open range existed along the highways at the time. The cow was destroyed with Blanding escaping injury thanks to the crash bars on the bike. The cycle patrols were scattered around the troop, but used almost daily where there was heavy traffic flow. He estimated riding the bike for about 100,000 miles. He recalled a couple of incidents with the bikes. He and Bill Rimmer were returning from a Public Assembly inspection in Silver Creek, when they observed a car parked with its lights on. Their vision was impaired from the lights before they suddenly realized the car was stopped on the road and standing next to it was

Sergeant Pappy Lee. Not having enough time to stop, they sped by missing Lee and the car by inches. The incident was never mentioned until one day, Rimmer said something about taking the bikes to Batavia. Lee made the remark that at the speed they drove, it wouldn't take long.

One of their duties was to escort military convoys through the troop area. A 50 to 75 vehicle convoy would be met at the Pennsylvania State line and travel at a snails pace with many stops along the way. It would take all day to travel to the Rochester area where another escort would pick up the convoy. They then had to travel the 150 miles back to Westfield. The reward was sore behinds and exhaustion.

While stationed at Wanakah, a truck driver woke Blanding up at 6:00 AM to report the station garage burning. The building was totally destroyed and right in the middle looking like a skeleton was Blanding's motorcycle. It seems that the BCI had placed a smoldering car seat in the garage as evidence from arson the night before.

NEW DAYS
During May 1963, a motorcycle training school was held at the Troy Airport to prepare both new riders and refresh experienced riders for the coming summer season. Troop "A" experienced riders included Troopers Jerome R. Brakefield, Robert J. Fisher and John T. Allen. Inexperienced riders were Milton C. Bartlett, James E. Wilson, Douglas W. Hedges and Richard E. Haberer.

Retired Trooper Douglas Hedges provided the following recollections about his motorcycle days. He and Trooper Richard Haberer from Troop "A" attended the motorcycle session held at the Troy Airport from May 6 – 10, 1963 and were housed at Troop "G" Headquarters, Loudonville, N.Y. They were trained on Harley's with training consisting of learning to ride the bikes. Hedges was an experienced rider having owned a motorcycle before becoming a trooper. The hardest lesson for him to learn was keeping his feet on the footpads. He was used to dragging his foot on the ground on turns. After training, he was assigned as the junior rider to Trooper Jerome Brakefield at Clarence. They were called Mutt and Jeff for obvious height reasons. Hedges was 6'5" and Brakefield 5'11" tall. He had to drive to Sydney Headquarters to pick up an old pair of breeches and putts and then had them tailored. (For some reason, older troopers had large bottoms) His plate number was # 1. He and the Governor were the only persons to have that plate number. Riding bikes was great. Supervisors didn't know what their duties were so they never handled complaints, just traffic work. They worked in the Clarence patrol area that was located in Northern Erie County. Motorcycles were only used during daylight hours with Brakefield working steady days, because he was the senior man. Hedges said he never wrote many tickets, but just his presence on the road made drivers more cautious. Hedges motorcycle days ended, when he was involved in an accident on Route 5 near the top of the East Clarence hill. A car turned in front of him and he was unable to avoid the collision. He laid down the bike striking the rear of the car suffering a broken back. There was no motorcycle patrol during winter months. The bikes were taken to Albany where they were checked over and maintenance performed before being returned in the spring.

Troop "A" had two motorcycles, one at Clarence and the other at Athol Springs. After his accident, Trooper Thomas O'Brien replaced Hedges.

The motorcycle patrols were phased out in 1966, because they were deemed too dangerous after several troopers were seriously injured.

HAZ-MAT PROGRAM
During 1984, a Hazardous Materials Unit of twenty troopers was formed to insure that hazardous and dangerous materials were carried and transported in a safe and lawful manner. The unit was

charged with seeking out shipper's who used inferior or unsafe equipment, untrained handlers and inexperienced drivers. Federal DOT studies showed that one of every ten vehicles transported hazardous material and two of every five violated at least one regulation. During the first year, the unit conducted 12,072 inspections resulting in 1,608 citations being issued. First Haz-Mat troopers from Troop "A" were Troopers John J. Kelly and Albert S. Kurek.

MARKED PATROL CARS

The newest car in the fleet until World War II ended was the 1940 Chevrolet. Most were two door sedans painted white with black hoods to cut down on the suns glare. The words Traffic Division above the state emblem and New York State Police below were located on the side door panels with a red flashing light placed in the grill. Due to war production, new cars were not available. When the automobile industry changed from war production back to automobile production, new cars were in great demand. The late 1940s trooper cars came in whatever color was available at the time. Only the letters "**STATE POLICE**" in large bold print was located on the door panels and just above the windshield. A combination red light/siren was located on the left front fender.

During the early 1950s, troop cars were ordered and delivered in basic gray.

CAR COLOR CHANGED – 1955
In 1955, the color of the Troopers Patrol Car was changed from basic gray to black and white. This was done to make the patrol car more visible to the public. The vehicle of choice was the Ford four-door sedan. The words State Police were located on the front of the hood with lettering New York State Police located on each front door panel with the state seal in gold located in the center. The combination red light/siren was mounted on the roof. In the same year patrol cars on the Thruway were painted blue and cream and, for the first time had sirens and flashing red lights installed on the roof.

1956 PATROL CARS – WBTA EDITORIAL – JAN 8, 1956
The 1956 Ford patrol cars were especially designed and made to meet the needs of the time with extra power under the hood. The car could reach speeds of 125 MPH and was built especially for highway patrolling. The new models were equipped with power brakes and power steering that was much heavier duty than regular models. The conservative gray color gave way to a bold black and white that made it easier for people to distinguish. Large bold black lettering with "STATE POLICE" was placed on the front, rear and sides of the cars. These colors and markings were done in an effort for the Troopers to be more easily recognizable in case of an emergency. Another innovation was having the siren exposed on top of the patrol cars along with a red light that flashed on and off. The siren had been mounted under the hood. Another first was the placement of a spotlight on the outside driver's side of the car. The new cars were put in service as the older one's wore out. These special built cars were not available for sale to the public.

On March 10, 1956, Trooper John J. Andrews was stationed at Henrietta, N.Y. where he did thruway patrol. He was assigned the only specially built, one of a kind, 1956 Ford patrol cars used by police in the state. It was an experimental model. It looked like any other stock model car except for a few additions. It had a four-barrel carburetor, an oversize eight-cylinder engine and an overdrive transmission. The car weighed 3200 pounds and was capable of speeds up to 120 miles per hour. Andrews had pursued and caught a speeder traveling 95 miles per hour. When queried, he said the needle hit the 120 mark and he still had plenty of pedal left.

1960 PLYMOUTH BLACK AND WHITE

What I consider to have been one of the slowest, most cumbersome patrol cars in the Division was the 1960 Plymouth Sedan. It was low to the ground, looked and drove like a tank and utilized push button transmission control. The push button panel was located to the left of the steering column in the dashboard and was difficult to view and access. "Park" was a lever that you pushed up or down and it was on the left side of the transmission buttons. Troopers from across the state took pleasure in going through the buttons one at a time destroying many transmissions. The Division finally had all the buttons removed except reverse and drive.

1962 PLYMOUTH BLACK AND WHITE

The 1962 Plymouth powered by a 383 horsepower motor was one of the fastest patrol cars in the fleet. It would get up to 60 MPH in a few seconds and was capable of chasing down almost anything on the road. The rear end sat higher than the front giving it a bird dog appearance. The only fault was its light rear end weight that created fish tailing on wet or snow covered roads. While stationed at SP Allegany, my night patrol partner was Trooper Mike Clayson from Hinsdale, N.Y. The cars speedometer was round faced with a top speed indicated at 120 MPH. Route 219 between Bradford Junction (Route 17) and the Pennsylvania State line was as straight as an arrow and about eight (8) miles in length. Mike enjoyed early morning drives on that stretch of road where he would "open it up". The speedometer indicator would push past the 120 MPH marker back to the zero indicator. We estimated our speed at about 140 MPH.

1965 PLYMOUTH BLACK AND WHITE

During the spring of 1965, the Division of State Police tested three Chrysler Corporation products on the Thruway. They were equipped with extra heavy – duty frames, brakes and related items. A Plymouth Fury I was mounted on a 119-inch wheelbase. The vehicles were equipped with transistorized ignition and heavy-duty automatic transmission for testing purposes. All 1965 Plymouth vehicles purchased had an extended wheelbase of not less than 119 inches and were equipped with a hand throttle. Testing was completed using disc brakes and transistorized ignitions. The ignition improvements reduced electrical interference aiding in better radio reception. New York State Police lettering was found on both front door panels with a single round red and white oscillating bubble light affixed to the roof.

During 1965, the division had 1,200 vehicles in service that traveled 47,472,150 miles. That was equivalent to 1,899 trips around the world at the equator.

1966 FORD BLACK AND WHITE

In the spring 1966, the Division of State Police purchased 800 new 1966 Ford troop cars under an open bid contract. The cars featured a 390 cubic inch V-8 engine, padded dash and sun visors, front wheel disc brakes and a special toggle switch that permitted disabling the rear deck lights. Tinted glass was also part of the package. A laminated maintenance schedule that was more detailed than recommended for normal use was included. The cars weighed 3,500 pounds.

1973 PLYMOUTH FURY

The 1973 Plymouth Fury was one of the most powerful troop cars ever. It got to top speed rapidly, but their big engines were heat producers making them uncomfortable during summer months. The single oscillating roof light was red and was cylindrical in shape.

1974 DODGE AKA THE TIAJUANA TAXI

New blue and roadside yellow Dodge cars were purchased in 1974. 344 were ordered for assignment across the state. The color was intended to make them more visible. When received, the cars were outfitted with Vascar speed detectors and new twin gumball lights and sirens. They were mounted on the new roof- rack providing better visibility and audibility. A survey taken at the NYS State Fair a year earlier resulted in a 5 to 1 ratio in favor of the new color combination.

The last black and white patrol cars were retired in 1977.

AIR CONDITIONING

Air conditioning was first introduced with the purchase of the 1978 Plymouth Fury. 297 cars were delivered with air conditioning and immediately placed in service. Division planned to replace one-third of its fleet of 1500 in 1979. The replacement cars would have air conditioning installed. It was anticipated that by 1981, all cars would have air installed.

1984 DODGE DIPLOMAT

In 1984, the Dodge Diplomat was phased into service replacing the blue and gold patrol cars. The color was changed to a dark blue with the lettering State Trooper spelled out in reflective yellow across the front fenders and trunk lid with the state police seal placed on each front door panel.

1946 FORD

1952 Ford Patrol Car

VIC SANTA - 1950S

BOOK IV — ENFORCING THE LAW

GAMBLING

HISTORY OF GAMBLING IN UNITED STATES

The United States has had a long history of allowing some forms of legal gambling and a degree of tolerance of illegal gambling. Different attitudes towards gambling were enforced. The Puritan-led Massachusetts Bay Colony outlawed not only the possession of cards, dice, and gaming tables (even in private homes), but also dancing and singing

In other colonies, settlers brought with them the view that gambling was a harmless diversion. Gambling was a popular and accepted activity.

The Virginia Company of London, the financier of Jamestown in Virginia, was permitted by the Crown to hold lotteries to raise money for the company's colonial venture. The lotteries were relatively sophisticated and included instant winners.

All 13 original colonies established lotteries, usually more than one, to raise revenue. Playing the lottery became a civic responsibility. Proceeds helped establish some of the nation's earliest and most prestigious universities. The following Universities were beneficiaries of the lotteries, Harvard, Yale, Columbia, Dartmouth, Princeton and William and Mary. Lottery funds were also used to build churches and libraries. Ben Franklin, John Hancock, and George Washington were all prominent sponsors of specific lotteries for public works projects.

Once the war of independence started, the Continental Congress voted a $10 million lottery to finance the war. The lottery had to be abandoned, however, because it was too large and the tickets could not be sold.

Notable among the later lotteries was a private lottery passed by Congress in 1823 for the beautification of Washington D.C. Unfortunately, the organizers absconded with the proceeds and the winner was never paid.

Wagering on horse racing was a popular form of gambling. The gambling was limited to a few friendly bets between owners of horses and their partisans. The first racetrack in North America was built on Long Island in 1665.

Casino gaming started slowly. Taverns and roadhouses would allow dice and card games. The relatively sparse population was a barrier to establishing gaming houses. But as the population increased, by the early 1800s, lavish casinos were established in the young republic.

Increasing evidence of fraud and dishonesty in the operations of lotteries was found. In 1833 Pennsylvania, New York, and Massachusetts put an end to state authorized lotteries. By 1840, most states had banned lotteries. Nevertheless, the tickets from a few states were shipped around the country by mail or smugglers. The prohibition also led to the creation of illegal lotteries.

Lotteries were targeted for prohibition, but gambling in posh clubs was still legal in New York. Horse racing survived unscathed.

The gold rush brought a huge increase in the amount and types of gambling to California. The market for gambling space was so strong that a mere canvas tent, 15 by 25 feet, cost $40,000 annually, payable in advance with gold dust. Gambling was so widespread that by 1850, both the state and cities were licensing gambling establishments to raise money.

Laws against gamblers and gambling began to be enacted. State laws were weak and had little real effect on gambling. The statutes outlawed specific games, making the laws difficult to enforce as new and unnamed variants were used and only light penalties were provided. In 1860, all banking games were banned. (Banking games are those where the player bets against the house) Initially, the laws tended to focus on those who ran the games, not the players. In 1885, this was changed so that it was illegal to play. Finally in 1891, the statutes made the penalty for playing equal to the penalty for running the game.

In California, where most gambling was now illegal, the first slot machine was invented and premiered in San Francisco in 1895. It was not specifically outlawed until 1911.

The South turned to lotteries to generate revenue to rebuild the war-ravaged region. In 1868, the Louisiana Lottery Company was authorized and granted a 25-year charter. A carpetbagger criminal syndicate from New York bribed the Legislature into passing the lottery law and establishing the syndicate as the sole lottery provider. The Louisiana Lottery was an interstate venture with over 90% of the company's revenue coming from outside Louisiana.

Scandals and antigaming sentiment led to additional state and federal legislation against lotteries. By 1878, Louisiana was the last of the legal lotteries in the country. By the end of the century no state permitted the operation of lotteries.

Horse racing was also plagued by fraud. The odds and payouts were often faked. The parties taking the bets, known as the bookmakers, often owned horses and were able to influence the race. "Ringers," horses that were fraudulent substitutes and were either much quicker or slower than the expected entry, were often raced.

Scandals and the rise of Victorian morality led to the end of legal gambling. By 1910, virtually all forms of gambling were prohibited in the United States. Prohibition did not stop gambling. There were many types of illegal gambling houses.

The great depression led to legalization of gambling. Legalized gambling was looked upon as a way to stimulate the economy. Massachusetts decriminalized bingo in 1931 in an attempt to help churches and charitable organizations raise money. Bingo was legal in 11 states by the 1950s, usually only for charity purposes.

Horseracing and pari-mutuel wagering began to make a comeback. During the 1930's, 21 states brought back racetracks. New laws and automated systems made horse racing much more honest than during the 1800s.

The crackdown on illegal gambling forced the likes of New York mobster Benjamin "Bugsy" Siegel to move to the West Coast. His role was to expand gaming and bookmaking operations for organized crime. Publicity forced him out of California so he relocated to Las Vegas.

Mobsters financed many casinos in Nevada. Most notable perhaps was the Las Vegas Flamingo that Bugsy Seigel opened in 1947. The lavish casino opened with such stars as Jimmy Durante, Xavier Cougat, and George Raft entertaining the many guests. The Flamingo helped establish Las Vegas as the destination for high roller gamblers to come and practice their skills.

During the 1950s, the Senate Committee to Investigate Organized Crime in Interstate Commerce held a number of hearings on criminal influence in the casino industry. The committee found widespread evidence of skimming, which sheltered gambling profits from taxes. The result of the committee's findings was a crackdown on criminal influence and a cleansing of the casino industry. Eventually, the mob sold their casino interests to lawful individuals and publicly traded companies.

From 1894 to 1964, there were no legal government-sponsored lotteries operating in the United States. Despite the illegality, numbers was quite popular with about $5 billion wagered in 1960.

Growing opposition to tax increases was a leading factor in establishing state-run lotteries in the 20th century. In 1967 New York sponsored a state run lottery.

In 1978, New Jersey became the second state to legalize casino gambling in an attempt to raise revenues.

GAMBLING IN NEW YORK STATE

The New York State constitution contains an absolute prohibition against gambling in New York State. Below are the only three exceptions.

THE STATE LOTTERY

The lottery exception was written into the constitution when voters approved the Amendment on November 8, 1966, becoming the second state in the modern era to authorize a lottery; implementing legislation followed. The constitutional exception provides that "no lottery or the sale of lottery tickets, pool-selling, book-making, or any other kind of gambling, except lotteries operated by the state and the sale of lottery tickets in connection therewith as may be authorized and prescribed by the legislature, the net proceeds of which shall be applied exclusively to or in aid or support of education in this state as the legislature may prescribe . . . shall hereafter be authorized or allowed within this state; and the legislature shall pass appropriate laws to prevent offenses against any of the provisions of this section".

PARI-MUTUEL WAGERING

The pari-mutuel wagering exception dated back to 1939. It permitted pari-mutuel betting on horse races as may be prescribed by the legislature and from which the state shall derive a reasonable revenue for the support of Government.

In 1970, New York State expanded pari-mutuel wagering to include Off-Track Betting,

the first state to do so. The purpose of the OTB's was to support local government, particularly New York City, to displace illegal bookmaking and to aid the horse industry. In 1973, seven geographic OTB regions were established. Six permitted off-track wagering. They were Capital, Catskill, Nassau, New York City, Suffolk, and Western.

In addition to thoroughbred racing, New York State had seven harness racetracks located at Batavia, Buffalo, Monticello, Saratoga, Syracuse, Vernon, and Yonkers. In 1981, simulcasting began in New York State, on an experimental basis; simulcasting is the "live simultaneous video and audio transmission of a race from an originating racetrack to a receiving port located elsewhere for the purposes of pari-mutuel wagering". In 1990, simulcasting was made permanent.

CHARITABLE GAMBLING

The charitable gambling exception became part of the state constitution in 1957 and was added to in 1975 with games of chance commonly known as: (a) bingo or lotto, in which prizes are awarded on the basis of designated numbers or symbols on a card conforming to numbers or symbols selected at random; (b) games in which prizes are awarded on the basis of a winning number or numbers, color or colors, or symbol or symbols determined by chance from among those previously selected or played, whether determined as the result of the spinning of a wheel, a drawing or otherwise by chance. In 2002, the level of charitable gambling in New York State was approximately $461 million.

ARRESTS

CRAP GAME RAIDED
On September 9, 1946, troopers led by Lieutenant Richard Walter broke up a dice game making two arrests at the annual Eagles Outing at Cook's Paradise Grove, Millersport Highway and Transit Road, Amherst, N.Y. Frank Manns, 76 Kentucky Street and Harry L. Granger, 64 Days Park, Buffalo, N.Y., operators of the under/over game were charged with gambling. Dice, gambling equipment and $230.00 were confiscated. Both were released without bail to appear at a later time before Lockport Justice Harry J. Kelley.

LEROY LEGION SLOTS SEIZED – 1953
Troopers seized six slot machines during a raid of the Botts-Fiorito American Legion Post. It was said to be the only place in the county where slots were still operating. Three of the dime and three of the nickel variety were seized as well as a lottery fishbowl. Charged was the Leroy Servicemen's Club Inc. who ran the home. Leroy Attorney Louis P. Brady Jr. was president of the club. Troopers E. A. Bogucki, R. M. Barrus and Sgt. G. S. Wood conducted the raid. Mr. Brady entered a guilty plea to the charge before Leroy Police Justice Francis Dougherty and was fined $100.00 suspended. The contents of the machines contained $150.00 that was turned over to the Genesee County General Fund. The slot machines were destroyed.

OAKFIELD-ALABAMA GAMBLING – MAY 1953
On May 5, 1953 Troopers seized bowling shuffle board games used in conjunction with a lottery at the Arnold House Hotel owned by Ward Berg, the Country Grill near South Alabama owned by Margaret Waterstreet and the Alabama Hotel owned by Benjamin Schoemaker. It was contended that the operation of the shuffle bowling game in conjunction with offering a chance for prizes constituted a lottery. It was alleged that any person who paid 10 cents and scored 200 in the game received a chance to pick a ticket from a stick and certain numbers won prizes. There were 1,000 tickets on the stick with only 15 prizes. Troopers Malcolm Grant, W.W. Eckhardt and Edmund Bogucki, conducted the raids. A jury trial was held before Oakfield Justice Albert Avery with Berg being found guilty. He was continued on bail.

BATAVIA GAMBLERS NABBED – AUGUST 10, 1956
State and City Police conducted a raid at the Liberty Street Smoke Shop, 102 Liberty Street, Batavia, N.Y., an alleged gaming establishment. Charged with bookmaking were the shop proprietors, Joseph Lobello, 33, 5 Maple St. and his father-in-law, William Yates Sr., 52, 210 Ellicott Street. Two others in the building, Nicholas Martino, 47, 10 Ellicott Place and Frank Pelligrino, 42, 106 Osterhout Street were charged with Disorderly Conduct. They were arraigned before City Judge J. Vincent Serve with all but Yates pleading guilty.

Martino was sentenced to 6 months in the Monroe County Penitentiary and fined $250.00

Lobello was sentenced to 30 days in the Genesee County Jail and fined $500.00

Pelligrino was sentenced to 10 days in the Genesee County Jail and fined $100.00

Yates posted $500.00 bail for a later appearance

Batavia Police Lieutenant G. Samuel Baudanza, Patrolman James Aquino and Edward Santora along with Troopers George Wood and Robert Powell, conducted the raid.

STATEWIDE GAMBLING RAIDS – OCTOBER 1958
An early morning statewide raid by 200 troopers and local police at 79 locations was hailed a powerful blow against organized crime. It was the largest raid ever in the state. Locally, Salvatore Valle, 41, Highland Park, Batavia, NY was charged with being a common gambler, when arrested at 1243 Clifford Ave., Rochester, N.Y. He posted $500.00 bail. He had been previously arrested on November 29, 1958 at his 306 Ellicott St., Batavia, NY toy store. He pled guilty before Judge J. Vincent Serve, was fined $500.00 and given a three month suspended sentence. Valle was sentenced to 6 months in the Genesee County Jail in 1945 for related gambling charges.

LEROY GAMBLERS – 1959
Leroyan's Thomas W. Brown, 64, 8 Church Street and Vincent Allen, 39, 25 North Street, Leroy, NY pleaded guilty before Police Justice Emmett E. Keenan to a charge of bookmaking with Brown paying a $50.00 fine and Allen a $25.00 fine. Brown was using the outside sill of a window at the Baltimore and Ohio Railroad Station as a desk. Runners would appear to do business from the Leroy industrial plants. 150 betting slips including wagers on Yonkers and Batavia Downs on them and $217.50 was confiscated.

OLEAN – MAY 1960
"CARD GAMES" – greatest fund raising idea ever for clubs and non-profit groups. Elite Vending Company, Box 511, Olean, N.Y. This Olean newspaper advertisement led troopers and Olean Police to raid the company warehouse located at 133-137 Adams Street. Confiscated were an estimated 10 million lottery tickets, several tons of punchboards, other games of chance and 23 slot and 30 pinball machines. Questioned were warehouse owners Wallace DaStaf and Charles Handmore of Olean. The company had a mail order list of 5000 customers filling orders by parcel post. Sgt. William Lombard in charge of the raid indicated it was the largest punchboard haul ever in New York State. No arrests were made. It was illegal to possess, sell or distribute games of chance. It was a misdemeanor punishable by a one-year jail term and $500.00fine.

MOUNT MORRIS - APRIL 1961
James Guarino, 50, Sonyea Road, Mt. Morris, N.Y. was charged as a common gambler and maintaining a gambling establishment by Sheriff James Emery and Trooper Sergeant George Wood. He posted $500.00 bail for a later court appearance. He was arrested the result of a holdup during a dice game a month earlier at a garage he owned. At that time, three masked men armed with shotguns held up the participants a dice game taking between $3000 & $4000. They then made them remove their trousers to delay pursuit. Guarino was arrested on a similar charge in 1959 and was fined $25.00 by Judge Robert Wier of Mount Morris.

LIMA – MAY 1968

Lima Town Justice Harold A. Hennessy donated $1.00 to the volunteer firemen of Livingston County, when he levied that amount in a fine against the Hook and Ladder Company Number 1, Livonia, N.Y. for illegal possession of slot machines. Attorney John J. Carey pleaded guilty to the charge in behalf of the Hook and Ladder Company from which State Police Investigator Thomas Salvemini seized three slot machines. The slot machines, two nickel and one quarter play have been with the fire company since 1932. There were to be held for thirty days, then would be destroyed.

Judge Hennessy stated that possession of the slot machines was illegal and was not to be condoned. He further noted that since the slot machines were used only once per year and that any profit from them was used to benefit the community for the purchase of new equipment.

Without the volunteer fire companies, our small villages would be in serious trouble and we owe a debt of gratitude to the firefighters who give their time freely. Therefore, I am fining the defendants $1.00 and will pay the fine myself.

1949S SLOT MACHINES
DESTROYED

JOE PLEAKIS - LYMAN
"BUD" MILLS - 1951

MURDERS IN WESTERN NEW YORK

During the nineteen-sixties, New York State revised its Penal Law and Code of Criminal Procedure. A conviction for Murder 2nd Degree was now punishable by a term not to exceed twenty-five years and Murder 1st Degree punishable by life imprisonment with a few exceptions where the death penalty could be imposed.

Attempts to obtain case dispositions in some instances were unsuccessful because none were available for review. The New York State Department of Correctional Services does not maintain records for inmates released more than twenty-five years ago.

SCHMIDT DOUBLE MURDER-BOSTON, N.Y. - 1944
On July 12, 1944, Jacob Schmidt and his brother Lawrence were killed instantly when gunned down by shotgun blasts as they started their day. The killings took place at a cottage on the Black Creek Road, Boston, N.Y. Wounded was Miss Edna Halladay, age 29, employed by the Schmidt's as a housekeeper. Jealousy was apparently the motive. The assailant, 29-year old Blasdell resident Walter Nowicki wanted to marry Miss Halladay. Nowicki who was married but separated was trying to obtain money from Miss Halladay for the purpose of obtaining a divorce. According to Halladay, Nowicki shot her first from outside, through a kitchen window. Injured, she and Jacob Schmidt's wife ran into an adjoining room and hid under a bed. Nowicki entered the house and shot Lawrence Schmidt who was sitting on a davenport in the living room. He then shot Jacob Schmidt, as he got out of bed and entered the kitchen. Nowicki then went out into the yard where he placed the gun barrel against his chest and the butt to the ground triggered the shotgun killing himself.

LYDIA C. WARNER – SILVER CREEK – 1946
On March 10, 1946, Lydia C. Warner, age 50 of 22 Adams Street, Silver Creek, N.Y. was found lying unconscious at the Dunkirk, N.Y. Nickel Plate railroad tower where she was employed as a night operator. Members of a train crew found her at about 6:30 AM. No entries had been made in her log for several passing trains with the last entry at 12:47AM. She was taken to Brook's Hospital where it was determined her worst injury was internal caused by a broom handle being driven into her body. She was also suffered a broken nose, jaw and collarbone and possible skull fracture.

A blood smeared broom handle was found at the scene bearing fresh fingerprints. A couch and wall were blood splattered. Brocton District Attorney Edwin G. O'Connor led the investigation.

Lydia Warner died three days later, but not before identifying her assailant, as Leo J. Mleczko, a 28 year old Middle Road resident. He was a decorated war hero that was also employed by the railroad, as a section hand. Troopers Richard Walters, Harold Debrine, Eugene Hageman, William Kirwan, Edmund Broughton, Frank Easton and Dan Bily aided in the investigation. Mlezcko was arrested and after extensive questioning, admitted guilt. He was found guilty after trial. His defense was that he did not recall events of the evening having been out drinking with several companions. It is believed that the conviction was appealed and reversed sometime in 1950. This could not be verified. (Dunkirk Daily Observer 3/14/46)

RAYMOND PLYTER BODY FOUND AT BERGEN, N.Y. - 1946

On July 25, 1946, 16 year-old Charles Wood, while riding his bicycle along the Ausblin (Dublin) Road, Bergen, N.Y. was attracted by what he termed a strong odor coming from the bushes. His curiosity led him to the discovery of a body later identified as 25 year-old Raymond Eugene Plyter of Shortsville, N.Y.

The State Police were called with a detail led by Inspector Eugene O. Hageman responded to the scene located on the George Reynolds farm 4 miles east of Byron. No identification was found on the body that was clad in denim overalls, work shirt and worn work shoes. Two bullet wounds to the head were found making the case a murder. Both bullets were recovered during the autopsy conducted by Dr. Joseph Tannenberg at the Bohm Mortuary. The body was severely decomposed making fingerprint identification impossible. Methodical review of bits of information and evidence gathered at the scene led to the body being identified four days later, as Plyter. Aided by Inspector Ed Doody of Troop D, the investigation centered at Plyter's home and employment in Ontario County. This eventually led to the arrest of Floyd Edgar Martin Jr., age 21, of Walworth, N.Y. charged with First-Degree Murder. Martin provided a statement admitting shooting Plyter twice in the head with a .22 caliber rifle. The motive proved to be jealousy and robbery. Martin and Plyter were long time friends with Plyter living with the Martins while working at various local farms. He became angry with Plyter when he put his arms around Martin's fiancé while they visited with her and referred to her as a whore. Plyter also saved his money and had a substantial amount in savings and uncashed checks.

On the morning of July 19, 1946, Plyter was in the Martin's barn doing milking chores. Martin, hidden in a stall, shot him where he sat. He then shot him a second time from close range to make sure he was dead. Death was instantaneous. Martin removed $300.00 in cash and checks from the body and then wrapped the body in a blanket & burlap sack, placing it in the trunk of dead man's Plymouth Coupe. He then set out to dispose of the body. He drove around in the dead man's car all day, finally locating a desolate wooded area on the Dublin Road. He drove back to Rochester, N.Y. where he got rid of the rifle by tossing it into the Genesee River.

On July 23, 1946, Martin without question by bank officials withdrew the savings of $450.00 from Plyter's bank account and cashed his checks. Investigation led to Martin's arrest on August 1, 1946. He was taken into custody at the Garlock Packing Company, Palmyra, N.Y. where he just started employment.

He was arraigned before Newark Peace Justice Parke M. Reeves who ordered him held for Grand Jury.

Martin was described as "well known and well thought of in the Walworth area" with no bad habits. He didn't smoke or drink, was an excellent athlete and a U S Navy veteran.

On November 7, 1946, he was convicted in Wayne County Court and sentenced to die in the electric chair. Two days prior to the scheduled execution, Governor Thomas E. Dewey commuted his sentence to life imprisonment. He spent twenty years in prison.

On September 14, 1966, Martin was freed. State Supreme Court Justice Jacob Ark granted a dismissal after hearing arguments by Public Defender Thomas J. Gilmore Jr. that Martin was without legal representation when he made his confession twenty years earlier. The United States Supreme Court ruled in another similar case that evidence obtained in this manner was inadmissible in court. On July

26, 1966, a Supreme Court Order ordered a new trial, citing the violation of the right to counsel, as the reason.

Batavia Daily News Editorial on August 2, 1946
There is no clock-punching by the men of the state police – no overtime emoluments for them – no bonus for excellence on the job. Their reward is the plain but substantiated satisfaction of a job well done and the confidence of a grateful public.

Their most recent achievement that is distinctly of commendable caliber began in the early afternoon of July 25th when a town of Bergen youth came across the body of a man, trussed in sacks and a blanket and abandoned in the weeds along the Dublin Road not far from the youth's home.

Two bullet holes were in the skull. Murder was the inescapable conclusion. Clues even to the identification of the victim were meager.

There were a blank deposit slip of a Fairport bank in the man's overalls pocket and a watch attached to the overalls by a leather thong. Hence, Fairport was the first port of call, as the state police investigators went to task.

Only one inquiry was made before the BCI agents came to the Fairport farm implement store, the proprietor of which said he once employed a man answering the description deducted from the decomposed remains.

Place after place was fitted into the puzzle by painstaking and methodical development of each lead, a procedure that was pushed day and night at the sacrifice of sleep and days away from families on the part of the State Police.

Six days of grueling pace produced the answer – a signed confession from a close friend of the victim that he had committed murder to obtain his chum's money. This accomplishment speaks for itself. It is a crime of detection achievement of distinction. Inspectors E.O. Hageman and Edward J. Doody and their men of the Troop A, Batavia barracks have again won the confidence of a grateful public.

LENA McQUEEN ROBINSON – 1948
On September 13, 1948, the body of Mrs. Lena McQueen Robinson, age 78 was found dead in the blood-smeared bedroom of her farm home on the outskirts of Scio. She had been raped and brutally beaten. She was the widow of oil producer Clarence Robinson who died 16 years earlier. A son, Paul McQueen of Allentown found the body when he stopped for a visit. Troopers Joseph Heilig and James Kirwan were assigned the initial investigation. It was determined that the murder took place on September 10 TH. While securing evidence at the crime scene, Trooper Heilig located a billfold lying on the floor near the foot of the bed. It identified Maurice Holshouser, age 26, a carnival worker and part time handy man as the owner. Holshouser had worked as a painter on the Robinson farm and was familiar with Mrs. Robinson's routine. An immediate wanted alarm was sent over the police teletype network describing the crime and Holshouser. Mrs. Robinson's 1937 Buick Sedan automobile was missing and believed to have been taken by the killer. Virginia State Police found the car abandoned near Ruckerville, Virginia and preserved it as evidence. Based on developed information, a request for Holshouser's arrest was sent to the North Carolina State Police. He was located at the home of his wife in Yadkinville, North Carolina. He readily admitted to the crime. Recovered were a diamond ring, several checks made out to Mrs. Robinson and an Elgin watch. Investigators Dan Bily and John Sage were sent to North Carolina to interview Holshouser and returned him for arraignment and trial. Holshouser was found guilty after trial presided over by Allegany County Judge Hamilton

Ward Hamilton of Belfast, N.Y. Heilig recalled the sentence to be a term of 20 years to life in a state prison.

(Recollections of Former Trooper Joe Heilig) (Wellsville Daily Reporter dated 9/15/48)

WILLIAM LARSON MURDER – JULY 2, 1948

Shortly after midnight on July 2, 1948, 55-year-old William Larson of Kuckville, N.Y., an attendant at the Veteran's Hospital, Batavia, N.Y. was returning home after his shift, when he was ambushed on the Quaker Hill Road 5 miles south of Albion, N.Y. He was the father of thirteen children ranging from age 5 to 25.

Passing motorist Melville Bort of Batavia, N.Y. was attracted to the headlights of the car about 30 feet off the road in a field. He thought it to be an accident until he observed bullet holes in the car. He immediately alerted the State Police with Sergeant Harry Adams of the Gaines substation responding. Investigation noted that two shots from a shotgun were fired at close range with one shot passing through the door striking the victim in the shoulder. A second shot pierced a window lodging in the upper section of the car. A blood trail was found on the roadway for about three tenths of a mile prior to the car going off the road. The front seat was blood soaked with a large pool of blood on the left running board. It appeared Larson while wounded attempted to drive away going into a field, when he lost consciousness. A State Police detail consisting of Inspector Harold Kemp, Sergeants George Wood and Harry Adams, Corporals Clarence Pasto and Elner Anderson and Troopers John Sage, Hanrahan, Frank Lachnicht, Gibbons and James Kerwin immediately went into action conducting hundreds of interviews. In less than 29 hours, troopers made an arrest charging 33-year old Lloyd G. Inman, who roomed at the William Wirt residence, 219 Washington Street and his 33-year old girlfriend Virginia Devereaux Ostrander of 118 South Clinton Street, Albion, N.Y. with 1st Degree Murder.

Details revealed that Inman was married to Larson's oldest daughter, Gladys and blamed Larson for their marriage breaking up. On July 1st, he had his girlfriend Virginia drive him to the Larson home to see his infant son but upon arrival, Gladys took the child into the house and refused his pleas. Angered, he made the decision to get even with his father in law. That evening, both he and Virginia returned to their separate residences. At about 10:00 PM, both sneaked out with Inman carrying his shotgun. They drove to the

VA Hospital and waited near the gate for Larson to leave. With Ostrander driving the car and Inman in the rear seat, they followed Larson as he departed. About a mile south of Barre Center in a deserted area, Ostrander pulled along side the Larson car and Inman discharged both barrels of the shotgun into the car. Inman watched through the rear window, as the Larson car gradually veered off the road into a field. They drove directly to the Erie Barge Canal where they disposed of the shotgun, then returned to their rooms. Trooper interviews of the family led to Inman and Ostrander being brought in for questioning at about 5:00AM. They were separated and questioned throughout the day by different investigators. They continued to deny any knowledge of the murder. The turning point came late in the afternoon, when Inman was taken to see the victim's bloodstained car. At about midnight, Ostrander provided a written statement to District Attorney J. Kenneth Serve that was completed at about 2:00AM. Inman followed also providing a written statement. At 5:45AM, both were arraigned before Justice of the Peace Milton Kast. They were confined to the Orleans County Jail pending Grand Jury action. Inman was found guilty of Murder 1st Degree in 1948 and sentenced to die in the electric chair. Governor Thomas E. Dewey commuted the sentence to life imprisonment. On July 23, 1965, Inman represented by Albion Attorney Curtis Lyman appealed his conviction before Acting Supreme Court Judge Philip Weiss of Batavia. Lyman contended that the long period of questioning before trial, failure to provide counsel, only one meal served the suspect in a 24 hour period, lack of sleep, fear of physical force and denial of medical attention all showed Inman's statement involuntary.

ARTHUR ANHEIER MURDER – ELBA, N.Y. 1950

During the fall of 1950, five foot tall Stephen Lewis, a resident of Byron, N.Y. had declared to his wife that he was going to Rochester, N.Y. where he could make a lot of money, as a salesman. He was described as a basically lazy person with an ego who fancied himself a ladies man. He had held several jobs including farming, but any money he had came from hustling local boys at the pool tables. He had married a woman with three sons from her previous marriage.

After several employment rejections, Lewis took a job selling vacuum cleaners door to door. During the course of this employment, he met and was smitten by Irene Anheier, a co-worker that had recently separated from her husband, Arthur of Elba, N.Y. She was working to earn a living while in Rochester. Irene kept company with Lewis, but was a highly moral person and rejected all of his advances and intentions. He took these rejections, as a sign that she really, truly loved him. He thought that if he were also separated, that she would agree to live with him. He returned to Byron where he advised his wife that he had fallen in love and that their marriage was over. Returning to Rochester, he found Irene packing her suitcases. She told him that she was going back to her husband. Lewis rationalized this setback to suit his own conceit. She was desperately in love with him, but felt too sorry for her husband to leave him.

Lewis sent letter after letter and bombarded her with long distance phone calls none of which she answered. Her silence made no difference, as he was sure she loved him. On a Sunday afternoon, Lewis arrived at the Anheier house where he declared to Arthur that he loved Irene and that he should do the sporting thing and divorce her. Arthur had been most patient to this point, but he insisted that Lewis no longer upset his wife and with this, picked him up by the collar and seat of his pants and threw him out the door.

On November 23, 1951 the deer season had just opened in Genesee County. At about 6:00 AM, Arthur Anheier left home to go to his job in the gypsum mines at Oakfield, N.Y. A shot rang out with a deer slug striking Arthur above the heart killing him instantly. Irene finding Arthur in a pool of blood called for an ambulance and the police. Troopers Sergeant George Wood and Claude Stephens arrived within minutes and secured the scene. It was first believed to have been a hunting accident. A detail of troopers beat the woods confiscating the shotguns of any hunters found in the area for comparison with the fatal slug while Inspector Harry DeHollander interviewed the hunters. He concluded that none were responsible for the death. The coroner provided his report and from this, it was determined that Arthur had been shot intentionally from close range, as there was gunshot wadding in the wound. The projectile entered his body at an upward angle indicating a small person had fired the shot.

At about 5:00 PM, Sergeant John M. Long was at the scene searching for clues, when the telephone at the Anheier home rang. Long answered it. A male voice asked for Irene with Long advising she was under a doctor's care and not available. The person then said " tell her not to worry, everything is going to be all right for the future" and hung up. Long immediately called the telephone operator identified himself and had the phone call traced. The phone call had originated in Rochester, N.Y. He immediately notified Inspector DeHollander who along with Rochester Police Department detectives went to the address provided and arrested Stephen Lewis. Genesee County District Attorney Wallace Stakel prosecuted Lewis, charged with 1st degree murder. Although he admitted to the murder, Lewis under law was required to plead not guilty. A trial resulted in his conviction with Lewis being sentenced to the death penalty. The conviction was appealed as a matter of law. It was denied. On

January 22, 1953, Lewis entered the death chamber at Sing Sing Prison where at 11:02 he was pronounced dead.

From November 26, 1951 to May 5, 1952, Irene Anheier was held at the county jail as a material witness. Upon release, she was compensated $3.00 for each day she was held.

(Real Detective Yearbook # 102 – 1969)   (Genesee County Clerk's Records)

NANCY BRIDGES MURDER – ALEXANDER, NY 1951

On June 5, 1951, Jerome Rozborski, age 17, Alexander, N.Y. was hunting along the Darien-Alexander Townline Road, when he discovered the body of a murdered girl. The victim was identified as 15-year-old Nancy Bridges of 111 East Ferry Street, Buffalo, N.Y., a Fosdick Masten High School student. Her maimed body was found in underbrush 20 feet off the road. Rozborski, who resided on Route 20 a short distance away first found a pair of leather shoes along side of the road. Looking more closely, he saw a spot of blood, then a blood trail leading across the road. He followed the blood trail into the underbrush where he observed an arm protruding and black hair. He ran immediately to a neighbor and called the state police.

Captain J.B. Lynch, Sergeants C.E. Cobb and G. S. Wood, Corporals C. Pasto and W.E. Rimmer and Troopers J.C. Moochler and M.B. Grant conducted the investigation. District Attorney Wallace Stakel and Sheriff Forrest Brown were also at the scene. The investigation turned to the City of Buffalo after the girl was identified, with city detectives John C. Rapp and John P. Revelle conducting interviews of the family. It was learned that family problems led to the slaying. The victim's sister Frances had left her husband Wallace P. Ford Jr., age 30, moving back to her parent's home with their infant son. Nancy was sent to the store, when Ford came along and questioned her about his son. Apparently Nancy told him that the family was going to keep the baby, enraging Ford. He then picked up a rock and struck Nancy in the head knocking her unconscious. He placed her in the back seat of his car and drove around for some time. Fearing arrest for striking her, he drove to the Town-line Road location where he placed the still unconscious girl on the road, then drove his car back and forth over her body. He then dragged the body into the underbrush. Dr. Joseph Tannenberg conducted an autopsy stating that death was the result of the automobile crushing her chest and puncturing her lungs. Wallace P. Ford Jr. was charged with Murder 1st Degree and readily admitted to the crime. He was arraigned before County Court Judge Philip Weiss and held for Grand Jury.

On November 30, 1951, Wallace Perry Ford Jr. was found guilty after trial of Murder in the 1st Degree in a trial presided over by Justice Hamilton Ward of Buffalo, N.Y.

CASSON CHURCH MURDER – ADDISON, NY - 1955

On September 9, 1955, the body of 54-year -old Casson J. Church was discovered in the trunk of a 1935 Chevrolet automobile owned by him and his son Basil. The body was clad only with socks and a T-shirt and displayed a bullet wound to the head. The automobile was found abandoned on the Thurston-Goodhue Lake Road with a flat front tire. Basil Church discovered the body when he learned the car was abandoned near Goodhue Lake. He had a friend, Bernard Ellwood drive him to the location. Using a spare key, Basil tried to start the car, but the battery was dead. He told Ellwood that he would change the tire, and then be pushed for a jump-start. When he opened the trunk for the spare, he found his father's body. Driving back to Addison, they called the Sheriff's office with Deputies Charles H. Reynolds, Forrest Herrington, Katner, and Nichols responding to the scene along with District Attorney Domenick L. Gabrielli. Preliminary interviews determined that because of the wide range of Casson Church's activities, help would be needed. Casson was estranged from his wife and had many lady friends throughout the area. This led police to believe it was a crime of jealousy or revenge. The troopers sent Inspector Harry DeHollander, Troopers R.K. Clark, R.H. Meachum, Ed Nearing, John Moulthrop, Gerald Schusler and George Wood to assist. Interviews were conducted in Olean, Wellsville, Scio, Addison, Savona and Elmira. Family members, friends, gas station attendants, bars and restaurants were all attended to with little information learned. He had been to several bars over the weekend, but his activities could not be determined after Saturday night, September 3rd. Finally, a bartender in Savona recalled Church being at the bar late Saturday night and leaving with a stranger. He provided a description recalling the stranger had big ears and a large nose. This eventually led to the stranger being identified as Floyd Brewer living on the Green Hill Road. Brewer initially denied having any knowledge of Church. A preliminary search of the immediate area found remains of clothing in a pile of ashes and a belt buckle. Confronted, Brewer admitted to killing Church. He said that they had been drinking at a bar in Savona on Saturday with both men getting intoxicated. Church had insulted him during the evening and continued to poke fun and insult him as he drove him home. Exhausted, they both fell asleep. Brewer got up at about 4:00 in the morning, took a .22 caliber rifle and shot Church in the back of the head while he slept on a cot. He then took the bloody mattress and clothing and tried to burn them. On September 12, 1955, Floyd Brewer was charged with Murder 1st Degree. He was convicted, but a disposition could not be determined.

SOUTHERN TIER MURDERS – 1957

During December 1957, a short- lived crime wave resulted in robbery and murder in the Corning and Horseheads area of the southern tier of New York. It started with a .32 caliber pistol being stolen from the car of security officer Henry Green of Elmira, N.Y. on December 11th and ended on December 27th with the arrest of 17 year- old Frederick Paul Sommer Jr. The Sommer's were a respectable family residing at Cameron Mills where Frederick attended Addison School. He quit school having completed the 7th grade and left home getting odd jobs at Horseheads, N.Y. None of his jobs lasted very long and he wound up living at an Inn in Horseheads where he did odd jobs for his room. He was flat broke, when he concluded that the only way to get money other than to work for it was to have a gun and a car and steal it.

On December 13th, Sommer was walking along Route 17 near the intersection of Route 328, when Cecil Stratton, the father of nine children stopped and offered a lift. Stratton was on the way to the hospital where his wife had given birth earlier that day to another son. Sommer accepted and along the way pointed his gun at Stratton in an attempt to rob him. Stratton said he had less than $2.00 and was ordered to drive out of town to the Tompkins Corners area. There they both exited the car where according to Sommer, Stratton kicked the gun from his hand and a struggle ensued. Stratton attempted to flee into the woods. Sommer picked up the gun and fired with the shot striking Stratton behind the ear. The body was dragged into the woods and Stratton's car abandoned on the Kahler Road where it was found two days later. Stratton's body wasn't found until December 27th when a 14-year-old Murphy Hill Road youth on his way home came across the body.

On December 17th, Bob's liquor store on College Avenue, Elmira, N.Y. was held up and $31.00 cash taken. On December 20th, George Berbary, another liquor storeowner was held up at gunpoint and $91.00 taken from the register and another $9.00 from his wallet. On December 26th, a Canisteo Street restaurant at Hornell, N.Y. was robbed at gunpoint and $200.00 taken. The descriptions of the perpetrator in each of the robberies were similar including a handgun of either .25 or .32 caliber.

Also found on December 26th was the body of Corning resident Leo Wallace Brown by a resident driving along the Barnes Hill Road near the Chemung County airport. He had been shot under the eye. Police were notified and the body taken to Arnot-Ogden Hospital for an autopsy. Brown's wallet contained no cash, but had a registration issued to Brown for a blue 1953 Cadillac. The car was not located. An all points bulletin was dispatched for the car. At about 1:15 AM, on the 27th, Trooper

Robert K. Clark & Painted Post Policeman Robert L. Boyle on patrol observed the Cadillac driving on Main Street. The car was stopped with Trooper Clark approaching the driver side and Boyle observing from the passenger side. The driver later identified as Sommer pointed his gun at Clark, but when he saw Boyle on the opposite side, dropped the weapon and surrendered. Taken into custody, he was interrogated by Trooper Lieutenant Kenneth Weidenborner and admitted to the robberies and killings. The tall, thin curly blonde haired Sommer said he killed Leo Brown and Cecil Stratton so that he could steal their cars to be used in holdups and robberies. Sommer was convicted of Murder and sentenced to from 40 years to life imprisonment. He was paroled in October 1975. (True Detective Magazine – April 1958)

MEDINA, N.Y. - DOUBLE MURDER – 1961

In the early morning of January 22, 1961, two Shelby Center, N.Y. youths were checking their muskrat trap lines along the Blair Road just south of Medina. It was a frigid, blustery day with visibility limited, when they saw the headlights of a car down a farm lane that was not moving. They thought it might have been someone in trouble so they proceeded to investigate. The car was empty, but as they proceeded around the corner of an outbuilding, they came across the bodies of a man and woman drenched in blood. Both were dead, lying face up with a thin layer of ice formed on their bodies. The State Police were called with Inspector James W. Russell responding to the scene. The victims were identified as 27-year-old Jose Torres residing at the American Hotel, Middleport, New York and 26-year-old Noreen Russell of West Center Street, Medina, New York. The investigative team was made up of Lieutenant Charles E. Cobb, Sergeants Claude Stephens, John Sage and Charles Davidson, Troopers Fred Penfold, Donald Smith, Henry Panus, Nick Fitzak, Ted Georgitso and Daniel Geiger.

Observations at the scene noted that Torres had been shot four times and Russell once. The car was a 1957 Chevrolet and was mired to its axels in mud. Bloodstains on the seat indicated Torres had been driving and was shot in the back, then twice in the chest and his body dragged behind the building. The girl had apparently tried to flee by running down the lane only to be shot dead. Her body was also dragged behind the building. Shell casings were secured and marked for evidence, fingerprints were taken from the car and plaster casts of footprints made.

Medina Police Chief William Hammond made his office available for a command base along with veteran Patrolman Don Vanderlean to assist. The investigators were split into three teams to conduct interviews and look for additional evidence. One group went to Middleport where Torres resided, another to the Russell apartment and the third to the crime scene. Over 60 interviews were conducted with no leads developing. All interviewees agreed that Torres was a very nice, likable and friendly person. Torres had been employed in a canning factory along with other migrant seasonal farm workers. There seemed to be a code among the migrants about not talking to police for no information was forthcoming. The coroner's autopsy reported that Torres had been shot twice in the back and twice in the chest while Russell had been shot under the left armpit with the bullet piercing her heart. There was no indication of rape. Finally late the first night, Inspector Russell received a phone call from an unidentified man who advised that he had been at the Green Front bar on Main Street the night before. He said Torres, Russell and Artemio Rodriguez were talking and the three left together at about 10:00 PM. Rodriguez lived at 443 Main Street, Medina.

Inspector Russell and a detail of troopers immediately went to the Rodriguez residence where he was interviewed and a search conducted. Found were a .38 caliber pistol, Torres' driver's license and his wrist bracelet. After intense interrogation, Rodriguez admitted to the murders and implicated 19-year-old Rafael Carde of 210 North Street, Medina. They admitted that they wanted Torres' car so they could drive to Florida. Rodriguez asked Torres if he would drive him to a girls home in the country. Torres agreed and the four got into the car and headed south on Route 63. Rodriguez had worked on the Zambito Brothers farm on the Blair Road and knew the area. When Torres refused to turn down a snowy farm lane, Rodriguez took out the gun forcing him to drive down the lane where he was shot in the back. Russell jumped from the car and started running, when she was shot. Both killers dragged the bodies behind the outbuildings. Carde became frightened and ran off on foot and returned to Medina. Rodriguez stayed at the scene. He got stuck in the mud when he attempted to drive out of the lane. The killings took place about 1:30am. With District Attorney Franklin Cropsey present, statements were taken and the defendants arraigned before Shelby Justice of the Peace Robert Brunkhorst who held them without bail for Grand Jury action. Rodriguez was convicted of Murder and sentenced to from 8 ½ years to life imprisonment. He was released on parole May 6, 2003. (Master Detective Magazine – June 1961)

CHAPELLE, WENDELL AND MARCIA MURDERS – 1964

Wendell, age 55 and his wife, Marcia Chapelle owned a 380-acre farm at Rathbone near Corning, N.Y. Wendell was also employed as the Steuben County Sealer of Weights & Measures. They were financially well off with Wendell owning and enjoying a collection of 30 antique cars that he kept in one of his barns. They had made plans to travel to an antique car show at Philadelphia, Pa on January 30 and return on February 2, 1964. On February 16th, concerned relatives notified the State Police at Painted Post, N.Y. requesting some measure of investigation. A uniform patrol along with a relative went to the farm to investigate. Both of the Chapelle cars were in the driveway, beds were unmade, dirty dishes were in the sink and their luggage was still in a closet. This was not normal for the neat Marcia Chapelle. A walk through the barns noted nothing unusual. Phone calls were made to Philadelphia and it was determined that the couple never arrived for the antique car show.

A man who rented a house from the Chapelle's and who was tending to their house and horses also reported them missing. Several checks were again made of the property and on February 20th, Sheriff's Deputies Larry Nichols and Jack Dartt located the frozen body of Marcia secreted under boards on the main barn floor. She was found lying on her side with her head wrapped in an old rag rug and burlap tied with twine. The next morning, the body of Wendell was found about 35 feet from where Marcia lay covered with bales of hay. The wall was blood splattered and covered with cow dung in apparent attempt to hide it. An autopsy determined that heavy blows to the head driving skull fragments into the brain had killed Marcia. Wendell was killed by a single shotgun blast.

The investigation proceeded with discretion and rather slowly, but in time a suspect was developed through the co-operative effort of Sheriff Theodore Katner and BCI Investigator Jesse Moulthrop. Troopers had interviewed a neighbor, Fred Rial on several occasions. It was learned that Rial had purchased several heads of cattle from Chapelle for $1300.00 that were picked up on January 30th. Rial then dropped by the Chapelle's caretaker, advised him that he had taken the cattle and instructed him to keep a check on the house. On January 31st, Rial picked up the caretaker and they went to the Chapelle farm. There the caretaker noticed both cars in the driveway, a pane of glass broken in a rear kitchen door, a rag rug used to wipe feet missing, dirty dishes in a sink, a lady's handbag on the table and a large brown stain on the kitchen floor. This was out of character for the Chapelle's leading him to comment that they must have left in a hurry. In the barn he noticed a sledgehammer, a crowbar and blacksmith's hammer, usually kept in a carport, on the barn floor.

On June 26, 1964, Fred Rial was taken into custody charged with Wendell's murder. The arresting officers were Sheriff Katner, Deputy Larry Nichols, Trooper Lieutenant John Monahan and Investigator Jesse Moulthrop. The very next day, the entire Chapelle farm contents went on sale at auction. Rial was indicted by a Grand Jury and charged with murder. Several motions and mental examinations slowed the trial process, but thirteen months after the murder on February 23, 1965, the trial commenced. The case was cracked through the investigative and interview techniques of BCI Investigator Moulthrop who noted every detail. Each time Rial was interviewed, a different scenario was presented to questions asked. The motive was finally determined that Rial was under financial stress and did not have the $1300.00 to pay for the cattle. He had borrowed the money several months earlier and was pressured by the bank to repay the loan, as promised. The loan was repaid on January 31st from monies received for the resale of the cattle. On April 1, 1965, Rial was found guilty on two counts of Murder in the 2nd degree.

What made this case outstanding and unusual was that the conviction was made strictly on circumstantial evidence with Investigators L.F. Taggart and J.J. Moulthrop of SP Bath playing a major role in the case.   (Inside Detective Magazine – July 1965 Issue)

MARY ELIZABETH CHAPIN – ALLEGANY, N.Y. - 1964

On June 17, 1964, Troopers Gerald L. Crocker and Thomas E. Griffith were sent to the Robert Foster residence, 29 North Second Street, Allegany, N.Y. to investigate the report of an injured girl. Arriving at the scene, they found 18 year old Mary Elizabeth Chapin deceased lying on a sofa with numerous head wounds caused by a blunt instrument. Chapin was the sister of Robert Foster's wife, Sandra. An investigative team comprised of Investigators Gerald Kitchen, Henry Panus, James L. Duval, Stewart Mills, Sergeant Eugene Redden and Troopers James J. Daly, William A. Reynolds, John P. Wilcox and David J. Schwartz responded to the scene.

Stephen Philip Foster, a brother to Robert Foster at the scene said that he had stopped for a visit and found the deceased. It was noted that he was freshly bathed and wore clean, fresh clothing. A bloodstain trail was found leading through the house to an exit. Stephen was told that he was going to be held as a material witness. Continued interviews led to consent to search at the residence of Stephen where blood stained garments and towels were found. He was again interviewed and admitted to killing Chapin with a crowbar. Stephen Philip Foster, age 26, 109 North Second Street, Allegany, New York was arrested for Murder 2nd Degree and arraigned before Allegany Police Justice Richard Kinney.

On October 25, 1965, Foster plead guilty to Murder 2nd Degree before Cattaraugus County Court Judge J. Richmond Page who imposed a sentence of 40 years to life imprisonment at Attica State Prison.

ANNA DELAMETER SIMRIL, CLARENCE, N.Y. - 1964

On October 20, 1964 Investigators George E. Karalus and Harold L. Eichorst responded to the report of a woman being killed at 4575 Harris Hill Road, Clarence, N.Y. This was the residence of the Verne and Anna Simril and their three sons. When they arrived at the scene, Christopher Simril, age 19 and Wayne Simril, age 16 met them at the door. When asked what had happened, Christopher replied that he had killed his mother with an axe. He indicated that the body was in a field at the rear of the house. Having confirmed that a murder had been committed, an investigative team comprised of Investigators Robert L. Tillman, Edward F. Stilwell, Eugene J. Fechter, James L. Duval, John L. Smith and Troopers George McCollum, Douglas W. Hedges, Joseph Paige and Walter H. Herbert responded to the scene.

The victim, 41 year old Anna Delameter Simril was found lying in the underbrush with a large wound to her neck caused by the long handled axe found next to the body. The cause of death was by a severe laceration, neck fracture and skull fractured in several places.

It was learned that Christopher Simiril had attended Oberlin College, Ohio where he attempted suicide on several occasions. At various times, he tried to end his life by taking an overdose of sleeping pills, stabbing himself with a knife puncturing a lung, slashing himself with a razor and jumping out of third story dormitory window suffering a fractured pelvis and clavicle. It was further determined that for what ever reason, he harbored deep hostility feelings toward his mother and was very resentful of her.

Christopher V. Simril was arrested for Murder 1st Degree and arraigned before Clarence Peace Justice Robert Smolka who committed him to the Erie County Jail for further proceedings. On April 7, 1966, a trial jury found him not guilty by unanimous verdict of insanity. He was committed to a state facility for the criminally insane where he was confined and treated for mental disease. (Buffalo Evening News)

BILLINGHAM MURDER – HUMPHREY, NY - 1969

On November, 26, 1969, Ira W. Billingham, age 24, Humphrey, N.Y. appeared at the East Aurora, N.Y. Police Department where he reported that he had shot and killed his mother, Ruby Billingham and the family dog. BCI Investigator's Henry Panus & Gerald Kitchen responded to the scene where the victim was found lying on the floor with gunshot wounds to her head. A 16-gauge shotgun with expended shells was found at the scene. During interview, Ira indicated that for several days, he had been hearing voices that told him to kill his mother. On the morning of the slaying, he got his shotgun and as Ruby stood in the kitchen, he told her that it wasn't necessary for her to suffer any longer and that he would have to shoot her. She attempted to hide under the kitchen table when he shot her. Ira then walked outside and shot the family dog. He then drove to the trooper stations at Franklinville and East Aurora, found no one there and proceeded to the East Aurora Police Department. On January 6, 1970 the Cattaraugus County Grand Jury indicted Ira on a charge of Manslaughter 1st degree. On January 8, 1970, he was sent to Mattewan State Hospital by reason of insanity for treatment of mental disease.

ALLEGANY HOUSEWIFE SLAIN – 1970

On October 20, 1970, 23-year old Carol Ann Fitzmaurice residing at the corner of Chapin and Five Mile Roads was found stabbed to death on her living room floor. Her husband, Daniel upon his arrival from work made the gruesome discovery. She had been stabbed 14 times in the abdomen and neck with death attributed to a severed aorta. The State Police were notified with a detail comprised of Lieutenant Douglas Parr, Sergeant Merle Van Skiver, Troopers Jim Rowley, Fred Porcello, George Knight, Tom Griffith, BCI Investigators Gerry Kitchen, Henry Panus and Bob McGinty responding to the scene.

She was last seen alive at about 1:00PM. An uncooked chicken was in the stoves oven indicating she was killed prior to starting her supper. A family friend, Melvin Pete Peterson, 42 North 2nd St., Allegany was across the street tending horses in a barn from about 4:20 to 5:50 PM. He reported that everything appeared normal and he heard nothing out of the ordinary. On October 21, Troopers Griffith and Knight while searching the five mile creek about 300 yards behind the Fitzmaurice home discovered a shiny, foot long knife in the water. It was felt this was definitely the murder weapon.

Although every lead was followed and several possible suspects developed for this crime, no arrest was ever made. It is possible that with new forensic advancements, the evidence could once again be reviewed and the perpetrator brought to justice. (Olean Times Union)

LORRAINE REDINGER MURDER – LEROY, N.Y. – 1970

On the morning of November 6, 1970, school bus driver John Brown of 55 Church Street, Leroy, N.Y, discovered the body of a young white female along Route 5, Leroy, N.Y. near Wicke's Lumber Yard. He reported his findings to the Leroy Police Department with Leroy Police Officer Charles O'Geen responding and securing the scene. Trooper Gerald M. Kalisz arrived at the scene and with the help of Sergeant Warden K. Barrows, conducted a preliminary search of the area and interview of local residents until the arrival of the coroner and state police investigators. Those interviewed recalled hearing what they thought was a car backfiring at about 1:30 AM.

The victim was fully clothed, approximately 20 years old with no identification on her person. She had been shot three times with a .38 caliber bullet. While conducting an examination of the deceased's clothing, a business card for "Ahimsa Trading Company", 1940 Craig Road, Pavilion, N.Y. was found in a pocket by Investigator John P. Wilcox. Investigators Theodore Georgitso and Winfield Duken traveled to the given address finding the location to be a "Hippie Commune". A post mortem photograph was identified by Daniel Snyder, Pittsford, N.Y., Steve Openhein, Scarsdale, N.Y. and Ned Nisson, Port Chester, N.Y. as being Lorraine Redinger, a post graduate student at the University of Rochester. She had come to the commune on November 2, 1970 with a male friend she introduced as Zygmunt Tobias. Redinger stayed at the commune for a few days. Tobias, a heavy user of LSD did not remain there. Redinger was given a ride back to Rochester, N.Y. on November 4th. They further reported that Tobias had traveled abroad during the summer months and that within the past three weeks while under the influence of drugs, had stabbed a female classmate while at her residence. It was learned that Lorraine Redinger, age 22, 304 Meyers Circle, Clearfield, Pennsylvania was temporarily residing at 189 Cottage Street, Rochester, N.Y.

The entire focus of the investigation now shifted to the Rochester, N.Y. area working round the clock. Senior Investigator Donald L. Smith was placed in charge of the investigation assisted by Investigators John P. Wilcox, Winfield R. Duken, Theodore J. Georgitso, Leonard P. Bochynski, John

W. Anna, William J. Cooley, Robert E. Burns, Richard F. Manns, Ralph D. Fuller William J. Tumulty, Richard C. Lewandowski, Michael Iaculli and Nicholas Fitzak.

Information gathered during the investigation pointed at Zygmunt Tobias as the primary suspect for the crime. Monroe County Sheriff Albert Skinner and Rochester City Police Commissioner John Mistretta were notified of the investigation.

It was found that Tobias resided with his parents at 128 Versailles Road, Rochester, N.Y. A former girlfriend, Elizabeth Barry reported that on October 19, 1970, Tobias had come to her on campus room and said something to the effect, "I have to kill you" and lunged at her with a knife. She fought him off receiving cuts to both hands requiring stitches. He then calmed down and left stating that he had to come back and kill her. She reported the incident to Campus Security who escorted her to the Rochester Police Department where a complaint was filed and warrant issued for the arrest of Tobias. He was arrested on October 21, 1970 and committed to the Psychiatric Section of Strong Memorial Hospital, Rochester, N.Y.

On November 2, 1970, Tobias was released from Strong Hospital. Elizabeth Barry had been told that Tobias had purchased another gun and was going to kill her. Campus security officers stayed with Barry in the event Tobias tried to contact her. Surveillance was maintained at the Tobias residence and other locations know to be frequented by him.

At 7:30 AM on November 7, 1970, Monroe County Sheriff's Deputy Bernard Fittos while on patrol observed the suspect's car parked at the Dorkat Motel, 3990 West Henrietta Road, Henrietta, New York. Motel office records indicated Tobias was indeed registered in room # 3. Troopers were immediately notified. A trooper detail entered room #3 finding Tobias sound asleep. He was placed under arrest without incident. A search warrant was obtained from Henrietta Town Justice Lawrence Sullivan for the search of the Tobias car seeking the weapon used to commit the murder. Investigator John P. Wilcox found a fully loaded .38 caliber Smith & Wesson revolver with 4-inch barrel and box of ammunition.

During interview, Tobias admitted knowing Redinger, but stated that because he was using drugs heavily, he had only vague recollections of events and denied harming her in any way. He was arraigned before Leroy Town Justice Leonard Ianello charged with Murder 1st Degree and committed to the Genesee County Jail.

An investigation by Investigator Duken took him to Wilmington, Vermont where the firearm used to kill Redinger had been purchased. Tobias bought the gun at the Parmlee and Howe Hardware Store on November 5th for $92.60. (It was later learned the monies to purchase the gun came from a student loan)

On March 17, 1971, Zygmunt Tobias was adjudged to be insane by Genesee County Court Judge Glenn Morton and committed to the Mattewan State Hospital for Criminally Insane.

Note – NYS Police Investigator Michael Iaculli who was part of the investigative team owned The Dorkat Motel where Tobias was arrested. Investigators were sleeping at the motel in adjacent rooms to Tobias, when his presence was made known by Deputy Fittos.

HALLET TRIPLE MURDER –JAMESTOWN, N.Y – 1973

On February 12, 1973, Trooper Investigator's David Carr and Philip Trapani were instructed to proceed to the Town of Busti where three bodies were found face down in a utility washroom. The dead were identified as Robert Hallett, age 49, his wife Grace, age 39 and eight-year old daughter, Ann. All were shot execution style. The bodies were found by a son in law of the deceased, Harry Lee Berry of Falconer, N.Y. Hallett was known to carry large amounts of cash that was absent and his 1973 Lincoln Continental car was missing. Investigators John Wilcox and Henry Panus conducted a crime scene search gathering evidence. The house had been completely ransacked with a small safe found opened and empty. Zone Sergeant Albert Whaley developed information that Hallett had an older daughter, Susan Hallett from a previous marriage residing in Detroit, Michigan. Investigator Donald Munch contacted the Detroit Police Department providing her address and information on the missing car. On February 13th at 2:15 AM, Detroit Police Sergeant John Click advised that he had located the Hallett's 1973 Lincoln parked in the lot where Susan Hallett resided with her boyfriend, Richard Parish. A surveillance of the car was initiated. Investigators Wilcox, Munch, Norman Minklein and Richard Olma were sent to Detroit. Upon their arrival, they found that Parish had been taken into custody when he entered the Hallett Lincoln car. Several hours later, Detroit Police also arrested Susan Hallett. At one point, there were over 40 troopers involved in the investigation.

On March 25, 1974, Susan Hallett and Richard Parish were found guilty of Manslaughter 1st Degree after a Jury trial presided over by Judge Lee Towne Adams. They were sentenced to imprisonment of three consecutive terms of 8 to 25 years. (Actual report)

SKI - RESORT DOUBLE MURDER – 1978

In early 1978, two maintenance workers employed a Cattaraugus County Ski Resort were found brutally murdered by workers reporting for work in the morning. The two had been preparing the slopes for the next days activities and apparently returned to the main building where they surprised their assailants in the process of chiseling open a safe. Captain Henry F. Williams and Lieutenant Raymond Slade determined the two had been forced to lie down on the floor and were shot in the top of the head. The safe containing $18,000.00 was removed from the site. A month later, Trooper Gene Adams found the safe at a dumping site in the Allegany River. The case has never been solved.

RONALD L. FISHER MURDER - 1980

On June 27, 1980, 32 year-old Ronald L. Fisher of South Dayton, N.Y. was blown from his motorcycle by a shotgun blast fired into his back. The killing occurred on the Hanover Road in the Town of Vellenova. Witnesses thought that a black van had hit Fisher knocking him from the motorcycle, but after arriving at Lake Shore Intercommunity Hospital it was found that he had been struck with several double-o shotgun pellets.

A week long investigation led by Trooper Captain Henry Williams and Senior Investigator Donald Munch led to the arrest of Joseph L. Debos, 32, 101 Travis Boulevard, Kenmore, N.Y., Otto M. Krasnewicz, 20, 14 Gale Avenue, Buffalo, N.Y. and Michael W. Lafferty, 30, 88 Kenton Road, Kenmore, N.Y.

Apparently, Fisher was dating the same girl, as Lafferty and he wanted to remove the competition. He hired Krasnewicz who drove the van and Debos who fired the shotgun to kill Fisher promising them $1,500.00. Lafferty who was unemployed took out a home improvement loan to finance the murder. Krasnewicz was convicted of Conspiracy 2nd Degree and Criminal Facilitation receiving sentences of 8 to 24 years and 2 to 6 years to run consecutively. Lafferty was convicted of Murder 1st Degree and Conspiracy 2nd Degree receiving sentences of 15 years to life. He was released on June 20, 2005. No disposition could be found for Debos.

BRENDA BROCKWAY McCOY - 1983

On the morning of May 20, 1983, Brenda Brockway McCoy, age 35, Lovers Lane Road, Corfu, N.Y. was leaving for work at the Batavia State Police Barracks where she was employed as a Secretary. Exiting her home, she was confronted by her brother-in-law, Lawrence (Larry) McCoy. He had been married to Brenda's sister, but now divorced, blamed Brenda for the breakup. Armed with a .12 gauge Browning semi-automatic shotgun, he shot Brenda twice striking her in the chest and left shoulder from close range. She fell to the ground mortally wounded. Her 13-year old son Mark, peering from a kitchen window saw the confrontation and woke his father, Gary who was a disabled Viet Nam Veteran. They exited the house through a rear door just as another shotgun blast was heard. They found Lawrence dead in the garage from a self-inflicted gunshot wound.

Trooper Mickey Schrader, receiving a complaint of shots fired patrolled to the McCoy residence unaware anyone had been shot. Upon arrival, he observed the slain Brenda McCoy lying in a pool of blood on the driveway near her car. He immediately armed himself. Gary McCoy came from the rear yard with Schrader immediately taking aim at him until satisfied that he was no threat. Notification was made with several BCI investigators responding. She had been employed as a trooper secretary since 1967.

EARLY HISTORY OF THE ELECTRIC CHAIR

The New York State Legislature enacted Chapter 352 of the Laws of 1886 entitled "An act to authorize the appointment of a commission to investigate and report to the legislature the most humane and approved method of carrying into effect the sentence of death in capital cases. " Under the old code of justice, every county had its hangman, every county jail its gallows. But separate executions in each jurisdiction seemed too inefficient as government became more centralized.

As for the method, it was, well, unpleasant. Dying men thrashed about, choking and wetting themselves.

The Electric Chair inventor Harold Brown had applied for the chair's patent and, thus, set out on a campaign to prove its efficiency. Using a prototype, Brown demonstrated the chair's capabilities on more than fifty cats and dogs. The New York commission (which was the first state to consider the new invention) needed more convincing. Brown replied by killing a cow before a panel of advisors. He emphasized his chair's ability by killing a horse. The panel was impressed. On June 4, 1888, electrocution became a legal means of capital punishment.

The state knew that they would need public support behind the method. In order to win over the public they sent Brown on tour with his chair. Brown traveled the state-executing animals in all of the major population centers. Animals were recruited for the show as he went along. In Albany, Brown executed an orangutan. Its hair caught on fire. August 6, 1890 saw the first ever-electric execution of a human being.

The history maker was William Kemmler of Buffalo, New York. On March 29, 1889 Kemmler killed his lover Matilda ("Tille") Ziegler with an axe in Buffalo, New York. He was the first to die in the electric chair. A group of doctors and reporters gathered for the historic occasion. Kemmler was jolted for seventeen seconds. It failed to kill him. Kemmler was unconscious but still breathing. The embarrassed prison officials electrocuted him again for seventy seconds. Kemmler thrashed and convulsed as the electrodes seared his head and arms, filling the room with the smell of burning flesh. Some witnesses fainted, while others fled the room. The killing took eight minutes.

While many critics rallied for the return of the gallows, New York remained faithful to the chair, executing two more criminals without incident. The most botched electric execution, however, was the fourth.

William Taylor was slated for execution on July 27, 1893. The first jolt of electricity caused his legs to stiffen with a force so great that they tore loose from the chair's ankle straps. Like Kemmler, Taylor was still alive. When the executioners attempted to send a second charge through Taylor's body it was discovered that the generator in the powerhouse had blown. Taylor was removed from the chair and placed on a cot. Officials kept him alive with chloroform and morphine so that an active current could officially kill him. An hour and nine minutes later Taylor was returned to the chair and given a more than adequate charge.

A 1903 execution at Sing Sing was the last reported botched electrocution. Fred Van Wormer was electrocuted and pronounced dead. Upon arrival to the autopsy room, however, Wormer began breathing once again. The executioner, who had gone home, was called back to re-electrocute Wormer. Upon his return, Wormer had officially died. Nonetheless, Wormer's corpse was set into the chair again and electrocuted with seventeen hundred volts for thirty seconds. He was the first dead man to be electrocuted.

THE FIRST WOMAN TO DIE IN THE ELECTRIC CHAIR

During 1926, Ruth Snyder had made several attempts on her husband, Albert's life at their home in Queens Village, according to Judd's testimony at a later trial. But by March 20, 1927, Ruth had enough. That night, she and Albert went to a party in Manhattan and returned to their home in the early morning hours. At about 7 AM, their daughter Lorraine awakened and found her mother tied up on the floor and her father unconscious in his bed. The little girl ran to a neighbor, who summoned the police. Albert was dead, his head smashed in by an unknown object. His hands were tied together and so were his feet. There was a length of wire wrapped tightly around his neck. When the neighbors tried to untie Ruth, she insisted on remaining tied up until the police responded. Investigation found that Ruth and her lover; Judd Gray had killed Albert for the insurance money that totaled over $100,000, an enormous sum in 1927. Both were arrested and convicted.

On January 12, 1928, Ruth Snyder became the first woman to die in the electric chair at Sing Sing prison in the 20th century. On May 9, 1927, Ruth Brown-Snyder and Henry Judd Gray were convicted of murder and sentenced to death. Over 1,500 people applied to witness her execution. At Sing Sing, executioner Robert G. Elliot, a distinguished looking gentleman who had been on the job for only a year, was upset. He had never executed a female before, but he realized the significance of the event. A few days before, he told the press, "It will be something new for me to throw the switch on a woman, and I don't like the job"

DRUG ENFORCEMENT

HISTORY

The first American anti-drug law was an 1875 San Francisco ordinance that outlawed the smoking of opium. It was passed because of the fear that Chinese men were luring white women to their "ruin" in opium dens. "Ruin" was defined as associating with Chinese men. It was followed by other similar laws, including Federal laws in which trafficking in opium was forbidden to anyone of Chinese origin, and restrictions placed on the importation of smoking opium. The laws did not have anything really to do with the importation of opium as a drug, because the importation and use of opium in other forms, such as in the common medication laudunum were not affected. The laws were directed at smoking opium because it was perceived that the smoking of opium was a peculiarly Chinese custom. In short, it was a way of legally targeting the Chinese.

Cocaine was outlawed because of fears that superhuman "Negro Cocaine Fiends" or "Cocainized Niggers" (actual terms used by newspapers in the early 1900's) take large amounts of cocaine that would make them go on a violent sexual rampage and rape white women. There is little evidence that any black men actually did this, if only because it would have been certain death. The United States set a record in 1905 with 105-recorded lynchings of black men. At the same time, police nationwide switched from .32 caliber pistols to .38 caliber pistols because it was believed that the superhuman "Negro Cocaine Fiend" could not be killed with the smaller gun.

Dr. Hamilton Wright is sometimes referred to as the "Father of American Drug Laws". Dr. Wright was the Opium Commissioner at the time and had previously become famous because he had "scientifically proved" that beri-beri was a communicable disease. Beri-beri is a vitamin deficiency.

The Harrison Act that "outlawed" these drugs was, on its face, a licensing law which simply required sellers to get a license if they were going to handle opiates and cocaine. As the Consumers Union Report on Licit and Illicit Drugs had said, it was doubtful that very many members of Congress would have thought that they were passing what would later be regarded as a general drug prohibition. The law even contained a provision that nothing in the law would prohibit doctors from prescribing these drugs in the legitimate practice of medicine.

In fact, even the people who wrote the Harrison Act and the Marijuana Tax Act in 1937 agreed that a general prohibition on what people could put into their own bodies was plainly an unconstitutional infringement on personal liberties. There was no fundamental reason why a constitutional amendment should be required to prohibit one chemical and not another.

The trick was that the bureaucrats who were authorized to issue licenses never did so, and there was a heavy penalty for not having the license. This heavy penalty required that the enforcing bureaucrats needed more staff and therefore, more power, which in turn required tougher laws. Over the years, through a series of court rulings, they gradually got the courts to change what had been well-established constitutional law. Specifically, they got the courts to accept the notion that it really was a tax violation when people got arrested for drugs, and that the fact that the government would not issue any licenses was not a defense. They also got the courts to bypass the old issue of whether the Federal Government had the right to control what an individual puts into their own bodies by creating the fiction that whatever the person puts into their bodies must have come as a result of some form of interstate commerce, which is regulated by the Federal Government in the form of taxes and licenses and, therefore, since the Federal Government is allowed to levy a tax, it is by rather indirect logic allowed to regulate what anyone may put into their own bodies.

Marijuana was outlawed in 1937 as a repressive measure against Mexican workers who crossed the border seeking jobs during the Depression. The specific reason given for the outlawing of the hemp plant was its supposed violent "effect on the degenerate races." The American Medical Association specifically testified that they were opposed to the law. When supporters of the law were asked about the AMA's view on the law before Congress, they lied and said that the AMA was in favor of the law because they knew the law would never pass without the AMA's endorsement. The law passed with the AMA later protesting, but the law was never repealed.

In both cases, newspapers across the country carried lurid stories of the awful things that these drugs did to racial minorities, and of the horrors that people of racial minorities inflicted on innocent white people while they were under the influence of these drugs. Later research has shown that not a single one of the stories used to promote these laws could be substantiated.

There never was any scholarly evidence that the laws were necessary, or even beneficial, to public health and safety and none was presented when the laws were passed.

The number of drug deaths in the US in a typical year is as follows:

Tobacco kills about 390,000
Alcohol kills about 80,000
Side stream smoke from tobacco kills about 50,000
Cocaine kills about 2,200
Heroin kills about 2,000
Aspirin kills about 2,000
Marijuana kills 0. There has never been a recorded death due to marijuana in the US
All illegal drugs combined kill about 4,500 people per year, or about one percent of the number killed by alcohol and tobacco. Tobacco kills more people each year than all of the people killed by all of the illegal drugs in the last century.

Alcohol and tobacco are the clear leaders. Some authorities have estimated that up to forty percent of all hospital care in the United States is for conditions related to alcohol.

As a medical hazard, few drugs can compete with alcohol or tobacco on any scale. A study at Rockefeller University in 1967 concluded "Tobacco is unquestionably more hazardous to the health than heroin."

Since the 19th century when Americans first discovered new wonder drugs like morphine, heroin, and cocaine, our society has confronted the problem of drug abuse and addiction.

When the 20th century began, the United States--grappling with its first drug epidemic--gradually instituted effective restrictions: at home through domestic law enforcement and overseas by spearheading a world movement to limit opium and coca crops. By World War II, American drug use had become so rare, it was seen as a marginal social problem. The first epidemic was forgotten.

During the 1960s, drugs like marijuana, amphetamines, and psychedelics came on the scene, and a new generation embraced drugs. With the drug culture exploding, new laws and agencies were developed to address the problem. In 1973, the U.S. Drug Enforcement Administration was created to enforce federal drug laws. In the 1970s, cocaine reappeared. Then, a decade later, crack appeared, spreading addiction and violence at epidemic levels. Today, the biggest challenge is the dramatic change in organized crime. While American criminals once controlled drug trafficking on U.S. soil, today sophisticated and powerful criminal groups headquartered in foreign countries control the drug trade in the United States.

State police drug enforcement had been minimal until the mid 1950s. Drug arrests were made for violation of the Public Health Law. In the spring of 1955, an investigation with Federal Agents was conducted in the Brentwood section of Suffolk County. Information provided to troopers resulted in a federal agent going under cover, but always in protective view of a trooper, developing contacts in the drug world. As a result of the four-month investigation, seventeen pushers & four distributors of heroine were arrested in simultaneous raids in New York City and Brentwood. This was the first multi-agency drug raid that the Division was involved in. It was the beginning of the long battle against illegal drug and narcotic distribution.

The 1960's gave rise to increased social unrest and rebellion against authority. A widespread acceptance of recreational drugs generated huge demands for illegal drugs drawing thousands into the illegal drug trade. The State Police were lax in drug enforcement with no drug related cases reported or any arrests for illegal drugs made during 1962 & 1963. In 1964, 32 drug cases were reported increasing to 403 in 1966. In 1968, a Narcotics Unit was created with arrests dramatically increasing to 2,984 arrests for the year. As the 1970s rolled in, drug use was at an epidemic proportion. The NYS Police Laboratory was buried with drug cases to the point that a backlog was created. A federal grant allowed for the hiring of fourteen additional scientists who worked two shifts to close the backlog. At the end of 1973, new get-tough drug laws were passed mandating life imprisonment for serious drug violations. Many dealers moved their operations to adjoining states with less severe laws. This resulted in a reduction in drug related arrests. The illegal use of drug continued to grow with cocaine and crack becoming the drugs of choice during the 1980s. It also ushered in the vicious criminal cartels that controlled the cocaine trade. Two characteristics that made these cartels dangerous was their use of violence and the wealth derived from the cocaine trade allowing them to buy the most sophisticated technology and weapons available in the world. The end of the 1980s assigned 300 specially trained troopers assigned as narcotics investigators with emphasis on identifying upper level dealers.

NARCO UNIT

A Division Narcotics Unit was established in 1968 to intensify efforts to root out the criminal sources of narcotics and illegal drugs. Fifty-one Investigators were assigned to the unit with twenty-six working in the New York City and twenty-five in the upstate area. By the end of the first year, 2,081 arrests had been made involving dangerous drugs valued at $41,811,465.

HENRIETTA, N.Y. MARIJUANA ARREST
On February 6, 1968, Trooper Ronald Martin stopped a car on Route 15 bearing California registration plates. He immediately smelled a strong marijuana odor and called for back up. Trooper John G. Meyers arrived almost immediately. They conducted a search of the vehicle finding 174.6 pounds of marijuana neatly wrapped in 2-pound packages. The value was placed at about $55,000.00 and was the largest drug bust ever in upstate New York. Both troopers were honored receiving the Rochester Police Department Distinguished Service Award. This was the first time the award was given to someone other than a Rochester Policeman. A distinctive gold bar pin was also presented and authorized by the Superintendent to be worn on the uniform.

DRUG RELATED ARRESTS

1969 – The largest drug manufacturing operation ever uncovered in the state was found in remote Orange County having the ability to produce LSD and hallucinogens valued at one million dollars.

150 pounds of hashish was seized in New York City and $250,000 worth of uncut heroine confiscated in Syracuse, N.Y. resulting in over 100 arrests.

A teddy bear shipped from Israel to a Buffalo resident was stuffed with one pound of hashish.

On May 23, 1969, an undercover operation by Trooper Investigators R.G. Dennis, J.J. Strojnowski and T.A. Constantine of the Troop "A" Narcotics Unit resulted in an early morning raid and arrest of thirty persons with an additional forty charges filed.

Materials seized were marijuana, heroine, hashish, drug implements, amphetamines, barbiturates, several revolvers, pistols, a sawed off shotgun and stolen property. This marked the first of its kind inter-agency drug raid in Western New York.

1972 - 7189 Drug related arrests were made.

NYS Police drug investigations resulted in arrests in Belgium where $25 million in annual income and 264 pounds of heroin was confiscated.

A smuggler was charged with possession of 1500 pounds of heroin and $1,078,000.00 in cash confiscated.

1981 – A homemade lab producing 10 pounds of methamphetamine valued at $1.4 million was closed in Franklin County.

1982 – 1,629 pounds of cocaine valued at $160 million seized in Suffolk County.

1985 – A Montgomery County farm was raided that served as a factory for producing $250 million of cocaine yearly. It was the largest cocaine factory ever uncovered in North America and was followed by two similar raids in Sullivan and Otsego Counties.

MARIJUANA

Marijuana is obtained from the hemp plant and is smoked in cigarettes or pipes or eaten. The texture of marijuana may range from fine to coarse. The color may vary between grayish-green to greenish-brown and with its continued use, the tolerance level increases making its dependence more likely.

COCAINE

Cocaine is an addictive substance, which comes from coca leaves or is made synthetically. This drug acts as a stimulant to the central nervous system. It appears as a white powder substance which is inhaled, injected, freebased (smoked), or applied directly to the nasal membrane or gums. Cocaine gives the user a tremendous "rush". These chemicals trick the brain into feeling it has experienced pleasure. The effects of cocaine occur within the first few minutes, peak in 15-20 minutes and disappear in about 1 hour. The immediate effects are what make cocaine so addicting. The user is willing to endure the lows in order to experience the highs.

Cocaine is highly addictive. Every use of the drug makes the addiction stronger. This addiction can begin almost immediately following the first use. The addiction to cocaine is very strong, therefore, withdrawal symptoms are likely to occur when a person is not using the drug.

CRACK

Crack is chemically altered cocaine and found as small, hard, white chunks. It is a stimulant to the central nervous system, is extremely addictive and is deadlier than other forms of cocaine. Anyone using crack can become an addict in two to three weeks, and in some cases, people who try crack become instantly addicted the first time they use the drug. Crack reaches the brain in less than 8 seconds and produces a "high" which peaks in 10-15 seconds and lasts only 15 minutes. This "high" is produced because crack tricks the brain into releasing chemicals that produce a false feeling of intense pleasure. This "high" is immediately followed by an intense "low".

ECSTASY

Ecstasy is an illegal synthetic, or designer, drug. Designer drugs mimic an already illegal drug by slightly altering the chemical composition. Ecstasy is also called MDMA, which stands for methyl enedioxymethamphetamine. The amount of MDMA needed to get "high" is close to the toxic dose. Ecstasy is similar to methamphetamine and MDA, which is another designer drug in its chemistry, therefore it may have similar affects to other amphetamines. Ecstasy acts as a stimulant to the central nervous system. Ecstasy can be found in a capsule or pill form, of various colors. It may also be in powder form.

Ecstasy is commonly used at "rave" party settings. "Raves" are all night parties known for their dance music and drug experimentation. Other names for ecstasy are wonder drug and XTC.

HALLUCINOGENS

Hallucinogens are man made, or grown naturally. Many hallucinogens are in the form of a white powder. They have no taste and are found as tablets, capsules, tiny sheets of paper, or liquid. Certain types of mushrooms and datura plants are also hallucinogens.

These drugs are injected, taken orally, or eaten. They produce radical changes in the mental state, involving distortions of reality and acute hallucinations. They also affect the way a person experiences their sense of taste, smell, hearing and vision.

Hallucinogens have no prescribed medical use and are made and sold illegally.

Large doses can be frightening and disturbing and tolerance may occur rapidly

Hallucinogens cause cross-tolerance. This means that the use of one hallucinogen causes and increases tolerance to other hallucinogens.

A dependence on hallucinogens is likely, but no withdrawal symptoms occur when use of the drug is discontinued. Hallucinogens radically affect the brain thus affecting the personality. Serious mental illness may occur. Unpleasant episodes (or "bad trips") may cause psychological damage and lead to suicide. They may affect the same user in man different ways during the same "trip". The effects of a "trip" may be experienced 15-30 minutes after use and the effects may last up to 24 hours. A person may re-experience effects of a "trip", days, weeks, or years after use of the drug. This phenomena is called a "flashback". If a high dose of the drug is used, a "bad trip" may occur which will be very unpleasant, frightening, and dangerous.

Hallucinogens may be used by those who mistakenly hope to attain transcendental, mystical experiences, which they believe will provide them with a greater understanding of life. Some people may remain permanently brain damaged or psychotic from the drugs and this condition cannot be reversed.

MIGRANT LABOR CAMPS

Migrant, seasonal, transient or farm labor, as it was known had been in existence for many years prior to regulation by the New York State Health and New York State Labor Departments.

Farm workers were needed for the survival of many farms during the growing and harvesting season to insure there would be no loss of crops and income. With the advent of the automobile and refrigeration, farmers were able to expand their market to an ever-increasing population.

As one travels about the countryside, you will find many-abandoned single railroad beds criss-crossing New York State. These were known as peanut tracks with a small railroad station found in almost every rural hamlet and town. These peanut tracks were used primarily to transport farm workers from the big cities to the farms for work during harvest and to transport produce to market. My father, born in 1905, related how he at age 8, his mother and two sisters would travel by train from Buffalo to Penfield, N.Y. during the harvest season to pick fruit in the many area orchards. They would stay in a tent or woodshed or in whatever was available for several weeks at a time. Everyone picked, but children were desired because they could climb the trees for hard to reach fruit. The workday was from sun up to sunset and the family was paid by the amount of fruit picked, usually only a few cents a bushel. My dad would say that the best fruit could always be found near the outhouse. I wonder why that was? Of course there was no sewage disposal, as we know it today. There were no labor laws restricting work by children and they were not required to attend school as they do today.

During the 1930s, new and amended Labor, Education, Health and Social Security Laws were introduced that changed the way farmers did business. A new breed of farm-laborer came into existence with the migration of African-American workers from the south traveling north during the southern off-season to work the northern farms. Farm workers were excluded from labor laws that guaranteed most other employees basic rights to overtime pay, disability insurance, a mandatory day of rest and collective bargaining.

In 1941, the War Management Commission brought the first black workers to Western New York as a group. The group was from Jamaica with most working in Orleans County. A few came to Genesee County where they picked beans for Frank Pixley in Bethany. Workers lived in two barracks style buildings on East Road and Ellicott Road. They were brought into Batavia on Saturdays to shop. It was not a pleasant experience, as only a few restaurants, taverns or shops would serve them. Segregation was still being practiced.

Since then, several thousand migrant farm workers came yearly to harvest potatoes, onions and fruit in New York State. Many came directly from home based communities in Florida. Others worked their way up the east coast picking strawberries, tomatoes and other crops along the way. In late fall, they returned to Florida for the winter citrus and tomato harvests. Farm work was hard stoop labor. Machines dug up potatoes and onions leaving them in rows. Workers moved along the rows bagging the potatoes, then hand loading them onto trucks for transportation to sheds where they were graded. Graders were paid an hourly wage and pickers paid by the amount of produce picked and bagged.

Crew leaders and farm labor contractors based in Florida recruited family groups and single men to work on the northern farms. They provided transportation, usually a converted, battered old school bus and contracted for work with local growers. Farmers built camps where the workers were housed. On more than an occasional instance, workers were charged for their transport, room, board and other fees leaving them in debt to the contractor.

In the camps, workers slept in small bedroom units, one to a family, or in a larger bullpen dormitory for single men. The communal kitchen or "commissary" was the center of camp life. Workers bought meals from the camp cook, often the crew leaders wife or another family member and ate together on long bench tables. The crew leader would also stock a makeshift store where tobacco, alcohol and other items that could be bought usually on credit at a cost in excess of store shelf prices. In their spare time, men would gather to play cards and listened to a jukebox or "piccolo" playing loudly in the background.

The life of a migrant or seasonal laborer amounted to a bare bones existence. Their entire social life was restricted to the camps because of lack of transportation. There was very little, if any interaction in the local communities. It was usually only the contractor or Crew Leader that realized any financial success earned through the exploitation of the workers.

1946 - The State Police were represented on the Governor's Interdepartmental Committee on Migrant Labor along with the Departments of Agriculture and Markets, Labor, Health, Social Welfare, Education, the State Youth Commission and Extension Service.

Information on the location of the camps, population and name of the owner or operator was supplied by the State Department of Health.

During 1946, there were a total of 265 migrant camps statewide with a total population of 14, 423 persons. Troopers made 225 criminal arrests at these camps.

Reported violations of law relating to gambling and unlicensed alcohol sale resulted in each camp being inspected at least every two weeks by troopers.

1950 - During the 1950s, state law required that all Labor Camps be inspected and licensed by the County Health Department. The health inspectors always requested the presence of a trooper during the inspection out of fear for their safety. Migrant laborers referred to the troopers as the "Big Hats" and always showed respect for their authority

1953 - Local citizens concerned with the welfare of the temporary residents created a Migrant Committee. They hired a young divinity student who traveled the camps serving the residents. The development of farm harvesting machines reduced the need for large numbers of workers. At the time, migrants that decided to remain in Western New York needed a sponsor to remain. Pixley sponsored many who became permanent, productive residents of Genesee County.

1956 - Due to a reduced farm labor force, pirating between labor camps was a common occurrence. On June 30, 1956, Genesee County farmers agreed to halt such practices and assist one another, when possible.

During 1957, a State Police report noted that there were approximately 450 labor camps in the eleven county Troop "A" territory. No arrests had been made in Genesee County in the past two years for violation of Chapter 15 of the Sanitary Code, 229 of the Public Health Law.

GENESEE COUNTY MIGRANT LABOR CAMPS

McNair Camp	Bethany, N.Y.
East Road Labor Camp	Bethany, N.Y.
East Pembroke Canning Company	East Pembroke, N.Y.
Todd Farm Labor Camp	Elba, N.Y.
Bergen Producers Co-Op Inc.	Bergen, N.Y.
Curtice Bros. Labor Camp	Bergen, N.Y.
Cook Brothers Labor Camp	Bergen, N.Y.
Walter Stewart Labor Camp	Byron, N.Y.
Grinnell Labor Camp	Byron, N.Y.
Oakfield Camp (Cannery)	Oakfield, N.Y.
Oak Orchard Village	Elba, N.Y.

All camps required health permits issued by the Genesee County Health Department and were inspected semi-monthly by troopers from the area stations accompanied by an official from the health department. An Inspection form MLC-1 was completed for each inspection. If the condition of the camp was other than good, i.e. fair or poor, this was noted on the inspection form. If the same condition existed at the next inspection, the Health Department at Albany was notified for appropriate action.

ARRESTS IN GENESEE COUNTY

1956	6 – Assault 3rd	2 – Disorderly Conduct	1 – Public Intoxication
	1 – Murder 2nd	1 – Petit Larceny	1 – Public Safety
	1 - Rape		

1957	3 – Assault 3rd	3 – Disorderly Conduct	1 – Public Intoxication
	1 – Murder 1st	1 – Murder 2nd	

1959 - During the farming season of 1959, it was reported that there were 10,019 migrant workers in the Troop "A" area.

Legislation was enacted requiring all Farm Labor Camps to be licensed by the County Health Department and that all Farm Labor Contractors and Crew Leaders be licensed by the NYS Department of Labor.

CRIMINAL ACTS
Criminal acts upon one another seemed to be way of life for the migrant worker. Larcenies, assaults and drunkenness were the norm. There were occasional violent acts resulting in death and serious injury. More often than not, the District Attorney would decline to prosecute these cases. He instead provided a one-way bus ticket out of town for the defendant, the rationale being that a bus ticket was cheaper than the expense of a jury trial. Below are of some of the more violent crimes perpetrated by migrant workers.

BETHANY, N.Y.
On June 5, 1948, 33-year-old Lee Stokes of the Fisher Labor Camp, East Bethany, N.Y. was stabbed to death by co-worker Henry Harris, age 33 during an argument. Trooper Clinton Salmon found Harris hiding in a bean field and arrested him. He was convicted of Murder 2nd Degree.

ELBA, N.Y.
In July 1953, migrant laborers residing in the "White City" area of the Elba muckland got into a cutting match with knives, resulting in Louis Nealy, 35 suffering a 4-inch deep laceration to his arm. State Police Sgt. George Wood charged his companion, Louis Sermons, 32 with Assault 2nd Degree.

On June 30, 1962, Lee Roy Valley, age 39, a migrant worker employed by Edwin Squires, Barre, N.Y. was arrested for Manslaughter 2nd degree. Earlier in the day, he shot and killed 37-year old J.C. Moss with a .22 caliber rifle, as Moss attempted to enter his cabin. Trooper Patrick J. Petrie, first on the scene, arrested Moss without incident. Investigator T.R. Salvameni Jr., Investigators Nick Fitzak, R. C. Fitzwater and Troopers L. P. Bochynski, Gerald Kalisz, Gordon Mosher and Theodore Georgitso assisted him.

On December 12, 1962, Valley was found guilty after trial of Manslaughter 2ndDegree. County Court Judge Philip J. Weiss imposed a sentence of 2 to 7 years at Attica Prison.

BYRON, N.Y.
On March 18,1954, migrant worker Walter J. Barter, 32 was taken into custody in Riverhead, L.I. by Federal Agents. He was charged with 2nd Degree Murder in the July 17, 1953 stabbing of co-worker James Dixon, 23 at the Grinnell Labor Camp, Byron, New York. Dixon whose neck was slashed with a butcher knife bled to death in a matter of minutes.

On June 8, 1969, Trooper Leroy J. Seitz responded to the report of a shooting at the John Rolle residence, Shelt Road, Byron, N.Y. He found Arthur Terrell Sr., lying dead on the kitchen floor from gunshot wounds. Rolle stated that the assailant entered his home, shot Terrell and left the scene in a black sedan. The investigation was continued with the arrival of Captain George Tordy, Lieutenants James C. Moochler and Raymond Slade, Investigators Donald L. Smith, Robert M. Barrus and John P. Wilcox and Troopers Bruce M. Buttles, Leonard F. Dayka, Daniel E. Geiger and Donald Kozlowski. Extensive interviews and search of the area identified the perpetrator to be John A. McDonald who resided at the Frank Weathers-Camp, Elba, N.Y. McDonald was located and taken into custody by Troopers Seitz and Buttles without incident. He had shot Terrell during an argument involving McDonalds wife. On June 8, 1969, McDonald pled guilty to a charge of Manslaughter 2nd Degree and was sentenced to a term not to exceed 10 years at Attica State Prison by Genesee County Court Judge Glenn R. Morton.

EAST BETHANY, N.Y.

On August 11, 1957, 43-year-old Fred Payton of the Hayes Labor Camp, East Bethany was shot and killed during a dice game dispute. Witnesses said that Eugene Marshall, 30 dropped a fifty-cent piece on the floor that Payton covered with his foot. They both stepped out of the room where Marshall took a pistol from a hiding place and shot Payton in the chest. Troopers Duane Roberts and Frederick Porcello conducted an investigation sending out a wanted notice. Genesee County Deputy Norman Mattice arrested Marshall later that day. He was held for grand jury action without bail.

COHOCTON, N.Y.

On September 23, 1957, migrant farmhand William Hampton, age 25, staying at the Schwingle Labor Camp on Pine Hill, North Cohocton, N.Y. died of stab wounds at the Wayland Hospital. Hampton upon returning from the fields got into an argument that accelerated with fellow worker Marguerite Betterson. It was alleged Hampton started beating Betterson with a chair and in self-defense, she picked up a knife and stabbed him to keep him away. Troopers Gerald Forster, Phil Smith and Corporal Raymond Slade investigated. Forster recalled arriving at the camp finding the victim in a pool of blood. His aorta had been severed. The ambulance used was a "hearse" with Forster accompanying the victim to the hospital. He died on the operating table. Grand Juries were used infrequently back then and witnesses would have been gone before one would be called so Corporal Slade asked for a coroner's inquest. It was determined to have been a justified self-defense.

HAMLIN, N. Y.

On December 5,1965, migrant workers Walter Martin and Albert L. Thibadoux residing on the Elmer Leverenz Farm, Lake Road, Hamlin, N.Y. became involved in a dispute over the moving of a bed in the migrant quarters. Martin armed himself with a piece of wood and Thibadoux with a kitchen knife that resulted with Martin being stabbed several times. One stab wound punctured a lung proving to be fatal. Trooper Ronald Junior and Investigator Nicholas Fitzak went to the scene assisted by Identification Troopers Joseph A. Paige and Harry S. Crosier. Thibadoux was placed under arrest by Trooper Junior and taken to the Clarkson station where he was interviewed by Investigators Donald L. Smith and Warren C. Sargeant. On May 16, 1966, he was found guilty after trial of Manslaughter 1st Degree. Monroe County Court Judge Harry Rosenthal sentenced him to a term of 5 to 15 years at Attica State Prison.

VEHICLE AND TRAFFIC LAW REGARDING MIGRANTS

1952 – The Vehicle and Traffic Law made no provisions for seasonal or migrant workers.

1957 – Vehicle registration – Seasonal laborers were exempt from June 1st to Nov 30th provided they showed proof of liability insurance ($10,000 minimum) and pay a $2.00 fee for a certificate to be affixed to the vehicle.

A driver's license was for the same period of time, but required the driver to be at least age 18. A $2.00 fee was charged for a drivers permit requiring a local address on it.

1960 - Legislation was added requiring a vision test be passed along with a sign recognition test.

1961 – There were 25,369 migrant laborers in the state. Troopers conducted 3,602 inspections in the 912 camps located within the state.

1963 - Proof of liability insurance was raised to $20,000.00 with license & registration required to be obtained within 7 days of entering the state.

1974 - Exempt status changed to April 1 until November 30 and registration & license to be obtained within 30 days of entering the state.

NO LONGER A NEED
With the increased development of farm harvesting machinery, sorting and packaging equipment and a permanent farm labor force, there was a lesser need for migrant workers. There are very few if any labor camps still in existence. Hispanics now make up what labor force there is, usually during the cabbage harvest with better quality accommodations provided by the employer.

1949 SHOOTOUT- ASSAILANT KILLED

CPL. TED MARTIN &
TPR.PUMPHREY
1949 SHOOTOUT -

1949 SHOOTOUT- TROOP CAR STRUCK

WARREN TERRYBERRY - ED LONGHAN?
ARSON SUSPECT

1959 - FATAL AA

1965 BATAVIA TRAIN DERAILMENT
GEORGITSO - DUKEN - SHAVER

TROOPER AL KUREK

JIM HOFMANN - HENRY HAAS - DOUG
MILLER
DRUG BUST

LeoKliszak. Donald Munch. Norm Minklein. Raymond Slade – 1968

TROOPER ERTIS "BUD" BRADLEY

BOOK V — HISTORIC TROOPER EVENTS

APALACHIN MOB RAID - 1957

The popular theory behind mob crime in this country is that it was an outgrowth of racketeering from the Prohibition days of the 1920s and 30s. The public tolerated bootlegging to satisfy their need for "booze". The bootlegging proved so profitable, that the gangs branched out into other activities. Over the years, they engaged in respectable businesses giving their criminal organizations a front of respectability, but all the time still dealing in drugs, prostitution, blackmail, gambling and murder. Federal crime fighters believed the gangs were local, individually operated entities.

Organized crime! Who ever heard about organized crime and its extended families during the forties and fifties? No one. But things changed when troopers paid a visit to the Apalachin, N.Y. "barbecue" of Joseph Barbara in November 1957.

New York State Trooper Sergeant Edgar Croswell had been keeping an eye on the sprawling 58-acre estate owned by Joseph Barbara who had reputed criminal ties since the 1940s. A year earlier, Sergeant Croswell had become suspicious of Barbara after he learned the identity of a houseguest who gave police phony identification after being pulled over for speeding. The speeder turned out to be notorious drug dealer Carmine Galante. He also learned that several other out-of-town gangsters visited Barbara while in the Binghamton area.

On Nov. 13, 1957, Croswell and his partner Vincent Vasisko learned that Barbara's son was booking rooms at a nearby motel. They checked out Barbara's home and spotted several out of state license plates.

The next morning, even more cars had parked on the garage apron and adjoining field. Treasury Agents Arthur Ruston and Kenneth Brown aided at the scene. While writing down license plate numbers of the newly arrived cars, they were spotted and all hell broke loose. Nattily dressed men in dark suits, fedoras and pointy-toed shoes including a Dapper Don of the era, Joseph Bonnano dashed into the woods throwing away guns and wads of money. Others, including Vito Genovese, climbed into their cars and tried to speed away during the confusion. Croswell set up a roadblock at the base of the hill on the only road leaving Barbara's estate. Any car trying to get to Route 17 would have to pass the roadblock. With reinforcements from surrounding town police departments, the troopers brought the occupants of the cars stopped at the road block and a dozen or so men seen running through the woods to the State Police Station at Vestal a few miles away. Each man was asked to identify himself, but Croswell had no cause to fingerprint and photograph them. Croswell quickly determined he had a group of ex-cons from around the nation, many with long arrest records. Little was known, if anything about the structure of La Cosa Nostra at the time. They didn't have any knowledge that they had detained at least 10 Mafia bosses, many under-bosses, capos and soldiers. 58 were identified.

No criminal activity had occurred and no arrests were made. A total of sixty men had been detained and questioned at the Vestal State Police Station. Of the sixty, nine had no criminal record. The others had a total of one hundred convictions and two hundred seventy five arrests. None were wanted.

"If they stood still, nobody would have touched them," Vasisko later recalled. "We would have just gone home."

The guest list was a who's-who of organized crime at the time: Stefano Maggadino, a Buffalo boss who suggested meeting in Apalachin rather than in Chicago was there to discuss the recent slaying of Albert Anastasia. Vito Genovese, who was emerging as New York City's top crime boss since Anastasia's assassination; Joseph Profaci, the Brooklyn boss who became the model for the book "The Godfather"; Carlo Gambino, Joseph Bonnano and many other crime bosses from Philadelphia, Cleveland, Los Angeles and even Havana, Cuba. The roster of those present conclusively established the ties between crime families nationwide and signaled the launching of investigations into the activities of all present.

When the story broke, congressmen, senators and other elected officials wanted to know who the men were and why they were there. The FBI had little information. The publicity that followed and years of hearings and investigation exposed many of the gangsters for what they were, rather that the simple businessmen they pretended to be. The real damage to La Cosa Nostra resulted from the embarrassment caused the FBI. Director J. Edgar Hoover reacted by ordering a massive intelligence gathering operation. They used illegal bugging operations against mobsters that could not be used in court, but gave the FBI knowledge of who and what the mafia was all about. Six years later, Joe (Joe Cago) Valachi, a mafia turncoat reinforced what they learned during public testimony.

Who knows how things would have turned out if not for good old- fashioned police work by Croswell and Viscanti. Croswell became a legend in the law enforcement community with troopers referring to him as "Apalachin Ed".

(Saga Magazine article by Mark Simonson – 1957)

GANGBUSTERS

On October 25, 1958, Governor Averill Harriman ordered a 50-man criminal intelligence unit set up within the State Police to ferret out organized crime in New York State be established. The new unit based in New York City was headed by Inspector John J. Quinn with a mandate to conduct a vigorous and forthright attack against criminal elements operating anywhere in the state.

The unit's members were chosen for their special competence and skill in handling criminal investigations. The unit would report directly to the Superintendent.

Seven functions of the unit were as follows:

Collect information on organized crime.

Assemble, evaluate & catalogue data.

Maintain constant surveillance.

Take proper police action when necessary.

Assist local law enforcement officials.

Cooperate with agencies outside the state.

Uncover conspiracies & relationships between criminals & local political & police officials.

EDITORIAL COMMENT – 1958

The state's criminal intelligence unit could become a mighty force against crime. It's unfortunate that the Governor just vetoed an anti-racketeering bill. It was argued that the unit was a weak substitute for a united action by the governor and legislature for a war on crime. The Apalachin convention disclosed holes in the law that were meant to keep organized crime under control. A flurry of investigations by grand juries and legislative committees has netted exactly nothing. The effectiveness of the new unit will depend entirely on the vigor of its members.

MAFIA BOSSES - WESTERN NEW YORK

The Western New York crime family controlled the territory encompassing Buffalo, N.Y., Youngstown, Ohio, Las Vegas, Nevada, Niagara Falls, N.Y., Rochester, N.Y., Toronto, Canada, Hamilton, Canada & Niagara Falls, Canada. They were identified as:

Giuseppe "Joe" DiCarlo Sr. (19?? – 1922) Boss – died

Stefano "Big Steve" Magaddino (1922 - 1974) Boss – died

Fredrico "Fred the Wolf" "Lupo" Randaccio (1970 –1974) Acting Boss – died

Salvatore "Sam the Farmer" Frangiamore (1974 – 197?) Boss - ?

Salvatore "Sam Johns" Pieri (197? – 1981) Boss – died

Josephe Pieri (1978- 1979) Acting Boss

Joseph "Lead Pipe Joe" Todaro Sr. (1981 – Present) Boss

HISTORY OF THE MAFIA IN BUFFALO, NEW YORK

The history of the Buffalo Crime Family revolves around the reign of Stefano Magaddino, later described as "the grand old man of the Cosa Nostra." He was an original member of the National Commission, which was created in 1931, and was a highly respected figure in underworld circles from New York City to Chicago.

Stefano Magaddino was born on October 10, 1891, in Castellammare, Sicily. Before leaving Sicily, the Magaddino brothers, Antonino, Pietro, and Stefano, were involved in a feud with the Buccellato brothers. During this time, Pietro was murdered and the other two brothers left for the United States, settling in Brooklyn. On August 16, 1921, Magaddino was arrested as a fugitive from justice involving a murder that took place in Avon, New Jersey. Shortly after this, Magaddino and Gaspar Milazzo were shot at as they walked out of a Brooklyn store. The attempted ambush resulted in the death of two innocent bystanders. Members of the Buccellato clan had made the shooting attempt. The retaliation would claim the lives of several Buccellato men. When police suspected Magaddino and Milazzo, both left Brooklyn for Buffalo and Detroit, respectively.

Once established in the Buffalo / Niagara Falls area, Magaddino ran a profitable bootlegging business due to the city's close proximity to Canada. The Buffalo family allowed the Cleveland Syndicate and Moe Dalitz's "Big Jewish Navy" to smuggle illegal booze from Canada through Buffalo. However, in 1933 when remnants of another Cleveland gang, the Porrello family, tried to muscle in on the Buffalo corn sugar business, guns blazed and the Porrellos were turned back losing their fifth family member in four years.

In 1930, the Castellammarese War was raging in New York City. The war pitted Salvatore Maranzano against Joe "The Boss" Masseria. Maranzano was from the Sicilian coastal town of Castellammare del Golfo from which the war took its name. When the war broke out, the Masseria forces, the larger of the two factions, boasted the likes of Lucky Luciano, Vito Genovese, Joe Adonis, Albert Anastasia, Tom Gagliano, and Tommy Lucchese. On the Maranzano side was Joe Profaci, Joe Magliocco, and Joe Bonanno, who was Magaddino's cousin. During the months of fighting, Magaddino helped the Maranzano cause by sending $5,000 a week. The war came to an end on April 15, 1931 when Luciano set-up Masseria to be hit in a Coney Island restaurant. Maranzano was murdered six months later on September 10, in his Park Avenue office.

Before Prohibition ended, Magaddino began peddling a non-alcoholic mixture called "Home Juice." The local Italian population was compelled to purchase the concoction that was sold door-to-door. The immigrants quickly realized that refusal to buy the product could prove detrimental to their health, in which case another mob-run business was available to cater to their needs, the Magaddino Memorial Chapel funeral home.

After Prohibition, the Buffalo family continued its money making through gambling, loansharking and labor racketeering. The family was also branching out - west, into Ohio and north, into Canada.

In the late 1930s, Magaddino was associated with John Charles Montana in the Empire State Brewery located in Olean, New York. During this period, Montana was said to be Magaddino's second-in-command. This leadership was further cemented by inter-marriage between the two families. Magaddino's son Peter was married to the niece of Montana, while a daughter was married to Montana's nephew.

Montana was born on June 30, 1893 in Montedore, Italy. Montana had a clean record until he was convicted of Conspiracy to Obstruct Justice as a result of his presence at the Apalachin meeting. He purchased a taxicab and would eventually own the largest taxi company in Western New York State through a merger of the Yellow Cab Company and the Van Dyke Taxi and Transfer Company. In 1928, Montana was elected to Buffalo city council and re-elected in 1930. The National Junior Chamber of Commerce named the civic-minded mobster "Man of the Year" in 1956. His connections to organized crime were exposed in the wake of the Apalachin disaster. Reports after this exposure tied him in with the notorious Joe DiCarlo. Montana died in 1967.

In 1945, Buffalo racketeer Joe "The Wolf" DiCarlo, who had been arrested 26 times and earned the title of Public Enemy Number One in Buffalo, went to Youngstown to muscle in on the numbers rackets there. During testimony before the Kefauver committee on organized crime, DiCarlo irritated committee members with his poor memory and flip answers. At the end of the questioning, Kefauver told him that he would recommend appropriate action be taken against him, to whom DiCarlo responded, "Thank you, Senator."

Magaddino had many enemies over the years and survived several attempts on his life. In 1936, a bomb intended for him was detonated in the wrong house and killed his sister. Another assassination attempt took place in 1958 when a hand grenade was hurled through his kitchen window but failed to explode. This attempt might have come from one of the angry mobsters who had attended the debacle at Apalachin. Rumor has it that Magaddino talked Vito Genovese into having the meeting at Joseph Barbara's New York home instead of holding it in Chicago. Many believe that Magaddino was one of the meeting participants who escaped through the woods when police arrived. The fact that law enforcement officials found some of his personal belongings left behind at the Barbara home helps to bolster this claim. Buffalo family members arrested at Apalachin were Magaddino's brother, Antonio, James La Duca, a son-in-law, John Montana and Rosario "Roy" Carlisi. In the 1990s, Roy Carlisi's bother Sam "Wings" Carlisi would run the Chicago Outfit for a short time.

During the early 1960s, two brothers, Albert and Vito Agueci, were engaged in narcotics trafficking in the greater Buffalo area. Albert, who had a home in Toronto, had at one time befriended Joe Valachi and helped him find a hiding place in Canada when he was on the run from a narcotics charge. The brothers, who were born and raised in Sicily, had the blessing of Magaddino and paid him a percentage of their drug profits. In return, they were to be provided with protection from other gang members and legal help if they ran into problems. On July 20, 1961, the Agueci brothers were arrested in New York City on narcotics violations. When Magaddino reneged on his promise to provide support, Albert Agueci's wife was forced to furnish the bail. Agueci soon made noises about getting even.

On November 23, 1961 the 38 year-old Albert Agueci was found on a farm near Rochester, New York. His badly mutilated corpse had an estimated 30 pounds of flesh carved from it. Agueci's jaw was shattered and half his teeth knocked out. Finally, he had been strangled with a clothesline, soaked in gasoline, and set on fire.

Vito Agueci was convicted on the narcotics charges and sent to the Atlanta Penitentiary to serve his sentence. While there, Vito Genovese provoked him into a personality conflict with Joe Valachi. This conflict ended with Valachi killing another inmate and eventually becoming a government witness.

Also during the early 1960s, Magaddino's cousin, Joe Bonanno, who had already been expanding his influence into Canada, Arizona and Sicily, decided to make a power play in New York City. Since the late 1920s and early 1930s, Magaddino had been a big supporter of his cousin. But now, Magaddino believed Bonanno, along with his other moves, was trying to muscle in on some of his territory in Canada. Magaddino at one time was rumored to be on a Bonanno hit list. Conspiring with Joseph Magliocco, who succeeded the Joe Profaci who died of cancer in 1962, Bonanno planned the murders of Carlo Gambino and Tommy Lucchese. They hired Profaci enforcer Joseph Colombo to carry out the killings. Colombo betrayed the two by going to Gambino and exposing the plot.

At a meeting of the Commission, Bonanno and Magliocco were called to appear. Bonanno refused to show up. Magliocco agreed and admitted his role in the plot. He was fined $50,000, stripped of his role as boss of the Profaci family, and replaced by Joe Colombo. Magliocco died of natural causes in 1963.

The Commission ruled that Bonanno had forfeited his position and installed Gaspar DiGregorio as head of the family. DiGregorio was Magaddino's brother-in-law and had been Bonanno's best man in his 1931 wedding. This decision upset factions within the Bonanno Family and instigated what became known as the "Banana War," which raged from 1964 to 1969.

On October 21, 1964, Joe Bonanno was kidnapped by Magaddino's brother, Antonino, and his son, Peter, on Park Avenue. According to Bonanno, during the time he was held captive, Magaddino had "succeeded in maintaining an air of mystery about the kidnapping." After Bonanno was released, he and Magaddino never saw each other again. The "Banana War" effectively ended in 1968 when Bonanno suffered a heart attack and retired, or was banished, to Arizona.

By the late 1960s, the aging Magaddino relinquished control of the day-to-day operations of the family's legitimate businesses like the Magaddino Memorial Chapel, the Power City Distributing Company of Niagara Falls, and the Camellia Linen Supply Company. At the same time, Fred "Lupo" Randaccio, who the Buffalo Police Department was reporting as the second-in-command after the death of John Montana, oversaw syndicate operations.

Randaccio was born on July 1, 1907 in Palermo, Sicily. His first arrest in the United States was in 1922 when he was 15 years old. Two years later, he was arrested again for gambling and bootlegging. In 1930, he held up a garage owner and received a ten-year sentence. Deportation proceedings were brought against him in 1956. The government dropped the case when they discovered Randaccio served six months in the U S Army in 1945 giving him automatic citizenship.

Lieutenants reporting to Randaccio at this time were John Cammilleri, who controlled labor and union racketeering; Pat Natarelli, Joseph Fino and Daniel Sansanese, overseeing the bookmaking operations; and Steve Cannarozzo, who handled the numbers rackets. Randaccio, described as a great organizer, traveled frequently to Hamilton and Toronto, Canada to review Buffalo controlled operations there.

In the early 1970s, family members felt that Magaddino was taking more than his share of the family profits. The crime family members came to this conclusion after Peter Magaddino's Niagara Falls apartment was raided and a suitcase containing $521,000 was found under his bed. This discovery helped lead to a breakdown of his father's leadership. Magaddino had had a variety of heart ailments for several years and died in a Lewiston hospital of a heart attack on July 19, 1974 at the age of 82. He had served as the family leader for 52 years, quite possibly a record tenure for a mob boss. At the time of his death, some splinter groups within the family had begun taking orders from the Bufalino Crime Family, which operated out of Pittston, Pennsylvania.

The Canadian operations started by the Buffalo family, continued on well into the 1990s, and were overseen for the most part by Johnny "Pops" Papalia until he was murdered in May 1997.

John Cammilleri was another ranking member of the Buffalo mob. Cammilleri was born in Campobello di Licata Gigenti, Italy in 1905 and arrived with his family in Buffalo when he was five years old. During the Depression, Cammilleri began his life of crime as a small time hood. As a thief he was arrested for grand larceny in 1930. Over the next few years his rap sheet grew and included arrests for Assault with Intent to Kill, Burglary, Robbery, and Extortion. In 1933, he was sent to Elmira Prison for 20 years.

Paroled by 1939, Cammilleri was back in Buffalo working for the Hod Carriers Local 210, although no one can remember him ever lifting a shovel. Years later, a U S Senate subcommittee described his position as handling union problems as a lieutenant for Stefano Magaddino's Buffalo Crime Family.

In 1944, despite his lengthy record and the fact that J. Edgar Hoover had personally written a letter to the Buffalo Police Department advising against it, Cammilleri was granted U S citizenship.

Cammilleri's influence in mob activities grew as he gained a reputation as a man that could be depended on to do favors for the friends of organized crime members. He stayed out of trouble until 1971 when he was caught lying to a grand jury about his association with local gangsters Joseph and Nicholas Fino.

In the early 1970s, Cammilleri had attained a certain degree of independence in some of his operations, which included construction companies, "maverick" work done on the Buffalo Federal Building, and a high-stakes poker game he ran. The local family leadership was growing concerned with this independence. In addition, his attempt to control the leadership of Local 210 brought him into direct conflict with Ron Fino, Joseph's son, who as the business manager of the union, was trying to separate it from the influence of the mob.

Local 210 had become a haven for organized crime members in Buffalo. This was transparent to the public until Cammilleri put the union on the front page in 1970 when he appeared at the building site of the new federal building on Huron Street. A Time Magazine article in September 1971, stated, "In his sharply tailored suits, pointed-toe shoes, dark glasses and pinkie ring, Cammilleri was an unlikely looking straw boss for an office building." The $14 million dollar construction project, which had fallen woefully behind, now moved forward without any further problems.

It was through Cammilleri's efforts that Ron Fino was elected, and for his reward he wanted a top spot in the Local. Ron Fino, never a gang member himself, turned down Cammilleri's request. Angered by this rejection, he took his demands to the family leadership of which Salvatore "Sam" Pieri was the acting boss in the wake of Magaddino's death. On May 8, 1974 Cammilleri pleaded his case at a meeting held in a Buffalo cigar shop. The council denied his requests and he stormed out of the meeting enraged.

Later that night, he dropped off a girlfriend at Roseland, a popular West Side Italian restaurant, and left to attend the wake of Frank "Blaze" LoTempio, Pieri's brother-in-law. Cammilleri returned to the restaurant, parked his car and was crossing the street when someone called out his name. Several shots rang out and Cammilleri was hit in the face and chest and died instantly. As restaurant patrons rushed outside to look, a car with four men inside sped down Chenango Street.

The FBI reported that Cammilleri's death sparked a wave of mob-related murders that lasted into the mid-1980s. During this period law enforcement officials say 15 murders and one disappearance have been linked to his killing, with only one case ending in an arrest.

Ron Fino later became a government witness and testified that his father was marked for death the same night Cammilleri was hit. Joseph Fino barricaded himself in his home for several days until he could arrange a sit-down with family leaders. Ron Fino reported that Pieri stepped forward and saved his father's life. Both Pieri and Joseph Fino have since passed away.

Cammilleri's murder has never been solved. However according to the FBI, Michael J. Alessi, a former county legislator and a nephew of Cammilleri, during an interview in 1981 put the finger on Vincent "Jimmy" Siurella as being responsible for the killing.

According to the Department of Justice, leadership of the Buffalo mob is still a family affair. Since the mid-1980s, Joseph "Lead Pipe Joe" Todaro, Sr. and his son run local organized crime operations. Todaro, Sr. was born in 1923. He was active in labor unions and this is where he may have picked up the nickname.

The Justice Department's most recent statement on this comes from a November 1994 report which the courts were going to use as basis of suit against the Laborers International Union of North America before Arthur Coia and his administration agreed to government control.

The 212-page report stated that, "Todaro Sr. has been the boss of the Buffalo La Cosa Nostra family and dictates the affairs of Local 210, despite the fact that he has never held an office or position in the union and has never had an official connection with the union." Fifty-two of those pages concerned alleged connections between the mob and local 210.

The FBI describes Todaro Jr., according to a story in The Buffalo News, as a life long criminal who, with his father, runs a Buffalo organized crime family responsible for murders, loan sharking, narcotics traffic, gambling and other assorted crimes.

Todaro Sr. is semi-retired and lives in Florida. His son runs one of Buffalo's most popular pizza restaurants, La Nova, and frequently donates large numbers of pizzas to various charities, including National Guard troops called up for Desert Storm a few years ago. He has never been convicted of a felony and his attorneys through the years have always denied FBI allegations about his mob connections. But this didn't make any difference to the hearing officer, Peter Vaira, appointed by the International to root out mob influence from Local 210. Out of 28 people accused of associating with the mob, he found charges credible against 17, including Joseph Todaro Jr. who resigned his job as a business representative for the local in 1990. It is believed mob activity although somewhat modified is still controlled by the Todaro family.

Portions edited from an article by Mario Machi, Allan May and Charlie Molino
Investigative Journalists

ROCHESTER, NEW YORK RIOTS – 1964

Friday night July 24, 1964 is a date that will live for many years in the memories of Rochesterian's. At 11:38 PM, a riot was born. Rochester's population totaled 318,000 with the black minority numbering about 35,000. Vandalism, looting and rioting befell the city. Criminal acts developed so rapidly, that city and county law enforcement agencies were unable to control the situation. A call went out for State Police assistance.

A RIOT IS BORN

The evening started out calmly with a street dance organized in the "Negro" neighborhood by local residents Helen Myricks and Carrie Stevens. The dance was sponsored by the Nassau Street Mothers Association to raise money for a small children's park. Teen-agers seemed to be enjoying themselves except for one boy who "was causing a fuss". Gene Stevens as well as others approached the young man identified as 20-year-old Randy Manigault of Nassau Street asking him to calm down. He refused the request so Stevens located two white Rochester policemen, Anthony Cerretto and Roger Bacon, advising them of the problem. As the policemen approached Maniguallt, he started yelling, swinging and resisting the officer's attempts to calm him down. He was placed under arrest and handcuffed. A struggle ensued with the officers and Manigault falling to the ground. The dance crowd turned on the officers yelling for them to take off the cuffs and let the boy go. The crowd was assaulted the officers in an attempt to free him. Detectives Dan Funk and Sal Arnone parked at Joseph Avenue and Nassau Street saw the incident, radioed for help and went to their assistance. They were met by a barrage rocks and bottles thrown from the crowd. Several police cars with sirens blaring and lights flashing responded to the scene. They were also met with a barrage of bottles, rocks, stones and bricks.

In less than 30 minutes, 50 policemen were facing 500 rioters. Now the looting began. Word spread like wild fire. During the early morning hours, a crowd of white youths appeared on one side of the street near the US Post Office facing a crowd of black youths who stood across the street. Fire trucks arrived stiffening their fire hoses with water pressure while under the protection of newly arrived Greece and Brighton Police officers. Their arrival squelched a potential racial riot. Dawn brought a scene of senseless, wanton destruction. After two nights of violence, there wasn't a black neighborhood that did not show scars of violence.

MAN KILLED

Saturday night brought new violence with rioting "Blacks" ignoring a dusk to dawn curfew. All area liquor and gun supply stores were ordered closed. Rioters fired shotguns and pistols in the air and hurled bricks and bottles. Looting spread to another black neighborhood and a few white sections. Judson Brayan, an 80 year old white man was clubbed in the head with a pipe, stumbled into the street and was struck and killed by a car that dragged him for over 100 feet. The driver seeing the rioters left the scene without stopping. It was reported that rioting was not as intense as the night before, but looting increased at many businesses within a short driving distance. Looters would drive into an area, break display windows, enter a business, take what they wanted and leave the scene in a matter of minutes.

POLICE CHIEF WILLIAM LOMBARD

Rochester Police Chief William Lombard (a former NYS Trooper) drove alone to the riot scene to reason with the crowd. It didn't do any good as various objects were hurled at him. Several black people helped him to escape the fury. His car was overturned and burned.

155

TROOPERS HELP REQUESTED
At 3:08 AM, City manager Porter W. Homer called the Governor's Office requesting state police help. At 5:08 AM, Superintendent Arthur Cornelius ordered 463 Troopers to Rochester. BCI men sent to Rochester to assess the situation were followed early on the morning of July 25th by the uniform force. The first 45 troopers led by Captain John P. Nohlen of Batavia, N.Y. arrived at 7:30 AM. Additional troopers arrived totaling 264 on duty by 9:30 AM. Troopers assembled and were housed at the Culver Road Armory. All 2,574 troopers in the state were placed on emergency alert. State Police Colonel John A. Roche was designated in charge of all police forces at Rochester. It should be noted that New York City police had quelled rioting the week before in the Harlem and Brooklyn neighborhoods of New York City.

Troopers were sent to the western city neighborhoods where on Saturday night they brought rioters under control through the use of high- pressure water hoses and tear gas. Two white men in a car were arrested for carrying guns. They had revolvers, as well as shotguns and rifles. Ninety-eight persons were injured including twenty-four police officers. Ninety-two persons were arrested and arraigned in City Court on charges including grand larceny, felonious assault and inciting to riot. The troopers basically in a defensive mode the first day took control on Sunday securing areas and arresting violators with strict enforcement of the curfew law.

NATIONAL GUARD ACTIVATED
Sunday saw the activation of the 1st Howitzer Battalion, 209th Artillery, New York National Guard under command of Lt. Colonel Gordon T. Cole. It was strictly a maneuver to serve as a show of force. A twelve-vehicle convoy led by Major William McNally drove through the riot areas and back to the armory. The unit would also supply transportation to police if needed.

HELICOPTER CRASH – THREE KILLED
On Sunday, July 26 at 3:00 PM, a Hughes 300 helicopter owned by Page Airways Inc. while observing the riot areas crashed into a house at 252 Clarissa Street killing two occupants. It then plunged to the sidewalk below where it exploded setting fire to the building. The pilot, 45–year old James B. Docharty of 5 Lilac Lane, Brighton was killed instantly. A critically injured passenger, Civil Defense Director Robert Abbott was removed from the burning wreckage by Troopers Sgt. Joseph Christian, Troopers John Ryan, C.M. Shekel and J.L. Schmidt along with City Patrolman Donald Williams. Another passenger, 31 year- old Robert Cannioto of Henrietta found in a dazed and shaken condition was treated for cuts and bruises. The occupants of the house were burned beyond recognition. They were identified two days later as 40 year old John Riley of Clarissa Street and 40 year old Willie Jones of 4 Eagle Street.

ROCHESTER CITY COURT
On July 29th, only a few problems were noted. City court Judges Thomas Culhane, Sidney Z. Davidson and James Sheehan presiding gave suspended sentences to some seven hundred defendants following their arrests over the weekend for mostly curfew violations. Sporadic looting and hostilities flared up until August 3rd, when all resistance was reduced to a level that could be handled by local police. The troopers were gradually withdrawn. During the ten-day rebellion, nine hundred seventy-six persons were arrested, one hundred two city police officers were injured along with five deputies and eleven troopers.

Trooper's duty hours while in Rochester were from fourteen to twenty hours daily. Those that stayed behind worked twelve-hour over-lapping shifts where possible and were available twenty-four hours daily.

MEALS FOR POLICE AND FIREFIGHTERS
The Salvation Army was the first to provide meals for the police & firefighters. They dispensed 10,000 bottles of soft drinks, 400 gallons of coffee, 12,000 hamburgers and hot dogs and 5000 sandwiches.

Canada Dry Corporation established a no charge soft drink & hot dog stand.

St. Michaels Church parish served 5,000 cups of coffee, 4,500 sandwiches, 1,000 cartons of milk, 80 gallons of ice tea and 1,500 roast beef dinners.

Valley Echo, a catering firm toured the riot areas providing for police and fed off duty troopers at the Culver Armory.

The Hudson Avenue Area Association operated a coffee bar and disbursed food donated by local area merchants.

TROOP A MEMBERS INJURED
Trooper John Anna - treated on location, when he was overcome by smoke while aiding at the scene of fire on Adams Street.

Treated at Strong Hospital were:
Investigator Henry Panus - 14 stitches for facial cuts and glass in his eyes.
Trooper James Mohn – 11 stitches for a laceration to his arm from flying glass.
Trooper Watson Hartway – relieved of duty, when struck in the chest with a full quart milk bottle.
Sergeant George Chromey – laceration and contusions from a scuffle during an arrest.

ROCHESTER TIMES UNION EDITORIAL
A front- page editorial of the Rochester Times Union dated July 27, 1964 Civil rights for any minority group has little or nothing to do with it. Rather, the rights of all 600,000 residents of this county are at stake. Police brutality has nothing to do with either. Rather, brutality to police is involved. Every hour that passes makes it more clear that thrill seekers, drunks and hoodlums seized a chance to run wild, to defy authority, to jeer police officers. During the first 48 hours, an undermanned police force followed a policy of tolerance and lenience and great patience. This city in recent years has set many examples of equal opportunities-from jobs to housing to education. Brotherhood has been practiced here. That message must be made un-mistakenly clear. Opportunity under the law belongs to every man. Immunity from the law belongs to no man.

AFTERMATH
Many business owners did not believe they could re-open due to the heavy loss of merchandise and damage done to their properties. A few examples are noted below:

Henry Weiss, owner of Miller's Liquor reported every bottle of alcohol stolen.

Paul Newman's meat market had smashed windows, doors and the meat cooler damaged with all meat that wasn't stolen spoiled.

George Cohen of George's Clothing Store estimated $34,000.00 in damage and loss of inventory.

Grossman Supply Company, an appliance company, was undamaged, because the upstairs tenants protected the property from looters.

LESSON LEARNED
State Police Colonel John Roche noted that the chief lesson learned was mobility. "We were set up for riot in one place when new battles flared up in widely separated areas and the problem was to get there quickly. The piece of equipment that could have been used was a windowless bus. Borrowed Rochester Transit Co. buses used by police only provided targets for window smashers. When troopers tried to race men to a trouble spot in cars, streets became congested. Parked police cars were an invitation to rioters to overturn or damage them."

RECOLLECTIONS
Comments were received from a number of members who were on duty at Rochester during the riot. While most were interesting and historical in a fashion, space limitation precludes verbatim repetition. In truth, a book could be written on just the stories from all those involved.

The comments received have been reduced to their highlights so that some personal experiences are included. Now retired Trooper Larry Francis and Monroe County Deputy Sheriff Harry DeHollander both mentioned being under the command of State Police Lieutenant Charles Cobb and being impressed by his leadership and forceful approach to circumstances. Lt. Cobb was a longtime member of the State Police and prior to that had served in the US Marines and was not a man to be trifled with. The Deputy, Harry DeHollander, was a nephew of another old time member of the State Police and his namesake, Harry DeHollander, (the elder DeHollander was long retired and not at the riot scene). Given Charlie Cobb's nature, he likely accepted Deputy DeHollander with the same spirit he would have shown the deputy's uncle, a fellow trooper. Deputy DeHollander was commendatory of Lt. Cobb. His quote was that "Big Charlie carried a big stick and was one hell of a guy to follow into the crowd." Larry Francis mentioned that he was amazed when Monroe County Sheriff Albert Skinner drove into the riot zone one night and passed out bologna sandwiches to those on foot patrol. He appreciated the sandwich but wondered if the Sheriff couldn't have been doing something more pivotal in the situation. The Sheriff, of course, did have more to do and his effort in this regard was likely his way of showing the troops from all departments he was interested in their welfare.

TROOPER LARRY FRANCIS
I was at Rochester during the riot and here are several things I remember:

Lieutenant Charlie Cobb was marching a contingent of men down one of the side streets near Joseph Avenue while we were being pelted with stones and glass milk bottles. When the Lt. felt we had had about enough of it and at an opportune time, he ordered us to break ranks and arrest our attackers. During the skirmish, Trooper Watson Hartway took a direct hit from a full glass milk bottle or brick in the chest and was seriously injured. The skirmish would have made a great movie scene.

I was in a tavern in the area (Henry's, I believe) with Sgt. George Zink and several other Troopers. Sgt. Zink ordered the place closed and obviously no one was going to listen. The next thing I knew, Zink vaulted over the bar, wiped out every bottle of booze with his nightstick, broke the mirror on the back bar, vaulted back over the bar and wiped out a Wurlitzer jukebox. About six patrons were removed from their bar stools and taken to the floor. He then stood up and said, "I said this placed is closed", troopers arrested them all.

I was working nights and walking the streets near Joseph and Vienna Street. The cold and very dry bologna sandwiches being dropped off, believe it or not, were a welcome treat.

While at the Culver Street Armory during the day (worked nights), Governor Nelson Rockefeller and Superintendent Arthur Cornelius came to pay us a visit and provide a press briefing. A bunch of us Troopers were gathered around, all ripe and sweaty, when I felt someone pull on the nightstick attached to my gun-belt. It was Rockefeller. He said to me, "Have you had to use this yet"? My response, "some" (what an answer). His response, "Hopefully, not too much more, we need to get this over. Thank you trooper and nice talking to you". He then took his turn at the microphones.

Several troopers were manning a road-check point at a cross intersection. Bronson Street was one of the streets. All vehicles that entered this intersection were ordered to shut off their lights and open the trunk and vehicle for inspection. The majority complied and were released immediately upon satisfying the inspecting troopers. Obviously, there are always those who did not wish to comply and paid the consequences. I recall several brand new and late model high-end vehicles having the headlights smashed out with batons and the trunks opened like sardine cans with crow bars. The occupants came out of those cars like rats jumping off a sinking ship. Instant justice and gratification all at the same time.

BCI Investigators Edward Longhany and his partner Karl Limner were assigned riot duty after Police Chief Bill Lombard's car was burned. They were housed at the National Guard Armory on Culver Road for about a week. Ed recalls telephoning his wife Lil to bring him some clean clothing, as his were filthy and torn. We were pushing the blacks back in the Joseph Avenue area and a policeman beside me got hit in the face with a brick or stone. He was falling backward bleeding. Just as I reached out to help him, I was hit in the left shoulder with a brick. It was very sore, but I didn't report it. It was quite an experience. The rioters threw whiskey bottles, broken plate glass and everything they could find at us.

MONROE COUNTY DEPUTY HARRY DEHOLLANDER
I was one of the first called in by the Sheriff to respond into the city to support the city police. I was there from beginning to end working on Joseph at Herman Street and on Herman and Henry Streets in the heart of the riots. I found that a top cover from a 30-40 gallon garbage can worked well when held up in front of your face or over your head to shield yourself from bottles and thrown glass. I believe it was the second or third night on the corner of Joseph and Herman Streets. Our little squad of about 10 officers made up of Rochester Police and Deputy Sheriffs were under the command of a State Trooper Lieutenant named Charlie Cobb. Big Charlie carried a big stick and was one hell of a guy to follow into the crowd.

TROOPER DOUGLAS HEDGES
Troopers were called to duty in the early morning, many woken from a sound sleep. They reported to SP Clarkson just west of Rochester. Sgt. George Zink met us and as soon as the first bus was full, off we went, all 44 of us. We got to the riot area, exited the bus and marched down the center of the street in a show of strength. We then spread out in a line, sidewalk-to-sidewalk and advanced through the trouble spot. Anyone that did not move out of our way was thumped, and then arrested. I spent five days sleeping in the armory. While marching down the street one night, I was hit on the arm with a rock. The arm was sore for months. In those days, you didn't cry about it, you just went about your business. My most vivid recollections of the rioting were of Captain John P. Nohlen and Lieutenant Charles E. Cobb leading the men into the riot torn streets. It was the way leadership was supposed to be, superior officers leading the way.

Rochester, N.Y. Riots. Clinton Avenue - 1964

BLIZZARD OF 1966

From January 31 – February 2, 1966, Western and Central New York recorded a record high 102-inch snowfall. Snow drifter to heights of 20-feet. Most weather experts regarded the storm as one of the worst in the century considering the drifting and general interruption of basic services. The greatest concentration of problems ranged from Batavia to Utica and from Watertown to Cortland and reflected the effect of winds blowing from Lakes Erie and Ontario.

Visibility was zero halting all motor vehicle traffic including snowplows in their tracks. Troopers somehow managed to make their way around abandoned and snowbound vehicles helping the occupants to safety in nearby fire-halls established as shelters or nearby residences. Medical assistance was provided in many instances including taking expectant mothers to hospitals and even helping to deliver several babies. Many troopers reported for duty by telephone. Using personally owned four-wheel drive vehicles and snowmobiles, troopers and volunteers provided assistance where it was desperately needed.

During the three day storm, 4,400 hours of overtime were worked by troopers from Troops A, D and T.

STORM DUTY
Following are some of the deeds performed by troopers during the storm:

Troopers Thomas W. Kennedy, Robert J. Szymanski, Eric W. Hammerschmidt and Anthony R. DiRienz assisted a pregnant Leroy, N.Y. resident about to give birth. Hospitalization was required due to an RH blood factor. They were able to drive to within a mile of the residence, then walked through heavy drifting snow and carried the patient to the troop car for transportation to the hospital.

Troopers Joseph A. Paige and Harry S. Crosier with the help of a town snowplow were able to transport a heart attack victim to a Batavia hospital. It happened to be the wife of retired Trooper Jacques Stickney. They also transported a victim suffering from a smashed finger.

A Rochester man had suffered a fatal heart attack while stranded in his car near Bergen, N.Y. Troopers Thomas Kennedy and Anthony DiRienz placed the body in the back seat of the troop car and were able to get to a nearby church where a priest administered last rites. Unable to transport the body by any other means, they slowly (the entire day) made their way to Batavia's St. Jerome's hospital where the victim was officially declared dead.

While escorting a hearse proceeded by a snowplow, Troopers Joseph Paige and John Wilcox rescued two unconscious men in a stranded vehicle, another man that had suffered a heart attack and delivered critically needed medication to a thyroid patient.

Investigators Donald L. Smith, Richard H. Hampson and Trooper William F. Schencke transported the county medical examiner to the scene of an unexpected baby death.

Troopers David M. Corbine and Charles A. Militello with the help of a county snowplow and road grader were able to reach the residence of Kendall woman where they helped give birth to the child after receiving telephone instructions. Some eight hours later, an ambulance and snowplow were able to transport mother and child to a hospital.

A Mendon man walked to the Thruway where he told troopers he had 27 people stranded at his home with little food. Investigators Donald L. Smith, Thomas R. Salvameni and Paul R. Rectenwald purchased and transported bread, meat & milk to the home.

Troopers Dougal L. Kear and Richard D. Farwell were able to get to the home of Walter Lambert and transport his wife to the Olean hospital where their son Mark Edward was born.

Troopers Donald L. Vogt and Robert Wojcik carried a female skier with a broken leg from Kissing Bridge Ski area to their troop car one half mile away and transported her to the Springville hospital for treatment

Trooper John J. Meegan carried an elderly woman unable to walk and pulled her husband behind from their stranded car to shelter in a nearby restaurant.

Sergeant William F. Mulryan and Trooper John Folino established a system of coordination at Williamson. An emergency unit was established at the Williamson fire-hall that contained beds, blankets, food, fuel oil, snowshoes and transport items to persons in need of assistance. A total of 35 requests were processed.

On January 30th, Trooper Larry D. MacConnell was instructed to investigate an accident at Thruway marker 388 known as the "rock cut". A minor two-car accident turned into a 60-vehicle accident nightmare, as zero visibility and continued traffic kept entering the area colliding with already damaged vehicles. Additional help was sent with ambulances carrying 26-injured persons to nearby Batavia hospitals. Some of the ambulances also became part of the accident. Lieutenant Alexander Gallion initiated a rescue operation that took more than 24-hours to complete. Troopers at the scene, along with several hundred occupants of stranded vehicles remained isolated without food and in some instances, without heat, as the storm immobilized the area.

When the visibility cleared and stranded motorists had been removed, the smashed cars and trucks that remained protruded from the white snow in helter-skelter fashion giving the appearance of a combat zone.

The Trooper – March 1966   NYSP Annual Reports – 1966

Blizzard 1966 – Thruway near Batavia, N.Y.

Trooper Thomas Phillips – 1966 Snowstorm – 100 car Accident

NY STATE PRISON RIOTS

GREAT MEADOW PRISON – 1955

On August 17, 1955, 174 rebelling inmates at the Great Meadow Prison refused to eat or return to their cells congregating in an outside yard area. They had armed themselves with boards containing spikes. They demanded to speak with the Commissioner who was escorted to the prison by the state police. In the meantime, sixty-five troopers were sent to the prison as a precaution. Arriving, the commissioner spoke to inmates over a loud speaker instructing them to return to their cells while promising that he would speak with each of them individually in the morning. They refused. The troopers along with a complement of prison guards entered the yard and marched on the inmates. A brief melee took place with the inmates subdued, searched and returned to their cells.

AUBURN PRISON RIOTS – 1970

An incident at Auburn Prison on November 2, 1970 occurred when militants seized a microphone and proclaimed a "Black Solidarity Day" that precipitated an inmate sit in. It was short lived with fourteen inmates confined to their cells as punishment.

On November 4, 1970, troopers were sent to Auburn Prison when rebelling inmates refused to return to their cells, failed to report to assigned workshops and prevented other inmates from doing so. By 11:45 AM, seven guards had been clubbed. Inmates armed with boards and pipes seized 30 guards as hostages. Prisoners had control of the entire prison with the exception of the administration building. 322 troopers were mobilized with an additional force of 300 guards and sheriff's deputies placed in a support role. Corrections officials refused to discuss grievances until all the hostages were released. The show of overwhelming force quickly ended the rioters desire to continue. At 3:30 PM, the first hostage was freed and inmates started returning to their cells without further incident. Approximately 450 inmates were actually involved in the rebellion.

ATTICA PRISON RIOTS - 1971

The story of the Attica Prison Riots have been told and retold through every media outlet known. These are my recollections.

BACKGROUND

In 1931, the most secure, escape-proof prison ever built opened in the little upstate village of Attica, New York. It was also the most expensive prison ever built. Construction had begun in 1929 and continued into the early years of the Depression. Attica State Prison was to be the solution to problems of prison uprisings. When Attica opened, it was widely hailed as the ultimate prison. Its wall alone, enclosing 55 acres, was 30 feet high, extended 12 feet into the ground, and cost $1,275,000 to erect. The prison contained four separated cellblocks, each of which could house some five hundred men in individual cells. The total cost of the prison eventually reached the sum of approximately $9,000,000. The New York Times reporting on the recent riots and the new prison under construction, stated on January 22, 1930, Whatever may be the outcome of that agitation, the immediate and practical answer to the convict revolts will be the new Attica prison. No other prison since Auburn has created the interest that Attica did when it was built. Shortly before it opened, Attica was hailed in the following article, which appeared in the New York Times on August 2, 1931: When the New York State Prison opens at Attica with its full quota of 2,000 convicts, it is said to be the last word in prison construction. There will be beds with springs and mattresses, a cafeteria, recreation rooms and an automatic signal system for inmates to contact guards. Doors are operated by compressed air, sunlight will shine into cells and every prisoner will have his individual radio. When Attica opened, over 130 years had passed since Auburn Prison was built; the population of New York State had changed vastly; the entire social structure of the nation had been dramatically altered; new laws and social conditions had altered the very nature of crime itself; theories of human behavior had been radically modified by the developing social sciences. In fact, everything had changed except the prisons. They were still built in the silent congregate style of Auburn.

In 1971, Attica Prison, just as any other prison, had the potential for serious problems. The facility built to house 2000 inmates had a population of 2,254 requiring double bunking. Its population contained approximately 75% street hardened black and Latino criminals who were well versed in events occurring in the outside world.

During 1970, National Guard troops had gunned down unarmed students protesting against the Vietnam War at Jackson State and Kent State Universities. Black leaders Malcolm X and Martin Luther King had both been shot and killed. When George Jackson, a Black Panther inmate was killed at San Quentin by guards on August 21, 1971, Attica prisoners organized a hunger strike. His book "Soledad Brother" was passed from prisoner to prisoner.

Politically aware Attica inmates were well organized and unified against what they felt was a repressive, very tough white prison guard authority made up of 383 guards. Black militancy was at its peak with other state facilities transferring black problem inmates to Attica Prison. (Department of Corrections policy at the time was to move difficult and problem inmates from one prison to another.) It was strongly felt that the earlier Auburn Prison disturbances were allowed to fester with the transfer of troublesome inmate leaders from Auburn to Attica. During July 1971, a group of inmates sent a manifesto of grievances to prison officials relating to inmate treatment and conditions. Commissioner Oswald said he needed time to review the requests.

On several occasions prior to the rioting, inmates had told guards that they (inmates) were going to take over the prison using force. The guards gave this information to their superiors, but no action was taken. When the riots were over, the date September 9th was found circled on many of the inmate calendars indicating the rebellion was not spontaneous, but a planned event.

On Wednesday evening, September 8, 1971, two inmates were placed in solitary confinement for fighting and another for throwing a can striking a guard in the head, then being forcibly removed from his cell. Guards sensed a tense and uneasy atmosphere and considered keeping all inmates confined to their cells the next morning. Instead, supervisors opted to continue with normal operations.

THURSDAY - RIOT DAY ONE

September 9, 1971 started out to be just another day. Residents of the Village of Attica went about their business as they had always done. The Attica Prison located just south of the village was the primary employer having a huge economic impact on the community. Guards and civilian staff reported for duty with no inkling of what was to soon take place.

Around 8:30 AM, the prison sounded an alarm of trouble by blasting the prison siren. This was a signal for prison guards within sound of the prison siren to report for duty as soon as possible. The inmates were rioting. The State Police at Batavia, N.Y. were notified and quickly mustered approximately 30 troopers who were detailed to the prison. I had been given the day off for the purpose of registering in the Criminal Justice program at Buffalo State Teachers College that day. Instead, a phone call canceled my leave directing me to report immediately for duty.

A group of "A" block inmates described by guards as "trouble makers" and "political militants" overpowered a handful of unarmed guards taking over control of a majority of the prison. As word spread of the takeover, other inmates armed themselves with homemade weapons, (razors, knives, spears, pipe's) and overran a large area of the prison. They set fire to the chapel, prison school and machine shop, as well as three other buildings. In less than thirty (30) minutes, inmates seized a majority of the prison taking forty-one (41) guards and prison employees hostage. Guard William Quinn had been severely injured and along with eleven (11) other guards and civilians was released to obtain medical assistance. Those held hostage were stripped of their uniforms and given prison clothing to wear. In this manner, they would be indistinguishable from the inmates.

Not all rioters were willing participants. In an article written by Buffalo Evening News reporter Bob Buyer on September 8, 1996, he recalled interviewing inmates in the "D" yard who told him that they were being forced into continuing with the rioting by other inmates who threatened physical injury to them if they attempted to leave.

I arrived at the prison shortly after 10:30 that morning with a group of hastily mustered troopers from Batavia. A detail of thirty (30) first responding troopers and prison guards using tear gas had regained the "B" and "C" blocks from rebel inmates. Inmates that were not part of the rebellion were confined to their cells. By noon, there were well over 200 troopers and guards at the prison. We all felt confident that we could and would soon enter and retake the prison from the inmates. Hastily made plans had been prepared and we were ready to enter the cellblocks, tunnels and catwalks. Instead, we were ordered to stand down by Prison Commissioner Russell G. Oswald who elected to negotiate rather than retake the prison. He reasoned that the hostage's safety was primary and any show of force could result in injury to them. Troopers and guards alike felt this was a mistake on Oswald's part. A small group had earlier taken back two cell block's with little, if any resistance. It was felt that the entire assemblage of officers should be utilized from the get-go with a deployment of men retaking each cellblock, yard and adjacent buildings one at a time. Firearms would be used only if absolutely necessary. The approximately 1200 rioting inmates had taken up a position in the "D" yard that was furthest away from the prison's main entrance. We (the assembled troopers) felt strongly that a show of force would be enough to show the inmates the futility of their position. Inmates initially were disorganized, but relished their limited freedom and control they had over the hostages. With the state electing to negotiate and having hostages as a bargaining item, the rioters gained confidence that they held a strong position.

Troopers and guards were assembled in a grassy area just inside the main gate while awaiting orders to retake the prison. Others took up positions on the prison roofs and upper floors of the cellblocks to observe the inmate activity. The order to retake never came that day. In the late afternoon, troopers were assigned to squads and assigned to sweep previously secured areas. I was on a detail with Captain George Tordy with an assignment to re-check the prison mess hall. While securing a room in the kitchen area, a voice was heard calling out, "*Al - - - Al, it's me Neil - - - Neil Jones, you remember me*" Somewhat stunned, I instructed Jones to show himself. A few seconds later, Neil appeared from his well-disguised hiding place. He appeared in good health and looked just as I remembered. I arrested him several years earlier for the larceny of funds from the Pembroke Thruway Restaurant that he managed. He was an easy-going, friendly man that you couldn't help but like. He had taken refuge out of fear when the rioting started. He was taken to a secure area by prison guards.

The evening passed into night and somewhere around 11:00 PM, we were relieved by a detail of trooper's arriving from the eastern part of the state. We went to our homes and only then did we learn details of the riot from television accounts. Commissioner Russell Oswald, NYS Assemblyman Arthur Eve, Buffalo News Reporter Bob Buyer and Attorney Herman Schwartz entered "D" yard and met with the rebels listening to their grievances. One demand was to allow outside observers into the prison to oversee the situation and act as negotiators. Oswald conceded to this request and 28 of 30 other demands presented by the inmates. He only refused the granting of amnesty, as he did not have the authority and the removing of Warden Vincent Mancusi, as he felt it would undermine prison authority throughout the system.

FRIDAY – DAY TWO

The second day was planned and organized. Troopers were assigned to designated locations with a 12-hour, 8AM to 8PM schedule established. The Salvation Army and Attica Lion's Club were permitted to set up food distribution centers just inside the prison wall where they dispensed coffee, water and donuts in the morning, as well as sandwiches later in the day. An old friend, Jim Hardie was working in the Lion's Club booth. We spoke briefly about the situation and what we expected to happen. It wasn't until after the retaking that I became aware that Jim's father, Elmer Hardie was one of the hostages and had been killed. He was a civilian supervisor instructing inmates in a trade that could be used once released.

My group included Sergeant Warden Barrows and Troopers Fred Walsh, Bill Sobolewski, Gerry Kalisz, Scott Saunders and Jim Lobur. We were issued .12 gauge shotguns and ammunition to be used only if needed to protect life. We were assigned to the upper level of "C" block. From our vantage point, we were able to see over the cat- walks into the back part of "D" yard. The hostages were not clearly visible. Inmates wearing football helmets and cloths covering their faces were wandering around the "C" yard breaking up everything in sight for use as weapons. They were piling debris across the catwalks similar to a beaver dam in attempt to build barricades that they thought would stop any advance by troopers. Sometime in the early evening, we were brought fried egg sandwiches and coffee. The sandwiches were made up of a square of egg (mostly the white) in equal size to the thick homemade bread it came on. We were so hungry, that the sandwiches actually tasted great. It was a long, dragged out day.

We heard that several other "celebrity negotiators" arrived during the day and met with the rioting inmates. There were 33 all together that included New York Times columnist Tom Wicker, New York Congressman Herman Badillo, State Senator John R. Dunne, Amsterdam News publisher Clarence Jones and others. They met with the inmates that night listening to their demands. We couldn't help but wonder what was wrong with Oswald to agree to that many negotiators. Whoever the inmates wanted they got. There was no way that large amount of "brain power" gathered at one location, debating every issue could be effective. The only issue they should have been concerned with was the health and welfare of the hostages and getting them safely released. I don't recall seeing anything written about the "good faith" observers going in and saying, ***OK, you made your point, the world is watching, you won. Everyone knows your demands. The state will have to act on them. They don't want another situation like this. There are a 1000 armed police out there and they will retake this place. You will be unable to stop them. Release the hostages and return to your cells peacefully.***

SATURDAY - RIOT DAY THREE

Our detail was again armed with .12 gauge shotguns and assigned to the metal shop located at the rear of the prison. Our day was relatively quiet. Learning from the day before, we brought various food items and a deck of cards to pass the time. We played either Euchre or Pinochle most of the day. At one point during mid morning, a voice boomed out ***"HOBBS COMING THROUGH"***. We all scrambled to our feet, as an elderly black inmate came limping in. He was Ernest Hobbs, a 72-year old trustee who worked in the garage area. Hobbs job was to keep the warden's car in tip-top shape. He had been in prison so long, that when released, he purposely committed a crime to get sent back to prison. On occasion, Trooper Henry Haas wearing his orange trooper raincoat would wander through looking for goodies to eat. We never saw another person until relieved that night. Again, the only news we heard was from the television reports that night.

I learned several days later that the only reason the metal shop and adjacent power building had not been taken over was because of a veteran officer assigned to the rear wall guard tower of the prison. He observed inmates running through an open area in pursuit of guards near the Power House. He fired a several rounds in front of the rioters and would have shot them if they continued. His actions saved Guard Roger Dawson and several other co-workers from being taken hostage and the building from being taken over.

We learned that Officer William Quinn died as a result of the injuries received on the first day of the riot. This changed the entire mood at the prison and removed forever any chance of amnesty from the negotiating table.

Late that evening, Black Panther leader Bobby Seale was allowed to meet with the inmates. He made a brief, self-serving, non-committal speech and left. Inmates had hoped for a strong statement of support for their cause and got nothing. The observer committee having met with Oswald the entire day took the 28 revised demands he agreed to back to the inmates. The proposal was rejected.

Several troopers had fashioned homemade slingshots and were propelling nuts and bolts into "D" yard. Several inmates that came into view taunting the troopers were sent scurrying from the slingshot barrage directed at them.

SUNDAY – DAY FOUR

Our same detail arrived in the morning and was again assigned to the metal shop. It was another long day of hurry up and wait with time passed by playing card games. Old Hobbs came along with ice cream for everybody. I never did learn where it came from. Everyone was getting frustrated by the length of time it was taking to resolve the riot. We just wanted to get it over with and get on with our lives. Several pleas were made to have Governor Nelson Rockefeller come to the prison and meet with the inmates. Rockefeller said no, that he would not appear, as it would establish a poor precedent in the event of future rioting. Oswald again appealed to the inmates to return to their cells.

MONDAY – DAY FIVE
THE RETAKING

Monday morning, September 13, 1971 was a misty overcast day yet quite warm for September. Arriving early that morning, we realized something was about to take place. The troopers we relieved were ordered to remain at the prison. Several National Guard trucks and ambulances were gathered in the front parking lot of the prison.

I recall Captain Henry Williams standing on the front step of the prison announcing to the troopers present that it was a grave and serious situation. Hostages were still being held and rioting inmates controlled part of the prison. An ultimatum was being to given the inmates to surrender or force would be used to take back the prison. If force was used, we were told to look out for one another first and if placed in a position where life was in danger, to use whatever force was necessary including use of our firearms. Lastly, let no one take your weapon meaning the inmates. Although outranked by others present, it was Williams who I believe ultimately made the decisions and was unjustly dubbed the scapegoat of Attica. He was the only supervisor that had personal knowledge of the troopers present, their abilities and how best to utilize them. Those that knew Hank Williams were aware that the well being of the troopers and the safety of the hostages were foremost on his mind. There was no thought of glory or heroism in his leadership role, only the idea to get the job done as quickly and safely as possible.

Captain George Tordy again sought out several of us for his detail that was made up of Fred Walsh, Bill Sobolewski, Gerry Kalisz, and Jim Lobur. Fred Walsh and I were given body armor and a tear gas gun to use. Our group was assigned to clear the "A" tunnel leading from the Administration Building to times-square of any and all obstacles. (Times Square was the center of the prison where all the tunnels and catwalks above come together) The tunnel was about 12 to 15 feet wide and about 200 feet long. Half way down on either side were exit doors leading into the "A" and "C" yards. The tunnel ended at times-square and was secured by heavy, locked steel gates. A guard would have been assigned there to allow for passage from area to area. The body armor was the old heavy ceramic armor and weighed a ton. It was stored in footlockers at the barracks and made available, as needed.

Our assault group gathered at the "A" cellblock gate of the tunnel that was kept locked. We could see some type of barricade near the side exit doors with times-square barely visible in the distance. At about 9:45 AM, we could hear a helicopter flying on the prison perimeter. The signal to go in was the cutting of all power in the prison that was coordinated with the dropping of a tear gas canister from a second helicopter into the "D" yard inmate stronghold.

We were given the go ahead with Walsh and I sending tear gas projectiles into the barricade, then further into the times-square area. I could see one or two inmates exiting the tunnel into the "A" yard. A guard then unlocked the gate and we proceeded into the darkened tunnel. We got to the barricade consisting of mattresses, wood, trashcans and table parts and pushed it to the side. As we passed the exit doors, a group of troopers behind us exited through them into the yards. We continued on to times-square where we found the steel gate locked. Our vision was obscured from the settling of the tear gas in the tunnels. I saw an inmate lying on the floor near the gate inside times-square and pointed him out to a detail of troopers that had entered unimpeded from "C" tunnel, through times-square and on into the "D" tunnel. Gasmasks were distributed to all taking part in the assault. Our assignment had been completed in just a few minutes. During the entry, I could hear the muffled pop- pop of gunfire in a distance that lasted for just a couple of minutes. No one in our detail fired a weapon other than tear gas. Some of the detail remained at the times-square gate while the rest of us went out into the "A" yard. I could see a helicopter flying above the prison with a repeated loudspeaker announcement telling the inmates to "put down your weapons, no harm will come to you". I later learned that it was Senior Investigator Donald L. Smith making the announcement from the helicopter.

The prison was retaken within minutes. A rescue detail entered the "D" yard rushing to the aid of the hostages. A second detail identified and separated inmates. The inmates were searched by guards, stripped naked and taken into the "A" yard. While in the "A" yard, the inmates were ordered to lay face down. A few guards were observed prodding inmates with their batons, but I never saw any outright brutality or torture.

Our detail was unaware that the hostages became human shields after the inmates refused an ultimatum from Oswald demanding their surrender. I spoke with several sharpshooters during the debriefing later that day. They were situated on the "A" and "C" block roofs with a powerful .270 caliber rifle with scope. They were in a position to see the blindfolded hostages and their captors standing on the "B" catwalk just prior to the retaking. The inmates were observed holding knives or a similar weapon to the throats of the hostages making threatening gestures. When the tear gas was dropped from the helicopter, sudden movements by the captors made the troopers believe the hostages throats were being cut and tried to stop the attempt by picking off their captors. It should also be pointed out that vision was quickly obscured with the dropping of the tear gas being spread downward by the helicopter blades and held there by the mist. It was similar to being in a heavy fog.

LIEUTENANT JOSEPH CHRISTIAN

Some years later, Joe Christian related his recollection while leading a hostage rescue team. He was the second man down a ladder from the catwalks into D yard. He wasn't aware of the depth of the trench dug by inmates on the inside perimeter of the yard. As he crossed the trench, inmates armed with homemade spears and clubs greeted him. He was hit in the back with a steel bar, knocked to the ground and was somewhat dazed. As he looked up, an inmate stood over him with a fire axe raised in the air ready to strike. At the same moment, he heard three shotgun blasts fired from above and the inmate fell to the ground, mortally wounded. Christian was hit in the left leg by the gunshot blast. As it turned out, he was the only trooper to suffer a gunshot wound during the prison retaking. In 2005, he was one of the Forgotten Victims of Attica awarded compensation from the state because of the injury.

TOM WICKER

Tom Wicker later wrote that when Attorney William Kunstler arrived, the group became more militant in thought, with Kunstler perceived as on the side of the inmate rather that remaining neutral. He said he never felt that the hostages would be hurt, because once that occurred the inmate bargaining power was lost. He recalled that entering and leaving the prison on several occasions gave him an opportunity to see the strength of the trooper force. He knew that if they retook the prison, there was no hope for the inmates. Many would be killed. He felt there was a failure on his part not to relate his feelings at the time. Inmates were making speeches about "dying like men". Wicker knew that some of them would die, but was fearful of harm or injury to himself if he spoke out. He wanted to say, "you are going to die, the troopers will come in shooting their guns and you will die." He said nothing. Wicker also related that he never observed such a bond of men with a mutual goal as he had with the rebel inmates. Blacks, Hispanics and whites joined as one with no racial barriers.

I wondered what rock Wicker was hiding under when he made this observation. The rebels killed three of their own and refused to allow inmates caught up in the turmoil to leave under threat of serious injury.

ATTICA LOGISTICS

When Troop "A" Commander Major John Monahan departed troop headquarters for the prison during the riot, he instructed First Sergeant Vernon Clayson to handle the routine troop matters and to find lodging for about 300 troopers. Clayson was soon made aware that more troopers were coming and reserved 600 rooms in area motels. Another bear of a job was setting up work schedules. Almost everyone wanted to go to the prison with many troopers calling and asking that a zone supervisors orders be overruled or requesting permission to cancel their annual leave and return to duty. It was allowed in some cases keeping in mind that we still had to maintain coverage in the troop area. Those left behind were required to do double patrol duty compensated with overtime pay. The only thing they missed by not being at Attica were the long and tedious days and nights of sitting around, the false starts and the dreary diet of fried eggs, hot dogs and hamburgers provided by the Salvation Army and other such groups. They also missed the commute to and from the motels and the evenings at the Holiday Inn bar (Yes, some had the energy to do some bar hopping.) Clayson was as busy as he had ever been keeping up with the normal matters, the inquiries from division headquarters and the media, plus relaying information from Monahan to the various troops, division headquarters and the National Guard. He managed to nap for three or four hours on a few nights but basically, he worked around the clock. He was sure I could still drive the twenty miles between troop headquarters and the prison in his sleep The Commissioner of Corrections was normally the man in charge and probably did the best he could, but his negotiations were a waste of time. Another waste was allowing entry to people like Arthur Eve, the black state legislator from Buffalo, whose appearance only emboldened the rioters further delaying a solution. The liberal attorneys William Kunstler and Bernard Schwartz did make some sense, but they were wasting their breath. The rioters were having their moment and played it for all it was worth. Another famous, or infamous, figure, one of the black panthers, Bobby Seales, showed up at the prison and was turned away. Then one of the genius prison officials, perhaps Oswald, changed his mind and invited him back. They would have invited the devil himself for some way out of the dilemma. A trooper was sent to locate Seales and return him for his royal appearance. A safe bet is that his first thought when the trooper stopped him was that he was being hassled rather than being summoned back for the negotiations. Another safe bet was that a thorough check on him and his companions, and probably even the vehicle, would have brought to light any number of felonious infractions. The negotiations came to nothing and the end came swiftly and violently. It was something like a military action, hours and days of waiting, then finally the killing began in earnest. Even Walter Cronkite used the military analogy, saying, "It was like a war except that only one side had guns." What did he expect, that they should have been treated courteously? They sought trouble and they found it. I don't believe that Monahan ever got the publicity he deserved. For instance, BCI Captain Hank Williams got more publicity and he was, at best, an assistant to Monahan. Captain George Tordy was also there as an assistant and led a tunnel detail during the retaking. Captain Tony Malovich led the first detail to go in. He was a former Marine and I don't think anything could have kept him back. There were two division deputy superintendents present, Bob Quick, an unapproachable and arrogant cold fish, and George Infante, a friendly, good natured guy, looking over Monahan's shoulder, ostensibly not to advise or judge but to observe. After the prison was retaken, Monahan came back to his routine duties seemingly unaffected. He completed his reports on the incident and went back to work as if the long and historical week was just another day at the office. Everyone else rehashed and recounted every minute of the incident over and over and over.

HOSTAGE RECOLLECTIONS

DEAN WRIGHT
Dean Wright, one of the prison employees taken hostage heard the gas being dropped and the shooting start. "I was scared to death - I said the Lord's Prayer to give me strength to die like a man.'"

We hostages spent most of the previous four days blindfolded with our hands and feet bound, soaked with rain, mud and human filth.

"There were two inmates behind me, one had what I thought was a knife to my throat," We were kept in a circle, blindfolded, with our hands and feet tied. "I heard a bullet go by and hit one of the men behind me," Wright said. "It sounded like you took a pumpkin and smashed it on a blacktop road. When he went down, I went down with him.

"All you could hear was shooting and screaming. The first thing I saw when they turned me over, about six inches from my face, was the barrel of a 12-gauge shotgun. Then somebody yelled, 'He's one of ours! He's one of ours!' and he left."

MIKE SMITH
Mike Smith was 22 years old and married with one child at the time of the Attica uprising. He had not finished college and had taken a job at a local prison while deciding what to do with his life, and had been transferred to Attica only six months before the riot. For Smith, as for many people in this upstate area, employment at Attica represented one of the best and highest-paying jobs in the vicinity. Despite the racial tensions at Attica, Smith maintained cordial relations with inmates. Nonetheless, during the riot he was taken hostage and subsequently wounded by police gunfire. When police overtook the prison, he was shot four times in the stomach by an automatic weapon. Smith spent the

following two-and-a-half years in a difficult recovery. He underwent a coloscopy, his weight dropped from 218 to 121 pounds, and he had to learn how to walk again. Attica State Prison declared him "physically incapable" of performing his duties and gave him partial disability retirement.

JOHN STOCKHOLM

John Stockholm, a 24-year-old father of two was escorting 41 inmates from breakfast through Times Square when he was struck with a pipe and knocked unconscious. Friendly inmates put prison clothing on him and hid him in D cellblock. They also hid Arthur Smith in an adjoining cell. Rioting inmates hearing news reports the next day realized they were missing two guards and sought them out. Stockholm was chosen as one of the eight hostages to be taken up on the catwalks overlooking D Yard and held with a knife to his throat in an effort to ward off the state's attack.

"They asked if I wanted to have a cigarette, because I was going to die 'like the rest of you pigs." I took the cigarette.

Still blindfolded, Stockholm felt his appointed "executioner" fall off his back after the shooting began. He hit the deck, and stayed there until the shooting stopped.

"You could hear the sounds and the smell of pain and death," Stockholm said. "They've haunted me for more than 30 years. I hear them and smell them in my nightmares."

FRANK STROLLO

Frank Strollo was a 29-year old prison guard working in the prison commissary with Officer Ronald Werner on the day of the riot. He was unaware of any insurrection until a surge of inmates rushed into the commissary knocking down the light wire protective barrier that protected it. He was beaten on the arms, back and side with makeshift weapons of the inmates but was not seriously hurt. Werner was struck several times in the face with his cheek being broken. They were both stripped down to their underwear and taken to the D yard where they were blindfolded. Sometime later, they were given prison clothing to wear. On the day of the retaking, Strollo said he was hit on the head by a pipe just as the firing started. He fell to the ground with his attacker laying over him in a protective manner. He heard someone yell out "Don't Kill Him". The next thing he knew, he was staring into the face of his brother, Trooper Anthony Strollo, a member of the rescue team. He was taken to a hospital for treatment.

AN INMATES PERSPECTIVE

In an article written March 31, 1972, inmate Frederick Wiggins serving a third term for embezzling, provides an insight from inside the walls. He questioned the motivation behind the riots and gives a different perspective from that outlined by the rebel leaders.

Demand for better food and less pork: The food was adequate and the demand for less pork was to satisfy the 3% Muslim population. The trays and glasses could have been cleaner, but it was the inmates who cleansed them.

Good jobs were given to whites of homosexuals: 2 principal clerks in the school were black, 6 of 7 in the library were black, 80 % of the instructors were black or Hispanic and the civilian head of the cell study program was black. It was not possible to give key jobs to more minorities because of the high percentage of illiteracy.

Inadequate medical care: I found the medical care adequate. You were taken care of, if you were really sick. Serious cases were taken to outside hospitals.

Lack of textbooks: The majority of inmates didn't care if they had a book or not. They were in class only because rules required attendance under a certain educational level or they were trying to impress the parole board.

More recreation: Each yard had baseball, basketball and football teams, Handball courts, weekly movies, card games, chess and checkers and home made weights. At night, there were three radio stations to choose from.

Guard brutality: I never observed any brutality. Force was only met with force. Remember that guards are surrounded by inmates all day armed only with a nightstick that would be of little use. There were no black guards.

Inmates are not treated with respect: Respect is something that is earned. A man is treated like a man if acts like one. The rebels talked about respect for their rights, then showed none when they killed Officer William Quinn. The rights of inmates Mike Privitera, David Schwartz and Kenneth Hess were trampled, when the rebels killed them because they did not agree with the rebellion.

Other grievances had to do with visitation, the segregation policy and having cellblock representatives to meet with the warden to air complaints and offer constructive criticism.

Did Commissioner Oswald handle the situation properly: I felt that after the situation had deteriorated, there was no alternative but to order the assault. I do feel that had he moved in with force the first day, September 9th, there would have been fewer casualties, if any. On the 9th, the rebels were disorganized and no one was dead so there would be no fear for surrendering.

Rebels killed a guard and three inmates prior to the assault.

Rebels brutally and repeatedly raped and sodomized young white inmates at knifepoint.

The inmates did have the hostages lined up on the catwalks with knives at their throats. The rebels had voted to kill them if their demands were not met.

THE FORGOTTEN VICTIM'S OF ATTICA

After the retaking, those civilian and guard survivors were directed to take six months off and continued to receive paychecks identical to their regular pay. The survivors and families were unaware that by cashing the checks, they were forfeiting their right to sue the state because the state had filed workmen's compensation claims on their behalf, without their knowledge or approval.

State officials urged widows to accept "benefits" as meager as $230 per month that was the same as if her husband had died a natural death, rather than being shot to death by his employer. Only Lynda Jones, the widow of slain prison clerk Herb Jones, refused the state's offer and retained the right to sue. She was awarded $1 million, more than a decade later.

Simmering frustrations among the survivors and families of the hostages finally peaked in January, 2000, when New York State paid $8 million to rioting inmates wounded during the retaking and another $4 million to their attorneys, ending more than a quarter-century of litigation.

Shortly after the inmate awards, a group made up of the widows of New York State Corrections Department employees killed during the 1971 riot at the prison, surviving hostages and family members formed **"The Forgotten Victims of Attica"** Members weren't resentful of the inmates, but of the state's refusal to acknowledge that its actions and guidance was financially and emotionally devastating to survivors and their families at a time that they were most vulnerable. Gary A. Horton, a prominent Batavia Attorney and Genesee County Public Defender voluntarily represented the Forgotten Attica Victims. A "Five-Point Plan for Justice" was formulated.

- An apology from the New York State acknowledging culpability for the deaths of hostages and physical injuries to its employees.

- Open state records on the riot and its aftermath previously sealed by Governor Hugh Carey.

- Provide counseling for survivors and families.

- Approval for a memorial service outside Attica Prison each September 13.

- Reparations to group members. It was noted that $125,000 was awarded to prisoner Frank "Big Black" Smith, who testified that he was severely beaten and threatened with castration during the riot's aftermath.

The state legislature passed a bill sponsored by State Senator Dale Volker (R-Depew) that would have given $50,000 each to the families of the 11 employees killed at Attica. The group refused the offer due to the state's refusal to admit any wrongdoing and the small amount in comparison to the inmate's award.

GARY A. HORTON

Gary A. Horton has earned the gratitude and respect of his peers, his community and those many defendants that he has represented over the years. A somewhat low key attorney, he would rather his office team be given accolades for the their work than himself. He is the son of a former New York State Trooper, Albert Horton who served the people of New York State with distinction from 1927 to 1953.

In January 2000, the Federal Courts awarded 8.5 million dollars compensation to inmates injured or killed during the retaking of Attica Prison in 1971 and 4 million dollars to their attorneys. Soon after, an editorial from the Batavia Daily News regarding the award was being discussed on a WBTA Radio talk program hosted by Debbie Horton, wife of Gary. A caller phoned in and only said, "You don't know the real story" and hung up. This led to a radio program being hosted on location in Attica Village a few weeks later. Many of the hostage's families were there and voiced their opinions. Although known to one another, they had never gotten together as a group. It was at this point in time that Gary who had accompanied his wife volunteered to represent the group who officially became known as the "Forgotten Victims of Attica".

Horton represented the group "Pro Bono" for over five years with 12.5 million dollars being awarded in the fall of 2005. The proceeds were distributed in various amounts taking all factors into consideration. For his efforts, Gary Horton won the gratitude and respect of his peers, but none more than from those he represented. Federal Court Judge Richard J. Arcara and the New York State Bar Association who presented him with the following citations recognized him for his many years of diligent work.

UNITED STATES DISTRICT COURT

2005 SPECIAL SERVICE AWARD

PRESENTED TO GARY A. HORTON

FOR HIS PRO BONO REPRESENTATION OF

"THE FORGOTTEN VICTIMS OF ATTICA"

HIS TIRELESS AND SELFLESS SERVICE TO PRISON

GUARDS KILLED OR INJURED DURING THE ATTICA

UPRISING WERE IN KEEPING WITH THE HIGHEST

IDEALS AND STANDARDS OF THE LEGAL PROFESSION

AND EXHIBITED A TRUE COMMITMENT TO THE SEARCH

FOR TRUTH AND JUSTICE.

06 OCTOBER 2005   **RICHARD J. ARCARA**

Because of his pro bono work in successfully representing the Attica Forgotten Victims, Genesee County Judge Robert E. Noonan nominated Gary A. Horton for the prestigious 2005 David S. Michaels awarded annually by the New York State Bar Association. Letters of support were sent by the Batavia Chapter of Former NYS Troopers, as well as 16 others supporting his nomination. On January 26, 2006 Horton received his due at a luncheon in New York City where his peers honored him.

DAVID S. MICHAELS AWARD

PRESENTED TO GARY A. HORTON

FOR HIS COURAGEOUS EFFORT IN PROMOTING

INTEGRITY IN THE CRIMINAL JUSTICE SYSTEM.

PRESENTED JANUARY 26, 2006

NEW YORK STATE BAR ASSOCIATION

PRISON EMPLOYEES KILLED

Elmer G. Hardie, born March 16, 1913, Industrial Foreman

John J. D'Arcangelo, born November 11, 1947, Corrections Officer

Edward T. Cunningham, born June 17, 1919, Corrections Sergeant

Herbert W. Jones Jr., born January 3, 1945, Senior Account Clerk

Richard J. Lewis, born August 1, 1929, Correction Officer

John G. Monteleone, born November 21, 1929, Industrial Foreman

William E. Quinn, born March 25, 1943, Correction Officer

Carl W. Valone, born June 11, 1927, Correction Officer

Elon Werner, born September 16, 1907, Principal Account Clerk

Ronald D. Werner, born December 3, 1936, Correction Officer, nephew of Elon Werner

Harrison W. Whalen, born July 9, 1934, Correction Officer

HOSTAGES

Raymond Bogart	James Clute
Robert Curtis	Richard Delaney
Richard Fargo	Elmer Huehn
Don Jennings	Gordon Kelsey
Frank Kline	Gordon Knickerbocker
Ronald Kozlowski	Paul Krotz
Larry Lyons	Donald Melven
Edward Miller	Al Mitzel
Royal Morgan	Anthony Prave
Gerald Reger	Al Robbins
Paul Rosecrans	Anthony Sangiacomo
Arthur Smith	Michael Smith
John Stockholm	Frank Strollo
Robert Van Buren	Frank Wald
Gary Walker	Philip Watkins
Walter Zymkowski	

INMATES KILLED PRIOR TO THE RETAKING

Michael Privetera – a cop killer whose mind had deteriorated to the point that he didn't know where he was most of the time. He was killed because he hit another inmate on the head with a stick. His throat was slit.

Kenneth Hess - his throat was slit and he was stabbed multiple times because he tried to get a note to negotiator telling of the atrocities being committed in the D-block galleries where negotiators didn't get to go.

David Schwartz – his throat was slit for no reason.

ATTICA RIOT FACTS

Survivors compiled a list of what they considered myths and facts surrounding the bloodiest action by an American government on U.S. soil since the Civil War.

Except for William Quinn, who died of injuries inflicted by inmates during the initial uprising on Sept. 9, all fatalities among the hostages were as a result of state gunfire during the retaking on Sept. 13, 1971.

No hostage was castrated.

After the initial uprising, no hostage was harmed by inmates up until the time of the retaking.

Death benefits received by widows were no different than had their husbands died a natural death.

Surviving correction officers and civilian employees held hostage were given time off with pay, not knowing the paychecks they received were funded by workmen's compensation.

All but one of these families unknowingly lost their right to sue the State of New York by accepting death benefits or workers compensation funds.

No one has ever been held responsible for what happened at Attica or its aftermath.

Several years later, Governor Hugh Carey granted blanket amnesty to everyone involved in the Attica Riot. After years of grand juries and litigation, he wanted the Attica episode to finally be put to rest. He felt this was the best way to resolve the issues.

I have learned that in the case of willful murder, amnesty can only be granted to named individuals. There being no statute of limitations for murder, the Wyoming County District Attorney or the New York State Attorney General can at anytime prosecute individuals if they find sufficient evidence to do so.

JUNE 21, 1972 - FLOODS IN SOUTHERN TIER

On June 21, 1972 at 5:30 AM, off duty trooper Jake Stewart living in the Village of Almond, N.Y. was awakened by a neighbor reporting that a man (later identified as John Ide) and his infant child disappeared in rapidly moving flood waters, when a boat they were in capsized while attempting to get to higher ground. Heavy rains during the night turned calm streams into raging rivers causing water to rise 65 to 70 feet. Torrential rains continued for the next three days and nights. Troopers from the Bath barracks led in the evacuation of all residents from the Village of Almond to the Alfred-Almond High School where they remained for the next seven days. Food and necessities were flown in by State Police helicopter. A State Police Command Post was established at Corning to co-ordinate all search and rescue efforts in the southern tier. State police helicopters completed many rescues and at the same time kept the command center informed of the direction of fast moving currents.

When the flooding subsided, troopers continued their search and recovery efforts of drowning victims. The bodies of John Ide and his daughter were never recovered.

Retired Trooper Louis Reitnauer recalled that when the flooding started, John Ide, his wife Dorothy and two daughters Amy and Rene resided above a service station he operated in Almond. They were upstairs when apparently a can of white gas stored in the garage tipped over, spilling the contents due to the rising floodwaters. John and his family evacuated the building using a small boat. On Main Street, the rapidly moving water level reached a depth of about 18 inches. The boat struck a utility pole, overturned and threw the four into the fast moving waters. Dorothy and Rene grabbed onto a tree limb and awaited rescue while John and daughter Amy were swept away. The floodwaters were captured in the Almond Dam several miles downstream, but the bodies were never recovered. Trooper Jake Stewart and a Hornell Fireman rescued Dorothy and Rene. Troopers working during the flood in Almond area were Jake Stewart, Lou Reitnauer, Ted Root and Paul Johnson who resided in the immediate area. The troopers worked until they literally dropped from exhaustion during the flood emergency.

1972 FLOODS - SOUTHERN TIER

1972 FLOOD - ALFRED ALMOND

UNITED PRESS INTERNATIONAL

Woman whose husband and child drowned is rescued from creek.

BLIZZARD OF 1977

Thursday, January 26, 1977, started out like most days on the flat plain north of Batavia where the new Troop "A" Headquarters was located. The sky during the morning was not unusual with a clear blue sky. Staff had planned on leaving work at noon, because the weather reports were predicting a snowstorm for later in the afternoon. Linda (McCabe) Beeman and Nancy (Pfaff) Smith were standing at the back (employee's) door, when both the front (visitor's) door and the back door blew open at the same time. It was unbelievable. The pressure was so great and wind so horrific with heavy snow, that their vision was completely obscured. Shortly before noon, Troop Commander, Major Richard Boland and F/Sgt. Vernon Clayson had gone to the nearby Treadway Motel for lunch. A few snow flurries began to fall, but that was not unusual for Western New York in January. Exiting the restaurant, there was no indication that a snowstorm was in progress because nothing seemed out of the ordinary. That changed abruptly. Crossing the New York State Thruway bridge on northbound Route 98, they were greeted by a curtain of heavy snow driven by wind gusts estimated at 70 mph. Traveling in a marked Troop car with Clayson driving, they continued their trek with all available lights turned on. It was like nothing ever before encountered. Thinking they might be able to see better by looking out the window, they ran the window down and were met by the blinding, swirling wind driven snow that practically tore the air from their lungs. Unable to see, Major Boland got out and walked ahead of the car to avert driving into a ditch or into another vehicle. They inched along for perhaps a hundred yards until coming upon a truck-car accident in the southbound lane. The barely visible drivers were standing in the road exchanging information. They advised that the vehicles were operable and were told to drive on into town and exchange their information there. Continuing northbound, they came upon a frightened young woman with two children stuck in a snowdrift. A vehicle behind her with three young men resolved the problem by driving her car into town. Finally turning onto West Saile Drive, the wind was now at their back and visibility improved. Entering the east driveway, they were met by a huge snowdrift. They both abandoned the car and ran to the safety of the building.

The temperature hovered around 10 degrees with a chill factor of minus 50 degrees.

Staff, members and civilians were concerned with the monumental storm and how it would affect their daily routines. Most believed it would blow over soon, however, it turned out that most remained until the storm subsided on Monday, January 31st. Staff secretary Brenda McCoy insisted on leaving even when told not to. She went into the parking lot with its blinding snow, but was unable to find her car or way back into the barracks. She finally made it back through a back door.

Dorothy Coughlin, an English teacher from Elba N.Y. returning home from Batavia drove to the barracks where she sought shelter. She had been grocery shopping and offered her groceries to those at the barracks. Thank goodness for her groceries. If not for her, nourishment would have been limited to food from a coin machine in the lunchroom. She had a ham, oatmeal and many other things that she prepared for everyone. I'm sure she recalled her adventure fondly even though she became the chief cook and bottle washer. Fortunately, a sufficient supply of coffee, bottled water, tea and hot chocolate were available.

The communication section supervised by T/Sgt. Gary Law handled radio and an overwhelming amount of telephone calls without letup for the entire period of the emergency. Clerical employees were utilized to handle the influx of calls from concerned citizens. People sought information on weather and road conditions, as well as seeking fuel, food and medicine. Calls were received seeking help in locating persons lost in the blizzard and seeking assistance for themselves after becoming stranded. Communications personnel were placed on a duty schedule of four-hours on - four- hours off.

They coordinated the hundreds of calls for help with civilians who volunteered their four wheel drive vehicles, snowmobiles and services during the emergency. Emergency services, highway departments and fire departments interacted where needed if humanly possible.

While most of the staff was occupied, Major Boland, Captains George Tordy, Hank Williams and Lieutenant Sam Slade conferred in their offices concluding that nothing supervisory could be accomplished, as trooper and civilian staff members were making decisions on dozens of telephones and radios.

Sleeping accommodations were varied with some sleeping in the bedrooms and others sleeping on the floor or chairs in the employee lounge. Beds were taken apart and the mattresses placed on the floor. Stanley Sochalec, the building maintenance supervisor had taken the day off and was unable to return for work due to the storm. The oil lines weren't functioning properly and had to be siphoned to get oil flowing. One line would start running and another line would fail. The lines were too small for the job. At least the generator for the building worked faultlessly although it did not provide electricity to some parts of the building when commercial power was interrupted. Late one night, the thermostat went bonkers with the temperature rising to about 90 degrees. It was very hot. On another occasion, the snow was blowing into the building through the heating units.

The front door was unusable because the drifting snow could not be shoveled fast enough to keep it open. The only accessible building doors were the east garage door & the patrol room door.

The only four-wheel drive vehicle at the barracks was the Troop "A" dog wagon assigned to Trooper Leon Dywinski who was at the barracks when the storm hit. Some troopers that made it back to the barracks told of their troop cars being stuck and completely buried in the snow. On the second day and desperate for toiletries and a change of under garments, Nancy Smith, Linda Beeman and Sergeant Walter Purtell convinced Trooper Dywinski to drive them into town hoping to find an open store. The mission was accomplished, when the Ames Department store's manager who was stranded accommodated them. They were able to purchase several needed items for those stranded at the barracks. They also found an open liquor store purchasing a few liquid refreshments.

The New York States Department of Transportation (DOT) left a light truck at the barracks for snowplowing purposes. It was a single axel dual wheeled truck with plow. Maintenance employee Russell Chilano and Trooper Dywinski got into the truck and proceeded to save the Barracks. They got about 10 feet from the building and according to Dywinski, "couldn't see crap". It took the better part of an hour to back the truck into the garage without hitting the glass panels on each side of the overhead door.

A short time later, a tandem axel 10-wheel State DOT plow with a wing was trying to clear the barracks driveway, when it got stuck. Trooper Leon Dywinski and Mechanic Bill Joyce did their best to free the plow without success. The two DOT employees, unable to leave, slept over night at the barracks.

Trooper Dywinski also struggled daily when going to the kennel less than 100 feet away from the main building to feed and check on the bloodhounds. He had to stand flat against the kennel wall and wait for the wind to subside so he could open the door.

Two Division helicopters arrived on Sunday the 30th, and were used for searches and observation. F/Sgt. Clayson volunteered to go along on one flight with Pilot Joe Bendo and Gary Law went out in the other aircraft. Bendo's skills were almost magical during the flight in adverse weather conditions. He couldn't recall the name of the other pilot, but his abilities were just as proficient.

The first employee to leave was Lana Cummings. Her husband retrieved her on a snowmobile on the second day of the storm. The next to leave was Captain Hank Williams. In typical Hank Williams fashion, he drove off into the wind and snow with his window down, heading for Buffalo. The others straggled out as best they could over the following days.

Trooper's Don Kozlowski and Fred Walsh caught in the storm stayed with Troop "T" Z/Sgt. Bob Minekheim at his home in Batavia. None being a masterful cook, it was decided that they would make a pot of chicken soup. The nearby Tops store provided a chicken for flavor. Bringing a pot of water to a boil, the entire chicken was placed into the pot, feet, head and all else. Needless to say, the soup was never consumed.

Investigators Henry Haas and Gerry Weiss managed to get stranded at SP Batavia. On the second day, they made their way to the Treadway Inn in Batavia. While there, they shared a room with Sgt Ward Barrows and few other stranded troopers. It was real cozy. On the third day, Haas decided to try and make it the seven miles to the Pike Road where he lived. He took the plowed Route 98 South turning onto Pike Road. He quickly found the Pike Road snow covered from hours of driving snow. He recalled that he had to continue, because it was impossible to turn around. It was difficult to determine where the road shoulders ended and the fields started. He used the telephone poles to his right side as a guide and managed to stay on the roadway. He came to a point where the "dirty" telephone company crossed the highway placing the poles on the left side. Needless to say, he drove fifty feet off the road way into an open snow covered field. He was thankful that he was in a Troop, BCI car, and radioed for a tow truck. An old pal, "Ajax" (Ira Hale) and his tow truck showed up and winched him out at no charge. He returned to the Treadway Inn where at least he had food & shelter.

Sadly, a number of lives were lost, some from exposure in and near their stranded vehicles. One death during the worst part of the storm, although not necessarily caused by the storm, was that of Investigator Nick Fitzak's mother in rural Orleans County. The family was cut off from help and while Fitzak called for help, there was no way to get in or out. Another incident left everyone with a feeling of helplessness when a man that called for help was found dead, because there was no way for help to get to him. When found, he was nowhere near where he thought he was.

Hundreds of cars were abandoned and completely buried by the snow. Nancy Smith recalled that after the storm passed, she found that the vinyl seats in her car had cracked due to the cold temperatures.

Major Boland instructed Nancy (Pfaff) Smith and Linda (McCabe) Beeman to leave the barracks on Sunday. Trooper Leon Dywinski drove them both to their Wyoming County homes in the four-wheel drive truck. He was able to maneuver the twenty miles of drifted roads. It was a long treacherous trip that took several hours. None of the roads were officially open with the wind still blowing.

Trooper Louis J. Lang was on patrol in southern Genesee County, when the blizzard struck. He personally transported over 100 persons to shelter in the Alexander Fire Department Recreation Hall that were forced to abandon their vehicles on the treacherous Route 20. With the able assistance of the Alexander and Attica Town snowplows, he was able to transport a woman who had miscarried and was stuck on Route 98 between Alexander and Batavia. He painstakingly got her to the residence of Attica Doctor Myron Williams for treatment and care. Dr. Williams made himself available and provided countless care during the storm's duration with little, if any sleep.

There were countless rescues and mercy missions performed by troopers, volunteers, hospital caregivers, fire departments and highway departments. Each a hero to the person helped in a time of need. Many unforgettable acts of individual bravery, unselfishness and kindness took place earning the respect and applause of the community.

Article Contributors:

Linda (McCabe) Beeman, Secretary/Nancy (Pfaff) Smith, Secretary
Howard Hartman, Communication Specialist/Vernon Clayson, F/Sgt., NYSP
Leon Dywinski, Trooper/Louis J. Lang, Trooper/Henry Haas, Investigator

STORM OF 1977
REAR DOOR AT TROOP HQ.

185

WINTER OLYMPICS LAKE PLACID, N.Y. - 1980

The accepted date of the first Olympics is 776 B.C. held at Olympia, Greece. The Olympic Festival was held every four years until 393 A.D., when Greece lost its independence to the Romans.

Baron Pierre de Coubertin of France revived the modern Olympic Games. They were held at Athens, Greece in 1896 with nine countries participating.

Winter Olympic events were held for the first time in 1920 at Antwerp, Belgium. Since 1924, these winter games have been held during February preceding the regular Olympic events at various winter resorts around the world. No Olympic Game's were held during 1940 and 1944 due to World War II.

PLANNING
The International Olympic Committee selected Lake Placid, New York, as the site for the 1980 Winter Olympic games. Lake Placid was also home of the 1932 Olympic Games.

On January 18, 1977, the New York State Police was assigned as the agency responsible for coordinating and planning of security for the games. Security included the physical security of athletes, trainers, coaches, officials and spectators along with traffic control, area policing and emergency services. It was anticipated that 54,000 spectators would visit the various venues daily. The emergency service detail was responsible for preparing a comprehensive document to be followed in the event of a disaster or serious disruption of events and to coordinate all rescue squads, fire departments and other services on a day-to-day basis.

The state police planning committee researched all areas of disaster and rescue methods and determined the level of emergency equipment and personnel that would be available during the event. Meetings were held with rescue squads, fire departments, the Red Cross, Salvation Army, Travelers Aide Society, hospitals and NYS Health and Transportation Departments. These meetings resulted in an operational plan tailored to the specific needs of each agency represented. The plan became a regional disaster plan after the Olympics.

It was determined that in all probability, the health department and local rescue squads were the core of emergency services and would be most used during the games. Training sessions were held giving various departments an opportunity to become familiar with one another and methods used. Training courses included hypothermia, triage, vehicle extraction and fighting propane fires. Because of the volunteer status of the local fire and rescue squads, arrangements were made to provide additional manpower. A 911 system was installed prior to the opening of the games that would ring directly into the command center.

SERVICES RENDERED
The disaster plan was used during the handling of a small aircraft crash near the Lake Clear Airport. The pilot and two passengers were airlifted to hospitals, but expired from hypothermia and injuries received during the crash. It was again used during the first five days of the games, when severe busing problems to and from parking areas left spectators stranded and exposed to the below zero elements.

From February 13th to 24th, rescue squads responded to 128 calls requiring hospital transportation, 134 automobile accidents and 134 other incidents. The fire department responded to 25 fire calls.

American Red Cross activity was centered at parking lots where 187 spectators were assisted with hypothermia, frostbite, lacerations and abrasions. Poorly marked buses and lack of scheduled busing and pick up locations in sub zero temperatures were primary causes.

The Salvation Army utilizing their mobile canteens served 26,146 spectators and staff personnel with hot coffee, soups and hot chocolates.

The Capitol District Travelers Aid Society assisted 994 with temporary shelter and transportation.

The Department of Transportation responsible for towing had 441 vehicles removed that interfered with the smooth traffic flow.

(FBI Law Enforcement Bulletin – April 1981 – Lt. Leigh Hunt, NYSP, Author)

OLYMPIC SECURITY DRY RUN - 1976

Anticipating the safeguarding of participants and spectators at the 1980 Winter Olympics, the Division assigned 225 troopers to a "dry run" protection of Olympic athletes training at SUNY Plattsburg for the 1976 Montreal Summer Olympics. During a three-week period, the detail provided protection for 700 athletes and coaches, as they ate, slept and trained at the complex. Additional security was provided when President Gerald Ford visited the athletes. A $335,000 federal grant funded the detail.

A combined unit made up of Division helicopters and the Mobile Response Team maintained perimeter security. The unit maintained electronic sensor monitors and practiced rappelling for special situations.

LAKE PLACID SECURITY

The 1980 Olympic Security detail was assigned to the very capable Inspector Nicholas Giangualano who coordinated the joint State Police, Secret Service (Gilbert Paraschos) and FBI (Ervin Recer) detail. Giangualano had earned a reputation for thoroughness and attention to detail. Training sessions were given in dignitary protection, counterfeiting, hostage negotiations and terrorist management. Manpower included 950 troopers, 160 conservation officers and 300 Pinkerton security guards. Due to extreme cold weather, work shifts were limited to an 8-hour day. Each trooper was on call for four hours at the end of each shift.

The US Army under the command of Colonel Van Halladay provided electronic underground sensors at key locations in and around the Olympic area. Two fences' each 12 feet high and spaced twenty feet apart surrounded the Olympic Village and were wired to detect vibration, climbing and cutting. Two radar units scanned the wood-line near the command center. Twelve monitor cameras videotaped the most sensitive areas.

Two supervisors from nine troop divisions attended early instruction and indoctrination meetings and were provided with maps, manuals and techniques. They returned to their troops where they provided training to an average of 100 troopers. The Olympic village, home of the athletes and coaches was converted to a state prison after the Olympics. A new facility at Raybrook 5 miles from Lake Placid was the Command Central headquarters. This facility became the Troop "B" headquarters after the Olympics.

An accreditation system using colors, letters and access area symbols were introduced. They were laminated and worn around the neck on a chain. Each contained identification information and areas the holder could enter.

187

Biosensor dogs were utilized to detect explosives and drugs. Nine troopers handled nine dogs that sanitized the Olympic Village prior to occupancy. They inspected all incoming cargo and deliveries, provided perimeter security and inspected athletes entering the village.

CAMP ADIRONDACK

Troopers and Conservation Officers were mainly housed at Camp Adirondack under the command of Captain Blake Muthig. These were two, three story brick buildings that previously had been tuberculosis sanatoriums converted to a state prison. In November 1979, PBA members found many unsanitary conditions where the 700-man security detail would be housed. Sixty to seventy troopers would be in an area serviced by only four showers, six toilets and six sinks. Another area would provide for twenty-two men with only one shower, one toilet and one sink. No storage or shelving was available for storage of personal items. A letter was sent to Governor Hugh Carey that resulted in six million dollars being spent to refurbish the buildings, repave roads and install a new water supply. Troopers dubbed it "Camp Swampy". Recreational facilities, a Rathskellar named " Home of 1,000 Animals" and cafeteria style dining facility were located within the housing units. A huge cafeteria opened around the clock provided hot meals and snacks and proved to be of excellent quality and quantity. The rooms were equipped with bunk beds and slept two, four or six to a room. On February 15th, this writer was designated as the Police Benevolent Association (PBA) representative assigned at the Olympics to help resolve any issues. A major complaint was the inability to get into Lake Placid five miles away due to lack of transportation. Off duty troopers had no access to events and were unable to mutually change shifts within the same venue.

I had never met Captain Muthig and found him to be by the book and a bit hostile toward me initially. He followed housing directives to the letter and resisted any deviation. He finally realized that I was there to work with him and made whatever subtle changes were needed to make everyone happy when possible. I'm sure he checked my credentials with Inspector Giangualano whom I worked for while he was at Batavia, N.Y. In short order, hourly bus transportation was provided for troopers to travel back and forth to Lake Placid while off duty, mutual shift changes within the venue were allowed and tickets as well as access to non-filled events were made available. The PBA established a check cashing service with a twenty-five dollar limit cashing several thousand dollars worth of checks.

Nine troopers were returned to their home troop from the Olympic detail. Three for disciplinary procedures receiving troop commanders punishment and six due to illness or injury.

TROOPER INJURED

Trooper Howard Finn Jr., was injured on February 13th, when he stopped a car driven by the owner of the Adirondack Inn. When asked for identification, he swore at the trooper stepping on the gas just as Finn reached into his window. Finn was dragged down the street for 100 feet. The man was arrested and charged with Assault 2nd degree. Finn was returned to his troop to recover.

MOON BOOTS

With bitter cold temperatures and below zero wind chill factor, one of the most important questions was how to keep the troopers on post without suffering frostbite and other related cold weather problems. The answer was "MOON BOOTS". They were made of from soft, pliable foam with about a 3-inch thick sole and wrapped above the ankle. They really were a lifesaver.

US HOCKEY TRIO VISIT SWAMPY

Troopers assigned to guard athletes adopted the USA Hockey team, as their own. On the eve of the game for a possible gold medal after beating the Russian team 4 to 3, this writer persuaded three of the USA Olympic Hockey players to visit Camp Adirondack and fete the troopers. Left-winger Phil

Verchota, second goalie Steve Janaszak and defensemen Mike Ramsey arrived to a standing ovation by the 150 troopers present. They signed autographs, posed for pictures and chatted with everyone. It proved to be a memorable occasion. This writer had earlier discussed their appearance with Captain Muthig and he agreed that it would be a good moral booster. It was better than anticipated. The next day, the US Hockey team won the gold medal by beating Finland 4 to 2.

TROOPERS TAKE CHARGE

As Slalom events ended at Mt. Van Hoevenberg, thousands of spectators moved slowly to transportation sites in the bitter cold weather finding no buses available due to a traffic-snarl up. Frustration soon turned to anger. Trooper John E. King (Brewster) climbed on top of a 55-gallon drum and began singing. Surprised spectators soon joined him in song after song until transportation arrived calming what could have been a serious situation. Trooper's sensitivity showed when they kept older persons and children warm in their trooper cars. Troopers also forced open a locked VIP lounge so spectators could come in from the cold.

A transportation plan had been adopted banning almost all cars from the Olympic area. Parking areas were established on the perimeter with buses available to transport spectators. Unfortunately, it was a disaster. The NYS Police informally took over transportation to get spectators to various venues as quickly and safely as possible. With unfailing courtesy and good organization, troopers imposed order on chaotic waiting lines, commandeered buses and put their communications to work getting buses dispatched. In the meantime, the NYS DOT contracted more buses to ease the situation. Major Bob Siek in charge of the Traffic Detail thanked each member of his detail for the admirable manner in which they carried out their duties.

On March 6, 1980, Governor Hugh Carey issued a unit citation to the NYS Police for distinguished service during the Winter Olympics at Lake Placid. Each member was cited for exceptional meritorious conduct, exercise in good judgement, restraint and initiative, which directly insured the safety and well being of all. A service bar was issued that was blue and white in color with the five Olympic rings in the center noting 1980 Olympics.

MY RECOLLECTIONS

I was fortunate in that I was there representing the Police Benevolent Association (PBA). This gave me the freedom to come and go as I pleased and I took complete advantage of it. I had security credentials, but was independent from the Division in that I had my personal car on location and wore civilian clothing. The credentials gave me access to almost all venues. The actual events usually took place in the afternoon or evening with mornings set aside for practice and warm ups by the athletes. I would take care of business with Captain Blake Muthig during the morning hours, and then was off to either the skating complex where I met Linda Fratianni and the team of Randy Gardner and Tai Babalonia, the US ice skating champions. The speed skating rink was at the rear of a school in Lake Placid and had access to the roof where I witnessed Eric Heiden win his five Olympic Gold Medals in speed skating. The greatest thrill of all was being able to witness the US Hockey teams victory over the Russian team and two days later, winning the gold medal by beating Finland. I had access to the locker room area where I would talk with coach Herb Brooks between periods. An interesting note is that he never entered the locker room between periods. He let the players make their own adjustments to their game plan. I was also fortunate to hang out with US Hockey players Steve Janaszak; back up goalie, Phil Verchota, left winger, Kenny Morrow, defensemen and Mike Ramsey, defensemen during their time off.

Just being a part of the Winter Olympics was awesome, but meeting and talking with the many athletes gave me memories that will forever be etched in my mind.

No 26827

ALBERT S. KUREK

TROOPER

NYSP

SECURITY
1980 OLYMPIC ID CARD

INSPECTOR N. GIANUALANO - 1980 OLYMPICS
W/ YUGOSLAV REPRESENTATIVE

1980 OLYMPICS HOUSING - CAMP SWAMPY

OLYMPIC HOCKEY PLAYES - CAPT MUTHIG- M.RAMSEY- S.JANAZAK- P.VERCHOTA- AL KUREK

1980 – WINTER OLYMPICS, LAKE PLACID, NEW YORK
USA vs RUSSIA HOCKEY - USA WON 4 TO 3

OLYMPIC HOCKEY PLAYER - MIKE RAMSEY

1980 OLYMPICS
FIGURE SKATER LINDA FRATIANNE
AL KUREK

DON MUNDY
AL KUREK
PAT O"REILLY

BOOK VI — BITS AND PIECES

1940 TID BITS

TROOPER QUALIFICATIONS - 1940

In the early 1940s, qualifications to become a trooper required the filling out of an application and returning it to Division Headquarters at Albany, N.Y. The candidate had to be between ages 21 and 40, at least 5'9" tall, free of all physical defects, physically strong and active. He could have no dental defects, no criminal record and required satisfactory hearing, excellent vision and an operator's license to drive in New York State. A minimal acceptable education was graduation from a Senior High School. Upon acceptance, the candidate had to be willing to serve anywhere in the state.

CAR THIEVES CAPTURED

On April 28, 1942, three Akron, Ohio youths were arrested after leading troopers on an hour-long chase at speeds in excess of 100 MPH. The pursuit started in Niagara Falls and led Troopers Albert J. Mazziotta and Florence J. Driscoll through the Tonawanda's, Buffalo, Amherst and Clarence. The car had been reported stolen at Akron, Ohio the night before.

TROOP "L" - 1943

Twelve troopers had patrolled Long Island since 1917 operating out of Bay Shore, Suffolk County and were commonly referred to as the "Sunrise Trail Detachment". In 1928, they were re-organized as the Long Island Detail of Troop "K" based in Babylon, N.Y. During 1943, Troop "L" encompassing Long Island was brought into existence with Troop Headquarters located at Babylon, N.Y. This was short lived, as the troop once again reverted to being Troop "K". Troopers were non - existent with policing taken over by the local sheriff's offices and the New York State Parks Police. It wasn't until January 1980, when legislation provided for a merger of the State Park Police into the State Police that Troop "L" was formally established, as it is known today.

TROOP "A" STATIONS – 1943

Batavia   -   Telephone Batavia 2200 – 2201 *

Substations	Telephone
Athol Springs	Wanakah 400 *
Clarence	Clarence 3181
Westfield	Westfield 346 *
Silver Creek	Silver Creek 193-W
Lewiston	Niagara Falls 8082 *
Newfane	Newfane 3711
Martinsville	North Tonawanda 1222-R
East Aurora	East Aurora 63-J
East Avon	Avon 3131 *
Pittsford	Pittsford 23
Churchville	Churchville 635
Gaines	Albion 63
Painted Post	Corning 1563 *
North Hornell	Hornell 1792
Friendship	Friendship 2121 *
Castile	Castile 14 *
Allegany	Allegany 191
Franklinville	Franklinville 4-R

*Denotes Teletype Station

TROOPER LAWRENCE C. NORSEN
On October 15, 1944, Trooper Lawrence Norsen escaped serious injury, when he leaped from his motorcycle as an automobile pulled in front of him. The car driven by Reverend Francis Sullivan of Albion, N.Y. was turning into the St. Joseph's Cemetery. No charges were placed against the 85-year-old priest, as it was raining and visibility was poor. Norsen was treated at Arnold Gregory Hospital for lacerations of the left knee, bruises and shock.

TROOPER CHARGED WITH BRIBERY
On December 8, 1944, Trooper Barnett Wagner Campbell, age 38, Syracuse, N.Y. was arrested for Accepting a Bribe in violation of Section 372 of the Penal Law. He was freed on $5,000.00 bail. It was alleged Campbell accepted a $155.00 bribe from a farm worker and his wife after their arrest on a minor charge. Campbell, a 7-year veteran trooper was stationed at Williamson in Wayne County. The case was transferred to Steuben County where Campbell pled guilty to the bribery charge on March 6th, 1945. Supreme Court Judge Lewis A. Gilbert sentenced him to Attica Prison for a term of one to three years suspended, placed him on probation to John Newton, Wayne County, N.Y. and fined him $250.00. At the time of his conviction, his occupation was noted as laborer indicating that he had already been dismissed from the State Police.

197

TROOPER CAR KILLS PEDESTRIAN – 1945

On October 27, 1945, John J. Bausch, age 67, 36 Columbia Avenue, Batavia, N.Y. was instantly killed when struck by a state police car near the intersection of West Main and River Streets. Corporal Percy Leitner was returning to the barracks and driving the State Police car. Leitner reported that he was traveling in an easterly direction at about 25 MPH, when Bausch ran in front of him from behind a parked car on the south side of the road. Leitner swerved to his right but could not avoid striking the man. Witnesses verified the accident description.

EMERGENCY TELEPHONE SERVICE

On July 1, 1945, the state police initiated a new 24-hour telephone service whereby a person could immediately call the troopers without charge in an emergency by simply calling or dialing an operator and simply saying, **"I WANT A STATE TROOPER"**

Captain Joseph B. Lynch announced that the following barracks would remain open 24-hours daily to receive emergency calls. Batavia, Athol Springs, Lewiston, West Henrietta, East Avon, Friendship, Westfield and Painted Post.

The program was designed to provide the public with an immediate and more efficient link to the troopers. Operators would send the calls to the nearest station. Previously, callers were charged for the phone-call before it was forwarded.

TROOPER JOHN BRADY

On January 17, 1946, Trooper John Brady received the **"Legion Of Merit"** from Major General Maxwell Taylor, Superintendent at West Point, N.Y. It was awarded to Brady for his work in breaking up a "Black Market Ring" in Algiers where he served as a Master Sergeant in the US Army during World War II.

SERGEANT CHARLES COBB HEADS BATAVIA POLICE

On February 11, 1946, Sergeant Charles E. Cobb replaced Batavia Police Chief Herbert L. Snyder, as the Department's Police Chief. The Batavia City Council made a request of the Superintendent of State Police to have an experienced officer assigned to help re-organize the department. Cobb made major policy changes and established a training center that each officer was required to attend.

CALEDONIA, N.Y. 1946

New York State Troopers are required to enforce all laws. One of many is the Conservation Law that was enacted to provide for the protection and propagation of wildlife. The "Poacher" was a serious menace to the efforts of preserving wildlife existence.

On the night of April 24, 1946, Trooper Andrew C. Fisher assigned at East Avon received a telephone call reporting shots being heard near the Genesee River at Caledonia, N.Y. After secreting his car in a wooded area, Trooper Fisher proceeded towards the river on foot. He apprehended one man in the woods who admitted that he and two companions were "jack lighting" geese by using a portable searchlight. The two companions were located and also placed under arrest. Confiscated were several shotguns, ammunition and ten dead geese. The geese are startled and become motionless, when a bright light is shined in their eyes. All three paid large fines.

CATTLE THEFT FINANCES HONEYMOON

Sidney James Hutton, age 28, Roanoke, N.Y. was charged with Grand Larceny, when he and his new bride returned from a honeymoon in the Georgian Bay area of Canada. On June 21, 1947, the unemployed veteran stole eight black and white heifers from his neighbors, Paul and Jay Legg of the Bethany-Leroy Road. The cattle valued at $900.00 were sold to a livestock dealer for $495.00. Hutton was arraigned before Stafford Town Justice Frank W. March and held for grand jury action. All the heifers were recovered. On November 8, 1946, Hutton pled guilty to a charge of Grand Larceny 2ⁿᵈ Degree and was sentenced to a term of one year in the Genesee County Jail suspended.

TROOPER EXAMINATION - 1948
An open examination for Trooper was given on September 15,1948 at several locations throughout the state. The starting salary was advertised at $1380.00 plus lodging, food or an allowance in lieu thereof and all service clothing and equipment. Approximately 100 immediate appointments would be made. Requirements were:

A United States Citizen.
Between the ages of 21 and 40 years.
Sound constitution.
Not less than 5 feet 10 inches in bare feet.
Free of physical defects.
Physically strong, active & well proportioned.
Weight in proportion to build.
No disease of mouth or tongue. No dental caries, unless corrected; no missing incisor teeth. Reject if more than three teeth are missing, unless they could be replaced.
Satisfactory hearing.
Color perception and satisfactory eyesight; no ocular disease.
Good moral character and habits.
Mental alertness and soundness of mind.
Minimum education, senior high school graduate or equivalent.
License to operate motor vehicles in the state.
No conviction for a crime.

The examination consisted of a written examination testing general knowledge; an oral interview to determine mental alertness, soundness of mind, initiative, intelligence, judgment, address and appearance and a physical examination. An investigation of moral character was also conducted.

ATTICA GAMBLING RAID
During February 1949, a detail of troopers comprised of Sergeants George Wood, Charles Cobb, Corporal Albert Horton and Trooper Charles Richmond, acting on numerous complaints raided the Ringwood's Smoke Shop, 8 Market Street, Attica, N.Y. where a stud poker game was in progress. Louis B. (Gus) Ringwood, age 48, the proprietor and eleven others were arrested. All were arraigned before Justice of the Peace Arthur Stephens with Ringwood paying a $50.00 fine as a common gambler and ten of the eleven fined $5.00 for Disorderly Conduct. One pled not guilty providing $5.00 bail.

Justice Stephens, an Attica Prison Guard refused to divulge the names of the participants stating that it would be embarrassing to them. He felt that publicity was not warranted, as no serious crime had been committed. He compared it to receiving a parking ticket.

KIDNAPPING
On December 23, 1946, Mrs. Lyle Mark, 40 Elm Street, found a twelve-year old Rochester girl crying in the streets of Batavia, N.Y. Her eye was badly swollen and she was bleeding from a cut under her eye. Investigation disclosed the girl and her brother had gone Christmas shopping in Rochester, N.Y. While watching a street vendor demonstration, they were approached by a man who asked if she

would like to earn $5.00 by babysitting his children for an hour. She agreed and got into his car. The boy was given a dollar and dropped off at a store and told to wait there for his sister. Once inside the car, the man drove directly out into the open country where he ordered her to perform unnatural sex acts upon his person. When she refused and began screaming, he struck her in the face causing her glasses to break, cutting her face. He threatened to hit her again. Badly frightened, she did as she was told. She was kept in the car until darkness being forced to commit acts of sodomy and other sexual perversion. He then drove to Batavia where he left her.

She gave a description of the man, as well as identifying his car as a Plymouth Coupe. It was learned that another girl had been approached earlier in the day, but refused to get into the car. Many other similar incidents had been reported to local police departments providing similar descriptions of the assailant and his car. Five cases were reported in Buffalo, N.Y.

On March 16, 1947, an eighteen-year old Brocton, N.Y. girl called police, when she recognized a man with two young girls at a local store. It was the same man that had enticed her into his automobile during September 1946, raped her and released her near a Dunkirk, N.Y. bus stop. Fearing criticism for getting into the car, she did not report the crime. She feared for the safety of the girls when she saw the man with his arms around the two girls. She notified the Brocton, N.Y. Police who detained and questioned the man regarding his attempt to entice the two twelve-year old girls into his automobile. During questioning, he was permitted to go to the bathroom at which time he jumped into his Plymouth automobile and fled the scene. The officer had gotten the man's name and wrote down the license plate number. The State Police were requested to assist. A criminal records check indicated the man had multiple arrests along the east coast and Canada and was a suspect in similar criminal acts. A loose surveillance of the suspect's home resulted, when information determined that he had left the area, but would soon return.

On May 9, 1947, Charles R. Dow, age 49 of Sheridan, N.Y. was arrested by Sergeant Donald Girven. After questioning and confrontation by many of his victims, Dow admitted to the many assaults attributed to him and admitted to many others that he could not clearly remember. He was arraigned in Genesee County on a charge of Kidnapping, Sodomy and Assault. He pled guilty to a charge of kidnapping and was sentenced to life imprisonment at Attica Prison. (1947 Annual Reports)

TROOPER CHARLES DAY
Charles A. Day, a trooper assigned at Troop "A", Batavia, N.Y. while on active duty with the US Army Military Police had risen through the ranks and upon discharge from the U.S. Army, had attained the rank of Colonel. In 1947, he re-applied for re-enlistment in the State Police and was the highest ranking military man in the organization. Day opted not to return to the troopers taking advantage of business opportunity.

LAST HORSE PATROLS
What had only 30 years earlier been the only means of transportation for the troopers was now another memory and part of their proud history and tradition. The early troopers patrolled exclusively by horseback traveling 15 to 20 miles daily. With the increase and development of the automobile and continued highway improvement and expansion, the horse was utilized less and less. They were used through the 1920s and 1930s during wintertime, when road conditions were not conducive to automobile or motorcycle patrol. The last record of miles patrolled by horse was recorded in 1947, when it was noted that 2115 miles had been patrolled on horseback.

TROOPER WORK SCHEDULE
Troopers were on call 24 hours a day. They had one night off a week and received a monthly four-day pass. They also enjoyed a four-week annual vacation that was required to be taken during winter months. Troopers that were assigned to substations were required to reside there.

TYPICAL SHORT NOTICE TRANSFER
This was an actual telegram advising Trooper William J. Byrne that he was transferred.

"WESTERN UNION TELEGRAM July 18, 1947 – 10:13 AM
TO: William J. Byrne – 31 Hollywood Ave, Massapequa, N.Y.

Your transfer to Fonda, New York is effective July 19, 1947, 0800 – Be at Windham on time.
Signed: F.G. Knight"

Trooper Byrne was a PBA representative.

BATAVIA MAN LOSES LEG IN HUNTING ACCIDENT
JANUARY 1949
Trooper Frank Lachnicht was credited with saving the life of 57-year-old Peter Falcone, 112 Jackson Street, Batavia, N.Y. Falcone was hunting rabbits at the Rose Road farm of Norman Bigler with his neighbor, Samuel DeFazio of 104 Jackson Street, when the accident occurred. Falcone said that he tripped over an old wire fence causing the gun to lurch from his grasp and discharge when it hit the ground. The .16 gauge shot struck and shattered his left leg above the knee. DeFazio ran for help with Trooper Lachnicht responding to the scene. He immediately utilized his pistol lanyard as a tourniquet to halt the bleeding. Falcone was taken to Genesee Memorial where it was necessary to amputate the leg.

RIMMER ENDS CRIME SPREE
On June 9, 1949, Trooper William A. Rimmer ended a short lived crime spree that included theft of a car from Buffalo, burglary of Whit's Gun Shop, Fredonia, and armed holdup of the Center Diner, Silver Creek, New York. Philip Logan employed at the diner phoned in the alarm giving a description of the car used. Trooper Rimmer on patrol near Wanakah observed the car and gave pursuit. The car speeded up for several miles before losing control on the slippery highway, skidding sideways coming to rest on its side. The uninjured occupants were taken into custody at gunpoint. Arrested were john R. Swanson, 17 and his cousin Viola M. Hauser, 16 of Buffalo, New York. A 15-year old youth was turned over to juvenile authorities.

TROOPER FRANK LACHNICHT – 1949
On August 13, 1949, at 11:40 PM, Troopers Frank Lachnicht and John Sage were detailed to investigate the alleged sexual solicitation by Fred Decapua and his wife, Santa at the Pat and Mac's Diner, Bergen, N.Y. At about 11:30 PM, Decapua was observed leaving the diner. Lachnicht attempted to stop the car, but it sped away. Lachnicht gave chase stopping the car on the Dublin Road a short distance away. As he approached the vehicle, the vehicle again sped away with Lachnicht jumping onto the running board. With Lachnicht clinging on the left-side running board, Decapua intentionally drove the car against trees knocking the trooper to the ground. He suffered a fractured pelvis and other minor injuries. Decapua, age 29 of Byron, N.Y. then fled the scene. Trooper Sage who had following in a second car found Lachnicht lying on the side of the road. He was transported to a Batavia Hospital by ambulance in critical condition. Decapua was arrested several days after the incident at Rochester, N.Y. He was arraigned on a charge of 2nd Degree Assault and two vice counts, one involving the

compulsory prostitution of his wife Santa and having lived of the funds that she collected from her tricks. He pled guilty to Assault 2nd, a felony and was sentenced on October 14, 1949 to a term of 2 1/2 to 5 years in Attica State Prison. The vice charges were reduced to a misdemeanor with a one-year sentence imposed to run concurrent with the Attica time. As a result of his injuries, Trooper Lachnicht was forced into disability retirement on February 1, 1952.

TROOPER SHOOTOUT – ALLEGANY COUNTY

During October 1949, Maine Game Warden Roland C. Abbott of Bethel, Maine and a Deputy Sheriff were investigating the complaint of a man acting in a strange manner at the Woodland Cemetery, Gilead, Maine. While being questioned, the man drew a .45 caliber automatic pistol from his pocket and shot the game protector. The deputy grappled with the man who dropped the gun, ran to his car and escaped. A search of the camping area disclosed a dead cat and two dogs that had been placed in a copper container, and then soldered it shut. Several personal effects identified the man, as 41-year-old William Furlong Howe of Portland, Maine. It appeared Howe was deranged.

On the early morning of October 11, 1949, Cuba Police Chief Thomas Musto noticed a man asleep in a car parked in the village. When he approached the car and roused the occupant, he was greeted by a sawed off shotgun pressed against his chest. The gunman took the officer's service weapon and attempted to flee in the chief's police car. When he found no keys in the ignition, he fired two shots at the officer. He then fired two shots into the front tires of the police car. He fled the scene stealing a car from nearby resident Fred Swift. Chief Musto gave the alarm by phone. In rapid succession, reports came into the Wellsville State Police station of three stolen cars from men on their way to work in the Cuba area. The last report was that an armed gunman had commandeered a car and forced the driver identified as William Hennessey, to chauffeur him.

At about 7:55 AM, Troopers Theodore Martin, age 48 and F.V. Pumphrey, age 23 observed and overtook the car. Howe seated in the rear of the car smashed out the rear window opening fire from a shotgun at the troopers. The trooper's windshield was smashed and both suffered minor wounds. With Howe's attention directed toward the troopers, Hennessey intentionally drove off the road and up a road bank hoping to roll the car over. Hennessey was thrown from the car that came to rest against a dirt bank on the opposite side of the road. Howe exited the car carrying two shotguns and an automatic pistol. The troopers likewise exited their car and a gun battle ensued. At the same time, Trooper John Cole drove on the scene. Unaware of the gun battle in progress, he halted his car between the troopers and Howe. Cole was warned of the danger and took refuge behind his car. In an attempt to take Cole's car, Howe ran to the car, threw the shotguns on the seat while continuing to shoot his automatic pistol. Cole crept along the side of the car, took aim and shot Howe trough the car window. Howe was instantly killed from a bullet to the chest. All three cars showed extensive damage after being struck with bullets during the shootout. Martin suffered pellet wounds to the legs, arm and head; Pumphrey suffered pellet wounds to his legs and arms while Trooper Cole was uninjured.

Howe, a former mental patient had been acting normally for several years. The catalyst for the above events was the result of Howe's pet cat to which he had been devoted for over thirteen years. He had left home to bury the cat and two pet dogs that he killed out of grief for the cat. The remains had been encased and exteriors coated with tar. Howe traveled to the Woodland Cemetery approximately 150 miles from his home where he was digging a shallow grave with his hands. He planned to bury the containers with the pet remains there. It was at this point that Abbott approached triggering the chain of events.

1950 TID BITS

CORFU AIRPLANE CRASH KILLS TWO – APRIL 24, 1950

On the afternoon of April 24, 1950, an airplane joyride turned to tragedy, when a plane crashed into a farm field killing the pilot, 24-year-old Robert L. Kerr of Medina, N.Y. and 26-year-old Robert L. Smith of Corfu, N.Y. The plane, a light Aeronica two place aircraft plunged immediately to earth after take off from a height of about 100 feet. The scene was a wheat field behind the home of Smith's parents and was witnessed by his mother and wife. Kerr was manager of the A and P store, Medina, N.Y. where Smith also was employed. Kerr flew from the Medina Airport to the Chris Fissler farm near Genesee Street, Corfu to take Smith for his first airplane ride. Benjamin Duschen, age 71, an Allegany Road resident said the engine appeared to quit and the plane plunged straight down just after take off. Genesee County Coroner Sidney McLouth arrived at the scene and pronounced Smith dead from a crushed chest and skull. Kerr died while enroute to St. Jerome's Hospital, Batavia, N.Y. also of a crushed chest and skull. Sergeant C.E. Cobb, G.S. Wood, Corporal A.S. Horton and Trooper M.B. Grant investigated the accident. Smith was a life long Corfu resident graduating from Corfu High School in 1942. He served in the US Navy from 1942 until 1945. Kerr was born in Toledo, Ohio.

TROOPER ROBERT J. CONWAY INJURED

Trooper Robert J. Conway, age 23 assigned at the Darien sub-station was injured on September 5, 1950 after striking a dog. He was patrolling motorcycle on Route 98, Alexander, N.Y., when the large dog owned by Mrs. Mary Mulcahy darted into his path. The dog was killed instantly. Conway suffering cuts and abrasions was treated at the scene and signed off duty to recuperate at his Castile, N.Y. home.

BUFFALO, N.Y. - COURIER EXPRESS ARTICLE - 1951

The State Police of Western New York function 24 hours a day, every day with 130 troopers assigned in the eleven county area. Headquarters for Troop "A" is at Batavia, N.Y. Unlike most city police departments, the troopers force is free of politics. Some members of city police departments get higher salaried jobs and choice assignments because they know the right politician. Troopers advance by having to pass a written examination prepared by executives of the department and not supervised by the Civil Service Commission. Superintendent John A. Gaffney is responsible for the appointment of Inspectors, Captains and a few Technical Sergeant ranks. Troop "A" is under the command of Captain Joseph B. Lynch and is divided into four zones. Zone 1 is at Athol Springs and patrols Erie, Niagara and Chautauqua Counties with Lieutenant Francis P. Dwyer in charge. Zone 2 is the Batavia Barracks covering Genesee and is under direct supervision of Sgt. Charles E. Cobb. The barracks also houses the Bureau of Criminal Investigation in charge of Lieutenant Harry M. DeHollander. Zone 3 is at East Avon and covers Livingston, Monroe, Orleans and Stueben Counties with Lieutenant Charles O. Mink in charge. Zone 4 is at Wellsville covering Allegany, Wyoming and Cattaraugus Counties with Lieutenant Richard T. Barber in charge.

(January 10,1951 – Edited version from Buffalo Courier Express)

BLISS, N.Y.

On March 22, 1951, Corporal Eugene Redden and Trooper Howard Smith on patrol in Bliss came upon a trio of men that were transferring slot machines from two smaller trucks to a larger truck while parked on the roadside. The three Buffalo, N.Y. men were arrested for Possession of Gambling Devices. They posted $500.00 bail before Peace Justice William Schaffner. Additional slot machines found in a nearby barn were also seized. On April 7, 1951, a representative of the Click Amusement Corporation, Buffalo, N.Y. appeared at court and was granted a request that the charges be dropped against the three individuals and placed against the corporation. This was granted. He then entered a plea of guilty and paid a fine of $300.00. The slot machines were destroyed.

ACCIDENT - YORKSHIRE, N.Y.

An out of control automobile seriously injured pedestrian Raymond King of Olean, N.Y. and wrecked the interior of a grocery store owned by Michael Dobbins at the corner of Routes 16 and 39. The car plunged through a front window narrowly missing Mrs. Dobbins sending shattered glass in all directions and coming to rest 25 feet inside the store. Trooper Lawrence D. McCall of Franklinville identified the driver as Marie Anderson age 42, 494 Doat Street, Buffalo, N.Y. She reported that a car pulled into her path from Route 39 so she took evasive action to avoid a collision. She pulled off the road where she hit pedestrian King who was hitch hiking and continued on through the yard of the Kittleson filling station before coming to rest in the store.

BLACK FRIDAY

On September 21, 1951, a terrific explosion took place in a residence on Buckland Avenue, Brighton, N.Y. completely destroying the house and killing two children that were in it. Almost immediately, other explosions took place completely destroyed eleven more homes in the immediate area and badly damaged twenty-eight other buildings either by explosion or fire. The Brighton Police Chief requested trooper help with troopers responding from both Troops "A" and "D". Evacuations, perimeter security and a communication center were manned for four days until the area was safely secured. It was determined that the explosions were the result of a faulty gas regulator system that had just been repaired and adjusted. A gas regulator valve had increased gas pressure into homes of about 2000 customers. The damaged buildings resulted from a pilot light or stove igniting the gas.

HUNTING ACCIDENT – HEYWOOD SHOT – 1951

A 1951 Thanksgiving-day deer hunt turned tragic, when 41 year-old Donald S. Heywood was found with a fatal bullet wound to the head. The scene was the Paul road farm owned by Heywood. Failing to return from hunting, a search was initiated with the body found the following day. Trooper Sergeant John Chambers looked into the death with a tip leading him to the adjacent DeFelice farm. Five days of intense interviews of hunters and neighbors revealed that Marion DeFelice along with his sons, Gasper and Angelo were also hunting on their farm adjacent to Heywood's. They had separated and were out of sight of one another. Gasper, age 16 armed with a .410 gauge shotgun thought he saw a fox resting on a brush pile. He took aim and fired one shot from about 150 feet away. He believed it was hit but fell out of sight. He never went to check. Not knowing where the body was found, Gasper was taken to show his location, when he shot at the fox. It was in direct line with where Heywood was found. After learning of Heywood's death and the fact that troopers were looking for a hunter using a .410 gauge gun, he became frightened and tried to destroy the gun. Trooper M.B. Grant found the barrel in a barnyard. Gasper was charged with hunting deer with an illegal weapon. He paid a civil compromise settlement of $62.50 before Justice Scott Stevens of Bethany.

LETCHWORTH PARK RESCUE

In April 1952, two troopers were dispatched to assist State Park Rangers at Letchworth State Park near Castile, N.Y. with a man reported stranded in the deep gorge. Arriving at the Wolf Creek area, a man was observed crouched down on a on a nearly perpendicular ledge 125 feet from the top. Ropes, floodlights and emergency equipment were taken to the scene. One of the troopers was lowered into the gorge on a rope to the stranded man. A rope was tied around the man and he was hoisted to the top of the cliff. A doctor at the scene treated the man for exposure and shock before sending him to a local hospital. The man later related that the previous day, he was hiking and slipped on loose gravel falling into the Genesee River. The rushing water washed him over a series of chutes like water falls dropping him 200 feet in distance. He managed to crawl ashore near the falls, but could not find a way out of the gorge. He started to ascend the gorge wall, but was unable to go any further due to rockslides. He spent the night clutching a tree on the ledge until the next day, when he got the attention of some hiking Boy Scouts who called for help.

OLEAN, N.Y.
On September 28, 1952, Corporal H.D. Smith and Trooper Robert Goundry turned cowboy in an unsuccessful attempt in rounding up three runaway horses. Mrs. Robert Benedict, 1358 Seneca Avenue said the horses had broken out of a pasture to frolic with a neighbor's horse. The troopers gave up after an hour of chasing the horses through the fields off of the Dugan Road.

LEROY, N.Y. ARSONS
During the summer of 1952, several fires occurred in the Village of Leroy, N.Y. Arsons were reported at the following locations:

June 09 - Glendale Lumber Co., Lake Street - $1500.00 damage
June 12 - Lake Street Storage Co. - $1500.00 damage
June 24 - Jell-O Foods Garage, North Street - $75,000.00 damage
June 25 - Barns on Crusher Road owned by James P. Clark, Myrtle Street
June 26 - Robert Acomb Farm – barns lost
June 27 - Leroy School Barn - $27,000 damage
June 27 - Fred Merica, 19 Church Street – loss of baskets and crates in a storage area
July 02 – Dr. Merton Skinner, 12 Church Street – minor damage
July 09 – Joseph Miceli, 15 Lake Street - $3,000.00 damage to small barn
Sept 12 – Stephen Reamer, Route 5 – Barns totaled - $80,000.00

A joint investigation by Trooper Investigator George Wood, Genesee County Under Sheriff Frank Gavel and Leroy Police Chief Al Messore resulted in the arrest of three Leroy boys' ages, 10, 13 and 15. They admitted setting several fires in the Village by igniting newspaper near the building they selected to burn. They did it for the excitement of seeing the fire trucks and watching the firemen fight the blazes.

An unrelated fire on June 12, 1952 caused $200,000.00 damage to five stores in the business district of Main Street. Two boys aged 7 and 8 years old admitted setting the fires by burning papers in an alley at the rear of the buildings.

On November 20, 1952, an 18-year-old Crusher Road youth was arrested and admitted setting fire to the Leroy School Barn and to a barn where his family rented. He had been in jail charged with killing a cow and wounding five others, when he was arrested for the Arsons. Revenge appeared to be the reason. He said that he was not being fairly treated by school officials or his landlord. He was adjudicated a Youthful Offender.

TOWN CRIER – BATAVIA RADIO WBTA – MARCH 15, 1953
The increase in the size of New York's State Police force will materialize through a law, which was born last week in Albany, should be instrumental in lowering the state's highway accident death and injury toll.

Three hundred (300) new troopers will be assigned to several areas of the state assigned to traffic duty. It has been no secret that the tremendous flow of traffic has been too great to cope with because of the trooper's undersized force. The troopers have been spread to thin over the vast Western New York area and have done a remarkable job dealing with wild and unthinking drivers. Still, the number of accidents has grown along with the increased motoring public. Troopers can't be everywhere; there aren't enough of them. The benefits of the new troopers should be apparent. The more patrols on the road the more sensible drivers become. The state cops will welcome their new associates and so will the motorists who enjoy living and are willing to obey the law.

RECRUITING EDITORIAL WBTA RADIO – APRIL 5, 1953

Young men looking for an interesting career offering plenty of action and a substantial amount of security would do well to investigate the future available in the ranks of the NYS Police. Governor Dewey recently signed a bill increasing the manpower by three hundred troopers. Competitive examinations have been scheduled for late April at Rochester, Jamestown and Buffalo in Western New York.

Youths in top-flight physical condition and who are mentally alert are urged to consider what state police service offers. The pay is good with uniforms, lodging and food paid for. Troopers receive retirements and disability benefits, good vacations and periodic leaves. There are no layoffs in the gray uniform. If it's security you seek, state police duty fills the bill.

Troopers work hard with long hours and under occasional rugged conditions. Law enforcement has a certain tone of adventure about it. It is not a dull occupation. There is a vast field of traffic control and enforcement into which many of the recruits will be assigned. Highway patrols are going to be more numerous as authorities strive to reduce accidents. The Bureau of Criminal Investigation (BCI) offers real opportunity. These crack, plain-clothes men are in charge of tracking down felons and criminals responsible for murders, robberies and the like. Uniform troopers of top ability are constantly being transferred to the BCI.

You are urged to pay a visit to Troop "A" Barracks in Batavia. Sit down and chat with some of the desk officers. Ask questions about life in the troop. Get the straight slant on what is required of a trooper. Remember, troopers work hard and constantly face danger, but it's a good life, healthy and rewarding in the service of the people of your state. Don't take our word for it, find out for yourself. Call the barracks anytime. Veteran troopers will be happy to answer any questions.

HARNESS RACING PERMITS

During the 1953 – 54 legislative sessions, a law was passed requiring everyone connected with the harness horse racing industry to be licensed by the NYS Harness Racing Commission. During a three-day period in May 1954, troopers fingerprinted more than 1000 employees at the racetrack. They included employees of the Buffalo Trotting Association, Stevens Catering Company, horsemen including owners, trainers, grooms and drivers. Corporal John N. Sage was in charge of the seven-man detail assigned.

GREAT MEADOW PRISON

On August 17, 1955, 175 inmates of the 1000 prison population refused to return to their cells. They demanded to speak directly with Prison Commissioner Thomas McHugh who accommodated them by going to the prison. He told leaders that no negotiations would be had until they returned to their cells. The inmates refused taking up weapons made from prison yard material. The State Police who had been notified and placed on alert directed 66 troopers to the prison. They along with prison guards entered the prison armed with nightsticks. A twenty-six (26) minute battle took place with the inmates subdued and returned to their cells. Fourteen inmates were injured, one trooper suffered cuts and bruises with two troopers suffering minor gunshot wounds from a shotgun blast accidentally discharged by a guard.

CLARKSON STATION BLAST – JULY 19, 1956

Four of six men injured when the state police post at Clarkson exploded were hospitalized and the other two were reported back on the job. The blast leveled the 2-½-story frame building causing an estimated $28,000.00 damage. Injured were Trooper Raymond Meyering with head injuries, Trooper Russell Shibley, a head injury, Trooper Frank Polewicz, a shoulder injury and Norman McFee, a State Public Works employee. Also injured and treated were DPW employee Arthur G. Osborne and Contractor Walter Van Ast.

Dean Henion of Brockport, N.Y, owned the building located at 3770 Lake Road.
The blast was apparently caused when the DPW crew broke a natural gas line while digging a pit for a gas tank just north of the building. The gas seeped into the basement and was exploded by a pilot light. The three troopers were inside the building and were blown clear of the blast. Polewicz who was asleep on the second floor was thrown 60 feet out a window. McFee operating the steam shovel broke or dislodged the pipe and was struck by flying glass. A section of the building slammed against the cab. McFee crawled out from the cab and saw one trooper lying on the ground, another laying on the porch and a third wandering around in a daze and bloody. The blast also knocked out windows and the plaster of adjacent private residences and blew one man off of a ladder. The injured were taken to local hospitals for treatment. (Rochester Times Union –7/20/56)

TROOPER EXAM

During October 1956, 155 Western New York Candidates took the examination for a position as Trooper. Starting salary was $2,900.00 with a food allowance amounting to $1,218.50 per year. Lodging was provided as well as service clothing and equipment.

FARMER INJURED

On June 14, 1957, Stephen Lee Morris, age 54, Franklinville, N.Y. was treated at Olean General Hospital for lacerations and body bruises. The injuries were the result of an accident that resulted when the southbound tractor operated by Morris made a left turn into the path of the northbound State Police car driven by Trooper Joseph J. Donovan, age 24. The injured was thrown from the tractor. The troop car sustained heavy front-end damage with only the front tractor wheel being damaged.

AKRON YOUTH SHOT DEAD

On January 28, 1958, twelve-year old David J. Massaro was shot and killed while watching television at a neighbor's home in the Town of Newstead, N.Y. Charged with First Degree Manslaughter was 24 year old Robert Clark, the Rapids Road neighbor in whose house the shooting took place.

Earlier that evening, the Massaro boy along with brothers Alfred, age 12 and Daniel Poole, age 10 began pelting the Clark house with snowballs. Words were had between Clark and the boys. The Poole boys were brothers to Clark's wife and went into the house to watch television, as they often did. Words again were had between Massaro and Clark. Clark took a .22 caliber pistol from a holster hanging over a chair arm, pointed it at Massaro and pulled the trigger. The gun discharged striking the boy temple above the left eye. He died two hours later in the hospital. Investigating were Sergeant George Wood and Troopers Harold Eichorst and Jack Smith.

KINGSTON, N.Y.
On March 6, 1958, Lieutenant Kenneth P. Weidenborner was placed on special assignment to re-organize the Kingston, N.Y. Police Department. At the request of the mayor, Governor Averill Harriman assigned his chief investigator Arthur Reuter to look into allegations of laxity and malfeasance in the department. As a result, Governor Harriman asked Police Chief Ray VanBuren to signify his intention to resign by March 15th. In six months, Weidenborner brought confidence and respect back to the Department by first looking into allegations of corruption and bias, drafting a set of rules and regulations and introducing an unbiased promotional examination.

LEROY BOY KILLED IN FARM ACCIDENT
On October 8, 1958, 7-year old Richard Glen Walters was injured, when his head struck a tree as he leaned out the window of a pick-up truck driven by his 11-year old brother. He died a short time later at St. Jerome's Hospital, Batavia, N.Y. where his father, Royal Walters, took him. Trooper Jack Braisington's report indicated that the truck driven by Robert Walters was turning into the driveway when a group of boys shouted. Both Robert and Richard looked back with Richard leaning out of the passenger side window. Robert lost control or the truck as he looked back with the truck grazing a tree. Richard was pinned between the tree and the door. Coroner R.L. Warn said death was the result of a fractured skull and broken neck.

SPEAR GUN FISHERMEN - 1958
Complaints at the Hulberton quarry owned by Gene DePalma led to the arrest of five men for using spear guns to take fish. Trooper Ted Georgitso and Conservation Officer Charles Robishaw investigating questioned the men and held them at the location until skin divers arrived to search the quarry. Trooper divers George Zink and Daniel O'Halloran entering the quarry located two spear guns. The spear guns had been dropped into the water just as the trooper car arrived. The five men were arrested and arraigned before Clarendon Justice of the Peace George Keople. A civil compromise was paid and they were released.

WHITESVILLE, N.Y. – TROOPERS FAMILY PERISHES
During the winter of 1958, Trooper Dougal L. Kear was assigned to the Clarence Sub-station, approximately 100 miles from his home. February 15, 1958 would have been his day off, but because of a severe statewide snowstorm, he was assigned to work emergency duty. It turned out to be a most tragic day for Kear. On February 15, 1958, his wife, Neva Kear, age 28, his son, Jeffery, age 5 and two step children, Sherry age 10 and Tommy, age 8 were asphyxiated in their home at Whitesville, New York. The storm plugged the chimney with ice and snow causing backed up gas fumes to fill the house. It was a tragedy that cannot even be visualized.

DISTURBED PERSON - 1958
The capture of an armed man in the Darien sector by State Police was in the finest tradition of the Department. It was a tense and anxious situation. Any moment, their quarry could have opened fire and killed or wounded one or more of the law enforcement officers closing in on him.

Trooper Robert Powell and Sergeant William Rimmer demonstrated exceptionally good judgment. Powell managed to get close enough to distract the man through conversation and then bring him down with a flying tackle. Sergeant Rimmer was quick to close in and complete the capture. The defendant was taken to Rochester State Hospital for mental observation. Needless to say, the public is most grateful and pleased to see a delicate situation so masterfully handled. The greatest beneficiary of all was the man himself. Excellent police work obviously saved him from what could have been a horrible fate. (Batavia Daily News)

IN 1958, THERE WERE 5 MILLION REGISTERED VEHICLES IN NEW YORK STATE.

FUGITIVE CAPTURED ON TONAWANDA INDIAN RESERVATION

On July 31, 1959, 20-year old escaped mental patient Theodore Holton's sixteen days of freedom came to an end with his capture on the Tonawanda Indian Reservation near Akron, N.Y. He had been under arrest for auto theft. He was described as armed and dangerous, which caused alarm to local residents. Escaping on July 12, he was observed in Medina, N.Y. on the 17th and at the Tonawanda Indian Reservation on the 20th, 21st and 23rd. On one occasion, Genesee County Deputy Merton Johns said Holton had shot at him, but Holton later stated that he only fired a shot into the air. Each sighting of the fugitive brought squads of patrol cars to the area only to be searched without success. On one occasion, he was so well hidden in a barn near Corfu, he was never found during a thorough search. On another occasion he put a note on Under-sheriff Sanford Bork's car saying "Ha, Ha. You can't catch me". Bork said he did find such a note. While in Corfu, Holton broke into the Ehmann Green house taking rifle bullets and while there, made a telephone call to a girl in Basom with the operator notifying troopers. That same week, a 1956 Ford sedan owned by Cecil Compton was stolen and found abandoned on the reservation. This was Holton's undoing. He drove to the reservation where he picked up a group of teenagers standing along the Bloomingdale Road and then dropped them off at various points after exhibitions of high speed driving and drag racing. He also bragged of his many escapes from police. The car was found with its motor burned out. Jean Printup (Tarandena) was one of the teenagers that went for a ride with Holton. She along with Beeman Logan Jr., Juanita Logan (Spring), Cheryl Sundown, Pete Poodry and Eileen Charles (Porter) piled into the car and were driven around the reservation. She said that Holton let each of them drive the car. They heard on the car radio that the troopers were looking for Holton and that the car they were in was stolen. On the morning of July 31st, a group of reservation residents concerned for the safety of their children went to the Clarence trooper's station reporting his presence on the reservation. Miss Jean Printup told Trooper Bert C. Musick that her brother residing near the Council House had chased Holton earlier that morning. Musick notified Inspector James W. Russell at Batavia with troopers converging on the area. Troopers met and traveled in unmarked cars to avoid recognition. Holton was seen near the Community Building, but a complete search was unsuccessful. As an afterthought, Trooper L. D. Mills shone his flashlight under stone steps leading into the building and there found Holton curled up, sound asleep with a .22 caliber rifle next to him. Mills reached in and grabbed the weapon ordering him out of the hiding place. He was defiant telling troopers to "Shoot me, I'm not coming out". The hiding area was so tiny, that the sidewall had to be chopped away to access Holton. Trooper Mills crawled into the crawl space, tied a rope around Holton's feet and dragged him out. After his capture, he said he got a kick out of watching the police look for him even taunting them with the notes and purposely being seen. He denied having entered any homes and said he stole no cars while free. He was again committed to Rochester State Hospital.

FORMER TROOPER MURDERS WIFE

In the fall of 1959, former New York State Trooper Gordon Starr, 28, admitted killing his wife in San Diego, California. A bride of three weeks, Jeanette, 28 was found strangled with an electrical extension cord lying on a bed. Starr was reading a mystery magazine, when police arrived. Starr had been an Elmira, N.Y. policeman for three years and a state trooper assigned at Albion for several months before resigning in about 1957.

1960 TID BITS

KISS RESULTS IN BEATING/TROOPER FIRED –WAVERLY, NY

On October 15, 1959, Trooper Henry Lembeck struck James G. Greeney, age 30 on the back of the head and pulled him from his car while in Sayre, Pa. He then forcibly took Greeney to Waverly, N.Y. where he kicked and beat him while at the trooper's barracks. Trooper Elton L. Cowan who was present did not intervene. The severe beating was the result of Greeney unknowingly kissing Lembecks "girl" goodnight the evening before. A civil action was heard before Court of Claims Judge John H. Cooke who ruled the state liable for Trooper Lembecks actions and with added weight given the case when Trooper Cowan took no action to stop the beating. In March 1964, Greeney was awarded $12,000.00 in damages. Cowen was given departmental punishment and Lembeck was dismissed from the State Police.

AUTO CHASE

On March 20, 1960 John Battaglia, 17, 6866 Broadway Road, Alden, N.Y. led troopers on a high speed chase in a stolen car that ended when he ran off the road into a snow bank. It all started when it was discovered that a burglary at the Zynda Pontiac Dealership, Alden, N.Y. had taken place. Money and a 1960 Pontiac were stolen from the show room floor. Trooper Eugene Fechter was investigating when he received information that the car was observed traveling eastbound on Route 20 into Genesee County. Corporal John Lawrence and Trooper Winfield Duken patrolling in separate cars observed the stolen car traveling east on Route 20 and gave pursuit. Speeds reached 120 MPH with a roadblock established at Corbin's Corners in Livingston County. The speeding car seeing the roadblock stopped, turned around and traveled back westbound. In the meantime, Trooper Duken who was forced to stop because of a flat tire just west of the Livingston County line heard the chase over his radio and could see Battaglia coming in his direction. He placed his patrol across one lane of traffic and removed the spare tire from the trunk of his patrol car, placing it in the other traffic lane. Battaglia traveling at about 100 MPH tried to avoid the spare tire, but hit it forcing him to lose control, striking eight guard posts before coming to rest in a snow bank. Unhurt, he was arrested by Trooper Duken and arraigned before Alden Justice George Wilson who committed him to jail pending Erie County Grand Jury action on a burglary charge.

SUSPECT KILLED BY TROOPER

On June 24, 1960, an Erie County Grand Jury reported a no bill against Trooper Stanley Paquadeck in the homicide investigation arising from the death of Kenneth Staufenberger. Trooper Paquadeck on routine patrol was in pursuit of a speeder at Sloan, N.Y., when the driver drove off of the roadway, abandoned the car and fled on foot. Paquadeck fired his service revolver in an attempt to have the man stop. The bullet struck Staufenberger killing him instantly. The Erie County District Attorney said that evidence indicated the warning shot ricocheted from some object and that the trooper did not intentionally shoot at the fleeing man.

HAMMONDSPORT POLICE CHIEF

In October 1960, Corning, N.Y. native Joseph F. Rowe, a former New York State Trooper was appointed Chief of Police of Hammondsport, N.Y.

BARCELONA, N.Y.

On October 2, 1960, a multiple fatal accident claimed seven lives. The accident occurred at 8:40 PM on Route 20 about 3 miles west of Route 17, near Barcelona, N.Y. The dead were identified as:

August P. Mason, 38, Mercer, Pa.
August M. Mason, 11, his son
James Shipton, 33, McKean, Pa., a driver
Joan Shipton, 33, his wife
James Shipton Jr., 6, their son
Louis DeLoe, 33, Emlenton, Pa., a driver
Clyde DeLoe, 18, a brother of Louis

The only survivor was Helen Mason, age 37, Arthur's wife. The DeLoe car traveling eastbound veered into the path of the westbound Shipton car on a slight curve where they met head-on demolishing both vehicles. Traffic was re-routed for over two hours.

FATAL HUNTING ACCIDENT

Over the years, hundreds of people have been shot and killed while hunting due to carelessness and negligence of the hunter. During the mid 1950s, the "Criminal Negligence While Engaged in Hunting Resulting in Death of Another" Law was passed.

Since its passage, there were very few convictions due to the difficulty in showing evidence of negligence.

On August 21, 1960, a city man was hunting in an area unfamiliar to him, when he shot at movement in heavy brush. What he shot was a young boy picking elder berries. The boy had been shot from a distance of 40 feet and was killed instantly from a gunshot wound to the head. The hunter was arrested and convicted of Criminal Negligence by a jury trial.

During 1961, eighty-four (84) hunting accidents were reported statewide resulting in three (3) arrests.

ROCHESTER, N.Y.

In February 1962, William A. Lombard, a member of the New York State Police since 1948 resigned to accept a position as Police Chief for the City of Rochester, N.Y. He was last assigned at Batavia, N.Y. as the Lieutenant Supervisor of BCI.

BATAVIA DOWNS GROOM KILLED – OCTOBER 18, 1962

An early morning fire at Batavia Downs Race Track resulted in the death of 30-year old horse groom John C. Jamison of Mercer, Pennsylvania. Trooper Investigator Edward Longhany and Batavia Police Officers Earl Davis and Matty Hamera investigated and found the cause to be faulty wiring in an electrical heater being used in a stall area. The fire started in Barn # 12 where the stable of William "Bud" Gilmour was housed.

Twenty-five (25) racing horses were also lost in the blaze.

BIGAMY CHARGED – 1962

Troopers were attempting to locate 33-year-old Horst Bogard "aka" Bragard of Cheektowaga, N.Y. to execute a warrant for practicing medicine without a license, bigamy and illegal entry. Investigator Henry F. Williams said that Bogard falsely claimed he studied medicine at the University of Heidelberg and performed operations and amputations at a New York City hospital and was now practicing medicine in Buffalo, N.Y. Williams started his investigation on the complaint of Giselle Bogard, the wife living in Canada who stated Horst had taken a second wife. Williams confirmed that he had indeed married Mary Ann Orsini on June 3, 1961 at Batavia, N.Y.

1964 DIVISION ARRESTS
During 1964, the State Police made 453,232 arrests.

432,701 - Traffic Violations.
 20,531 - Criminal Arrests.
 41,056 - Accidents Investigated.
  2,912 - Driving While Intoxicated Arrests. .

MOONSHINE IN SHERIDAN, N.Y.
In 1965, Investigator Gerald Forster received information that Sammy Lopez residing in the Town of Sheridan was selling moonshine to Puerto Rican migrant farm laborers in Brant, N.Y. An attempt to locate the sugar source for the still proved futile, as none was being used. Instead, fifty gallons of molasses was found that was being used to distill "Rum".

A search warrant was obtained and Lopez' home, a rural farmhouse, was raided. The still was located in his basement. A sample of the rum contents was secured as evidence, photographed and documented. The rum found in five large wooden barrels was destroyed on the spot with the heavy rum flowing onto the floor and into a sump hole that drained into a ditch at the rear of the house.

The local newspaper wanted a photograph of a uniform trooper destroying the barrels. Trooper Elmer J. Haas was selected to kick in a couple of barrels. The basement floor was covered with about two inches of rum that concealed the sump hole in the middle. Trooper Haas found the hole by falling into it, soaking him in rum. Sammy Lopez said he only ran the still to earn enough money to purchase a farm in Puerto Rico. Forster recalled that the rum was potent and made great charcoal fire starter. Lopez was prosecuted by Federal Authorities, paid a fine and was released.

ANGELICA BURGLARY
On March 9, 1965, Trooper William Goetschius was passing through the Village of Angelica when he noticed footprints in the newly formed snow leading to the rear of a local business. He followed the footprints and entered the building where he found two men breaking into vending machines. One ran out a side door and the other attempted to push by the trooper. A struggle ensued requiring Goetschius to be treated for facial cuts. One suspect was charged with Assault 2nd Degree and both with Burglary 3rd Degree.

DUNKIRK BOOKIE
In April 1965, off duty Trooper George Domedion was patronizing a Dunkirk barbershop that he frequented on several occasions in the past. Each visit led him to believe a bookmaker was operating out of the barbershop. Through his conversations, he was able to make a wager. He notified BCI investigators at Fredonia who raided the establishment making two arrests while confiscating $380.00 and betting slips. The barber bookie was fined $500.00 and given a ten day suspended sentence. Trooper Domedion hair was cut at another location after the arrest.

ALERT TROOPER
During the winter 1965, off-duty Trooper James L. Nashwenter traveling through the Village of Medina, N.Y. came upon a burning house. He dashed to the house alerted the resident, Mrs. Robert

Jones of the danger, then rushed upstairs where he found Stephen, age 5, Dennis, age 4 and Mark Jones, age 1. He cradled the youngest in his arms and led the children to safety.

ATTICA, N.Y. TRAIN DERAILMENT

On April 28, 1965, fourteen cars of a 104-car freight train derailed near the Favor and South Pearl Streets tearing up track and damaging two nearby cars with flying stone and cinder debris. The Erie Lackawanna train was en-route to Hornell, when the accident occurred. There were no injuries. The area was initially evacuated fearing possible explosion from an overturned tanker car containing 27,000 gallons of flammable liquid. The load was transferred to trucks and residents returning to their homes.

TROOPERS TOYS FOR TOTS

During the winter 1965, Trooper Jack Miller while assigned at Athol Springs started an annual toy give away to needy children by mending toys left in the station distribution box. In less than two years, his work turned into truckload proportions with students, senior citizens and other troopers combining to donate, collect, repair and distribute toys for Christmas. Based in Fredonia since 1966, the program continued to grow with distribution assistance provided by the Kiwanis Club of New York State. The program is such that two trailer loads of damaged toys arrive weekly donated by National Distributor K-B Toys and Hobby. No child is turned away with truckloads of toys going to children in disaster areas.

On December 15, 1977, Trooper Miller led a delegation on a 250-mile trip to Johnstown, Pennsylvania. Summer flooding had ravaged the city resulting in extraordinary high unemployment. The troopers carried with them toys in two tractor-trailers that had been donated by local Fredonia businesses, individuals and troopers. Both trucks bore the legend "Troopers Toys for Tots" and displayed a picture of a trooper carrying a bag of toys. The toys were presented to the local Salvation Army for distribution to needy children. It was felt that nowhere in the Northeast United States was there more of a need for free toys than this devastated community.

In 1977, Miller was honored for his efforts with the joint Chautauqua County Kiwanis and Knights of Columbus "Humanitarian Award" and the Salvation Army "Service Award".

When queried as to why he got so involved, he simply said: "I felt it would be an excellent way for troopers to interact with children." "The reward is seeing the tears of joy on the face of a child; that is truly the gift of Christmas."

NYCRR TRAIN WRECK – CORFU, N.Y.

On December 29, 1965 at 4:10 AM, a fast passenger train derailed without loss of life. Twenty-three persons escaped serious injury. A short piece of pulpwood wedged between switching tracks was responsible for the westbound derailment that left six persons in area hospitals and seventeen others treated at hospitals. The scene was on the NYCRR mainline about one mile east of Corfu, N.Y. The train was westbound from New York City to Cleveland with Buffalo, N.Y as the next stop. Uninjured passengers were transported to Buffalo, N.Y. by bus. Major John P. Nohlen, Captain John Cerino and Sgt. John Shaver headed the rescue effort aided by the Genesee County Sheriff's Department and over 100 volunteer firemen.

NEW ENGLAND MURDERER CAPTURED

In mid January 1966, Trooper Edward Gluch, while working radar near Silver Creek, N.Y. stopped a vehicle that just didn't look right. It turned out the 16 year-old driver, Frederick C. Lindner admitted to a murder that had yet not been discovered near Springfield, Massachusetts. He was charged as Fugitive from Justice and turned over to Massachusetts's authorities for prosecution.

TROOPERS MEET THE STORK
In February 1966, Thomas Heffernan, 8387 Jennings Road, Eden, N.Y. was taking his wife Joanne for a date with the stork. As they approached the Athol Springs Troopers Station, Joanne indicated she needed help immediately so her husband drove into the station driveway. Hurriedly explaining his emergency, Lieutenant Robert Charland, Sergeant Stanley Paquadeck and Trooper Dewey Rohl handled the situation, as they had been trained to do. They helped in delivering a healthy baby girl. Mother and child were then taken to Our Lady Of Victory Hospital where they were doing fine.

TROOPER ASSAULTED – CORFU, N.Y.
On March 14, 1966 at 9:00 PM, Trooper Donald F. Cochrane while on routine patrol stopped a vehicle for speeding in the Village of Corfu, N.Y. The violator was identified as 24 year-old William R. McCoy of Snipery Road, Corfu, N.Y. While standing outside of the patrol car issuing a citation, the irate McCoy punched the Trooper in the face. Cochrane was able reach into the patrol car and radio for assistance. Trooper Al Kurek responded immediately and upon arrival, found Trooper Cochrane and McCoy in a struggle, the radio hand-set cord wrapped around the Troopers neck. Kurek leaped from his patrol car and grabbed McCoy, throwing him to the hood of the car where he was handcuffed. Cochrane suffered facial contusions and a sprained finger during the struggle. McCoy was charged with Speeding and Assault 2nd Degree. He pled guilty to the speeding charge before Village Justice John Maha paying a $25.00 fine. He was committed to the Genesee County Jail in lieu of $250.00 bail for appearance before a Grand Jury.

BYRON, N.Y. ROBBERY
During the early hours of April 16, 1966, Kenneth Washburn was employed as a taxicab driver for Passlow Taxi, Batavia, N.Y. A regular customer, Drew Spikes, age 21 of Transit Road, Byron, N.Y. appeared at the dispatcher office needing the taxi service for a ride home. They departed Batavia with Spikes sitting in the front seat. As they traveled through the rural area, Spikes told Washburn to stop the cab. He then punched Washburn in the face taking $81.00 from his person. He then pulled Washburn from the cab, punched him several more times and drove off in the cab. Washburn went to farmhouse and summoned help. Troopers Donald F. Cochrane and Richard A. Schilling responded, conducted an immediate area search locating the abandoned taxi several miles away. A forty-man detail that included bloodhounds was assigned. Cochrane and Schilling observed Spikes running through a field gave chase and arrested him. On June 15, 1966, Spikes found guilty of Robbery 1st Degree and was sentenced to a term of three to ten years at the Elmira Reception Center.

MAN KILLED IN STRUGGLE WITH A TROOPER
On May 8, 1966 at 2:30 AM, Trooper Lee A. Pattison patrolling alone stopped a vehicle for traveling on the wrong side of the Sweden Walker Road just south of Brockport, N.Y. He was in the process of placing the driver, 25-year old Donald E. Jubenville under arrest for Driving While Intoxicated, when Jubenville jumped from the vehicle and fled. As Pattison started pursuit, 28-year old Lawrence F. Erbe, a passenger exited the car and began assaulting him. Erbe had grabbed the troopers blackjack and was trying to get his revolver. Jubenville joined the struggle with the revolver discharging striking Erbe in the abdomen. Erbe was pronounced dead on arrival at Lakeside Hospital, Brockport, N.Y. Troop "A" Commander Major John P. Nohlen said there was no indication of improper behavior on the part of the trooper. A Grand Jury cleared Pattison of any wrongdoing.

INVESTIGATOR GEORGE WOOD/TROOPER JOHN L. SMITH

On August 20, 1966, Investigator George Wood and Trooper John Smith were executing a warrant for a Parole Violation on Lanny H. Starkweather, age 24, Rapids Road, Newstead, N.Y. Starkweather tried to flee and was subdued by the troopers. Starkweather's aunt Hazel A. Cummings attempting to aid him attacked Trooper Wood who suffered mouth and facial cuts and Trooper Smith who suffered bites on his hand and cuts. Aunt Hazel was charged with assaulting an Officer. Both troopers were treated by a physician and released.

APPLETON FARMER SHOOTS GAS THIEVES

On December 4, 1966, Floyd Jesson, 49, 6800 Swigert Road, Appleton, N.Y. was charged with Assault 2nd Degree after an early morning shooting on his farm. Jesson was awakened and saw two men and a women-removing gasoline from his storage tank. He fired at them with a .22 caliber rifle as they fled. He was able to read their license plate number and called the troopers. Troopers J.J. Ryan and J. R. Johnson located the automobile a few hours later and arrested Richard Davis, 23, Lockport, N.Y., Edward Luce Jr., 20, Niantic, Connecticut and Lois Schurr, 20, Gasport, N.Y. for Petit Larceny. They pled guilty before Newfane Peace Justice Walter Reackhoff, were sentenced to a 30 day suspended jail term with Schurr also being placed on one-year probation. It wasn't until arraignment that troopers learned Jesson had shot Davis in the arm. He was taken to the hospital and the bullet removed. As a result, Investigator Harry Logan placed a charge against Jesson of Assault 2nd Degree. He was released without bail.

TROOPER'S SON BORN IN TROOP CAR

The wife of SP Clarkson Investigator Robert M. Barrus woke early on Easter Sunday morning 1967 and informed Bob that she was about to give birth to their child. Bob decided to take a shower (not a good idea at the time) just as the infant showed movement toward entering the world. In a rush, he helped his wife into his unmarked 1964 Plymouth troop car and proceeded to the hospital several miles away. Speeding along at the legal speed limit, he approached the intersection of Routes 19 and 31 just as the light turned red against him. His wife insisted he go through the red light, but Bob stood fast, not taking any chances. It finally turned green and he continued to Lakeside Hospital where his son, Tyler was born in the troop car at the hospital parking lot. What a difference a light makes. Tyler is now an Investigator with the Monroe County Sheriff's Office.

DOCTOR PAPARELLA APPOINTED - BATAVIA, N.Y.

On May 18, 1967, Dr. Jerome A. Paparella, 316 East Main Street, Batavia, N.Y. was appointed a Division Assistant Physician. He attended Wagner College in 1941, Cornell University and Hahnemann Medical School, Philadelphia graduating in 1948. He served in the US Army as an enlisted man in the mid 1940s, then as an officer in the Medical Corp from 1952 to 1954. He married the former Jean Petersen, had four children and resided in Batavia. In addition to his private practice, he was employed as the plant physician at Sylvania Products and Batavia Downs Raceway. He was Chief of Medicine at St. Jerome's Hospital, Batavia, N.Y.

TROOP "E" BEGINS OPERATION

On September 6, 1967 the re-organization of the State Police became a reality with the opening of Troop "E" Headquarters at Canandaigua, N.Y.

SHOOT OUT AT OLEAN, N.Y. - 1967

On the afternoon of October 26, 1967, troopers and police in the Olean, N.Y. area were alerted by an off duty Pennsylvania State Trooper that he was pursuing two men that had fled a Pennsylvania prison near Harrisburg earlier in the week. The pursuit started in Coudersport, Pa, continued into

New York State and ended on the campus of St. Bonaventure University near Olean, New York. The heavily armed pair, identified as 21-year-old Richard R. Gingrich of Annville, Pa and 21-year-old Gary Frederick Ayers of Elmira, N.Y. operating a stolen station wagon, abandoned the vehicle as they approached a state police roadblock. Trooper Harry B. Kowal captured Gingrich near the campus a few minutes later. Ayer, who was armed, fled into the Shay-Loughlen dormitory where he held several female students at gunpoint. As he moved to an upper floor and eventually the roof, Burns Campus Security Guard Robert Gaines, who was unarmed, confronted him. Gaines was himself taken hostage. After a short time Ayers left the dormitory with the gun still at Gaines head, located a campus station wagon and released Gaines. As he attempted to flee, he was fired upon with 11 bullets striking the vehicle putting it out of commission. Coming to a stop, Ayers came face to face with weapons pointed at him by Investigators Raymond P. Slade and Clare L. Jackson. He raised his hands and surrendered. After arraignment, both men were turned over to Pennsylvania authorities for prosecution. Warrants for Unlawful Imprisonment and Grand Larceny filed, as detainers.

ALBION, N.Y. SHOOTOUT

During February 1968, two Albion Village Policemen answered a complaint of a disorderly person at a local tavern. While taking the man into custody, a struggle ensued resulting in the sidearm being taken from one of the officers. The man began shooting wildly with the officers taking cover. Trooper Robert J. Gadsby, traveling through the Village, heard the shots and investigated. He got as close as he could with safety, then approached on foot where he took the man into custody at gunpoint.

MOTHER OF THE STATE POLICE

Miss Moyca Newell, the force behind the creation of a State Police in New York State died on February 25, 1968 at her Westchester estate. She and friend Katherine Mayo researched and wrote the book "Justice For All" describing the positive attributes of the Pennsylvania State Police. The book and their five-year leadership eventually led to the formation of a New York State Constabulary in 1917.

WHITESVILLE, N. Y. BANK ROBBERY

On May 7, 1968, the usually quiet Village of Whitesville came alive when the local bank had the distinction of being robbed. This was the first bank robbery in Allegany County since the 1930s. A lone robber armed with what appeared to be a tear gas pencil escaped with $1,300.00 in marked bills. Video surveillance cameras caught the robbery on film and a picture of the bandit was made and distributed locally. Investigators Stewart S. Mills, William Goetchius and Raymond "Sam" Slade were aided by a team of FBI agents in solving the robbery. The photos were identified as a bank employee's relative that had been in a mental institution. He was taken into custody at Erie, Pennsylvania with $865.00 of the marked bills recovered. He was turned over to federal authorities for prosecution.

GROOM SPENDS HONEYMOON IN JAIL
OCTOBER 16, 1968

Investigator George Wood had arrested William Rex Ogden, age 22, 38 Mill Street, Oakfield, N.Y. on a Parole Violation warrant in the City of Batavia. As they walked to the trooper's car, Ogden bolted from custody running handcuffed through the city taking refuge at the apartment of his friend, Elwood D. Mattison, 21, 43 State Street, Batavia, N.Y. Mattison was successful in breaking the chain links on the cuffs, but not the cuffs.

Mattison, who was to be married that evening, had borrowed a suit from Ogden. Batavia City Patrolman Robert Casper was tipped of Ogden's location and took him into custody without resistance. Mattison was permitted to be married, but was arrested as he exited the church, charged with Aiding a Prisoner to Escape.

YOUTH KILLED DURING HOLLEY STAKEOUT - JANUARY 21, 1969
Nineteen-year-old Bruce Clark of Buffalo, N.Y. was shot and killed during a liquor store burglary in the Village of Holley and four accompanies taken into custody during the early hours of January 21, 1969. State Police had the store staked out based on a tip from the Buffalo Police Department that a burglary was planned for the establishment. Three men entered the building during the night and were piling cases of liquor near the door, when they were ordered to halt by troopers secreted in the store. Clark bolted for the rear door and was ordered to halt by Investigator D.L. Smith. He continued to flee with a single shot fired by Smith. The shot struck Clark in the head killing him instantly. A straight razor was found next to his body. The other defendants were taken into custody by Investigators Theodore J. Georgitso and John P. Wilcox of the State Police and Orleans County Deputies William Schneider and Robert Parker. They were arraigned before Judge Clement A. Quarantello and held for Grand Jury. A coroner's inquest determined the shooting was justified. Smith did not intentionally intend to shoot the victim and his death troubled Smith until his dying days.

BURGLAR STAKEOUT – JANUARY 27, 1969
Having received information that a burglary would be committed at an East Main Road farm implement store, Trooper Investigators Warren Terryberry, Philip Trapani and Winfield Duken secreted themselves in the building while Investigators James Duval and Robert Barrus observed the building from a parked unmarked patrol car nearby. At about 7:00 PM, a car pulled up to the building, a passenger jumped out, kicked in the front door glass, unlocked the door and picked up two chain saws valued at $400.00. The troopers identified themselves, ordered the man to stop, but he didn't. The chain saws were dropped and the pair fled in their car. Duval and Barrus pursued and took them into custody at gunpoint a few minutes later. Burglary charges were filed against the pair identified as Ronald Wisniewski, 28, Depew, N.Y and Richard Gorski, 29, Buffalo, N.Y. On August 23, 1969, both were found guilty after trial. Wisniewski was sentenced to six years at Attica Prison and Gorski to a term of not more than three years.

ATTICA PRISON ESCAPE – MAY 10, 1969
On May 10, 1969, Attica Prison Warden Vincent Mancusi reported that inmates George Ody and David Withey had walked away from the State Prison Farm located just outside the prison main prison walls. Acting Troop Commander Nicholas Giangualano led a considerable police force at the scene that was made up of Deputies from Wyoming and Genesee Counties, Prison Guards, Bloodhounds and a helicopter. Investigator Leonard Bochynski was detailed to the prison to obtain a profile on the escapees. Designated search areas were assigned, however the searchers were hindered by heavy rain. The search went on throughout the night with the area contained by a constant police presence. The next morning a local farmer checking his barn noticed some hay bales in disarray. He notified troopers who responded immediately. Trooper James Kostecki found the two inmates hiding in the hayloft area hollowed out by the arranging of the hay bales. They were arrested and charged with escape.

THE NUTCASE
Stanley Sochalec, the Batavia Headquarters Maintenance Supervisor was one of the most intense individuals I've ever known and was wound tight most of the time. Despite this, he was a dependable man to have around. Recalling an occasion in1969, a nutcase came into troop headquarters to report that the FBI had inserted a radio device in his teeth. He was a huge, wild-eyed man and the deskman was unsure of what to do. Hearing shouting, First Sergeant Vernon Clayson came out of his office

just as the man was leaving. He exited the building and was on the driveway when Clayson caught up with him. Clayson grabbed his huge arm to get his attention just as the man swung the other arm at him. He managed to dodge the blow, then held the giant by both arms as best he could. Sochalec rushed to his aide immediately followed by Sergeant Gary Law. There were six or eight officers and enlisted troopers who made no move, apparently preferring to remain observers. Most of the road troopers always believed that Sochalec was a better man than those soft and timid headquarters types anyway. This is not to disparage the members of the patrol unit at troop headquarters as they were real troopers: Jake Lathan, Al Kurek, Fred Walsh, Tom Tucker, Bill Loft, Jerry Kalisz, Louie Lang and a few others were up to any situation, but were usually out on regular patrol, when some of these strange situations came up. The man was finally subdued and admitted to the Rochester Psychiatric Unit for observation.

ROUTINE CHECK NETS MURDER SUSPECT – FALCONER
While on routine patrol on May 11, 1969, Troopers C.W. VanEpps and R.C. Becker stopped a car with wired on Ohio license plates. The driver was arrested for multiple traffic violations. He was identified as Tai Salim of Cleveland, Ohio. A search of the vehicle revealed a .32 caliber gun, machete, marijuana, books on explosives and ammunition. He was arrested and committed to the Chautauqua County Jail in lieu of bail. A routine inquiry to the Cleveland Police Department determined that Salim was wanted for murder. Ballistics later matched the .32 caliber gun recovered during arrest to the murder victim. He was returned to Ohio and charged with First Degree Murder.

CHICKEN CAPER – LEWISTON – 1969
A coordinated effort by US and Canadian law men led to the arrest of four men for smuggling and the seizure of 6,800 pounds of contraband poultry medicine valued at $176,800.00. The medicine was identified as Zoatene and valued at $26.00 a pound. It was produced in Italy, shipped to the Bahamas and then flown to Toronto from where it was trucked to St. Catherine's where it was broken up into lots. Some was sent across the Niagara River by small boat and the rest by automobile across the Queenston Lewiston Bridge. The intent was to avoid inspection by the Food and Drug Administration and avoid payment of duty. The medication was found in bags at a campsite near Lewiston stored in a tent and trailer. Investigators Harold Eichorst, Frank Demler, Terry Reilly and Patrick Petrie conducted the investigation.

GRAND ISLAND POST OFFICE BURGLARY
On August 7, 1969, troopers responded to the report of unusual activity at the Grand Island, N.Y. post office. Three men were observed entering a safe where stamps and $250,000 worth of money orders were stored. Taking positions to block escape routes, the three were taken into custody, as they exited the building. They were turned over to federal authorities for prosecution.

TROOPER CAR HITS GIRL
On October 25, 1969, 12-year old Alice Marie Waldeck of Hinsdale, N.Y. was struck and killed, as she ran across Route 16 into the path of a State Police car driven by Trooper Gregory Snyder who was en-route to a complaint. He was unable to avoid hitting her who was with two companions. The accident occurred near the Hinsdale High School.

UNDERCOVER PRIEST – 1969
Information had been received from an informant that the "mob" had stolen a box of negotiable money orders in the midwest valued at one million dollars and they were being sent by air to Western New York. The shipment carried by courier was located at the Cleveland, Ohio airport where Lieutenant Raymond "Sam" Slade and Investigator Donald J. Munch had traveled to follow the package to

its final destination in Buffalo, N.Y. Arriving at Buffalo, the courier placed the package in a 25-cent airport locker and left the terminal. BCI Captain Henry F. Williams ordered an undercover surveillance of the locker utilizing a priest's clothing as a disguise. Investigator's Norman Minklein, Vincent Tobia and Munch dressed as a priest were assigned. Tobia was stationed behind a Rental Car counter, while Minklein assisted Munch around the airport in a wheelchair. After three days of continuous observation, the package was picked up by a taxicab driver who delivered it to the house of a person unassociated with the case. An immediate search was made of the residence with the package secured from the elderly resident. The taxicab driver when questioned said he had been paid $20.00 to pick up and deliver the package. The elderly resident didn't know why the package had been delivered to her. No local arrests were ever made. Munch recalled that Captain Williams had chewed him out for wearing his wedding band during the operation. He also commented on how sore his buttocks got after sitting in a wheelchair for three days. On the second day, Munch had Minklein take him into a men's room, because he wanted Minklein to sit in the wheelchair while Munch the priest pushed him around. Several visitors to the men's room thought it particularly funny that a priest and his aide would be arguing about who would ride and who would walk.

1970 TID BITS

NEW YORK, NEW YORK – MARCH 6, 1970
FOUR TROOPERS ARRESTED

On March 6, 1970, four troopers linked to a $650 million betting ring were arrested and charged with Interstate Transportation in the Aid of Racketeering. They were identified as Lieutenant Charles Cassino, Senior Investigators Eugene Curico, Vincent Malavorco and Louis Sabatini. The four acted in the role of protector and were rewarded with free vacations to Puerto Rico, automobiles, free tickets to fights, free meals and cash from the gamblers. It was Rockland County Investigator Joseph Colligan who infiltrated the ring accepting $1000.00 monthly from the gamblers and keeping his superiors informed. Also charged were Nicholas (Cock Eye Nick) Rattenni, age 64, Albert Paretti, age 52, Peter Variano and Michael Roman. It was Variano who offered to pay $1000.00 to insure troopers would not raid certain Rockland County operations. Bets totaling $30,000.00 were being made in each of several locations.

KIDNAPERS CAREER ENDED BY FLAT TIRE – JAMESTOWN, N.Y.

On May 6, 1970, troopers from the Falconer Station stopped 31-year old Kyle Sherrill, a Maryland construction worker for driving with an unsafe tire. He was issued a citation and directed to an all night service station. A file check proved negative. Unknown to the troopers, Sherrill had earlier that evening abducted 6-year old Carol Pierce from a suburban Buffalo, N.Y. playground some 80 miles away. Shortly before being stopped, he decided to dispose of the child and threw her from a bridge into a creek 52 feet below.

Uninjured in the plunge, she was able to swim to shore and slept in a patch of tall grass until daybreak. A passerby observed her walking along the roadway and took her to the Falconer trooper station. Unharmed, she described her ordeal and described the blue license plate, the flat tire and the fact her abductor had thrown a pop can on the floor. When the troopers became aware of this information, the Maryland State Police were notified and information from the traffic summons provided. They had similar unsolved crimes. Sherrill was taken into custody and confessed to 19 kidnappings in seven different states. He had been working at a construction site field office in Williamsville, N.Y.

TROOPER JACKING DEER

Trooper Leroy J. Seitz was an excellent trooper assigned at Batavia, N.Y. He did his job in an efficient manner and enforced the law to the letter. The only problem was that he didn't practice what he preached. In the fall of 1973, he borrowed a high-powered rifle from Batavia Town Justice Charles Barrett for use in a deer hunt in Pennsylvania. At the same time, there were reports from residents in the Town of Alabama of hearing gunshots at night and finding the remains of dead deer that had been shot. As it turned out, Seitz was spotting deer with a spotlight and shooting them for sport. A stakeout by the Conservation Department resulted in his apprehension and arrest. He was fined under civil compromise and the rifle was confiscated. The price was higher then he anticipated, as he was terminated from the State Police. The troopers have always maintained a high standard for conduct and to violate that standard was not unacceptable or tolerated. The rifle was returned to Justice Barrett.

TAXICAB BANDIT CAPER – 1971

During the winter of 1971, a 34-year old man entered a taxicab in Buffalo, N.Y. and instructed the driver to take him to a rural Erie County location. As they traveled, the man pulled out two pistols and declared he was going to rob a tavern. He selected a tavern in Hamburg, N.Y. and exited the cab with the driver who was under threat of being shot. As they entered the tavern, the cab driver ran for safety. The bandit also ran, but to the cab that he drove away. The troopers were called and established roadblocks and roving patrols. In relatively short time, Lieutenant George Elbel and Trooper Mike Kirkpatrick located the cab parked behind a tavern in Eden, N.Y. Troopers Joe Kwiatek, Albert Simmons and Tom Schultz joined them surrounding the establishment. The bandit was observed though a window, seated at the bar. He also saw the trooper looking in, pulled out a gun and fled into the rear kitchen area. There he ran into Trooper Schultz and returned to the bar area where he was met by shotguns and pistols pointing at him. He surrendered without further incident. It was later found that the pistols were toy cap guns that looked real. The bandit had three days earlier been released from Federal Prison where he had served a term for Parole Violation.

TROOPER HITS AND KILLS TWO PEDESTRIANS

On January 24,1973 at 6:30 PM, BCI Investigator Stewart S Mills, age 43 was driving a State Police vehicle east on Route 408 (Main Street), when he struck two pedestrians at Angelica, N.Y. The pedestrians were identified as William, age 84 and Ruth Schlau, age 64 of RD #1, Angelica, N.Y. Mills notified authorities with Lieutenant Douglas Parr and Troopers William Goetchius, Dennis Vespucci, Louis Reitenauer and John Cosgrove responding to the scene. Ruth Schlau was pronounced dead upon arrival at Jones Memorial Hospital. William died the next day. The Schlau' had walked into the path of the Troop car from the drivers side with Mills unable to avoid striking them. It was reported that alcohol and an unauthorized passenger in the trooper car might have been factors leading to the accident. An internal investigation resulted in Mills being reduced in rank and returned to the uniform force. Lieutenant Parr received a letter of censure for not securing the troop car as evidence after the accident.

PIPE BOMB INJURES HAMBURG POLICE OFFICER

On March 14, 1973, Hamburg, N.Y. police were sent to a residence after a suspicious wooden box was found on the front porch. The box contained a two-inch pipe with wire attached to the doorknob. A Hamburg Police Officer picked up the box. As he did so, the device exploded severing the left hand, a thumb and index finger on the right hand, caused loss of hearing in one ear and serious abdominal injuries. The bomb was intended for the tenant and was designed to go off when the door was opened. The BCI were notified and took over the investigation.

COIN COLLECTION STOLEN – OCTOBER 1973
In October 1973, a house burglary at Chautauqua County netted the thief a coin collection valued at $250,000.00 from a secure basement room. Investigators David Carr and Trooper R.H. Nelson investigated and developed a prime suspect, a repairman who had come to repair a washer. In February 1974, information was received that the repairman was trying to sell a coin collection for $70,000.00. Investigator Paul Wothe, SP Cortland, an avid coin collector, made arrangements to inspect the coins with the promise to buy it. Wothe wired with a microphone, made contact but the suspect became suspicious and broke off negotiations. Chautauqua District Attorney Charles Loveland directed that the suspect identified as Andy Lowell be arrested. State Police Investigators Donald Munch, Terrence Fiegl and Gerald Forster who staked out the site arrested him at "Al's Tire Shop", Falconer, N.Y. Fiegl and Forester apprehended Lowell just as he was drawing a .38 caliber handgun on Munch who confronted him. He was arraigned before County Court Judge Lee Towne Adams who set bail at $70,000.00. He denied any knowledge or possession of the coins, but proposed that if he didn't go to jail, he would try to locate the collection. Local publicity resulted in an informant telling of the suspect owning a house in Randolph, N.Y. with the coins secreted in a hidden basement area. A search of the house produced the coins. Other properties owned by the suspect were searched with 1,613 wrenches and other tools located that had been pilfered from his employer valued at $13,000.00. Claiming poverty, he was found to own a luxury car, a sports car, a cabin cruiser, a truck and three rental properties. He had been a suspect in numerous other residential burglaries, having first cased each place as a legitimate repairman several months earlier. He was convicted of Burglary and sentenced to Attica Prison.

TROOPERS RESCUE TWO FROM BATAVIA HOTEL FIRE
While on patrol on the night of March 17, 1974, Troopers Paul Lukasiewicz and Thomas Tucker discovered an early morning fire at Gentner's Hotel and Bar, West Main Street, Batavia, N.Y. After notifying firefighters of the situation, they attempted to enter the building through the first floor, but were thwarted by the fire and smoke. They then scaled a wall to the second floor entering a window where they found two elderly confused residents that they lead safety. The building was totally destroyed by the fire.

OLEAN SNIPER - DECEMBER 30, 1974
On December 30, 1974, 17-year old Olean honor student Anthony F. Barbaro secreted himself on the third floor of the Olean High School where for two hours he caused more human carnage than anyone could recall. Earl Metcalf, age 61, a school maintenance employee was shot dead when he responded to the report of fire on the schools third floor Student Union. Joe Kosidlo, another maintenance man, had accompanied Metcalf to the fire but fled when he heard shots fired and saw Metcalf fall to the floor. He immediately alerted police and fire authorities. Barbaro armed with several long guns including a high powered 30.06 with scope, sprayed gunfire from a third floor window on an unsuspecting public below. Engine No. 1 received the fire alarm responding to the school immediately. Pumper No. 42 was driven by Herbert Elmore with Captain John Snopkowski seated next to him. Seated in the back were George Williams and Greg Kwiatkowski. As they pulled in front of the school, a bullet shattered the windshield and struck Elmore in the head. The same bullet went on through the cab striking Williams in the seated in the back of the truck. A second shot hit 58-year old Neal Pilon, a Columbia Gas Company employee who had just exited his parked truck.

Unaware of the danger, Bud Fromme drove Engine No. 41 to the scene. A bullet smashed through the cab splitting Fromme's cap and scalp and striking Joseph Snopkowski in the stomach. Fire Lieutenant John Gibbons along with Firefighters David Nolder and Frank Ensell gave aide and protection to their comrades. Ensell attempted to help Pilon who was lying in the street, but several shots rang out with one hitting Pilon in the head killing him instantly. Twenty five-year old Carmen Wright Drayton, a passenger in a car driven by her sister was killed instantly when struck by bullets.

There were many innocent persons injured with many heroic instances of stranger helping stranger. Just before 4:00 PM, an M-48 military tank from the Olean National Guard Armory lumbered up the street. Knowing the immediate need, Unit Commander William Foss, unable to get authorization, ordered the tank to the scene. Police Chief Michael Luty had requested use of the tank to provide maximum protection and cover rescuers aiding the injured.

POLICE ACTION

From his vantage point, Barbaro shot and killed three innocent people and wounded several others as they went about their daily tasks. At about 5:00 PM, State Police Investigator John Stofer and Police Chief Luty worked out a plan to storm the school from the rear. Investigators Stofer, David O'Brien, Troopers Dale Butts and John Hayes along with Olean Police Officers Thomas Benton and James Connelly armed with shotguns and tear gas made their way to the third floor. They found Metcalf's body on the floor. On signal, Investigator O'Brien swung into the vestibule and fired a blasting hole in the frosted glass door. Simultaneously, a tear gas grenade was tossed into the room. O'Brien found Barbaro dressed in camouflage clothing hiding behind a desk. He offered no resistance when taken into custody.

THE CARNAGE

Dead were Earl Metcalf, 61, Olean, N.Y., a school custodian, Neal Pilon, 58, Olean, N.Y. a gas company meter reader and Carmen Wright Drayton, 25, Olean, N.Y. a young expectant mother. Eleven other persons suffered various degrees of gunshot wounds. They were:

Abdo, Albert J. Jr., Olean, N.Y. – Gunshot would to left elbow
Dutton, Wayne L., Hinsdale, N.Y. – Gunshot wound to right wrist
Elmore, Herbert V., Olean, N.Y. – Gunshot wound to skull & right hand
Fromme, William R., Olean, N.Y. – Gunshot laceration of scalp & forehead
Grosse, David A., Olean, N.Y. – Glass fragments to both arms
Limerick, Raymond C., Olean, N.Y. – Glass fragments scratches to legs and arms
McCutcheon, Larry J., Olean, N.Y. Fragment wounds to left thigh & right arm
Snopkowski, John M., Olean, N.Y. – Forehead laceration & fragments in left ear.
Snopkowski, Joseph J., Olean, N.Y. – Gunshot wound to stomach
Weidt, Earl R., Olean, N.Y. – Fragment wounds of chest and left eye
Williams, George H. Jr., Olean, N.Y. – Shrapnel wounds to left chest
Wright, Julius A., Portville, N.Y. – Glass fragments in both eyes

No reason could be given for the outburst. Barbaro was ranked #8 in a class of 290 academically and was a member of the schools rifle team. He entered a plea of not guilty when arraigned before Olean City Court Judge James Crowley and was remanded to the Cattaraugus County Jail without bail. He was indicted by a Grand Jury on three counts of Murder First Degree, but the trial never came to pass. At 6:00 AM on November 1, 1975, Barbaro was found hanging from his cell by a sheet. County Coroner Dr. Harry Law ruled the death a suicide by strangulation. No one will ever know what demons danced in his head causing him to do the unthinkable.

ALABAMA HOTEL ROBBERY – APRIL 22, 1975

On April 22, 1975 at 9:18 PM, four armed masked men entered the Alabama Hotel, Alabama Center, N.Y. forcing owner Agnes Woodward to place cash register receipts into a white bank bag. They then forced her and patron Donald "Whitey" Feitshans to lie on the floor while they made their getaway.

As they exited the front door, the owner's son, Timothy Woodward entered through a rear door, saw the bandits exit and pursued them, as they sped from the scene. He was forced to halt, when shots fired from the fleeing car struck automobile, but not before obtaining the license plate number. The car registered to Philip Skye, a Tonawanda Indian Reservation resident was found abandoned in a field on the reservation. Charges of First-Degree Robbery were lodged against Skye, age 27, and Faron Rueben, age 21 also a reservation resident. Two other youths were charged, but no reportable disposition could be found. Recovered were a .22 caliber revolver, an old Army rifle and a shotgun. The foursome were arraigned before Justice George Mills and ordered held for Grand Jury action. On July 15, 1976 both were found guilty of Second Degree Robbery and sentenced to a term in Attica Prison of no less than 3 1/2 to 10 years confinement.

BANK ROBBERS CAPTURED- JULY 1, 1975

A bank robbery in Monroe County led to two high-speed chases and the apprehension of the bandits. Genesee County Sheriff's Deputy Barry Garigan first spotted the bandits traveling in separate cars and gave chase. He notified the Batavia City Police and New York State Troopers providing vehicle descriptions and direction of travel. Trooper William F. Sobolewski joined the chase and after a five-mile pursuit, apprehended one of the robbers at gunpoint. As the second car sped toward Batavia, a roadblock was established near the city line. The bandit vehicle weaved its way through the roadblock, entered the city striking a car. It continued down Main Street through the city turning north onto Route 63 where it struck two other vehicles while traveling at over 100 MPH. First Sergeant Vernon Clayson and Sergeant Bill Stubbins joined the pursuit, as well as off duty Trooper Louis Lang who jumped into a troop car and gave chase. Lang managed to position himself directly behind the suspect vehicle. He followed along until the robber lost control leaving the roadway, rolling over several times coming to rest on its top. The uninjured black/male bandit fled on foot. A search by the Division helicopter resulted in the apprehension of the suspect by off duty Investigator Henry Haas and Trooper Mickey Schrader. Investigator Haas who had monitored the radio transmissions from his residence and Trooper Schrader who resided near the scene, both off duty, had responded to the location of the crash. The suspect was observed hiding next to a barn about a half-mile from the scene. In their haste to join the pursuit, Haas and Schrader failed to arm themselves. They took the bandit into custody by pointing only their fingers at him with a threat to shoot, if necessary. He surrendered without incident. Firearms used in the robbery along with $29,340.37 were found in the wrecked vehicle. During the robbery, Sergeant Gerald Thurley of the Gates Police Department had been held at gunpoint and his firearm and portable radio taken. As usual, after we did the legwork, the FBI came for pictures and news coverage. They even fetched the Buffalo TV station people to cover them taking the bumbling bandits away.

John Connor of the Batavia Daily News wrote:
"Good work". It was reassuring how quickly law enforcement officers rallied when the word was out that two bank robbery suspects were being pursued in the area." It concludes "police all did their part professionally and cooperatively in a real life dramatization of how important cooperation and communication are. This demonstration of law enforcement expertise, courage, dedication and risk taking should demonstrate that crime is not so profitable or worthwhile in this neck of the woods.

OPERATION ZINGER – 1976-1977

Opening for business on December 21, 1976, undercover troopers opened a store called Don's Buy and Sell at 1516 Pine Avenue, Niagara Falls, N.Y. Police Chief Anthony C. Fera decided to go after career criminals who were responsible for a multitude of burglaries in Niagara Falls and the immediate vicinity and requested the State Police help, because his men were known to the "bad guys". The "STING" was the first in Western New York.

The store was equipped with a hidden camera behind a two-way mirror to photograph each customer and a microphone was installed in the ceiling to record all transactions. The inside counter was reinforced with cinder block to serve as protection in case of a shootout. At all times, there was a Niagara Falls police officer hidden in the back room to operate the camera and was armed with a 12-gauge riot shotgun in case it was needed.

$9,500.00 funding for the operation was provided by Niagara County District Attorney Aldo Diflorio. When the storefront closed on March 14, 1977, all but $400.00 had been spent on more than 300 items having a retail value of $50,000.00. The net result was the indictment and arrest of 29 suspects who were responsible for 95% of the areas burglaries. All of the suspects entered guilty pleas in Niagara County Criminal Court.

Senior Investigator Donald Munch and Investigator Jack Gleason who ran the sting later recalled a few tense situations. A man came into the store with a bulge under his jacket with the intent of staging a holdup. One of the troopers laid a handgun on the counter quickly deterring the thought. On more than one occasion, they were actually accused of being cops, but conned the cons.

ATTICA PRISON MURDER
During 1977, troopers were called to the Attica Correctional Facility to investigate the rape-murder of a cook whose body was found stuffed in meat cooler. Investigators were able to penetrate the "inmate" code of silence and identify the murderer in less than 12 hours.

CLARENCE, N.Y – BURGLARY
On February 13, 1979, Troopers Albert Simmons and Charles Gibbs assigned at SP Clarence responded to a silent alarm at 8545 Main Street, Clarence, N.Y. indicating a burglary was in progress. A burglary suspect arrested at the scene was identified as Paul D. Weber, age 18, East Amherst, N.Y. One of the offices burglarized was the location of a CIA operation. With its "cover" blown by the unsuspecting burglar, the operation was relocated. Troopers Simmons and Gibbs received commendations.

PRISON STRIKE – 1979
On April 18,1979, Union Council 82, AFSCME representing New York States Correctional Officer's called for a strike due to an impasse in contract negotiations. 800 Troopers were mobilized and became immediately involved with perimeter security of the states prisons, traffic control and monitoring picket lines. The Division was placed on a twelve-hour workday for the sixteen-day duration of the strike that ended May 5, 1979.

Overtime costs were estimated at $2 ½ million. Unfortunately, 170 arrests were made for Disorderly Conduct, Trespass, Criminal Mischief and Harassment. Council 82 came under jurisdiction of New York's Taylor Law that made it illegal to strike without incurring fines imposed on the Union and loss of pay for striking members. Nevertheless, determined union members intent on improving working conditions persevered at considerable financial risk. Other Unions who refused to cross their picket lines supported them. 430 incidents were investigated.

A side note: The Batavia troopers had a close relationship with prison guards from Attica Prison. Years of friendly baseball and bowling competition resulted in many friendships and shared social activities with one another. Troopers assigned to the Attica Prison sector would often bring coffee and doughnuts to striking picketers with whom they sympathized while being mindful of their assigned duty to preserve the peace.

COMMENTS:
The efforts of the NYS Police to maintain order at state correctional and mental hygiene facilities have stabilized a potentially dangerous situation. The rapid deployment of state police permitted remaining staff, guard units and volunteers to maintain essential services in a secure environment. Hugh L. Carey, Governor

Thank you for the assistance provided by the NYS Police during a trying time. Your men have been a tower of strength and the assistance and cooperation received has been of the highest caliber. Superintendent Harold J. Smith, Attica Correctional Facility

Our local will be forever appreciative of the high degree of professionalism and sensitivity to the problems of Correction Officers exhibited by all members of the state police at Attica during the period April 18 to May 5. No one knows better than I the difficulties faced by your men here at Attica. Secretary Charles J. Biggins, Council 82, Local 1040 – Attica Correctional Facility

1980 TID BITS

OBSERVANT TROOPERS CATCH KILLER
In 1981, Troopers Thomas Fulton and Albert Gerhardt while on patrol in the town of Alden observed a green Ford Thunderbird traveling westbound on Route 20. Information received was that the vehicle was wanted in connection with a murder investigation. Fulton operating an unmarked patrol followed behind the suspect car while radioing ahead his location and progress. Lancaster, Depew and Cheektowaga Police established a roadblock in the Village of Lancaster utilizing a tractor-trailer to block the roadway. As they approached the village, a Lancaster fireman named Robinson listening to the situation develop on his police-fire monitor decided to help. With red lights flashing, he intercepted the Thunderbird attempting to force it to stop. The suspect driver turned onto Lombardy Street in the Village, then fled on foot into a vacant field on Parkview Drive. Fulton in close pursuit fired two shots at the suspect. A few seconds later, he heard a female voice saying, "He's right in front of you in the bushes". It was a sixteen-year old resident that had observed the chase from her window. Assisted by Gerhardt and a Lancaster Police Officer Pat Adino, the suspect was taken into custody at gunpoint without incident. He had been laying flat on his stomach removing rings from his fingers that had been taken from a murder scene in Boston, Massachusetts. He was identified as Daniel Richard Roberts who had previously resided in Clarence Center, N.Y.

It was learned that the suspect was an escapee from an Oklahoma prison and while at large, murdered and robbed a Boston man stealing his car, cash and jewelry. He then traveled west into New York State traveling to Clarence Center, N.Y. where he had previously resided. Along the way, he made a stop at Frankfort, N.Y. where he murdered an elderly lady in her home, stole money and her Green Thunderbird car. This was the car he was driving when pursued and captured.

He was convicted of Murder 1st Degree in both Massachusetts and New York and was sentenced to life imprisonment.

THE .22 CALIBER KILLER
During an 18-day reign of terror during the fall of 1980, six black men had been brutally murdered in or near the City of Buffalo, N.Y. The killings ended as quickly as they started.

On September 22, 1980, 14-year old Glen Dunn was shot three times in the head as he sat in a car in a supermarket parking lot. The next day, Harold Green was found shot in nearby Cheektowaga, N.Y.

and a few hours later, Emmanuel Thomas was found shot in Buffalo, N.Y. On September 24, Joseph McCoy was found shot in Niagara Falls, N.Y. Witnesses described the assailant as a white male. He had shot all four of the victims in the left side of the head with a .22 caliber gun. In early October, the body of Parler Edwards was found on the Thruway stuffed in the trunk of his car. He had been beaten and his heart had been cut out. The same night the body of Ernest Jones, a cab driver was found in a boat on the Niagara River. His throat had been slashed and his heart cut out. Newspapers dubbed the crimes the work of the "**. 22 CALIBER KILLER**". A multi agency law enforcement task force was organized and huge awards posted for the arrest and conviction of the "Demon" killer. Trooper Captain Henry Williams and Lieutenant Raymond Slade headed the eighty-man detail assigned to the case. Every man on the detail worked seven days a week, fourteen hours a day until Joseph Christopher was identified and taken into custody.

During the next few weeks, reports were received of similar attacks occurring in New York City. Five black men had been attacked with a knife while riding the subway with two victims surviving. Five attacks were reported at bus stops in Rochester and Buffalo, N.Y. with three victims surviving.

In early 1981, the US Army at Fort Benning, Georgia notified New York authorities that Army Private Joseph Christopher of Buffalo, N.Y. was undergoing psychiatric treatment for self-inflicted knife wounds. He was being in the stockade for attacking a black soldier with a knife. He had bragged to nurses that he had shot & stabbed several black men in New York. It was learned that Christopher had enlisted on October 15, 1980 shortly after the Buffalo murders stopped.

State police investigators were sent to Fort Benning where clothing, glasses and bus ticket receipts from Georgia to New York City and New York City to Buffalo were found. Search warrants were obtained for his Buffalo residence and nearby hunting cabin. Several .22 caliber shell casings were found that matched those found at the murder scenes.

Christopher was convicted and sentenced to 35 years to life for the New York City murders and on May 24, 1982, sentenced to 60 years to life for three Buffalo murders.

He subsequently died in prison, the victim of cancer.

PHONY ALLEGANY COUNTY DOCTOR
An unemployed Rochester, N.Y. fork lift operator found his way to a small Allegany County community where he established himself as a family doctor who made house calls and never charged more than $10.00 a visit. By the time the sham was uncovered, he had 600 faithful patients. He was charged with Practicing Medicine Without a License.

PENNSYLVANIA MURDER SOLVED BY DESKMAN
During the fall 1981, Trooper Michael H. Schrader received a call while working desk duty at Batavia. The caller talked for over forty minutes inquiring about various criminal punishments. Sensing there was more than was being provided, Schrader coaxed the caller into identifying himself. He and Investigator Louis J. Lang then interviewed him. After two hours of conversation, the man revealed that his grandson told him about a murder near Pittsburgh, Pa. and the taking of the victim's car after dumping the body. Inquiries to the Pennsylvania State Police indicated that they were unaware of any murders. The grandson was found hiding in a Batavia motel under an assumed name and was charged with a minor violation. He was interviewed and provided the following information: While hitch hiking from Florida to Pennsylvania with a 19-year-old couple, they were picked up near Pittsburgh. As they rode along, they stopped for a rest and the couple stabbed the driver to death, took $5.00 from him and dumped his body down a 20-foot embankment. They then took the victims vehicle. The Pennsylvania Troopers were made aware of the information obtained and short time later, confirmed

the finding of the body at the location described. The grandson provided information that the 19-year old couple resided in the City of Buffalo where they were located and placed under arrest. While statements were being taken, the first youth (Grandson) admitted that it was he who did the stabbing. They were extradited to Pennsylvania for prosecution.

FRANK CARROLL MURDER - 21 OCTOBER 1981
Trooper Senior Investigator Gerald Forster investigated an unsolved murder that had occurred in 1981. In the fall of 1981, a boy walking his dog discovered skeletal remains approximately 30-50 feet off a narrow dirt road, in a heavily overgrown pine tree plantation. It was a location that a person would not travel to unless familiar with area. The identity of the remains remained a mystery for 11 years. An intense investigation was conducted with numerous leads investigated. During the early stages of the investigation, fliers containing the facts of the investigation and composite drawings were sent to Police agencies throughout the United States, Canada and the Colorado B.C.I. that was a central repository for missing persons and unidentified victims.

Forster who retired on April 22, 1992 received a telephone call on September 15, 1992, from Lieutenant Larry Green of the Lake County, Ohio Sheriff's Office. Green was investigating a possible homicide with the victim identified as Frank Carroll. The killing took place in Lake County on February 2, 1980.

A witness had come forward stating that in 1980, she had helped her then boy friend Larry Schlee dispose of a body. She said the dead man was Frank Carroll and had been murdered by Schlee. She thought they had dumped the body in Pennsylvania, but couldn't be sure. Lieutenant Green had concentrated his searches in the Pennsylvania area without success. As a last resort, he contacted Chautauqua County Deputy Randy Vanderschaaff who was familiar with the unidentified body found years earlier. He in turn contacted the BCI unit at SP Fredonia and retired Trooper Forster. The body was positively identified as Carroll with Schlee arrested for his murder. Forster testified and acted as a consultant during the trial. Schlee was convicted and sentenced to 33 years in prison. During March 2004, Schlee was re-tried after appeal of his conviction citing new evidence. Retired Senior Investigator Forster was again called as a witness. Schlee was again convicted and again sentenced to 33 years with credit for time served.

TROOPER GEORGE H. LACHNICHT – December 1981
Trooper George H. Lachnicht stationed at SP Wolcott was preparing to go on patrol one morning, when an explosive device was detonated under the hood of his troop car. The bomb was detonated as he turned on the ignition key. Lachnicht suffered severe burns to his lower legs and numerous cuts and bruises that covered his entire body. He is the son of former Trooper Frank Lachnicht. The case was never solved and remains an open investigation.

PAUL LUKASIEWICZ AND WILLIAM HUBERT
During the winter of 1981, Troopers Paul Lukasiewicz and Bill Hubert (Orchard Park) on night patrol stopped to assist an Erie County Deputy at an accident scene. While parked with lights flashing, an intoxicated driver traveling at a high rate of speed struck the troop car in the rear forcing it into a guardrail. Lukasiewicz suffered small bone fractures in the neck and compression of vertebrae. Hubert suffered neck and back injuries that affected the use of his arm. Both were treated and recuperated at home.

TROOPER RENDERS CPR - SAVES A LIFE - 1982
Trooper Gerald Wienckowski was enjoying lunch at Zorba's Hot Dog Stand, Cheektowaga, N.Y. when a woman entered seeking help for her husband who had collapsed in the parking lot. Trooper

Wienckowski went to his aide administering mouth-to-mouth resuscitation. The man identified as Thomas Chiarmonte of Depew, N.Y. recovered fully. Wienckowski recalled that the incident was both gratifying and nauseating. He said that during the mouth-to-mouth resuscitation, the victim vomited into his mouth, which he instantly spit out. It didn't bother him at the time, but several hours later, when he thought back, he himself became ill and vomited. He related that several days later, Chiarmonte, the owner of a jewelry store called him and wanted to personally thank him. He was so appreciative of the trooper saving his life that he offered him "free lifetime service to have his watch cleaned."

AKRON, N.Y. MAJOR FIRE - 1982

During the winter of 1982, Trooper Philip Attea was called to investigate the strong smell of gasoline at a fuel distribution center. An unknown person attempting to steal gas had allowed 1500 gallons of gasoline to spill onto the ground. The owner was contacted and together with the Akron Fire Department, a cleanup procedure was commenced. About three hours later, a worker accidentally ignited a spark causing the entire fuel compound to catch fire. The firemen and workers had to sprint for over 100 yards to keep from being engulfed in a massive fireball. The fire ignited 5 storage tanks containing 50,000 gallons of gasoline, kerosene and diesel fuel, as well as two 24,000-gallon storage tanks containing highly volatile ethylene glycol. Trooper Attea, Akron Patrolman R.S. Farrington and Erie County Deputies evacuated 1000 residents in the near proximity of the fire. The fire was contained within the fuel compound grounds with no injuries resulting. It was declared officially out 24 hours after it started. Damage and loss of commodity was placed at $500,000.00. Twelve Fire Departments were on the scene in addition to a Medivac helicopter with trained medical technicians and seventy-five police officers for security purposes.

V. TOBIA - J. STOJNOWSKI - J. GRESENS
M. OROURKE - T. CONSTANTINE

CAPTAIN DAN FOX & ELK

DAN FOX

229

CAPTAIN DAN E. FOX
BINGHAMTON, NEW YORK 13901

TROOPER JOHN HAWLEY FUNERAL - 1974

LOUIS MACRI 1970S

Troopers Quiz Holton After Capture in Akron

—Photo by Dick McWain, Batavia.

TROOPER KARL LIMMNER   THEODORE HOLTON   SGT. WILLIAM RIMMER

BATAVIA, Aug. 1—Theodore Holton, escaped mental patient, told troopers, "I'm not going to come out alive!" before he was flushed from beneath some steps on the Tonawanda Indian Reservation in Akron on Friday. But Holton, who escaped from the Rochester State Hospital on July 12, was very much alive today in the Genesee County Jail. He waived preliminary examination Friday evening before Peace Justice E. Harry Miller on a charge of illegally possessing a weapon and was held for the grand jury.

Patrick O'reilly, John Kelly, PhilipCharnot at SP Lewiston – 1974

1944 – CAPTURED JAPANESE MINI SUBMARINE –
TOURED THE UNITED STATES TO RAISE MONEY FOR
WAR BONDS

R. Walters. C. Cobb. C. Bailey. J. Nohlen. K. Weidenborner. J. Long. G. Schusler – 1963

Art Rich. Alex Larson. Mrs Dorothy Johnston. Larry Kelly. Ray Schasel. Richard Brecht.
Walt Rosenow. Bart McFarland. Glenn Courlis. Bill Rimmer. Harvey Gregg.
Wes Eastman. John Murphy. Joseph Lyons. Red Cross Training - 1943

E.HAMMERSCHMIDT- E.GLUCH - J.CEFERATTI
GOVERNOR NELSON ROCKEFELLER

SP WELLSVILLE - 1969 -- B.INGALLS- LT.URANITIS
A.ASTON-T.STOFER-L.AUSTIN-H.HATCH- J.JOHNSON
G.KNIGHT-R.NITCHE- C.GOOCH- J.HAYES- G.ADAMS
P.CARLSON- J.COSGROVE- V.BARON

Jim Mohn, Norman Wright, Chief Everett Parker, Bob Szymanski
at Tonawanda Reservation — 1964

BOOK VII — HUMAN INTEREST

TROOPER RECRUIT IN 1957

I enlisted in NYSP on 2-14-57 and was assigned to Troop A Headquarters, Batavia, New York. John P. Ronan was the Troop Commander and Charlie McDonald was the "First Shirt" (First Sergeant).

Young rookie troopers were frequently the subject of those dreaded File 14's (Teletype Message) and were routinely transferred from station to station. The NYSP reason or "party line" for the transfers was that they did not want us troopers "to become too familiar with the local population". Another theory was that the transfers gave both the local young ladies and the new young troopers a change of scenery and sometimes a means of escape!

Coming from a metropolitan area, I found the falling and drifting snow to be incredible. Snow was near the tops of telephone poles in many areas. It was both a physical and cultural shock to me.

The first few weeks of our barracks duty (I arrived there with 8 other recruits) and the anticipated thrills of being a New York State Trooper consisted almost exclusively of dressing in fatigues daily, washing every headquarters window inside and out, vacuuming floors, dusting everything in sight that did not move, mowing grass, working in the Quartermaster, hand washing every Troop car assigned to Headquarters and the cars of visiting "important" people (Zone Lieutenants and BCI types) whenever they visited the building.

Each and every day, regardless of snow, rain or temperature, Captain Ronan's black 1957 Dodge Troop car had to be washed and carefully detailed and then re-parked very carefully in the very first horse-stall immediately adjacent to the back door. (The indoor parking garages were converted horse stalls).

NOTE: A very intense internal investigation never really confirmed the identity of the guilty party who, when parking Ronan's car after being washed, apparently parked it with the front wheels turned sharply to the left. When the Troop Commander attempted to back his vehicle out of the stall, a significant amount of damage was done to the right front of his Troop car.

Recruits were the prime suspects, but as the investigation widened, it was noted that other headquarters troopers occasionally parked Ronan's car after being washed by the recruits. Eventually and without the benefit of an accident report (a dreaded File 3) and at no cost to the State, Ronan's car was repaired. The matter was closed with an informal rule being implemented that any trooper parking Ronan's car was to make a blotter entry to that effect.

We lowly recruits were also assigned to vacuum, dust and clean Ronan's private one-man bedroom. The assignment gave us a rare opportunity to confirm some personal facts about our feared Troop Commander. By observing the contents of his chest of drawers, we were able to confirm that he did indeed wear only powder blue boxer shorts, meticulously stacked in the top drawer with a sachet of perfume scent placed between each pair of shorts. This discovery sent us Aqua Velva and Brill Cream types into hysterics and caused us to speculate wildly on the subject of Ronan's (if you will excuse the expression) masculinity.

On occasion, we recruits were permitted to pose as real New York Troopers by being ordered to get into "full pack" i.e. .45 Colt revolver with 6" barrel (cross draw of course), lanyard, breeches and puttees, stetson, sam brown belt and full length overcoat. (We were actually issued spurs, but never got to wear them).

Our duties in full pack were to chauffer Corporal Jim Moochler or Sergeant Billie Rimmer to the Batavia Post office or some other location. On one occasion, myself along with another recruit, Moochler and Trooper Duane Roberts participated in the "heroic" rescue of two elderly ladies who were marooned in their home because of complete blockage of the roads by snowdrifts. They were in need of their prescription medications, food and water.

Accompanied by a newspaper reported and photographer who duly recorded our heroic mission, the four of us loaded a large sled, strapped on full size snowshoes and set out to the ladies house that was about two miles from the nearest open road. (Two of us pulled the sled while two of us acted as rear brakes).

I cannot recall how many times we tripped (unless you walk totally bow legged, this is inevitable), overturned the sled and fell. We never did master the drill of efficient sled pulling which absolutely requires a high degree of co-ordination between the front duo and rear duo.

One of the very best troopers at Batavia was Sergeant John Long. He was the Communications Sergeant when I got there. It was my pleasure to know him and on occasion to work for him. Which leads me to a story about him.

About every other day, two of us recruits would report to the communications room and drag two or three heavy canvas bags, loaded with old teletype messages out for destruction. They were placed in the Troop's black Chevrolet pickup truck and taken to the city dump for burning. They were burned because the NYSP did not want the public to read them.

On one occasion, a fellow recruit carefully backed the pickup truck as closely as possible to the fire. I stood on the tailgate and proceeded to empty the contents of the bags into the fire. The wind suddenly shifted and blew hot flames, smoke and ash into my face causing me to let go of the bag. The bag fell into the fire and was totally consumed within minutes. We both saw our short careers in NYSP also going up in smoke for carelessly burning State Police property. Returning to headquarters, we fearfully related our tale of woe to Sergeant Long. Instead of the expected tongue-lashing and a written report of our misdeed, Sergeant Long told us not to worry and to not say anything about the incident. He somehow got the bag replaced without any written report. I am convinced to this day (I certainly was then) that Sergeant Long had just saved my career in troopers.

After my stint at Batavia, I became the subject of a number of File 14s (transfers). One was never sure as to the real reason for a station transfer. Explanations were never given, you just went. Arriving at each new station, you were given a quoted warning, "Hey, kid, don't unpack, you wont be here that long".

At various times and for varying lengths of time, I was stationed at the following locations:

SP Clarence - Corporal Ron Dennis was the station commander. I worked with Trooper Jack Smith (my senior Trooper), Bill Peterson, George Watt (to my knowledge, the only full blooded Indian in troopers) and BCI Trooper Bud Driscoll.

SP Lewiston - BCI Sergeant Charlie Bukowski, Corporal Chester Chwala, Troopers Ray Benson, Frank Demler, Eddie Pawlak and Bob Fisher.

SP Avon - Sergeant Mike Norsen, Lieutenant Vernon Voight, BCI Sergeant Claude Stephens, BCI Trooper Pete Koenig, Troopers Doug Carpenter (my senior trooper), Lou Ruberto, Jake Williams and Lennie Bochynski.

SP Bergen - Trooper George Zink and Jerry Brakefield.

SP Henrietta - Sergeant George Clune was the station commander.

I also did a short stint at SP Wellsville during the 1957 milk strike in the southern tier.

I was transferred to another troop where I completed my career and retired from the NYSP.

The author of this article chose to remain anonymous:

TROOPER HUMOR

ALCOHOL CONSUMPTION – 1950s

Trooper Harold "Hi" Moose was assigned to desk duty one evening, when he received an unusual telephone inquiry. The male caller wanted to know if it was okay for troopers to drink beer while on duty in uniform. Trooper Moose asked the reason for the inquiry and was told that the caller had just observed two troopers at a local tavern eating a sandwich and washing it down with a beer. The troopers next question was "did the man know if they paid for what they ate and drank" and was told that they had. Moose then stated that there was no problem, as long as they paid for it and hung up. (Troopers are not permitted to consume alcoholic beverages while on duty)

NEVER MISS BREAKFAST

Trooper Robert E. Minekheim was stationed at SP Gaines (Orleans County) during the 1950s and was sweet on a waitress working at a local restaurant. He planned his work schedule daily so that he could be with her for a short time before her shift started. One morning, his routine was interrupted when he was forced to make an arrest. Instead of continuing with normal procedure, he put that on hold by handcuffing the prisoner around the station flagpole while he went off for his romantic interlude. Returning an hour later, he continued the arrest process.

BREAST PRINTS

Sometime during the late 1960s, Lewiston, N.Y. troopers experimented with a new method of body identification. They believed that no two female breasts were alike and were determined to prove it. A willing female participant was found reporting to the station in the middle of the night. With breasts bared, she was quickly covered with finger print ink administered by hand. The station had four large, flat frosted light globes that were used to take the impression. Her breasts were gently pressed to the glass and an impression taken. The globes were then returned to their original position. Arriving for duty in the morning, Z/Sgt. Charlie Schwartz observed and spent the entire day trying to determine what was on the globes before he had them washed. He never did learn what they were. Finding no other willing females to bare their breasts for comparison, the experiment was ended.

GETTING A CONFESSION

Investigator Ralph Fuller (Wrights Corners) arrested a child predator for the molestation of young children. The suspect denied any knowledge of the crimes, but had been identified by several of the young victims. Fuller did not want to have the children put through any emotional trauma so he needed an admission for conviction. He ordered the suspect to take off his socks and shoes, marched him to the front of the station handcuffing him to the flagpole. He told the suspect he would have to remain there until he confessed. Fuller then left. Returning several hours later, the suspect readily admitted to the crimes.

THE SLEEPER
Trooper Richard Hampson (Henrietta) was sent to Syracuse about 70 miles away to pick up a prisoner. As they entered the troop car for the return trip to Rochester, Hampson handcuffed the prisoner to the steering wheel and instructed him to drive the car. He then got into the back seat of the car and went to sleep. Arriving at the Henrietta station, the prisoner was taken to the sleeping quarters on the second floor, handcuffed to a bed while Hampson again went to sleep. Troopers arriving for duty found the bewildered prisoner wide awake still handcuffed and the trooper sound asleep. Oh yes, Hampson was Narcoleptic. (a sleeping disorder)

NUDE INTERVIEW
Investigator Ronald Dennis had a theory on confessions that he applied in serious and violent crimes he investigated. He would force a suspect to strip nude under the guise of personal security and safety, then would conduct the interview. It was his personal feelings that a naked man couldn't lie.

STRIKING LABORERS
Trooper Joe Law (Thruway Buffalo) was sent to the scene of a labor union strike involving about sixty picketers. Arriving in a marked patrol car, he advised the strikers in his authoritative voice that if any of them stepped foot on thruway property, they would be arrested for trespass. He repeated his promise several times, adding, "just try me" each time. Returning to the troop car, he gave one more loud warning just as he entered the rear seat of the troop car and closed the door. The scolded picketers roared in delight at the sight. There was the embarrassed trooper, in full uniform, climbing over the front seat desperate to leave. (The rear doors were intentionally made un-operable from inside to prevent prisoners from escaping)

BIGGEST PILLOW
The Wyoming County night patrol was probably one of the quietest areas for activity in the state. Troopers Martin Hockey, Freeman Shaw and Larry Francis routinely volunteered for the night shift. There was a reasonable amount of activity for the first two hours of the shift, but after that it was lights out. Each vied for a position in the rear seat, as it was the most comfortable place to spend the night. Part of the un-issued equipment was a personal pillow. All three agreed that most use came from the super-sized pillow owned by Larry Francis. On more than one occasion, he would immediately locate himself in the back seat claiming squatter's rights. Francis commented that he slept more with his partners than he did with his wife.

TROOPER SLEPT WITH HIS SISTER
Trooper James Green (Fredonia) having a dry sense of humor enjoyed getting a reaction from his co-workers, when he told them he slept with his sister. The fact was that he really did, but not in an immoral sense. Jim's mother married his wife's father after their spouses had passed making Jim's wife his stepsister.

STAG NIGHT
The night patrols in Genesee County would meet early in the morning at the "Big E" Restaurant, East Main Street, Batavia, N.Y. owned by Jack and Francis Bennett. Jack would leave a back door key under an ashtray in his bakery trailer for police. The Troopers, Genesee County Sheriff's patrols and Batavia City Police would meet, exchange information and have a light meal there every morning. On one occasion it was decided that a review of evidence should take place. The evidence consisted of X-rated movies confiscated during a trooper raid on the East Pembroke Fire Department during a Stag Night. The date designated for movie night was well attended by not only Genesee County patrols, but Orleans and Wyoming Counties as well. The projector was placed on the eating counter

with a white window shade on the front door serving as the movie screen. The evidence had been closely scrutinized for about 30 minutes, when Patrolman Frank Lachnicht entered from the rear. He informed us that there were 5 or 6 cars parked across the street with occupants watching the movies from the outside. As it turned out, the thin window shade made viewing clearer from the outside than the inside with passing motorists taking advantage of the free show.

THE KEYS – SP LEWISTON

In 1967, Sergeant James C. Moochler was promoted to the rank of Lieutenant and assigned as Commander of Zone 1 at Lewiston, N.Y. He supervised the Batavia, Albion, Wrights Corners and Lewiston stations. He was affectionately referred to as "The Mailman". He resided in the Batavia, N.Y. area and would drop off and pick up memorandums, mail and paychecks on his way to and from Lewiston. On several occasions, he was overheard commenting on items missing from his office. He couldn't understand how that could happen as his door was always locked. The only extra keys were secured in a locked wall locker assigned to Zone Sergeant William Stubbins. While Moochler was away, the three Zone Sergeants, Stubbins, Charlie Swarts and George Convery decided to make the office as secure as possible for the new boss. They retained the services of a carpenter to install a new steel tamper proof door and doorjambs. A locksmith was hired to install new door handles and locks. The three were very pleased with themselves. As luck would have it, a local fruit farmer making his weekly delivery of apples stopped at the station. Convery purchased a basket of apples for the lieutenant locking them in the lieutenant's office. Returning to duty the next day, Moochler entered the office only to find a basket full of apple cores. An unsuccessful investigation was conducted to find the culprit or culprits who ate the apples and determine how the locked office was entered. The secret was never revealed until now. Retired Trooper Thomas J. Fulton recalled that the locking handle on Zone Sergeants Stubbins locker was faulty and could be opened without a key. At the end of the day, Stubbins would hang the spare office key in his locker, close the door, place his lock through the handle and check the lock to make sure it was locked. Everyone except the Sergeants knew of the faulty handle. Some of the troopers would enter the lieutenant's office, access his files and remove any derogatory information that could effect the annual performance evaluations. The secret of the faulty lock was the best-kept secret in Troop "A". Now you know the rest of the story.

COMPLAINT

First Sergeant Vernon Clayson was speaking on the telephone one afternoon just as Major John Nohlen came by and stopped. Clayson was spelling Nohlens name slowly and precisely to a man that wanted to send a letter of appreciation. When he hung up, Nohlen inquired what it was all about. Clayson told him that it was some guy with a complaint and I told him to go screw himself. He then wanted my name so I gave him yours. With that Nohlen almost lost his false teeth as he turned and left talking to himself.

SPORTS QUIZ BUST – 1970s

Sgt. Bob Minekheim along with Troopers Gerry Broska and Kevin Walsh were the most knowledgeable troopers in Western New York, when it came to sports trivia. They were selected to appear on a live locally broadcast sports trivia television show pitting them against an equally knowledgeable team. Channel four-television sports caster Van Miller served as moderator. The trooper's team practiced diligently for weeks. Minekheim was selected as the team captain and was the only team member that could push a buzzer indicating they knew the answer to a question. As the day of the event arrived, they felt confident they could answer any question posed. Now it was time for lights, camera and action. As the moderator posed each question, the buzzer for the trooper's team never sounded. Minekheim's hand completely covered the buzzer, but he was observed staring at the camera in what appeared to be a stupor. He had developed stage fright and was unable to answer any questions let alone press the buzzer. The competition soundly defeated the troopers who never answered one question correctly.

MALICIOUS COMPLIANCE
Captain George Tordy (Batavia) was very much impressed by the enforcement of Division Memorandums and on one occasion, selected the subject of File Checks, as his pet project. A file check was simply calling a persons name or license plate number to the communication section for them to check through the computer to determine if the person or vehicle was associated with a reported crime. He forwarded the directive to each station adding that each member of the troop would conduct file checks daily. Trooper William Gethoefer working the midnight shift proceeded nightly to the local motels calling in the license plate of every car parked there. Several days later, Captain Tordy called him into the office, admonished him for conducting too many file checks and handed him a memorandum. The memo stated that his **Malicious Compliance of a Directive** would not be tolerated and would be made part of his permanent record. Apparently, one of the less diligent communication people had complained about the large number of requests.

RUSSELL CHILANO – GROUNDS KEEPER
Russ Chilano was hired to do to odd maintenance jobs and was no ball of fire, but was a good guy. He just hated washing cars, mowing the lawn, changing light bulbs, trimming hedges and plowing snow, basically, everything he was hired to do. Russ was caught sleeping in the garage on several occasions, but nothing was said until one day F/Sgt. Vern Clayson took a picture of him sleeping, than woke him up. Russ denied he was asleep and demanded to see the Troop Commander, because he was being hassled and harassed. Vern said okay, as soon as I get the film developed showing you asleep and my notes on all the times I caught you sleeping. He quickly changed his mind with the incident soon forgotten. His wife Veronica also worked at the barracks and got into a routine of taking breaks when the different office girls took theirs. She was taking three in the morning and three in the afternoon. As a result, Russ became a more conscientious worker and Veronica was given a choice of when she wanted to take her one break each morning and afternoon.

THE DRUNK
Batavia Judge E. Harry Miller spent an evening at Heveron's Hotel in East Pembroke arriving home in a disheveled condition and a mess on the front of his jacket and pants from an upchuck. As he walked in the door, wife Mary demanded to know what had happened to him. Being a quick thinker, he told her he was returning from church, when a drunk came staggering down the street, bumped into him and caused the mess all over him. He went one step further and informed her that luckily, a trooper came along, witnessed the entire incident and arrested the man for public intoxication. The drunk was going to be arraigned before Harry the next day. Harry vowed to sentence him to the maximum. Make sure you do that Harry, commented Mary, because the man also pooped in your pants.

RUNNING TROOPER
There is a policy of checking on any stalled vehicles on the highway when the temperatures drop in the single digits or below. In the wee hours of the morning, a state trooper responded to a call of a car off the shoulder of the road. The trooper located the car with its engine still running stuck in the deep snow. Pulling in behind it with his emergency lights on, the trooper walked to the drivers door only to find a man passed out behind the wheel with a near empty bottle of booze on the seat. The trooper tapped on the window waking the driver. When the man saw the rotating red lights in his rear view mirror and the trooper standing next to his car, he panicked. He jerked the gearshift into drive and hit the gas. The cars speedometer was indicating 20-30-40, then 50 MPH, but was still stuck in the snow with its wheels spinning. The trooper having a sense of humor began running in place next to

the speeding, but stationary car. The driver was totally freaked out believing the trooper was actually keeping up with him. This went on for about 30 seconds when the trooper yelled at the man ordering him to pull over. The driver obeyed, turned his wheel and stopped the engine. Once out of the car the drunken driver asked about the trooper's special training and just how he could possibly run 50 MPH. The man was arrested still believing that a trooper had outrun his car.

RAVEN
During the 60's and 70's, Thruway Buffalo had a fictitious character known only to him called the **RAVEN.** He brought relief from the tension of the job to the forty plus troopers assigned there. Lieutenant Alexander Gallion, the Zone Commander was usually the focal point of the Ravens antics. If the Lieutenant posted a memorandum on the bulletin board, it was usually burned in just a few minutes with only the thumbtack remaining. The raven would leave notes for the dry cleaner to shorten the length of a pair of trousers or sew chevrons onto a trooper's shirt. He would fill a troopers boots with water soaking the trooper, when he went to use them. Materials and records wound up missing only to be found where they shouldn't have been. He would scratch a likeness of a raven's claw on the lieutenant's door to the point of the door having to be replaced over the years. On one or two occasions, the raven would send a memorandum to the local newspaper to be printed for all to see. No one really knew who the Raven really was or was it more than one person? Only the Raven knows!

FOLLOW THAT TROOPER
Trooper Philip E. Carroll was a tall thin man who always wore the finest clothing and drove a new Lincoln Town Car to work. Major Richard Boland, the Troop "A" Commander was convinced Carroll was doing something illegal. No trooper could live that lifestyle on a troopers pay. He was so convinced of wrong doing that he had a BCI investigator drive from Jamestown 90 miles away to Batavia in an unmarked trooper car to follow Carroll for several days. Carroll recognizing the car almost immediately led the poor investigator to every back road in the county including many he had never been on himself. Frustrated, Boland assigned Carroll to work desk duty. Each day Boland was on duty, Carroll would have his wife bring him lunch that was eaten at the desk. When his wife wasn't available, he would order a meal delivered from a local restaurant. The meals varied and would either be steak, lobster, scallops, shrimp or chops with all the trimmings and dessert. The major seeing this became increasingly frustrated with the trooper. Unknown to Boland, Carroll's wife had an inheritance that left them well off.

MIDNIGHT AUTO SUPPLY
Trooper Richard "Jake" Lathan was a full time farmer and a part time trooper. He always worked the "C" shift so he could tend to his farming during the day. On one occasion, he drove a tractor into a new troop car (while on duty) damaging a rear door. Concerned with reports and possible censure and punishment, Jake calmly returned to Troop Headquarters with his well-stocked toolbox. It being nighttime, he proceeded to the rear of the barracks where approximately 60 new troop cars were lined up in three rows waiting to be placed in service. He found the midnight auto supply to his liking and selected a troop car in the middle of the third row and methodically removed the door replacing it with his damaged door. Several months later, the car was being placed in service, when the damaged door was discovered. A thorough investigation failed to determine how the door was damaged.

TRANSPORTER CAR
Each troop had an unmarked car that was designated a transporter car. T/Sgt. Gary Law (Batavia Communications) resided in Lancaster, N.Y. and would occasionally drive the car home. One evening in February, Law attended a promotional party at the Batavia Treadway Inn. While on his way home

via the NYS Thruway, he ran off the roadway striking a guardrail causing considerable damage to the right side of the car. Early the next morning, Sgt. Jim Kasprzak (Clarence) called the writer to determine if anyone could quickly repair the damage. My good friend and neighbor, Keith Hammond, an auto repair specialist said he could. With two salamanders for heat, Hammond went to work on the car with the temperature below the freezing mark. The car was brought in at 9 AM and ready for pick up at 3 PM. It of course now sported many pounds of fiberglass and new paint. Total cost of repair was $125.00. Writer picked up the car returning it to Clarence, but not before driving off the roadway to get the new side soiled. Just as I exited the car in the rear parking lot at Clarence, Z/Sgt. Richard Hendricks drove in. He walked over to me and asked if the car I had driven in was the transporter car, as he would be taking it to Albany the following week. He inspected the car by walking completely around it and inquired about a dent in the center of the rear bumper. (It had nothing to do with Law running off the roadway). Hendricks said he would make a blotter entry to note the damage to the bumper. Kasprzak and I thought it humorous and Law was petrified. When I told Hammond about the inspection, he commented that he guaranteed his work for at least thirty miles or thirty minutes. We never did learn how long the repair job lasted.

LIE DETECTOR

Western New York had its share of migrant laborer related serious crimes. It usually wasn't difficult getting a confession, but occasionally, devious methods were used. One method was to blindfold and handcuff the suspect, then walk him down several stairs and have him step onto a low profile wooden soda pop case. A two or three foot length of clothesline was then placed loosely around his neck and the wooden box moved by kicking it. It gave the impression of being lynched. The suspect usually out of fright would provide a detailed account of the crime and would be placed under arrest. More often than not, the County District Attorney would provide a one-way bus ticket out of town to the defendant.

THE EYE BALLS

"Trooper Tom" was known throughout the Division for the matching blue eyeballs tattooed on the cheeks of his posterior. The tattoos came into play early one morning, when Trooper Tom and his friend, Jimmy (not a trooper) decided to take a trip south. While traveling through Pennsylvania several hours later, they were stopped by police. Having no form of identification on their person, the tattoos were offered as proof of identity. They persuaded the police officer to telephone Troop "A" Headquarters to verify the fact that Trooper Tom was indeed a New York State Trooper. Trooper Leonard Dayka assigned to desk duty that morning verified the famous eyeball tattoos and their location. Can you imagine the look on the trooper's face, when he saw the full moon with eyeballs?

MISSING MARIJUANA

The evidence locker at the old East Main Street barracks was located on the second floor in the BCI room. It was nothing more than a clothes closet with a hasp and lock on it. Several pounds of marijuana packaged in paper bags were secured in the evidence locker. Several months had passed with the case now going to trial. The District Attorney called for the evidence to be produced, but it could not be found. Records were checked and double-checked, but still no marijuana. Investigator Donald L. Smith was determined to find the missing marijuana. He emptied the evidence locker and found bits of the paper packaging in various locations within the closet. Then he found the culprit. A dead mouse and mouse droppings everywhere. The mice during the winter had eaten the marijuana. Needless to say, the case was dismissed for lack of evidence.

WORLD WAR II ACTIVITIES OF STATE POLICE

On September 6, 1939, President Franklin Delano Roosevelt declared a national emergency. The FBI was designated to coordinate all matters of internal national security. During early 1940, a complete survey of police personnel, equipment, transportation and communications facilities of the entire state except New York City was made.

CRITICAL FACILITIES INSPECTED
On July 24, 1940, Governor Herbert Lehman designated the state into eight mobilization districts. The troop commanders of seven districts that were the same geographically as the troop areas were designated coordinators. Plans were put in place to inspect various critical facilities on a daily, weekly or monthly basis. These included war plants, fuel storage areas, highway and railroad bridges, electric power stations, explosive magazines, canal locks and airports totaling 710 throughout the state.

INVESTIGATIONS FOR THE FBI
11,348 investigations were conducted and reports submitted of persons and organizations suspected of being engaged in subversive activities. These included Nazi, Fascist & Japanese sympathizers, Communist agitators and selective service delinquents.

MILITARY INTELLIGENCE INVESTIGATIONS
4000 investigations were conducted for the Army and 673 for the Navy. These included subversive investigations, confidential civilian and army personnel investigations and location of Japanese aliens.

OTHER AGENCY INVESTIGATIONS
6194 investigations were conducted for the Immigration Bureau, Treasury, Communication Commission, Marine Corp, Coast Guard, Department of Labor and several other state and federal agencies.

CONVOYS AND ESCORTS
The state police conducted convoy escorts of 2,699 military movement, 1,674 high explosive shipments, 228 vital war materials and 1,335 miscellaneous war materials.

Troopers purchased War Bonds in an amount of $181,195.00.

MEMBERS KILLED IN THE ARMED FORCES
Corporal Earl E. Wilkerson, Troop A – US Army Air Corp

   Killed in airplane crash May 24, 1942

Trooper Peter J. Formosa, Troop B – US Army

   Killed January 13, 1943 in motor vehicle crash

Trooper William O. Johnson, Troop B – US Navy

   Killed May 1, 1945 during action in Pacific

Trooper Milton Ratner, Troop C – US Army Air Corp

   Killed while bombardier during Sicily invasion

Trooper Bryant F. Stickles, Troop C – US Marine Corp

  Killed September 11, 1944 during action on Saipan Island

Trooper Charles E. Hover, Troop G – US Army

  Killed June 5, 1945 in airplane crash over northern Italy

EUGENE REDDEN
Retired Sergeant Eugene Redden gave the following account of one of his WWII experiences.

"I was a member of the Counter Intelligence Corps during the Second World War doing security work in the little villages as the Japanese were retreating from Burma. When the war ended, my unit was sent to Calcutta where we interviewed American prisoners of war who had just been released from the prison camps in Thailand and French Indo-China. When the interviews were completed, two of us were sent to Saigon to gather information on the Japanese guards who had mistreated the American prisoners of War. Gunfire was starting to become a common thing as the Vietnamese were killing the French at every opportunity. We had permission to leave at any time that we saw fit and decided to get out of there as soon as possible. The risk was too great so we hoped we could the next airlift flight out. In the early hours of September 26, 1945, we went to the airport to catch a flight that was to arrive at 9:00 A.M. The plane did not arrive on time so we stayed with a group of Americans also waiting for a flight out. The leader of the group appeared and advised us that the flight would be going to Calcutta, but was delayed so he invited us to his home for a meal. There was plenty of rifle fire going on around us so my partner and I declined his invitation. We stayed at the airport just in case the plane came in early and wanted to depart quickly. The man and his driver left. While returning to the airport, they were confronted by a native roadblock. The man now accompanied by an Army Major exited the jeep and spoke to the natives in French. It was a big mistake as they were immediately shot and killed by the natives who believed they were hated Frenchmen. As it turned out, I later learned that the man was Peter Dewey, a nephew of Governor Dewey. He had distinction of being the first American killed in what was to become Viet Nam.

TROOPER CHARLES W. JERMY
In a ceremony held in October1946, Trooper Charles W. Jermy, 36 Montclair Avenue, Batavia, New York was awarded the New York State Conspicuous Service Award for exceptional meritorious service. He was the first trooper from Troop "A" to enlist during World War II earning the Bronze Star, Purple Heart and a battlefield commission for heroic action during the battle of Ardennes. He was a member of the 334th Infantry, 84th Division.

WESTERN NEW YORK TROOPERS AND CIVILIAN STAFF MEMBERS THAT DIED OR WERE KILLED WHILE EMPLOYEES OF THE NEW YORK STATE POLICE

TROOPERS KILLED WHILE ON-DUTY
SERGEANT HARRY A. ADAMS

Harry A. Adams, age 55 of Medina, N.Y. was killed on September 1, 1951 when struck by a car while investigating an accident in Orleans County. An autopsy indicated he died of a ruptured artery and cerebral concussion, fracture of both legs and rib fractures. The accident happened on the Sawyer Road in front of the Colony Labor Camp and was witnessed by Trooper C. Leo Watkins who was with Adams. They were investigating a hit run accident at 9:30 PM, when a rapidly approaching car driven by George Hayes, age 31, of Palmetto, Florida, a migrant worker, struck Adams who was directing traffic. Adams was thrown forty feet, with Watkins narrowly escaping being hit. Trooper Watkins arrested Hayes at the scene on a charge of Criminal Negligence Homicide. Lieutenant William Stevenson, Corporal Kenneth Hemmer, Sergeant Donald Girven and Trooper John Sage conducted a follow up investigation.

Adams was a 28-year veteran enlisting in December 1923. He was in charge of the Gaines Station at Orleans County since 1932. Sergeant Adams was very popular and was mentioned several times as a candidate for sheriff. There were some who were of the opinion that he overemphasized petty crime, but he held the belief that small crimes unpunished lead to bigger crimes in the future. He was a victim of the mixture of alcohol and gasoline, a condition he had fought against for many years. He resided in Medina, N.Y. since 1933 and was survived by his wife, Margaret, sons Robert and John and daughters Virginia and Nancy. He was buried at Boxwood Cemetery, Medina, N.Y.

TROOPER RICHARD J. ROSA

Richard A. Rosa, age 30, 32 Goodyear Street, Buffalo, New York was killed in a motor vehicle accident on December 31, 1964. He was en-route for duty on the night shift when the accident occurred. He was north bound on Cedar Street, Batavia, N.Y. when for some undetermined reason he pulled sharply to the right striking a telephone pole. He then continued over a stone pile with the car-rolling end over end coming to rest on its top. He was crushed in the front seat suffering a fractured skull according to Coroner Dr. Dominic Cultrara. His wife Esther, a son Thomas and daughter, Cynthia Ann, survived him.

TROOPER JAMES D. CONRAD

On November 11, 1966, Trooper James D. Conrad, age 30, Prattsburg, New York was on routine patrol early in the morning, when a tractor-trailer truck made an improper left turn into the side of his troop car. The accident occurred on Route 15 just south of the Village of Cohocton. He was killed instantly. A trooper since June 18, 1962, he was assigned at SP Bath. His wife, Jesse Mae and five children Deborah, William, Anna, Betty and a 2-month-old infant, survived him.

SERGEANT JOSEPH GRANIC

On October 2, 1972, Sergeant Joseph Granic, age 33, 18 Baker Street, Andover, New York was instantly killed in an off duty auto accident. The accident occurred in the Town of Porter, an area he was unfamiliar with. He failed to stop for a stop sign and was struck broadside by an un-coming automobile. He was a native of Lackawanna, N.Y. He enlisted in the troopers on April 2, 1962. His wife Suzanne and three children, Joanne 12, Joseph 8 and Matthew 5, survived him. Burial is at Gate of Heaven Cemetery, Andover.

TROOPER JOHN W. HAWLEY

On 25, 1974, Trooper John Hawley, age 35, 750 Baseline Road, Grand Island, New York suffered a heart attack in the driveway of his home while conducting minor maintenance to his car. A few years earlier, he suffered an injury to his leg in a snow mobile accident that apparently created a blood clot that caused his demise. He became a trooper on June 18, 1962. His wife, Judith and children Rand 12, Sandra 11 and Patrick 10 survived him.

TROOPER RAY C. DODGE

On July 1, 1974, Trooper Ray C. Dodge, age 28 was mortally wounded by a shotgun blast at close range. He had responded to a simple property line dispute on Seneca Lake. As he entered the cottage of one of the disputant's, a shotgun pointed at him held by a Chadwick Little greeted him. While attempting to knock the gun away, it discharged striking Dodge. He was able to fire six rounds striking Little in the legs and chest. Dodge died the next day. The property owner recovered from his wounds and was charged with murder. As a result of this altercation, trooper weapons were upgraded from the traditional .38 caliber revolver to a .357 caliber magnum. His wife, Terri Gifford Dodge, survived him. He was buried at the Karr-Fairview Cemetery.

INVESTIGATOR THOMAS L. BUCK

On March 19, 1981, Investigator Thomas L. Buck, age 36 died of infectious hepatitis. He contracted the hepatitis during an arrest at Hanover, N.Y. He was securing a hypodermic needle as evidence, when he punctured his finger with the needle. In 1972, he was diagnosed with the infectious hepatitis. Continued episodes of liver dysfunction resulted in a disability retirement on August 1, 1979. His enlistment was May 5, 1968.

TROOPER GARY KUBASIAK

On August 30, 1982, Trooper Gary Kubasiak, age 32 was dead on arrival at Tri-County Hospital, Gowanda, N.Y. following a shoot-out, when responding to a domestic dispute. Charged with the killing was 33-year-old James J. Swan, Route 62, Dayton, N.Y., an ex-mental patient at Gowanda State Hospital. Troopers answered the call of a domestic dispute with Investigator Timothy Howard, a nearby resident responding. Kubasiak and his dog Donivan were also summoned to the scene from his nearby residence. Swan was known to and knew both officers and it was felt the personal contact was needed to handle the situation. Kubasiak along with "Donivan" entered the home through a rear kitchen door identifying himself and was immediately shot three times with a .30-.30 rifle. The shots struck Kubasiak in the abdomen, chest and hand killing him instantly. Investigator Howard had climbed into the house through a window and confronted Swan almost immediately after hearing the rifle fire. Swan holding the rifle was ordered to drop the weapon. Instead, he whirled pointing the rifle at Howard. Howard fired three rapid-fire shots with one shot striking Swan in the chest. Howard seeing Kubasiak wounded on the floor went immediately to his side rendering first aid. In the meantime, Swan not seriously wounded barricaded himself in a side bedroom. Sergeant George Berger entering the residence and not seeing Swan conducted a room-to-room search. Opening a bedroom door, he was confronted by Swan holding a shotgun pointed at him. Swan pulled the pulled the trigger but the gun misfired. A few minutes later, Swan surrendered without further incident. Investigator Gerald Forster recalled that District Attorney Larry Himelein was able to prove that Swan was legally sane at the time. He was convicted of Murder and sentenced to a term of 35 years to life imprisonment. An honor board made up of Deputy Superintendent Donald G. Brandon, Chief Inspector Nicholas G.

Lecakes and Deputy Chief Inspector Frederick D. Thumhart selected Trooper Kubasiak, Investigator Howard and Sergeant Berger to be recipients of the Brummer Award.

It was recalled that several years earlier, Swan had fired a weapon at a Deputy Sheriff and had eaten his own excrement while in jail. Deputies concluded that he didn't like the taste after the first time, because he only smeared it all over the jail cell walls during this arrest. While awaiting sentencing, Swan ended his life by hanging himself while in the county jail.

His wife Melody and sons Ryan, 9 and Randy 6, survived him. Both sons are now New York State Troopers.

TROOPER BRIAN N. ROVNAK
Trooper Brian Rovnak, age 39, Millbrook, N.Y. was killed on February 2, 1983 while on duty when his troop car ran off the I-84 interstate rolling over an embankment in East Fishkill, New York. His partner, Edwin Garcia was hospitalized with head injuries. He enlisted on May 6, 1968. He was born and raised in Buffalo, New York. His wife, Christine and children Dennis 11 and Dennis 9 survived him.

TROOPER ALVIN P. KURDYS
On September 15, 1987, Trooper Alvin P. Kurdys, Buffalo, New York was instantly killed when struck by a speeding car on the New York State Thruway at Pembroke, N.Y. He was the pick-up man on a radar detail when the radar detected a car traveling in excess of 100 miles per hour. Trooper Kurdys stepped to the edge of the highway in an effort to stop the vehicle. The speeding car lost control striking him with full impact. Born at Jersey City, New Jersey, he graduated from Lafayette High School, Buffalo. He had been a trooper since 1970. His wife Sandra and children Kimberly, 18 and Jonathan 14, survived him. Burial was St. Matthews Cemetery, Gardenville, New York.

TROOPER LAWRENCE P.GLEASON
Trooper Lawrence Gleason, age 28, Hornell, N.Y. was shot and killed on February 12, 2002 while investigating a domestic complaint at Crown Point, N.Y.

TROOPER ANDREW J. SPERR
On March 1, 2006, Trooper Andrew Sperr, age 33, Rochester, N.Y. was killed in a gun battle at Big Flats, N.Y. Sperr, alone had confronted two men in a pickup truck who opened fire on the trooper. He was mortally wounded although wearing a bullet- proof vest, but not before returning fire wounding his assailants. The two assailants sought medical treatment, which led to their arrests. It is not known if Sperr was aware that the two had just robbed the nearby Chemung Canal Trust Company.

TROOPERS KILLED WHILE OFF DUTY

CORPORAL EARL R. WILKINSON
Corporal Earl L. Wilkinson, age 34 died in a military aircraft crash on May 24, 1942. He enlisted on 1929.

LIEUTENANT GERALD D. VAINE
Lieutenant Gerald Vaine, Hornell, N.Y. died of natural causes on January 31, 1951 while in New York City. His wife, Marion Kelleher Vaine, survived him. Burial was at St. Andrews Cemetery, Hornell, New York.

CORPORAL LEO MELLODY
Corporal Leo Mellody, age 44, Batavia, N.Y. was killed on December 19, 1951, when he accidentally discharged a firearm he was cleaning while at home.

TROOPER C. LEO WATKINS
On December 14, 1957. Trooper C. Leo Watkins, age 50, 52 Wadsworth Avenue, Avon, New York died unexpectedly of a heart attack. He was a 27-year veteran of the state police assigned at the Avon station. His wife, Ann and daughters Marcia Ann Barrett and Faye Marie survived him. Burial was at the East Avon Cemetery.

TROOPER ALBERT J. PERRY
On January 1, 1962, Trooper Albert J. Perry, age 26, Rossburg, N.Y. was killed in a two- car accident near Warsaw, N. Y. while off duty. He had recently been assigned at the Clarence Sub-station. His father was the late Adelbert Perry, a Trooper from 1927 to 1932 and his uncle, Albert Perry, Adelbert's twin was also a trooper. His enlistment was June 1961.

TROOPER ALLEN R. WISE
On January 15, 1962, Trooper Allen R. Wise, age 29, 166 McConnell Avenue, Elmira Heights, N.Y. was killed, when his sports car ran off of the road and overturned. The accident happened on Route 17E near Big Flats, N.Y. His enlistment was August 29, 1957.

TROOPER GERALD R. CROCKER
Gerald R. Crocker, age 28, Olean, N.Y. died of cancer on May 25, 1963 after a long illness. His enlistment was May 19, 1960. His wife Mary Joan and children Ricky 9 and Berry 7 survived him.

INVESTIGATOR RALPH C. FITZWATER
Ralph C. Fitzwater, age 49, Penn Yan, N.Y. died unexpectedly on June 27, 1965 from a heart attack. His enlistment was July 1, 1940. His wife Elinor Burr Fitzwater and three daughters survived him.

SERGEANT JOHN C. MURPHY
Sergeant John C. Murphy, age 52, Rexville, N.Y. died of a heart attack on October 3, 1964 while at home. He enlisted July 1, 1935. His wife Helen and children James and daughter Mrs. Thomas Gibbs of Hornell survived him. Burial was at St. Mary's Church Yard Cemetery, Rexville.

TROOPER GEORGE C. DOMEDION
On June 3, 1967, Trooper George C. Domedion, age 28, Fredonia, N.Y. was killed instantly when the vehicle he was driving passed under the rear of a tractor-trailer that had pulled onto the roadway into his path. The accident occurred on the NYS Thruway in the Town of Hanover. His enlistment was April 2, 1962. His wife Christine and three sons, George, Mark and Michael, survived him.

TROOPER RICHARD L. WELTZ
On March 17, 1970, Trooper Richard L. Weltz, age 30, Hamburg, New York was killed instantly, when he apparently fell asleep, drove off the roadway and struck a tree and telephone pole. The Accident occurred on Route 219, Hamburg, N.Y. while he was returning from a pistol match. He was an outstanding marksman, having won many international awards. His wife, Lorraine, survived him.

TROOPER WALTER R. NEWMAN
Trooper Walter Newman, age 36, Hunt, N.Y. was killed on April 12, 1970, when he apparently fell asleep and struck a tree with his pickup truck. He enlisted on July 1958. His wife Barbara Getman

Newman, a daughter Holly 9 and son Todd, 6, survived him. Burial was at Mumford Rural Cemetery, Mumford, New York

TROOPER KENNETH F. KIRSCH

Trooper Kenneth Kirsch, age 32, Buffalo, N.Y. was killed instantly on September 22, 1970 when he apparently fell asleep while driving and struck a tractor-trailer head on. The accident occurred on Transit Road, Cheektowaga, N.Y. He enlisted in 1962.

TROOPER FRED D. BARTLETT

Fred D. Bartlett, age 29 on August 31, 1972 died while swimming at Waterport, N.Y. He dove into a swimming area on July 12, 1972 striking his head on a rock. He was a native of Bolivar, N.Y. His enlistment was March 6, 1967. His wife Diana and children Fred Jr.5, Mark 3 and Julie 2 survived him. Burial was at Maple Lawn Cemetery, Bolivar.

TROOPER KENNETH R. EARLE

Trooper Kenneth Earle, age 36, Chazy, New York was killed instantly on July 17, 1976, when struck by a vehicle while riding his motorcycle. He was a native of Gowanda, N.Y. His enlistment was June 26, 1961. His wife Sandra Jean and daughters Darlene 15, Marlene 12 and Charlene 10 survived him.

INVESTIGATOR NICHOLAS FITZAK

Investigator Nicholas Fitzak, age 48, on October 23, 1977 from an apparent heart attack while at home. He enlisted Aug 1, 1953. His wife Anne and children Gretchen 18, Jennifer 16, John 12 and Thomas 9 survived him.

TROOPER EUGENE B. ADAMS

On May 4, 1980, Trooper Eugene Adams, age 43, Limestone, New York was making repairs to his personal car, when he succumbed to carbon monoxide poisoning. His enlistment was June 18, 1962. His wife Nancy and three children survived him.

INVESTIGATOR ROBERT K. VANSON

Investigator Robert Van Son, age 45 died on August 18, 1980 from a heart attack. He was last assigned at Canandaigua, N.Y. His enlistment was June 13, 1963.

COLONEL HENRY F. WILLIAMS

Colonel Henry F. Williams, age 56, Hamburg, N.Y. died of cancer on December 5, 1986. He enlisted in April 16,1952. His wife, LaVonne and six children survived him. Burial was at Lakeside Cemetery, Hamburg.

TROOPER WILLIAM ERNST

William Ernst, age 46, Buffalo, N.Y. died on July 2, 1987 by his own hand. He was stationed at SP Clarence. His enlistment was February 24, 1966.

TROOPER ANDREW D. BRIGGS

Andrew D. Briggs, age 22, Dansville, N.Y. was killed on April 22, 1989, when his automobile ran off Route 17 overturning at the Town of Howard. His enlistment was September 19, 1988. He was buried at Forest Lawn Cemetery, Dansville.

TROOPER CHRISTOPHER P. GERWITZ
Christopher P. Gerwitz, age 34, Rochester, N.Y. was struck and killed on July 22, 1997 when struck by a car while riding his bicycle.

INVESTIGATOR JAMES H. KNOTT III
Investigator James Knott, age 54, Newfane, N.Y. suffered a fatal heart attack at his residence on November 29, 1998. His enlistment was 1970. His wife Nicki and sons Kenneth, James IV and Matthew survived him. Burial was at Corwin Cemetery, Newfane.

TROOPER STEVEN C. CROGLIO, age 24, Clarence, N.Y. was killed on October 24, 1999
in an off duty two-car accident at Catskill, N.Y. His enlistment was November 1991.

TROOPER LAURIE J. KALICKI
Trooper Laurie Kalicki, age 37, Batavia, N.Y. died on November 8, 2000 after a lengthy illness. Her enlistment was 1989. She was buried at Grandview Cemetery, Batavia.

INVESTIGATOR JOSEPH P. VALVO
Investigator Joseph P. Valvo was shot and killed on October 24, 1992 while visiting the residence of a friend estranged from her husband. The husband entered the home while in a jealous rage shooting Valvo.

CIVILIAN STAFF MEMBERS WHO DIED WHILE EMPLOYED BY THE NYS POLICE

SECRETARY BRENDA M. McCOY
Brenda McCoy, age 35, Corfu, N.Y. was shot & killed by her brother in law on May 20, 1983. She had been a secretary at the Batavia barracks since May 31, 1967. Her husband Gary and son Mark, 13 survived her.

SECRETARY ELIZABETH ALLEN
Elizabeth Allen, a Zone 4 Secretary died in 1989 of cancer after a long illness. The NYS Police had employed her since 1966.

COMMUNICATION SPECIALIST JOHN P. PRIOLO
John P. Priolo, age 47, Batavia, New York, a Communications Specialist at SP Batavia died of cancer on November 26, 1993. The NYS Police employed him since 1966. He was an avid carpenter. His wife Linda and children Michael and Susan survived him. Burial was at St. Joseph's Mausoleum, Batavia.

COMMUNICATION SPECIALIST RITA HYNES
Rita Hynes, age 48, a Communications Specialist at SP Batavia died of cancer on July 13, 1996 after a short illness. She resided with her husband at Elba, N.Y.

AUTOMOTIVE MECHANIC NICHOLAS A. MERICA
Mechanic Nicholas Merica, age 45, Leroy, N.Y. died by his own hand on May 12, 2006. He had been treated for deep depression. He started his employment in 1986.

ASSOCIATIONS

NEW YORK STATE TROOPERS POLICE BENEVOLENT ASSOCIATION (PBA)

SYNOPSIS

The PBA came into existence during 1943 through the efforts of Troopers on active Military duty in and around the New York City area. The common thread was the seeking of better working conditions and hours of duty for the trooper. Division Headquarters and the Governors office thwarted the PBA in every way. Troopers returning to the ranks after WWII joined the PBA. Active PBA members or elected PBA officers were relegated to menial barracks duties, ie: washing urinals, scrubbing floors etc or were constantly transferred on short notice without recourse. Legislation seeking better working conditions was introduced with popular support for its passage from civic, church and individuals throughout the state, however, the Governor vetoed it. Division Headquarters reactivated a long dormant Troop Civic Association using it in an attempt to slander and undermine the PBA. Getting recognition was a long drawn out ordeal with many PBA officials resigning from the PBA and the Division of State Police due to the high amount of directed scrutiny and disciplinary punishment.

COMMENT

Constructing a history of the New York State Troopers Police Benevolent Association (PBA) has been a difficult task. This report is comprised from notations, memorandums (partial and complete) and news articles that were retained during the formative years. It is believed that a group life insurance program provided to the membership gave the PBA its financial base. A group policy was negotiated for with an insurance carrier that ultimately, proved cheaper for the members, then the purchase of an individual policy. A few cents per thousand was charged going to the PBA.

THE FORMATIVE YEARS

In October, 1943, Paul McCusker, President of the New York City Port Authority PBA and Walter A. Caddell, an attorney friendly with troopers discussed the organizing of a Trooper's PBA. The purpose was to alleviate certain distressing conditions, as they existed in the State Police organization.

On October 11, 1943, Thirty-five troopers then on active military duty attended a meeting held at Hotel King Edward, 120 W. 44 Street, New York City. They agreed to organize a PBA. A temporary board of officers was established with William H. Barfoot chosen President, Frank Fitzgerald Secretary and Carl Wichmann treasurer along with John Nadig and Milton Brandeis as officers. Walter Caddell was selected as Executive Secretary. Within a month, 80% of all troopers became members of the organization.

On December 9, 1943 a members meeting was held with the discussion focused on whether non-coms would be permitted to vote and hold office. No determination was made at this time. It was agreed that dues would start in January 1944 and that if there were insufficient funds after the first of the year, a special assessment would be made. Membership dues were $1.00 if paid monthly or $3.00 for six months, which included a death benefit. These dues were not enough to provide for all the activities of the PBA. Temporary trooper delegates were initially appointed until January 1, 1944. The first PBA address was 55 Liberty Street, New York, N.Y.

MEMO SENT TO ALL TROOPERS

The following is an excerpt from a memorandum sent to all members of the state police by the PBA with a return address of 38 Park Row, New York 7, N.Y. "IT IS A NEW DAY". The old regime is dead. The day of a trooper genuflecting before anyone is definitely gone. Your PBA is only exercising a right that belongs to all free white American workers. It is a God-given right of organizing to protect your homes, your wives and children and to advance your common welfare. The PBA, as an organization has always encouraged loyalty, obedience and respect for proper authority, "BUT NOT SERVILITY".

YOUR DELEGATES ARE:
Troop A – Romie Laurence
Troop C - Edward J. Smith
Troop D - Robert Flaherty
Troop G – Edward Blaney
Troop K – Harold Nikola

We were all members of the Association of State Civil Service, but this group can never represent the State Police. It is the same group that refused the troopers a chapter, when it was most needed. We believe that it now seeks the right to act as your spokesman or agent. One organization has to go. We suggest you make it clear perfectly clear that they are not the voluntary choice of the troopers even if resigning from the chapter is necessary to make your position clear. A report of grievances and conditions affecting morale and efficiency was sent to Special Assistant Attorney.

General E. Scully by the PBA delegates and officers. It was the result of an inquiry made among all troopers deemed to seriously affect the general welfare and efficiency of the troopers. A copy was also sent to the Governor's Secretary. No reply was received.

In early 1944, the Troopers PBA was Chartered by New York State and incorporated under the Not for Profit Corporation Laws. Officers and Troop Delegates were elected from active duty troopers in the various troops. Edward J. Blaney was elected President & Nicholas E. Dale, Secretary. Within a short time, 95% of all troopers were members of the newly formed PBA. Walter Caddell remained Executive Secretary. The PBA notified Superintendent John Gaffney and Mr. Paul Lockwood, Secretary to the Governor of the purposes of the PBA and offered its co-operation in reporting real conditions within the State Police, as were found at the time. All efforts to meet with Mr. Lockwood or Superintendent Gaffney were met with silence. As time passed, it became evident that the PBA organization was not to be recognized. The PBA then prepared legislation requesting an investigation. Lack of legislative support ended the quest.

PBA BULLETIN DECEMBER 1944

The following is a condensed version of a bulletin sent to all troopers the result of a meeting held at Albany, N.Y. on December 27, 1944. Former Chief Inspector Albert B. Moore attended the meeting and volunteered to aid in the preparing PBA proposed legislation. Representatives attending the meeting did so on their own time. It was stated that the PBA would eventually bring great benefits to its membership and their families and at the same time do a great service to the citizens of the state by freeing the State Police from an improper administration with its tight control and restraints. President Laurence stated that he had sent a letter to the Superintendent requesting an interview in behalf of the PBA that had not been answered. Apparently, the policy was to ignore any matter they are out of sympathy with.

PBA Resolutions adopted were a legislative program and the continued support for Sergeant O'Hanley in his fight to prevent denial of his legal rights. Details of the legislative program would be provided in the near future. It was requested that all members get in contact with members of the Senate and Assembly personally or through friends to seek remedies for the deplorable working conditions of the troopers. Contact Granges, Farm Bureaus, Benevolent Associations giving the troopers plight. When legislation is underway, a nominal tax will be imposed on every member. It is unconceivable that any trooper will have to be urged to do his bit in this respect. Forget about things that are merely personal, such as disagreements with your brother officer. In unity lies our strength. Loyalty to your PBA officers is just as proper as loyalty to official authority.

In 1945, Blaney and Dale left the State Police in their own best interest with Roman J. Laurence (Troop A) unanimously selected as President. Persistent rumors that the PBA would not be recognized, because Mr. Caddell, an outsider was acting for the troopers led to Caddell resigning his position. The result was no change at all. The PBA was still not recognized, as a representative of the troopers. The PBA continued to have the Trooper's interests at heart and encountered warm and enthusiastic support from the vast majority of State Troopers.

The PBA agenda was that of basic, everyday natural entitlements of man. It asked for recognition of the trooper's rights as a man to normal home and family life with reasonable working hours and placement within reasonable distance of his home. The PBA recognized the right of the State to maintain the trooper on duty status even when he is out of uniform and at home, and to order him wherever a real emergency demands. The PBA does not recognize the necessity of keeping all troopers in what amounts to a constant emergency status.

Through a campaign of publicity and Legislative action, the PBA sought a square deal for the ordinary trooper

POLICE CONFERENCE OF NEW YORK AND THE PBA

On September 6, 1945, a joint meeting of the PBA Board of Directors & PBA members was held at the New York City offices. Present were William Barfoot, Frank Fitzgerald, John Nadig, Carl Wichman, Milton Brandeis, Walter Caddell, S. Nicherson of Troop B, Trooper Dale of Troop K, Elliott Johnson of Troop L and Harold Myers of Troop G. Barfoot reported on his attendance at the NYS Police Conference held on August 21st at Poughkeepsie, N.Y. Although President Laurence had communicated previously about PBA representatives being permitted to attend the meeting and explain the difficulty troopers faced in carrying on PBA affairs with opposition from superiors, difficulty was had in gaining admittance. It was clear that the attitudes of the Conference directors that the troopers were persona non grata. (The NYS Police Conference was comprised of Police Associations from throughout the state that represented small Departments joined together for mutual benefit)

A NYS Police Conference convention held in 1944 unanimously adopted a resolution wherein Secretary Keresman would personally see Governor Dewey to determine why the trooper's PBA was being suppressed by Superintendent Gaffney to wit: transfer of active PBA men, attempts to form a company union at state expense time. For whatever reason, the attitude had changed in that it was now felt that the PBA had failed to see Superintendent Gaffney personally or neglected to act itself in requesting recognition. Barfoot pointed out that the PBA had made both written and oral requests that went unanswered. President Laurence tried to speak with Mr. Lockwood by phone, taking vacation time to do so. When he returned home, he found he had been transferred 40 miles from his home then followed by a second transfer further away. Superintendent Gaffney in attempting to form a company union handpicked delegates who were called to Albany on State time and expense using the states teletype system to do so. All efforts for the PBA to have the same privilege were denied with the one asking usually transferred or otherwise disciplined. Keresman further criticized the PBA for having Caddell, an outsider acting for the troopers. Caddell had removed himself from all activities a year earlier and had only once again, at the urging of former President Blaney, acted for the troopers or else have the PBA collapse. Barfoot reported that it was obvious to him that Police Conference was run by J.R. Sprague, a Nassau County politician and that he Mr. Lockwood had succeeded in dominating the meeting getting any sympathy for the Troopers PBA smothered by the conference delegates. Barfoot's impression was that Political bosses who criticized the PBA and led a smear campaign dominated the NYS Police Conference against Caddell in his fight against the Governor's office. He felt the Conference was unmanly in their failure to support the trooper's cause and suggested the troopers withdraw from the Conference. The Board of Directors unanimously agreed to drop from the Conference. The with drawl was a form of protest against the domination of the conference by certain politicians who were opposed to the trooper's move, as well as a protest from the attitude and servility to the powers that be, it certainly did not echo the sentiments of the policemen the conference was supposed to represent. The PBA was supported by a majority of the individual Conference PBA's while attempting to get a resolution passed for an investigation into the trooper's affairs. The Conference officers acted as if the trooper's fight was a bit too dangerous to get involved in.

On January 10, 1946, a PBA meeting was held at the De Witt Clinton Hotel, Albany, N.Y. with the President and Five Troops represented as follows: "A"- H.J. Morse, "C"- H. F. Knapp, "D"-L.W. Johnson, "G"-John Falle and "L"- William Byrne :

It was determined that a stronger PBA must be had in spite of Executive (Governors Office) opposition. Since the boss's held the upper hand over the trooper's welfare, an open fight would not be advisable. It was decided to establish a central office in the Albany area. The Trooper Rules and Regulations allowed for a 90-day period where a member could be away from active duty. William Barfoot was selected and agreed to act as PBA Executive Secretary during the 90-day time frame to act in an appropriate manner and revive the PBA activity. It was felt that the administration would be in power for only one more year, but a lot of harm could be done during that time to men who openly acted in behalf of the PBA. A plan was laid to acquaint the public with the facts about the trooper's conditions and the efforts to prevent the men from having their own organization. The board adopted a program initiated in Troop A, as follows:

Pension laws amended to provide for twenty and twenty-five year retirement at the option of the pensioner. (Similar to the pension plan held by New York City)

No transfers out of troop unless with the consent of the trooper or for temporary purposes in case of emergency.

When a trooper is transferred such distance away from his home and family making it necessary for him to move, that such expenses be paid by the state.

Decent hours and salary commensurate with the hours on duty. At present, the wage scale is much below that recognized by the government for menial and unskilled labor.

To further the reviving of PBA activity, arrangements and funding were made to send a monthly letter to all members. The temporary address and clearing house would be the address of William Barfoot, 49 Lafayette Avenue, Coxsackie, N.Y. Full authorization was given the President and Executive Secretary to take whatever steps Necessary to further the welfare of the PBA.

Trooper H. Moose made a motion that delegates from the respective troops be made members of the Board of Directors. Seconded by William Byrnes. William Byrnes made a motion that passed unanimously for Mrs. Roman Laurence to be appointed secretary to the President to be paid $5.00 weekly from the General Fund.

McCADDIN PUNISHED

In February 1946, Trooper John McCaddin was confined to the Hawthorne Barracks because of his PBA activities. He was placed on a detail washing floors and cleaning lavatories. He was told by Captain Glasheen to give up his membership in the PBA or resign as a trooper.

Early in 1946, Senator Walter J. Mahoney, Buffalo, N.Y. proposed a legislative investigation with a view of improving troopers working conditions. He further introduced a resolution requesting a joint legislative committee be formed to investigate the operation of the State Police, duties of troopers, method of promotion, rules & regulations, working conditions and rates of pay. An appropriation of $15,000.00 was recommended with a report due by March 15, 1946. Since its inception, the State Police have never promulgated any set of rules and regulations governing the conduct of troopers. The State Police have been inferentially criticized with an exceptionally high number of resignations.

In March 1946, the Assembly Ways & Means Committee killed a six day 48 hour workweek bill. The reason provided was that it would have necessitated the tripling of the force making the cost prohibitive. Assemblyman Wilson C. Van Duzer and Senator Walter J. Mahoney introduced the measure.

On June 18, 1946 PBA members met at the Wellington Hotel, Albany, N.Y. Present were R. Laurence "A", H.F. Knapp "C", Spellman "D", John Falle "G" and John McCaddin "K". Laurence made a motion to amend the by-laws in that only members with the rank of trooper be eligible to hold office in the PBA, but all members be allowed to vote in any PBA matter or business. John McCadden seconded it and it was approved.

John Falle made a motion that it be the policy and principle of the PBA that no strike action be taken by its members. This was seconded by McCadden and approved. A motion was unanimously passed to expedite matters in the payment of death benefits and bills. It was that only the signature of the President be necessary on all checks to permit with drawl from the general fund.

On October 7, 1946, the PBA met at the Wellington Hotel. In Attendance were President Laurence, H.J. Morse & G.J. Schusler – "A", H.F. Knapp – "C", E.A. Kappeser – "D", J. Falle & W. Byrnes – "G" and John McCadden – "K". Walter Caddell attended as an advisor in a legal capacity. Also present as the newly appointed PBA Chaplain was Catholic Priest Ralph J. Garvey.

In 1946, President Laurence had been recently dismissed from the NYS Troopers and provided the following details of his dismissal. A Captain Greer of the US Navy had traveled from Buffalo, NY east and left his cap in a restaurant. He sent a letter to the State Police requesting them to attempt to locate his cap and mail it to him. Trooper Laurence was given the task, located it and sent it to Greer placing his home address on the package. Sometime had passed, when Greer in appreciation sent a letter thanking Laurence and enclosed a check for $5.00. Mrs. Laurence who thinking it a donation to the PBA endorsed it and put it into the PBA opened the letter general account. As a result, Laurence was terminated for accepting a gratuity.

Due to his dismissal, Laurence felt it best, if he stepped down and left the room so that the Executive Board could meet in open discussion. After meeting, the members felt the Laurence had been dismissed solely because of his PBA activities, that no evidence was presented to support such "trumped" up charges and he was dismissed by authority of Superintendent Gaffney. Since he was no longer a member of the State Police, Laurence could no longer retain his duties with the PBA without action by the Board of Directors, therefore, E.A. Kappeser moved that the Association By-Laws be suspended and Laurence be regarded as an officer of the Association until the matter was finally settled. Seconded by John McCadden and approved. John Falle then made a motion that Roman Laurence be designated & authorized to represent the PBA in such matters as his office may designate and in particular, to travel throughout the state and further organize the PBA. He would be compensated in an amount not to exceed $400.00 monthly. This duty was without salary. Laurence appealed his dismissal and was represented by William J. Mahoney.

On November 8, 1946, Romie Laurence sent a letter to William McCadden about the finance's of the PBA. He noted that on November 7, 1946 the PBA had approximately $38.00 left with an indebtedness of $477.00 for last years Conference Cards. William Mahoney was paid $500.00 and $400.00 paid to Laurence for the month of October, as previously agreed to. It was felt that the members should pick up the slack to be accomplished by the delegates. Many have already donated $5.00, but others needed prodding. Money was desperately needed to continue the work of the PBA.

THE TROOPER'S CASE IN 1946

Base pay was $900.00 a year plus a 30% bonus bringing their earnings to $1,170.00 a year. A rookie trooper works 573 hours a month or 6,876 hours a year that brought his hourly rate to slightly more than 17 cents an hour. Approximately 60% of troopers are the maximum of $2,562.00 a year and an additional $3.50 a day food allowance, which would bring their maximum to $3,587.00 a year. Paycheck deductions include $16.00 a month toward pension for top ranking men. The take home pay for a rookie is only $44.00 semi-monthly.

Work hours – Six, eight-hour shifts a week was sought with the right to live with their families. Troopers received only 4 days off a month plus a 28-day vacation. A few troopers assigned at headquarters are home more than one night a week. Officers lived at home and could be reached for duty. Why couldn't the troopers do the same thing?

Medical coverage – Medical care is provided those injured on duty, but if you become ill at home, a letter is received warning that failure to report for duty will result in removal from the payroll.

On January 4, 1947, "The Tablet" the official newspaper of Brooklyn's 110,000 Roman Catholics published an article prepared by Chaplain Reverend Ralph J. Garvey describing the trooper's plight and requesting support for proposed legislation of shorter work hours and better working conditions.

On October 11, 1947 a discussion was held on a legislative program for 1948. Present were President Laurence, John Falle, W.R. Spelman and John McCaddin. The following were agreed to:

An amendment of the present 20-year retirement to include ½ half of salary and maintenance after completion of 20 years service.

A bill to provide the hours of duty of members of the Division of State Police, including the rank of Sergeant at a maximum of six eight-hour tours of duty per week, to be effective July 1, 1949.

Amendment of the Executive Law to place the Division under the direct supervision of the State Civil Service Commission in regard to entrance and promotional examinations.

A bill to provide enactment of the former Morrit-Lyons Resolution to provide legislative investigation and study of the operations of the Division, with particular attention to working conditions of the trooper.

Enactment of a bill to grant all members of the Division the right to appeal to the Supreme Court from a determination of the Superintendent wherein disciplinary charges are sustained.

A Welfare Committee had been established to conduct annual dinners, dances, special affairs, provide entertainment and to solicit public support and contributions for the benefit of the Association.

THE TARGET
The Target was the official newspaper of the Trooper's PBA. I could find no information of when it was initially published or when it was last printed. Volume 6, No 4 was published in July 1947 and Volume 8, No 2 in February – March 1949 both consisting of 4 pages. Only 1000 Target's were printed for distribution. The 1947 publication had a caption "HOW CAN I HELP". It was suggested that when the reader was finished with the Target, it be forwarded to the editor of the local newspaper for possible printing and exposure of the trooper's plight to the public. It further noted that it was the job of every PBA member to get the widest circulation possible by passing the Target around among fiends.

Notes from a meeting held on May 10, 1949 at the Wellington Hotel, Albany, N.Y. In attendance were President Roman Laurence, John McCaddin, Father Garvey, Dr. Douglas, H.F. Knapp, John Falle, Wally Spellman, Ernie Goodspeed, Corporals Russ Reeves, B.F. Butler, R.D. Flaherty and R.C. Wylle.

Welfare Committee Financial Report - $3,479.21
General Account - $8,114.85 - most of monies invested in bonds.
Number of troopers employed in 1948 – 695
PBA membership in 1948 - 455
PBA membership in 1949 - 681

Benefits paid since August 1947 - $4,694.98
Motion made by McCadden – resolved that Troopers PBA members upon retirement receive $10.00 for every year of continuous membership.
Hospitalization benefit - $25.00 for immediate family: Maximum of 4 weeks.
Married – wife and children
Single – mother-father

President Roman Laurence rendered his resignation at the meeting wishing to express appreciation to all members and friends.
A notation was made to hire a stenographer.

1950 - ASSOCIATE MEMBERSHIPS IN WELFARE COMMITTEE
It appears that sometime in or prior to October 1950, an Associate Membership program was initiated. The following was disclosed in letter prepared by Walter Caddell.

Associate members names would be kept on file at the office. Please impress upon them that only a few are issued and we are more than careful to whom they are given. In this way, we will have people pleading for them. Only those concerned with recent, effective police work by decent policemen are eligible for membership. Associates are pledged to keep us informed of abuses by policemen, phonies or fakers against policemen and they agree to Co-operate in the interest of justice. Caddell also advised that he was preparing a booklet for Associates emphasizing the importance of integrity and loyalty to Christ's principles. (Commandments)

The committee had the right to revoke anyone's membership.

TROOPER CIVIC ASSOCIATION

The Division of State Police was composed of six troops. Each troop maintained its own Civic Association that was originally planned for benevolent purposes, such as buying flowers for sick or deceased members or the purchase of newspapers, magazines and radios for Troop Headquarters and sub-stations. Troop Headquarters Staff with an NCO regularly attaining the office of President usually selected the officers of these Civic Associations. Troop Headquarters equipment was used for printing and distributing of bulletins, letters, ballots and other communications and were performed, as part of the official duty of the individual assigned. With the formation of the Troopers PBA, the Civic Associations were gradually phased out. There was no reason to maintain them since the PBA did everything previously administered by the Civic Associations. A flower fund was established and all Troop members were asked to join by donating $1.00. Sometime during late 1948, it was announced that the members in charge of the flower fund were re-activating the Civic Association. The Troop G Civic Association elected Sgt. J.J. McNamee President. In January 1949, the Civic Association sent a petition to Governor Dewey denouncing articles written in the PBA bulletin, The Target. In brief it praised the Governor and State Police hierarchy for raising salaries, reducing hours of work and striving to better the troopers working conditions. It accused the PBA of unjustified personal attacks on administration stating that it did not represent the feeling of the majority of troopers. McNamee sometime later stated that he did not draft the petition and had no knowledge of it. The article had apparently been drafted at Division Headquarters in an effort to discredit the PBA who were trying to get positive trooper legislation passed at the time.

1961 ISSUES
During August 1961, the PBA sent a letter to the Governor charging the Superintendent with violating Rules and Regulations by changing rules pertaining to examinations for promotion. Under the new formula, 20% weight would be given to the written examination and 80% weight to the officer's evaluation. This would make future promotions solely under the control of the Superintendent subject to his likes and dislikes.

During December 1961, the PBA sponsored two legislative bills. The first was for a forty-hour workweek and the second for an optional 20-year retirement. The seed planted, both were implemented a few short years later.

1969 - PBA MOVES FROM NYC TO ALBANY
The PBA offices had been located in New York City since 1944. In 1969, Sergeant George Zink, SP Henrietta was elected to the position of President replacing William Courlis who served as president for eight years. Also elected were Owen P. Honors, (Syracuse) William Thompson, (Malone) Vice President and George Head (Lake George) Treasurer. Seth Towse, (Loudonville) a former assistant attorney general was appointed counsel.

Zink was responsible for having the PBA offices moved to Albany, N.Y. He felt it was the logical place to be. Every trooper comes to Albany occasionally and the new location would bring the PBA closer to its 3000 members, as well as near the legislature, government officials and Governors Office. Offices were established at 284 State Street, Albany, N.Y. In 1972, the PBA relocated to 12th floor at 112 State Street, Albany, N.Y.

ATTICA COUNSEL
In June 1974, a Grand Jury was empowered to investigate the actions of troopers assigned to the Attica detail. The PBA instructed all of its members not to appear without benefit of counsel. PBA

attorneys were made available at no cost to the member. A further note urged members not to talk "off the record" as there was no such thing.

COLLECTIVE BARGAINING

THE CONDON-WALDIN ACT OF 1947

The Condon-Waldin Act was a law passed by the New York State Legislature in 1947 prohibiting strikes by public employees and imposing severe penalties. Striking employees were penalized by being fired. They could only be re-instated under a three-year pay freeze and five-year probation.

New Yorkers awoke on New Year's Day, 1966, to find that thirty-five thousand transit workers had walked off the job. The 12 day strike was called off, when Mayor Lindsay agreed to a generous settlement and arranged for the state legislature to pass a retroactive waiver of the law that resulted in no sanctions being taken against strikers. That 1966 strike acted as the catalyst for the Taylor Law, New York State's foundational labor relations legislation. A blue ribbon panel was appointed by Governor Nelson Rockefeller to "make legislative proposals for protecting the public against the disruption of vital public services by illegal strikes, while at the same time protecting the rights of public employees." The panel, chaired by George W. Taylor, a professor of industrial relations and a well-known arbitrator of industrial disputes, issued a report whose recommendations would form the core of the 1967 Public Employees' Fair Employment Act, popularly known as the Taylor Law. While it maintained the strike ban, the new state law recalibrated the penalties for striking to make them more enforceable and set up a whole labor relations structure to help resolve disputes before they escalated.

THE TAYLOR LAW

(Public Employees' Fair Employment Act)

Civil Service Law, Article 14 - Section 200

The Public Employees' Fair Employment Act (Taylor Law) was enacted in 1967 guaranteeing the right of public employees to organize and bargain collectively with their employers: Provisions included:

- The right to representation by employee organizations (unions) of their own choosing;
- The requirement that public employers (including school districts) negotiate with their employees and enter into written agreements (contracts) with their employees' chosen representatives;
- Procedures for resolution of contract disputes (impasses);
- Prohibition of improper labor practices by either side;
- Creation of the Public Employment Relations Board (PERB) to administer the law;
- The requirement that bargaining unit members who choose not to join a union pay an agency fee, and that use of the fee for political and ideological purposes only incidentally related to bargaining to which the agency fee payer objects is subject to a rebate procedure.

While the Taylor Law grants public employees the right to collective bargaining, it denies them the right to strike. The penalties for striking are loss of pay for each day the employee is on strike, plus a fine of an additional day's pay for every day on strike and potential discipline for misconduct. A 1982 amendment mandated that if a collective bargaining agreement expires, its terms and conditions continue until a new contract was in place.

Like Condon-Wadlin, the Taylor Law uses a broad definition of strike activity, making it a crime for public employees and their unions to "cause, instigate, encourage or condone a strike." An employee is presumed to be on strike if he or she "is absent from work without permission" or "abstains wholly or in part from the full performance of his duties in his normal manner" during a strike. The courts have held that the law even prevents employees in certain situations from stopping voluntary work. The penalties for violating the strike ban remained severe. A union that encourages or condones a strike loses its right to deduct dues from members' paychecks. The law directs government officials to file for a court injunction against any union or individuals that "threaten" to violate the Taylor Law. Judges have the authority to levy fines against the union or those individuals for ignoring a court order. Individual strikers can be disciplined for misconduct under the Civil Service Law. "On the positive side, the Taylor Law granted public employees the right to unionize and to bargain collectively, a right denied in many states. In the event of an impasse with management, it provided for mediation and arbitration. The state Public Employment Relations Board was created as an independent agency to administer the law and act as a referee in disputes. The Taylor Law marked progress on the national stage for public employees, who had been left out of the 1935 National Labor Relations Act that gave collective-bargaining rights to private-sector workers. New York State became the seventh state in the nation to grant collective-bargaining rights to public employees.

FIRST ELECTION UNDER TAYLOR LAW
In the summer of 1968, the state police were the first state agency to hold an election under the Taylor Law. The election was to determine who would represent the troopers for collective bargaining purposes. On July 1, 1968, the Public Employees Relations Board (PERB) established two bargaining units, one for members below the rank of Lieutenant and a second made up of lieutenants, captains and majors.

Representation was sought by the Civil Service Employees Association (CSEA), Council 50 of State, County and Municipal Employees, AFL – CIO and the Police Benevolent Association (PBA). There were 3,044 members eligible to vote with only 2,720 ballots returned. The results were Council 50, 1,323, CSEA 209, PBA 1,068, no organization 72 and invalid 48. A majority vote was required that was had not been met. This resulted in a run-off election between the two highest vote getters, the PBA and Council 50 with the PBA winning 1,498 to 1,3,17. Pending an appeal, the PBA was not immediately certified, but was recognized for the purpose of negotiations. The PBA had also been chosen to represent the commissioned officers unit.

FIRST CONTRACT NEGOTIATIONS
In 1969, the first contract negotiations resulted in the most significant piece of legislation beneficial to the trooper. It was the agreement of a 20-year retirement bill. The state police pension plan was revised by legislative action that implemented a negotiated agreement between the state OER and PBA. Changes called for a mandatory retirement age fixed at 55 with goals to be reached by 1974. It also permitted retirement at half pay after twenty years of service instead of twenty-five years and provided for additional benefits for each year of service between the 20th and 30th years.

Previously, no benefits accrued after 25 years. The move toward the 55 - year retirement began in 1969 with those who reached age 60 or were over that age. Each year thereafter, the retirement was mandatory one year earlier. Among those reaching first year mandatory retirement were Deputy Superintendent Albin S. Johnson, Major Harold T. Muller and Deputy Chief Inspector John J. Quinn. Beneficial to the state was the maintenance of a younger force and increased opportunity for promotion within the ranks.

The 1969 agreement applied to all but 16 management positions. The two-year contract also included salary increases Averaging 5 ½ % each year, death benefits, health insurance, relocation expenses, vacations and holiday and overtime pay.

REPRESENTATIVE ELECTIONS

The Taylor Law provided for an election of a bargaining representative. If a petition was filed and an election held, it was monitored by the Office of Employee Relations (OER) and the Public Employee Relations Board (PERB) who certified the election results. An election could be held every two years. The main adversaries were the PBA, CSEA and Local 1908, Fraternal Order of Troopers. These elections proved to be time consuming and costly to all involved.

An election held in late 1970 to determine a representative for collective bargaining was won by the PBA, 1484 to 1360 for the Local 1908, Fraternal Order of Troopers. The unit composed of lieutenants; captains and majors selected the CSEA as its agent over the PBA by a vote of 58 to 19.

The 1971 negotiated agreement by the PBA was twice rejected by the membership before being approved 1467 to 1150. It provided for an increase in starting salary for troopers from $8,631 to $9,771. Later that year, Council 50 AFL/CIO was elected to represent troopers for the next two years. In September 1973, the PBA was re-elected as the collective bargaining agent for members below the rank of lieutenant by a vote of 1490 to 1154.

ISSUES IN THE SEVENTIES

On August 5, 1977, the Commission on Judicial Conduct notified the PBA that it was conducting an investigation into the practice of "ticket fixing" and reduction of tickets by town and village justices. The PBA provided counsel for every member that was subpoenaed to appear before the commission.

1979 proved to be a tumultuous year in the PBA. In January 1979, Charles Stuart ("F" Troop) and Fred Porcello ("A" Troop) initiated contract negotiations with the state. Porcello noted that Stuart conducted negotiation meetings on his own and failed to provide progress reports to the board of directors. In February 1979, Stuart was elected PBA President and no longer was involved in negotiations. As President, Stuart supported radical ideas for that time frame. He supported legislation to merge the Parkway Police into the State Police with a rider on the Bill to provide 26 weeks organizational leave for himself, as President. The Parkway Bill passed without the organizational leave attachment. He further pushed for binding arbitration. As it turned out, years later, the PBA president is now granted full time organizational leave and binding arbitration is part of the negotiating process.

Stuart angered BCI members who were in contract negotiations by hand delivering a letter to OER demanding they cease and desist in all PBA matters unless he approved of the attorney being used. This action stopped all negotiations, grievances and court actions for three months. He further fired one of the office staff that he believed was involved in a conspiracy to "Overthrow the President". She was rehired, as the President had no power to hire of fire without board approval. Between January and August 1979, PBA Treasurer Steve Sleurs detected irregularities in Stuart's Delegates and Presidents expense vouchers, as well as other spending without board approval. An independent audit verified his findings. Stuart resided 31 miles away yet his expenses exceeded those for board members residing 350 miles away. He elected to ignore warnings by Sleurs that drastic measures would be taken if he continued spending without documentation and board approval. The situation came to a head, when Stuart declared that as President, he would "Do it my way". A complaint was prepared and warrants issued resulting in Stuart being arrested for larceny by Sleurs and BCI board member Don Greely. The Board of Directors suspended Stuart as President. He filed suit in State Court alleging False Arrest and in Federal Court alleging violation of his civil rights. The criminal case was presented before the Albany County Grand Jury who failed to indict. A short time later, both civil suits were dismissed. As a result, a recall vote resulted in Stuart being dismissed as PBA President. He retired from the State Police in 1980.

In 1980, the finger pointing, bickering and arrest of Stuart took its toll on the make up of the PBA the following year. One half of the board of Directors failed in their bid for re-election or chose not to run. Elections held during the fall of 1979 resulted in several incumbents being ousted. Bob Gillespie replaced Charlie Stuart in "F", Al Kurek defeated Fred Porcello in "A", Anthony Moore replaced Don Mundy in "C", Mike Rusyniak replaced Fred Klein in "D", Dick Tweedel replaced Paul Johnson in "E", Roland Wildey replaced Ed Birmingham in "K" and Dick Hussey replaced Joe Stinton in "T". Roland Russell of the newly formed Troop "L" also came aboard, as a delegate.

AL KUREK'S TENURE 1980 to 1985

In 1979, I ran for the elected position of Troop "A" delegate to the PBA. At the time, the PBA reputation was that of party boys with a lot of dissention and turmoil among board members. I ran against and beat then long time incumbent Frederick Porcello (Allegany) in a two-man election. I had worked with Fred many years earlier and had a great deal of respect for him. My running had nothing to do with Fred personally, but was about the direction of the PBA and lack of feedback to the field. Board members had recently arrested PBA President Charles Stuart and had him removed from office. The charges were later dismissed. Fred's aspirations to become the PBA President was nullified with his election loss. In January 1980, I attended my first meeting in Albany, N.Y. Board meetings were held on the third Thursday of the month with travel expenses and lodging paid for by the PBA. Board members stayed at the Silo Ramada Inn on Western Avenue. Each troop had a delegate plus an officer delegate, BCI east and west delegate and an NCO East and west delegate. Association officers were elected from the board by the board. Delegates received a monthly deposit into their troop account of $1.25 per member of their troop. This was used for retirement gifts, social gatherings and family assistance at the discretion of the delegate.

Under the leadership of newly elected President John Canfield, an active role was taken in public relations with members visiting legislators on an almost daily basis to determine who would be supportive of legislation beneficial to the State Police. This was a complete turn around, as many legislators had never met a trooper and did not know what the PBA stood for. These early visits eventually led to the formation of a Political Action Committee within the PBA. Board members purchased tickets to legislative fund-raisers and attended informational meetings held by legislators. Soon, these legislators were calling the PBA office for our input into specific trooper legislation. Members met with Lieutenant Governor Mario Cuomo for lunch on occasion at his request. Led by long term Senator Dale Volker, a former police officer, Western New York legislator's supported all trooper legislation introduced.

There were four board members from Western New York. Myself, Michael O'Rourke (BCI West), Donald Barnes(Officers) and Patrick O'Reilly (NCO West). In 1980, we initiated a Troop "A" picnic that was held at Emery Park, East Aurora, N.Y. catered by Amidor Ortiz. This was a first of its kind and brought both retirees and active troopers together in a social atmosphere. Picnics were held every year until I retired in 1985. They were now known as the Troop "A" Legislative Picnic with local politicians and state legislators invited guests. These were all day affairs now held at Kloc's Grove in West Seneca with three hundred in attendance.

In about my second year as delegate, I appointed Roger Giuseppetti, Batavia Communications, as my alternate delegate. I established a station delegate system with every Troop "A" station represented. I would call and provide Roger with updated information and he would relay it to the other delegates. Being stationed at Troop Headquarters, I had benefit of first hand knowledge and kept members up to date. I established a policy with Troop "A" Commander Major George Tordy that resulted in all the station delegates meeting with him in conference on a monthly basis to discuss troop problems and issues within the troop. These proved to beneficial with several policy changes being made and improvements made in radio communications that was a primary safety issue concern.

The backwash of Attica continued with Grand Juries indicting inmate after inmate for violent crimes committed during the uprising. A second Grand Jury looked into any wrong doing on the part of law enforcement. During these investigative hearings, the PBA provided an attorney who was present at all times to consult and advise. The attorney fees were in excess of $250,000.00 draining the PBA treasury. Several years later, legislation was passed reimbursing the PBA for attorney related expenses. During these trying days of endless hearings and inquiries, Trooper Jeffrey Gustafson under advise of PBA Attorney Bernard (Bud) Malone took a position under the Fifth Amendment (Self Incrimination) and declined to answer any questions. The hearings being held in Rochester, N.Y. resulted in Judge William Quigley citing Gustafson for Contempt of Court and committed him to the Monroe County Jail. PBA representatives Richard Tweedel and Albert Kurek sat with him for several hours until Malone arranged for his release. The charges were later dismissed. After all was said and done and millions in dollars spent in court related costs, Governor Hugh Carey declared blanket amnesty for everyone involved. No one was ever prosecuted.

One of the duties of a delegate was to represent members at grievance or disciplinary hearings and provide counsel, when required. There was only one occasion during my tenure where a trooper's job was at stake. I was in Albany, when I was told to report to the office of Deputy Superintendent Robert Quick in the "Ivory Tower". Quick was absolutely irate, as he related an incident involving a Troop "A" member. Apparently, Trooper Thomas Paluch (SP Boston) and several other troopers while on duty had traveled to Chefs Restaurant for a farewell dinner in honor of retiring Trooper Thomas O'Brien. While returning to SP Boston, Paluch, a passenger in a marked troop car "**mooned**" a female Thruway Toll Collector at the Ogden Street exit. She was outraged and placed an official complaint against the trooper. Quick was outraged that a trooper representing the people of New York State should do such a thing and felt there was no place for this type of individual on the job. I looked into the complaint and yes; Paluch was the man in the moon. Reporting back to Quick, I pled a case of high productivity (100 plus traffic tickets a month), the building of an addition for an elderly in law that he cared for and the fact that in his many years, his performance evaluation was outstanding with no negative comments. Quick looked me square in the eye and asked me if I thought Paluch should stay on as a trooper. I told him that I did. The PBA was in contract negotiations at the time with one of the issues being a reduction in personal leave days from 5 to 3 days for new hires. Quick told me that if I supported the reduction, he would discipline Paluch, but not fire him. I spoke with the PBA attorneys and was advised that Division could arbitrarily change personal leave for new hires at any time, as it would have been terms of their employment and the PBA did not represent persons not on the job. It was pointed out that there were other issues more important than personal leave on the table so I agreed to Quick's request. Paluch was suspended for a short time, but continued as a trooper until his mandatory retirement. It was pointed out on several occasions by a few new troopers about how I sold them out during negotiations. I continued to serve as PBA Vice President and Troop "A" delegate until my retirement in 1985.

PBA PRESIDENTS

WILLIAM H. BARFOOT	1943
EDWARD J. BLANEY	1944
ROMAN J. LAURENCE	1945 TO 1949
?	
TED DELUCA	
WILLIAM COURLIS	1961 TO 1968
GEORGE ZINK	1969 TO 1970
WILLIAM A. THOMSPON	1971
PATRICK J. CARROLL	1972 TO 1976
GLEN E. HELD	1977 TO 1979
CHARLES STUART	JAN-SEP 1979
ROBERT E. O'CONNOR	SEP 79 TO JAN 80
JOHN CANFIELD	1980 TO 1985

ASSOCIATION OF FORMER NEW YORK STATE TROOPERS

HISTORY

The Association of Former New York State Troopers, Inc. originated some years previous to 1951 with the forming in New York City of a social club of ex-troopers principally from Troops "K" and "L". In 1951, this club decided to expand and form a statewide organization to be known as the Association of Former New York State Troopers. It was incorporated as such on November 14, 1951. Anthony J. DiGiovanna, Justice of the Supreme Court of the State of New York, signed the authorization. The petitioners for the incorporation were John J. Levy, George R. Homa, John H. McCaddin, James Bree, Howard G. Poppe and Michael J. Codd. The petition was dated in Brooklyn, New York. Only those members that served in the State Police for a minimum of one year were eligible to join. The purpose of the organization is to promote friendship, instill loyalty to each other, to stimulate intellectual advancement and to hold fraternal meetings and gatherings on a footing of equality.

In addition to the chapter in New York City, local chapters were initially formed in Poughkeepsie, Albany and Oneida, N.Y. Within a few short years, all areas of the state were represented. Officers of the state association were elected by majority vote.

BATAVIA CHAPTER

In the early spring of 1955, Edward J. Doody was approached by George R. Homa of Brooklyn who had been elected president of the state association, asking that he interest himself in the establishment of a local chapter in Batavia, New York. Ed consulted with a number of former "A" troopers and they

267

decided to look into the matter. On April 15, 1955, John E. Stuerwald of Schenectady, vice president of the state association, wrote Ed on the subject and sent a copy of the constitution and by-laws of the association. The area to be covered by the new chapter would be the ten counties of Western New York to include the cities of Rochester, Buffalo, Lockport, Batavia, Olean, Jamestown, Niagara Falls and Dunkirk. A meeting was held in the American Legion rooms in Batavia, New York on May 20, 1955 with the following persons in attendance:

Chester W. Acer	Edward J. Doody	Albert R. Perry
Leslie C. Benway	Frank A. Easton	Donald J. Libera
Joseph W. Brandstetter	Andrew C. Fisher	Arthur L. Rich
Albert C. Butler	Guy W. Hamm	William T. Silage
William E. Cannon	Joseph P. Heilig	Stanley N. Smith
Devillo H. Chamberlain	Albert S. Horton	Herbert G. Southworth
Edwin B. Chamberlain	Harold L. Kemp	William J. Szymanski
John S. Cole	Harold E. Kramp	Samuel J. Vint
John L. Costello	Frank A. Lachnicht	George L. White
Harold L. Debrine	Norman H. Lippert	Oscar H. White
George V. Delaney	Edward B. Miller	James A. Wolcott

Mr. Stuerwald came to Batavia to address the meeting and explain the purpose of the association, namely, to promote friendship and provide mutual assistance and welfare among its members. The result was that those present voted to form a Chapter. Preliminary plans were drafted and temporary officers appointed headed by Edward J. Doody to be assisted by George L. White and Norman Lippert. It was then decided to hold an organization meeting in Batavia on June 28, 1955 at which time those desiring to unite with the new chapter would fill out application cards, pay dues for the last half of 1955 and elect permanent officers for the year. The first officers elected were Edward J. Doody, President, Oscar H. White, Vice- president, Norman H. Lippert, Treasurer, George H. White, Corresponding Secretary and Stanley N. Smith, Recording Secretary.

(This document is printed, as originally written by Winfield W. Robinson, Association Secretary)

CHARTER MEMBERS OF THE BATAVIA CHAPTER

Acer, Chester W.
Anderson, Elner F.
Andrews, Montagu
Balling, Leon F.
Barton, Albert J.
Beach, Harold W.
Benway, Leslie C.
Bertman, Algird J.
Blount, Curtis L.
Bogucki Jr., Edmund A.
Brandstetter, Joseph W.
Bund, Edward P.
Cannon, William E.
Carmichael, Jay
Chamberlain, Devillo H.
Chambers, Harvey L.
Coakley, Kenneth H.
Cole, John S.
Dahn, Edward M.
Delaney, George V.
Donnelly, George W.
Doody, Edward J.
Dunn, Wilson H.
Easton, Frank A.
Fisher, James P.
Fortner, Lyman D.
Foster, David C.
Girven, Donald S.
Gormley, Joseph A.
Greer, Thomas
Hamm, Guy W.
Heilig, Joseph P.
Hoar, John J.
Horton, Albert S.
House, Willis S.
Keefe, Lawrence C.
Kemp, Harold L.

Kinne, Donald T.
Kramp, Harold E.
Krick, John D.
Lachnicht, Frank A.
Lathan, Calvin A.
Laurence, Roman J.
Lengeman, Nelson E.
Leone, Sebastian
Librock, Irving E.
Lippert, Norman H.
Manhold, William P.
Martin, Theodore F.
McGaughey, Arthur D.
McConnell, Lester J.
McFarland, Bart F.
Miller, Edward B.
Molinaro, Clarence L.
Ogden, Casimer F.
Perry, Adelbert E.
Perry, Albert E.
Pettinger, Earl P.
Phelps, Edgar J
Rich, Arthur L.
Rimmer, Edward A.
Robinson, Winfield W.
Rogers, Henry G.
Rooney, Leo J.
Rosenow, Walter
Rowe Jr., John F.
Rowe, Joseph F.
Saelzler, Eugene H.
Sharrow, Edwin W.
Smith, Stanley N.
Smith, Silas W.
Sullivan, Gerald R.
Szymanski, William J.
Verplank, Harold J.

Vint, Samuel J.
Ward, Edward P.
Waterman, Clayton
Weinstein, Julius
Wheeler, Lynn H.
White, George L.
White, Oscar H.
Wolcott, James A.
Woodward, Eugene

On August 25, 1955, Ed Doody in a letter to Norm Lippert suggested naming the chapter the Niagara Chapter or Genesee Valley Chapter. It was determined at a membership meeting that it would be simply known as the Batavia Chapter. On August 31, 1955, Secretary George White sent a check in an amount of $88.50 representing dues for the Batavia Chapter. Yearly dues to the State Association were $6.00 a year. Meetings were initially held monthly at the American Legion, Bogue Avenue, Batavia, N.Y. At some point, meeting were moved to the Batavia Elk's Home where sometime during the 1960s, many records stored in the basement were destroyed due to flooding. Meetings were again held at the Legion and since 1994, have returned to the Elk's home.

Through the 60s and 70s, yearly functions included a dinner dance held at either the American Legion (Joe Brandstetter was Steward) or Batavia Elks home in the spring and a summer picnic held at Como Lake Park in Lancaster, N.Y. or at Harold Silloway's airfield in Hamlin, N.Y. Silloway's was preferred, as he owned and flew his own airplane and would take members for short rides weather permitting.

The Chapter fell on hard times during 1978 –79 after the deaths of President Henry Rogers and Secretary Charles Richmond. The Chapter had 118 members, however only five or six were attending meetings. This was attributed to the membership aging, residing out of state or not wanting to drive the distance to a meeting. The majority of members resided in Buffalo, Rochester and the Southern Tier and felt it too far and expensive to travel for a meeting.

State Association President John Everhardt in a letter dated September 5, 1979 noted that the relationship with the association had "suddenly been going down hill". In 1978 –79, Jim Duval was elected President, Oscar Lazeroff, Vice President and John Wilcox, Secretary-Treasurer. Meeting dates and activities were scheduled, however attendance was small and slowly dropped off. At the end of 1979, no one could be found to run for office so the current officers were re-installed. In May 1980, Jim Duval resigned for personal reasons. Attendance at meetings consisted of two members. This was attributed to the formation of the Niagara Frontier Chapter in the Buffalo area that reduced the chapter roster by 40 members. There was confusion in the collection of dues for 1980 with no membership cards being sent to the Batavia Chapter by State Treasurer Ertman Crouse. It appears to this writer that Treasurer Crouse, himself was the cause of the confusion by not sending membership cards and decals to the Chapter, believing the Batavia Chapter to be defunct. The confusion was due to formation of two new chapters from the existing Batavia membership. Crouse let it be known that the Batavia Chapter was defunct and was to be a part of the Genesee Valley (Finger Lakes) Chapter. At about the same time, a deposit check was lost and checks returned for insufficient funds. This confusion resulted in the Batavia Chapter barely staying in existence in 1980.

The Niagara Frontier Chapter formed in 1980 followed by the Finger Lakes chapter in 1981 reduced membership in the Batavia Chapter from 118 members to an all time low of 40 members. A considerable amount of dissention and hard feelings resulted. The membership reduction devastated the Batavia Chapter to the point that no elections were held for the year 1980. Newly elected State Association President J.J. Lawson commented that the childish bickering between the State Board and Batavia Chapter members be stopped and settled immediately. (Dispute was about amount owed to the State for dues & decals based on membership) Initially, Batavia Chapter members did not want to allow the formation of a Finger Lakes Chapter so soon after losing members to the Niagara Frontier Chapter. Lawson stated there was too much dissention among the membership and that he would end it by approving a new chapter, if a proper petition was submitted. A petition was submitted and approved.

The Batavia Chapter successfully recruited new members from the Class of 1962; the troopers largest manpower increases ever, that were now retiring. The State Police have a 20-year retirement plan with many young troopers taking advantage and pursuing second careers. Meetings continued to be held at the Batavia American Legion on the third Wednesday of the month. In about 1994, chapter meetings returned to the Batavia Elk's Home now boasting a membership in excess of 100 members. The meetings start time was changed from 8:00 PM to 6:30 PM with the Chapter providing a meal at no cost to the membership. The meals consisted mostly of beef on weck, pizza and chicken wings or Italian sausage sandwiches with a brief business meeting following the meal. Al Kurek serves as the chief chef with Louie Lang the alternate in preparing the meals for Chapter members.

A monthly newsletter is sent to the membership usually one week prior to a meeting. Those that have computers are provided with up to date information regarding member & trooper activities. Approximately 75% of the members are on the e-mail listing saving the chapter many dollars in postage fees and time.

In about 1998, the Batavia Chapter initiated an associate membership. Associates members are current troopers that are eligible to retire, retired civilian staff employees and those eligible to retire and retired conservation officers that worked closely with the troopers. We were all part of the state police family and by doing so; continue our close friendships and bonds from years gone by.

The chapter has been very active socially. Several dinner dances billed as Xmas in March were held at either Christina's Restaurant or the Treadway Inn at Batavia, N.Y. We enjoy a family picnic each August held at Ed Longhany's "Woody Acres", Leroy, N.Y. We have had law enforcement beef & beer parties and several years ago, initiated a law enforcement golf outing that is held the second Thursday of September each year.

BATAVIA CHAPTER PRESIDENTS

1955 – 56	Edward J. Doody	1957	Stanley N. Smith
1958	Elner F. Anderson	1959	Henry J. Wise
1960	Clarence J. Molinaro	1961	Henry G. Rogers
1962	George W. Donnelly	1963	Charles F. Maguire
1964 – 65	Clyde E. Nelson	1966	Clarence J. Pasto
1967	Arthur L. Rich	1968	Donald S. Girven
1969	Claude A. Stephens	1970 – 71	William C. Tiffany
1972 – 73	Harold L. Silloway	1974	Albert S. Horton
1975 – 76	James E. Harrer	1977 – 78	Roy J. Wullich
1979 – 80	James L. Duval	1980 - 81	Oscar Lazeroff
1982 – 85	Ray A. Chudoba	1986 – 87	John P. Wilcox
1988 – 91	Albert S. Kurek	1992 – 93	Leonard P.Bochynski
1994 – 95	Peter C. Detoy	1996 – 97	Ronald Junior
1998 – 99	Richard C. Tonzi	2000 – 05	Frederick R. Walsh

FINGER LAKES CHAPTER

In April 1981, a request was made for the formation of a Genesee Valley Chapter for members residing in the Rochester area. Eighteen (18) Batavia members transferred to the new chapter. On June 20, 1981, the officers of the newly formed Finger Lakes Chapter were sworn in at Utica, N.Y. during the state association meeting. The first elected officers were: Oscar Lazeroff, President, Edward J. Murphy, Vice President, Kenneth Hulbert, Treasurer and William Schencke, Secretary. The chapter meetings are held on the third Tuesday of the month at various locations within their geographical area. Meetings are dinner meetings and normally include spouses and friends. A summer picnic is held, usually in August at one of the member's residences.

ALLEGHENY MOUNTAINS CHAPTER

In February 1987, retired trooper Stewart Hill, Olean, N.Y. expressed interest in the formation of a Southern Tier Chapter. An organizational meeting was held at the Olean Town Hall on March 10, 1987 with enough interest shown, that a petition was prepared for the establishment of the Allegheny Mountains Chapter. The Chapter was chartered on July 1, 1987 having 28 charter members. The first officers were Stewart Hill, President, Richard Haberer, Vice President, Philip Smith, Treasurer and James Rowley, Secretary. Stewart Hill has been overwhelmingly elected president each year since the Chapters conception.

Meetings are held on the second Tuesday of each month at 8:00PM except the summer months of June, July & August. The Chapter met initially at the Eagles Nest, Olean, N.Y., but has since relocated to the American Legion on Route 16, Hindsdale, N.Y.

CHAPTER EVENTS

Special events include an annual steak bake normally held the second Saturday in June honoring a deceased member of the state police. 2005 was the 18th consecutive year for this event with all profits donated to local area youth organizations.

The Chapter provides a yearly $200.00 scholarship to a High School Senior from Allegany, Cattaraugus and Chautauqua Counties that is entering the Criminal Justice field. Payment is only given after successful completion of the first semester.

The Chapter provides annually to the SPSP program where a less fortunate youth from the area is sent to the State Police Academy for a week of summer camp.

The Chapter sponsors an annual hockey game at the Olean Recreational Hockey Center between the Buffalo Sabres Alumni and local troopers with proceeds donated to local youth programs.

BARON STEUBEN CHAPTER

On June 17, 1995, George Ott, a member of the Finger Lakes Chapter presented a petition with 31 signatures requesting the formation of a new chapter to be known as the Baron Steuben Chapter in the Southern Tier area. Approval was granted with a Charter presented at the Tally Ho Restaurant, Kanona, N.Y. during the first Chapter meeting held on July 12, 1995. The first elected officers were: George Ott – President, Ken. L. Yergens – Vice-President, John A. Kulikowski – Treasurer & Jan Ketchum – Secretary/Clerk. Monthly meetings are held at the Tally Ho on the third Tuesday of the month.

Charter members of the Chapter are: Steve Bigger, Robert Chura, Robert K. Clark, James S. Cortese, David Day, Fay Faucett, Gary F. Forshee, Raymond G. Granston, Paul T. Johnson, Robert W. Jones, Jan Ketchum, John A. Kulikowski, Keith Lawton, Robert McGinnis, Ken McKillup, Bernard H. Marro, W. Narby, Ron Nixson, George W. Ott, Bill Recktenwald, Paul Recktenwald, Louis J. Reitenauer, Dick Rice, Don Robinson, Don E. Sanford, E.H. Schusler, Gerald J. Schusler, Richard E. Swan, Leon Taggert, Raymond E. Wells, K.L. Yergens, and Robert F. Yorio.

In 2004, the Baron Steuben Chapter elected Bridgette Lamphere to replace long term President George Ott. Bridgette is the first female retiree to hold office in the AFNYST. Other newly elected officers are Larry Francis, Treasurer and Emmett Milks, Secretary.

In 1997, the chapter hosted a very successful AFNYST Re-union at Corning, N.Y. Captain Ed Haag, the Zone 3, Bath Commander provided a great presentation of the history of the state police with troopers wearing authentic period uniforms.

NIAGARA FRONTIER CHAPTER

James F. McDermott, Richard Manns and George Mills of Buffalo, N.Y. appeared before state association board meeting on June 21, 1980 requesting advice and aid in forming a new chapter to be known as the Niagara Frontier Chapter. A petition was presented at the next board meeting. The Chapter was approved in the Fall of 1980 with George Mills elected President, Jim McDermott Vice President, Frank Demler Recording Secretary, Robert Shanahan Corresponding Secretary and Dick Lewandowski Treasurer. Meetings were initially held at Lewandowski's Blue Collar Tavern in West Seneca. As the Chapter grew, meetings were moved to the Airways Hotel near the Buffalo Airport, until it was demolished for expansion. Meetings were then moved to the Airways new location at Main Street & Kensington Avenue, Amherst and most recently, at Magruders Restaurant, Depew, N.Y. meetings are held on the first Wednesday of the month. The Chapter grew form 26 members to the present membership of 267. Activities include sponsoring of Troopers Helping Hands, an annual chicken barbecue in June and a gala Christmas party in December.

FORMER TROOPERS HELPING HANDS

MAKING WISHES COME TRUE FOR TERMINALLY ILL CHILDREN

The Niagara Frontier Chapter initiated the desire to help terminally ill children by forming the Western New York – Make – A – Wish in 1983. A threatened lawsuit filed by the Make A Wish Foundation for name infringement resulted in a change of names to what it is today, The Former Troopers Helping Hands.

The Former Troopers Helping Hands, Inc. was incorporated in New York State on September 26, 1986, as a Not-For-Profit Organization. Contributions made are deductible. The original officers were Maurice "Mo" Gavin, the ramrod, Gregory Wildridge and Chapter President James McDermott. The Helping Hands mission is dedicated to fulfilling the wishes of all children and young adults with life-threatening illnesses and their families. In 2003, wishes were granted to 13 children & their families.

In 1987, Shane Conlan, the Buffalo Bills rookie linebacker and son of Trooper Daniel Conlan was selected as the winner of the 1987 OLD SPICE/NFL ROOKIE OF THE YEAR SWEEPSTAKES. Conlan designated the Helping Hands, as the recipient of the cash award that totaled $26,000.00

Throughout the years, requests for wishes have been put before the board for consideration. The Helping Hands program provides the means for participants to temporarily escape the reality of medical treatment into an experience where their wishes are fulfilled.

Having no paid staff, time and resources are donated by the board members, the membership and friends. Funding comes from many sources: cash donations, designated donations to the United Way and SEFA on Helping Hands behalf, corporate and benevolent service organizations, fund raisers and golf tournaments sponsored by individuals and civic groups, veterans posts, volunteer fire departments, the law enforcement community, donations and memorial contributions from other chapters and individuals plus an annual membership available to all for a ten dollar donation. Helping Hands does not use professional fund- raisers, telephone solicitations or mass mailings to solicit funds. Over ninety five percent of all donation dollars received go directly to fulfill a participant's wishes.

If you are interested in donating to this worthy cause, donations and membership applications can be gotten by contacting the "Former Troopers Helping Hands", P.O. Box 432, West Seneca, New York 14224 / Phone 716-824-0088. A yearly membership can be had for as little as $10.00.

JOHN NOHLEN - RAY SLADE - DICK BOLAND
HANK WILLIAMS

HANK WILLIAMS - SAM SLABIK - 1970

BOB KOENIG - TED GEORGITSO - BOB
MINEKHEIM
BERGEN STATION - 1955

1964 BOWLING TEAM - A. DIRIENZ- S.SOCHALEC R.CHUDOBA- F.WALSH- J.DUVAL

1968 – TROOP "A" BASKETBALL TEAM – FRONT – THOMAS TUCKER, WARDEN BARROWS, ERTIS (BUD)

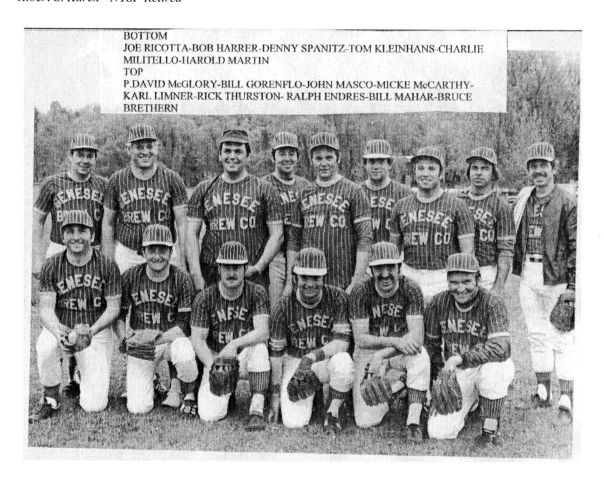

BOTTOM
JOE RICOTTA-BOB HARRER-DENNY SPANITZ-TOM KLEINHANS-CHARLIE
MILITELLO-HAROLD MARTIN
TOP
P.DAVID McGLORY-BILL GORENFLO-JOHN MASCO-MICKE McCARTHY-
KARL LIMNER-RICK THURSTON- RALPH ENDRES-BILL MAHAR-BRUCE
BRETHERN

JIM LOBUR-GERRY WEISS-GERRY KALISZ-CHUCK
RECCIO -- BILL LOFT -- WARD BARROWS --RAY MOTYKA
TOM TUCKER-FRED WALSH-BOB MINEKHEIM-BOB
HUMMEL -- JERRY SCHLAGENHAUF -- PHIL CARROLL

1965 BOWLING TEAM -
K.LIMNER - J.NOHLEN
H.SMITH-R.MINEKHEIM-
G.KALISZ

KEN BLACK - RON HADSALL - BILL
ERNST - JIM CEFERATTI - JOE MULLINS

S. PAQUADECK-W.RIMMER-E.LONGHANY-CARMEN BASILIO
W.MURPHY-J.CAPPACI-R.POWELL - 1958

BOOK VIII — PROFILES

MONTAGU ANDREWS - 1925 TO 1954

Montagu "Monty" Andrews was widely known throughout Western New York for his photographic and fingerprint work that figured in the solving of thousands of cases.

He was born in Braintree, England in 1893 where he attended Essex High School. He then served five years in the British Army, as member of the Royal Fusiliers. During WW I, he was with the British Expeditionary Force in France and Belgium and held the British War, Meritorious Service and Victory medals. Coming to the United States, he enlisted in the New York State Police on July 15, 1925. He was promoted to the rank of Corporal on April 1, 1927 and assigned to the new Troop "A" identification bureau. He single-handedly built up a Troop "A" file of fingerprints and photographs where it contained 15,000 identifications. He attended the State Police School at Troy in 1927 and the Institute of Applied Science at Chicago. He resigned on February 15, 1928 to take a position as a detective with the Delaware, Lackawanna and Western Railroad. He was re-appointed to the troopers on February 1, 1931. He was a charter member of the newly formed Bureau of Criminal Investigation (BCI) on July 1, 1936. Monty retired on June 1, 1954. He was presented with a special ring containing an amethyst stone and bearing a state police shield and engraved with his service record. He was married to the former Teresa Aquino, daughter of Mr. and Mrs. Nicholas Aquino of 62 Swan Street. They had three children, Gordon, Shirley and Montagu Jr.

SERGEANT WILLIAM J. ANSLOW – 1943 TO 1969

In 1943, the Capitol Security Detail was created at the request of Governor Thomas E. Dewey. Sergeant William Anslow, a trooper since 1933 was the first trooper selected as guard to the Governor's office, a position he held until his retirement on December 30, 1969.

When he started, it was a one-man detail with no relief. He sat at a desk outside the second floor Red Room (governors office) from 9:00 AM until the governor left at usually 8:00 or 9:00 PM. He wore a pistol but never had to use it, as it was usually a quiet area. In 1948 he was one of five troopers that accompanied Governor Dewey as he barnstormed the country during his presidential campaign. As his bodyguards, they stood near him on the platforms and were frequently the targets of a misdirected thrown egg.

During his tenure, he served for Dewey, Averill Harriman and Nelson Rockefeller. He found all of them and their wives to be friendly and easy to talk with. The busiest time at the Capitol was during night legislative sessions and during clemency hearings. The regular night sessions were discontinued in 1964 and clemency hearings diminished with new revisions to capital punishment laws.

Sergeant Anslow and his wife, Mildred were honored guests at the Governors 1969 staff Christmas party held at the Governor's mansion. Sergeant John A. Mainello of Brunswick, N.Y, replaced Anslow.

VERNON J. CLAYSON - 1956 TO 1978

RECRUIT
After completing an Air Force enlistment and returning home, I saw a notice at the Post Office that the Division of State Police was seeking applicants so I obtained an application at the sub-station in Allegany, N.Y. The Trooper that gave me the application was Bob Jackson who is still around

but now retired. I submitted the application and soon received a letter advising that the written test would be given at Jamestown, N.Y.

After passing the examination, I was instructed to travel to Batavia for a physical examination that I passed handily; I was standing upright and breathing. I looked over the applicants and thought very few of them looked like I pictured Troopers and that included the Troopers monitoring the examination who seemed even more miscast, out of shape and not especially sharp in appearance and conduct. One applicant, Vic Santa, had his foot in a cast from a skiing accident but he passed. It occurred to me later that he might have used the cast to be tall enough. Not sure I was actually interested, I was so casual about the whole business I had even taken a girl friend along for the ride and she waited patiently in the car while I took the physical. I remember Vic Santa because we talked during the physical and then went to lunch together. He didn't stay in the State Police very long, eventually moving to Florida where he joined the Dade County Police.

The next step in the application process was an interview with the Troop Commander, Captain John Ronan, and a lieutenant whose name I don't recall. I apparently answered the questions to their satisfaction and was told I would be notified of the results shortly. On the way out of the building, I passed the old First Sergeant who had directed me into the presence of the even older men but it appeared he had lost interest, as he was sound asleep at his desk. I learned later he was Charlie (C.Z.) MacDonald and it was a regular thing for him to fall asleep at his desk. Years later I stopped to see him when he was working at the Desert Inn in Las Vegas and he fell asleep while talking to me. I have to say now they weren't really old, they were in their late 40s and early 50s, and seem rather young from my present perspective, here in 2006.

A few days later, Investigator Eugene Redden interviewed me and conducted the required applicant background investigation. I thought he was much more impressive and professional than the Troopers I had encountered earlier. A few weeks later I received a letter telling me that I had met the qualifications and to report to the Troop Headquarters at Batavia on May 10th, 1956. That day arrived and I started my State Police career.

There were 33 in my recruit class. We quickly became acquainted, especially those whose names were closest in alphabetical order, as we were usually called in that sequence. In my group it was Chidsey, Chura, Clayson and Cleere. The age limit at the time was 32 but those older than that were allowed to subtract their military time. Jim Duval was one of the oldest in the group. He had been a bus driver in New York City. He became a BCI man and retired as a Senior Investigator and office administrator at Troop Headquarters. He returned to driving buses after his retirement, albeit school buses. I was one of the younger guys and wondered why such "old" guys wanted to be a Trooper. After completing a number of forms that served enlistment and administrative purposes, we were sworn in. The first items issued us were plain gray work clothes called fatigues, socks and uniform shoes. (Old timers will remember that the socks were black with white toes and heel and basically indestructible.) One member of our class looked at these issue items and declared he had not enlisted to do menial work and resigned immediately. No one attempted to dissuade him. We were led through the headquarters offices, Communications, Troop Clerk, Bureau of Criminal Investigation, and the Traffic Section; the duties performed by each were briefly explained. In those days, there was a kitchen and dining hall at the headquarters, which served meals to employees stationed there. We were fed with the regular staff that, in my mind, looked at us balefully, as if we were all interlopers. Troopers in the field were paid a per diem for meals amounting to about $4.20 for every day worked that was in addition to the regular pay. My regular pay in 1956 was $2700.00 annually; with the per diem it was a decent wage. (You have to remember that a cup of coffee was a nickel and a couple of eggs or a hamburger with coffee was around forty-five cents at the time.) Benefits of being stationed at Troop Headquarters, in addition to being served meals, were shorter workdays. Headquarters staff members worked more regular hours and were allowed to go home after their shift. Members in the field lived in one of the many substations, had two days off each week with one extra day a month usually combined with the two days. The workweek was well over 80 hours a week. A day off wasn't quite a 24-hour period. You worked until 3:00 PM and had to be back and ready to work the next day at 10:00 AM. When I say we "lived" at the substations, it was actually just a place to sleep. A normal workday was from 7:00 a.m. until 10 or 11:00 PM. While still at Troop Headquarters, we listened to lectures, washed cars, cut grass and raked leaves and other menial tasks. These duties ceased when we were issued uniforms. We were given old style uniforms which consisted of ill-fitting breeches with puttees, shirts and jackets without shoulder patches, old black rubber raincoats and Stetson hats, all of which were obviously used, if not nearly worn out. Dressed, we were a sad looking group. We were soon issued used leather equipment, belts, a holster, a rusting and antique looking .45 revolver and moldy ammunition and then required to stand formation for inspection by Captain John Ronan and the First Sergeant, C.Z. MacDonald. The Captain looked at my weapon and asked when I had cleaned it last, I told him I had never cleaned it as I had just gotten it five minutes before. He ignored me but the old First Sergeant glared at me. We next were required to qualify with the ancient firearms. The range was little more than an overgrown field that was adjacent to a dump; it may even have been part of the dump. The firearms instructor was the Assistant Troop Clerk, Jim Moochler, I think he was a corporal at the time. The vehicle used, as the range car was a 1930's van style ford. It probably wasn't safe at any speed yet I recall it was used for several more years.

In the evenings, a few of us rode with an experienced Trooper on his patrol. I apparently drew one of the department's party animals. He drove as rapidly as he could from the back of one tavern to another and entered briefly while I waited in the car. Each time he came back to the car, he smelled stronger of booze. Eventually he tired of this "patrol" and we returned to the headquarters so he could talk to the people on the evening shift in the communications section that seemed as bored as he was while I sat in the hall looking at the wall. His name was Malcolm Grant who was eventually fired short of completing twenty years for passing out drunk at the wheel of a troop car. I also rode with another old-time trooper, Charlie Richmond, whose primary duty was being the troop headquarters car mechanic and all-around handyman. He was okay, just smelled of automobile lubricants and cigarettes. One memorable day, we were transported by bus to Sidney, N.Y. halfway across the state. We were picking up new troop cars to drive back to Batavia. We were like kids with new toys, kings of the road with people moving aside as our line of Troop cars passed. This was cool despite the presence of Trooper Duane Roberts, always self-important, who supervised the assignment. The next day, Bob Chura, and I were told to take one of the new cars to the Wrights Corners substation and stay there for a couple of days. On the way, we were maniacs, taking turns driving the car at high speeds, really full of ourselves. At the Wright's Corners substation, I rode with Phil Trapani, a seasoned veteran of two or three years. As opposed to the headquarters patrols, he actually worked at law enforcement, stopping cars and writing tickets. I felt foolish in my ill-fitting old style uniform when I approached motorists on my own as Trapani was wearing the new style uniform, a lighter weight and color with a shoulder patch. The first of the hapless individuals I encountered was named Berger Lillieberger. Who could forget a name like that? He responded politely to my request for his license and registration despite my sad sack attire of loose fitting breeches, too large shirt and too small Stetson. The metal clips holding the puttees came unfastened each time I alighted from the car so I had to bend down and connect them before I could approach the motorists. I did commence to feel better about the State Police, however, as girls were smiling and waving, in retrospect I'm sure Phil was the attraction. This made me aware of a benefit that had not been discussed in any briefings. Girls liked Troopers. I left Batavia a short time later. We recruits were given station assignments for training with experienced Troopers and I was sent to SP Athol Springs, a zone headquarters station on the lakeshore near Hamburg in Erie County. This was both an enlightening and humbling experience.

ATHOL SPRINGS
Arriving at Athol Springs, I was told to ride around with Jack Steinmetz who introduced me to the streets of the Village of Blasdell, and later with Maurice Gavin who patrolled only back roads. Neither spoke to me all the while we were together with no cars being stopped and no complaints or investigations assigned to us. It was plain to see they were merely killing time. They did go home for lunch, leaving me in the car to entertain myself. My first night patrol was with the more active George Mills. The first night together, we investigated a triple fatal accident, caught three burglars in a gas station and wrote a number of tickets. I learned more in one night with Mills, than with any other trooper at the station. Harvey Gregg was the Sergeant and "Chink" Smith the Lieutenant. I recall the Lieutenant and Investigator Dick Walters going out to check on Trooper Clint Salmon who had called in sick. They found him dancing at the Arcade, N.Y. American Legion. The pleasure they got from catching and writing Salmon up was beyond my comprehension, they seemed especially pleased to report that he was dancing to Sweet Georgia Brown. Thankfully, I was only there for two months before being assigned to SP Gaines.

SP GAINES
I found the troopers at Gaines to be friendly, casual and sociable, as well as lackadaisical. Charlie Henderson was the station commander and Bob Minekheim the Senior Trooper. Henderson had been at the physical examination as a monitor and was even heavier than I recalled and his weight was the butt of many of Bob Minekheim's jokes. One day, riding with Minekheim, he announced we were going to his parent's home for lunch and off we went. I didn't realize they lived in Syracuse some 100 miles out of the patrol area. Others at Gaines were Ed Gluch, Merle Van Skiver, Warren Terryberry and Dave Baker. Many of the troopers hired during 1954 – 55 had enlisted as "Provisional", a procedure allowing enlistment without having to take an examination. This was at a time when it was difficult to recruit members and I believe most of those entering in those years were hired under the provisional policy. If they were of age, passed the physical and background investigation and survived one year of evaluation, they were sent to the State Police School. While at Gaines, I was issued new uniforms that actually fit and was soon off to basic school myself.

BASIC TRAINING SCHOOL – TROY, N.Y.
Troopers were lodged at the Hendrick Hudson Hotel with classes commencing on November 12, 1956. Lodging and meals were provided with both being more than decent hotel fare. Classes were held at the nearby Masonic Lodge while the YMCA was used for physical exercises and drill with the local armory used for firearms training. Classes were from 9:00AM to 8:50PM with study after that. Nearby "Dukes Bar" was a place we could go for a few beers. The local gals would also gather there to check out the new troopers in person, having already looked over our personnel records to see who was single. My roommate was Jim Cortese, but not for long. He made fun of my lack of marksmanship with the .45 caliber revolver resulting in a few physical confrontations. It wasn't long before I was assigned to another room. Classes were given by a number of senior members with Lieutenant Handville and Sergeant Viehl being all business and the most impressive. Handville was a large and hard man. While conducting exercises on removal of a reluctant motorist from his car, he took me out of the car as if I were a child; something other recruits were unable to do. We graduated just before Christmas and I returned to Gaines for duty. The Gaines station was relocated and renamed SP Albion in January 1957. I believe I was sent there only to help in the moving, because I was reassigned to SP Bergen a few weeks later. Ralph Wulff was the trooper in charge at Bergen with Ted Georgitso and Reggie Perry also assigned there. In May 1957, I was transferred to SP Allegany.

SP ALLEGANY

Sergeant John Murphy was in charge at Allegany and from the old school. He wanted less said and less done to attract less attention to himself with an apparent purpose to limit his own responsibility. The only urgency on his part was that he wanted the floors shiny, new troopers were not supposed to disturb the status quo. Gene Redden, Ed Kwiecen and Joe Pleakis were also assigned at Allegany and were the responsible, mature and level headed individuals there. Bob Ennis was also there along with Merle Van Skiver who worked the night patrol. If you worked night shift, you were allowed to go home when off duty while the rest of us had to actually stay at the station unless we were on a day off. There was no deskman at night with the junior man getting the privilege of sleeping next to the phone. It was usually me. We went to a sixty-hour workweek in 1960 with the thought that eight hours would be on patrol and four hours on standby at the station. The station commander would send us off on some errand or assignment during standby so in reality, there wasn't any standby.

Lieutenant William Keeley became the Zone Commander in about 1957 and established a top ten list for tickets written during each month. Sergeant John Shaver replaced Murphy at Allegany and was a pleasure to work for. He was the most devoted advocate of the State Police that I knew. He appreciated active workers and since I was always in the Lieutenant's top ten list, he didn't bother me with menial tasks. He wasn't petty or a dictator, but you knew he was in charge. I was sent to Thruway Buffalo in 1960 where I worked for six months. I was then assigned to SP Falconer where Ed Kwiecen was the station commander. I was there a few months working with Gene Byrne, Carl VanWagenen, Herb Johnson, Bob Keyes, Cliff Lee, Jack Arnet and Jim Burns. The latter two were my kind of men, you never knew what they were going to say or do and it was not wise for anyone to cross them. I was sent back to Allegany, my favorite all time station assignment. The names are muddled as troopers rotated in and out, but I recall working there with George Abare, Frank Conway and Gene Redden as station commanders, Bob Bartlett, Jim Rowley, Fred Porcello, Bob McGinty, Henry Panus, Jerry Kitchen, Tom Griffith, Bob Johnson, Larry Austin, Bob Bubbs, Bill Reynolds, Jack Tuttle, Stewart Hill, Gary Knight, Greg Snyder, Tom Stofer, Jerry Crocker and my brother, Milford Clayson. I enjoyed working with this bunch as none were as bitter or angry as the old timers I first worked with. One of the new Lieutenants was Nicholas Lecakes who was devoid of humor. His uniform was impeccable except for his hat that seemed too small for his head. His priority was making sure every trooper's daily activity sheet was filled in correctly. Other lieutenants were Clayton Bailey and George Tordy. Both thought that trouble followed me. When I took the Sergeant's exam my score ranked me 28th in the state but the final ranking for appointment took into consideration your annual performance rating that counted for 70% of the final grade giving the favored few a huge advantage. I wound up 126th on the list and was one of the last to be promoted from that list. I believed it was all about personality and seeking your superior's favor, something I would not do. A few years earlier, Sergeant Howard Smith rated my personality as unsatisfactory on the annual performance rating. It may be the only such rating in the Division and was a proud accomplishment for me. I was never anyone's man.

PROMOTION

I was promoted to Sergeant on May 4, 1964 and initially assigned to SP Horseheads but that was changed to SP Wellsville where I stayed for about a year. I was then transferred to SP Allegany as the Station Commander. No one told Gene Redden that I was replacing him and would be in charge of the station. I felt sympathy for Gene, as I believed it was Divisions method of trying to force the old timers to retire. Gene wasn't the only one treated in this manner. Sergeant Dick Hastings was assigned desk duty in Batavia requiring travel of 100 miles round trip daily. He replaced Corporal Larry Norsen who drove back and forth from Clyde, N.Y., a similar distance. Lieutenant John Sage was assigned to Bath, N.Y. a distance of over 100 miles from his home and on and on and on. Redden never showed any bitterness and retired in May 1967. He still resides in Hinsdale, N.Y. and is beating the actuarial tables having been retired for thirty-nine years. As Station Commander, I was a stickler for orderliness and set up the administration of the station to Division specifications. In August 1966, I was promoted to the rank of Zone Sergeant that I felt was the most useless rank in the State Police. I never understood why Division would take a productive Station Sergeant and promote him to that rank as it had little responsibility and even less accountability and there were three of them to a zone. In 1967, I was designated Acting First Sergeant replacing Anthony Malovich who was on assignment at the Academy.

FIRST SERGEANT POSITION

On January 4, 1968, I was permanently promoted to the rank and assigned to Batavia.

I'm told that my competition for the position was BCI Investigator Robert Tillman. He opted not to go back into uniform so the position was mine. Tillman was a former Navy fighter pilot and a few months later, was designated the Division Chief Pilot. Although John Nohlen was the Troop Commander, it didn't take me long to learn that the real power was Captain Nicholas Giangualano. He knew finances, administration and supervision and the power that came with them. While Nohlen listened to civilian employee's opinions, Giangualano considered them help, to do what they were hired to do. He didn't concern himself with minor incidents, electing to let the trooper in the field handle situations they were trained for. It was no wonder he was placed in charge of organizing security for the 1980 Winter Olympics at Lake Placid.

In the ten years I was First Sergeant, I participated in basketball and softball with the Batavia Barracks teams. I loved basketball and while at Allegany, had troopers playing a couple of times a week at the local school gymnasium while their troop cars were parked out back. The teams at Batavia were very competitive playing in leagues with local jocks. As First Sergeant, I would call the Academy prior to a recruit class graduation and find those who were athletic and coming to "A" Troop, and based on their abilities would make their designated station assignments. We had many championship teams and always finished near the top in our leagues. We even played basketball against other troops and stations and always won, but we did meet our match with an Air Force team from the Niagara Falls area. They were too tall in basketball and too good with card games and at fighting, all in the spirit of competition of course. It was a memorable evening, only one of our teammates suffered a black eye.

MY BOSSES
MAJOR JOHN P. NOHLEN

When I first arrived at troop headquarters, Nick Giangualano was a captain and for all intents and purposes ran the troop. Major John P. Nohlen was the Troop Commander but mostly a figurehead. He joined the State Police on July 15, 1936 and retired December 30, 1970. A graduate from the old school, he was a gentleman with a good heart who always provided a source of amusement. He tried with all the goodness in his heart to be a conscientious and sincere leader but this was offset by his appearance and actions. He was 6' 5" tall, gangly and awkward and seemingly had no control over his feet or false teeth. His teeth chattered when he spoke and when he was really excited they would slip part way out of his mouth. As he traveled from office to office, he would bump into desks, file cabinets and people in his haste. Everything to him was a crisis especially when Division Headquarters called. He would walk around muttering "Albany Wants" or "Albany is Asking". The break room at the old barracks was in the basement with a low ceiling. Nohlen would come down and try to be one of the boys talking about fishing and sports although he knew little about either. Coffee came from a vending machine with Nohlen always fumbling to put change in the slot and usually dropping coins on the floor. He would gather them up and try again and again always having difficulty hitting the coin slot. Succeeding, he would take a test sip then grimace in pain at the hot coffee, drink the remainder in two or three gulps, stand up and hit his head on the low hanging pipes. His knees buckled on several occasions, but he never went down. He would sometimes run through the barracks yelling "robbery, robbery" after reading a teletype message, it not mattering if it occurred hundreds of miles away. He was more dangerous driving then anywhere else. I was riding with him one day, when he decided to pass another car. He passed the car, but stayed out in the opposing lane while all the time paying more attention to me than the road. Finally, I told him that we weren't on the thruway and he had to move over. On another occasion he was traveling to an incident with siren going full blast even when he stopped at red traffic lights waiting for them to change. The State Police was his life. After retiring he moved to the Albany area where he slid into Alzheimer disease.

JOHN MONAHAN

In January 1971, John Monahan came on board as Troop Commander and was the complete opposite of John Nohlen. I learned to respect Monahan early on. He had been a First Sergeant and understood the position and made it clear he would work through me, often to the exclusion of the captains and lieutenants. In effect, a word from me was a word from him. As troop commander, he was totally in command, giving the captains jobs to do rather than leaving them at loose ends trying to find something to do and usually ending up in the way. More often than not, we took our coffee breaks, lunches and trips to the field without any of the officers. Some of the civilian employees had taken advantage of Nohlen's old fashioned and gentle manners but Monahan treated them as the help, nothing more. He didn't repeat himself or ask their opinion. I liked that. He stayed about a year then one day came in and said, "Let's take a ride, First." He was silent for a while and then told me that I wasn't to repeat it to a soul but he was retiring. A few days later he came in, shook my hand and departed as if taking vacation and never came back, everyone but me was surprised. I liked that and did something similar when I retired. He was a hell of a man.

ARNOLD BARDOSSI

When Monahan left, Arnold Bardossi became the troop commander and the madness began again, a malady probably caused by troop level officers having too much time on their hands, a condition which had been suspended while Monahan was there, came back in earnest. Major Bardossi wasn't a bad guy; actually he was funny and good-natured. His main fault was that he, like Nohlen, believed that the nearest thing to God was division headquarters and all things, good and bad, came from that celestial and radiant region and the all-wise deities that dwelled there. A call from the lowest ranking boob in any office at division level was sufficient to cause either of them, Nohlen and Bardossi, to mobilize all hands in the troop, sworn and civilian, to respond without question. While Nohlen had the good fortune of having Captain Giangualano to keep things level, Bardossi had some captains that were even more conscious of division as an almost spiritual entity than he was. He also had some that had only self-interest, plus some who hadn't the faintest clue what they should do or what was expected of them and some were just treading water while they waited for the next transfer or promotion. While Bardossi was a funny and good-natured individual, lunchtime often turned into embarrassing feeding frenzies. It didn't matter what else was going on or how busy I was, at about 11:30 AM, he would come into my office, hat and coat on, and announce, "First, it's time to mangiare." Then, without fail, he would say, "Don't get between the lion and his kill." If one of the captains were around he would invite them but if they hesitated in the least, for whatever reason, whether talking to someone in person or on the telephone, they were quickly forgotten and he would say, "Let's go, First." After a few times of being left behind, they would make themselves available regardless of what they were doing. On one occasion, a waitress brought our four servings on a tray, balancing it in one hand as they do. Bardossi was either in a hurry or perhaps he believed he was helping the waitress, grabbed his plate off the tray which unbalanced the tray and sent the other three lunches cascading down on Tony Malovich. This was bad enough but when he saw what was happening he shouted "Hey" which drew the attention of all the other diners in the restaurant and they became witnesses of the tray and lunches falling onto Malovich, doubly embarrassing him. The girl apologized and she and Malovich cleaned up as best they could, then she left to refill our orders as Bardossi said, "You guys don't care if I start before you, do you?" On another lunch run we thought we should try the new Your Host restaurant. While waiting for our meal, an unknown young man sat down with us and was greeted cordially by Bardossi. I asked the guy what he thought he was doing and he said he always sat at this table. I told him he could move or I would move him and he left. Bardossi seemed surprised at my rancor but remarked on my table manners in the incident many times, always in good humor.

During the early period of minority recruiting a young black man came to troop headquarters and at first glance he looked to be a good candidate, clean cut and trim. It being lunch time, Bardossi invited him to lunch, I mentioned that nothing stopped him at lunch time, and off we went with Bardossi and the candidate discussing his future with the state police. I endured it through lunch, becoming more suspicious of the man as the minutes passed, but when we got back to the office I said, "I'll tell you what, slick, give me your name and date of birth, I will tell you what your real chances are." Bardossi looked shocked. I'm sure he envisioned a civil rights complaint, but the dummy gave me the information. A criminal records check came back in a few minutes showing a long rap sheet with convictions for a variety of felonies and lesser crimes.

One day much to the delight of most of the men at troop headquarters, Bardossi seriously offended the fine ladies working there. He was scheduled for his annual physical part of which required a first morning urine sample. After talking to some of the secretaries and clerks while holding an empty sample vial, he excused himself and soon returned holding a full vial. He then resumed the conversation with them, all the while shaking that fluorescent yellow and increasingly frothy vial in full few. It was truly hilarious; they couldn't take their eyes off that vile container while pretending to carry on a conversation. He was totally unaware of their discomfort and seemed to think nothing of my laughter. He died shortly after retiring. Most of the division members who attended his funeral were ordered to go but I went of my own free will. I thought of the others as hypocrites who befriended him while he was in office and became disdainful after he was gone. To me he was a funny, good natured individual who loved the state police and pretty much allowed me to have my way in most matters.

RICHARD BOLAND

Richard Boland who brought new challenges replaced Bardossi. He wanted more than respect for his rank, he wanted worship for his exalted position. For several months he came into my office about 9:00 o'clock each morning to see what was going on but I was usually on the telephone with more calls waiting so he would hang around for a minute to get a word in. He evidently tired of this and finally said, "I think it would be more appropriate if you came to my office to brief me." I said, "I don't know, I'm awful busy." He stopped coming over and I relented a little and tried to go to his office around 10:00 or 10:30. We had our best interaction at lunch but they were totally unlike the wild and unruly lunches with Bardossi, we mostly talked troop business. I think he may have thought he was running things, or wanted to run things, whichever, I still did things my way. He had one obsession other than himself, which was part of the hallway between the garage and the offices. It had a space of about fifteen feet of vinyl tile, likely because the designers knew that foot traffic from the garage and outdoors would soon soil and destroy any carpeting. Anyway, he endlessly complained about this being dirty, I guess because a red carpet had not been placed for his arrival each morning. I told Stanley Sochalec that I didn't care what he did the rest of the day so long as he polished that damned hallway for the great man's entrance. I don't think that anything achieved by anyone in the troop pleased him more than seeing that hall polished and shiny, although he may have been more pleased when I retired a few years later.

RETIREMENT

I kept my retirement plans to myself as I had witnessed too many lame duck supervisors awkwardly enduring the time from announcing their retirement and the day of departure. I sent my retirement papers directly to the retirement system from Arizona, as there was no requirement that they be processed through the division. Sending them through channels was at best only a courtesy and I had no desire to be courteous to that bunch at troop headquarters. My official retirement date was July 27, 1978. The last day at troop headquarters I told three people I wouldn't be back, Gary Law as he was a close friend, Joe Abate because I liked him and thought one officer should know and last, but not least, I told Stanley Sochalec, the quartermaster. I thanked him for his help and loyalty and told him that I had the highest regard for him and that he was one of the best men in the State Police, bar none. I drove away without looking back. While I am proud of my time with the State Police, I have to admit I was a lone wolf of sorts, more so after getting promoted and leaving the work-a-day role of a trooper. I've mentioned before that I envied those on the road who were actually doing police work and I meant that. It still seems to me that most of the supervisors I encountered were more interested in personal aggrandizement than in actual leadership. I've made it obvious who they were and I disliked them intensely. I really cared less what most of the civilian help thought. I tried to remember that subordinates were fellow employees, equals, and not the enemy. A few may think that I wasn't always successful in that regard but there are many who will vouch for my effort. Despite the years at troop headquarters, I was, and always will be, an old Allegany station trooper. There were times when the hours, days and years dragged, but in retrospect, my twenty-two years flew by too swiftly.

When I enlisted 22 years earlier, I had little idea of the purpose of the New York State Police. Early on, an older trooper, Ed Kwiecien, told me what the purpose was. Speaking of our superiors he said, **"We are here to vacillate in their radiance."** There were obvious law enforcement duties, much of which were serious and worthwhile in some instances, but I found the essence to be as he declared. **"We are here to vacillate in their radiance"** was the one and only factor that never changed. Ed Kwiecien was a wise and discerning man.

(Retired First Sergeant Vernon Clayson resides in Las Vegas, Nevada where he documented his recollections in book form called "Trooper Catch 22". His story provided the basis for this article and was edited by him.)

CHARLES E. COBB – LIEUTENANT - 1929 TO 1966

Charles E. Cobb was one of he most highly respected troopers in the Division of State Police. Cobb was born January 1, 1907 in Rochester, N.Y. He served with the U.S. Marine Corp assigned to the famous "Devil Dogs" from 1925 to 1929 earning honors on the "All Marine Football Team." Enlisting in the Troopers on July 1, 1929, he reported to Troop "A" on September 3, 1929 for duty. He resigned to attend North Carolina State University where he graduated and returned the state police 1932. He was promoted to Corporal on July 1, 1936, Acting First Sergeant on June 2, 1937 and Sergeant in 1939. He was last promoted to Lieutenant in 1953 and re-assigned to Malone, N.Y. until his return to Troop "A" at Henrietta in 1962. He retired on October 2, 1966. He and his wife Mary made their home at 106 Hart Street, Batavia, N.Y. until 1977 when they moved to Florida. He died in October 21, 1998 at age 92 and was buried at Mt. Albion Cemetery, Albion, N.Y. His wife, Mary, who has since passed away and two sons, Thomas L. Cobb of Bear Mountain, N.Y. and Charles E. Cobb Jr., Cobleskill, N.Y, survived him.

On February 11, 1946, the Batavia City Council in a special session requested the Superintendent of State Police to appoint an experienced police executive to act as the temporary head of the police department to help re-organize it. Captain J.B. Lynch appointed Sergeant Charles E. Cobb to the position. Two days later, Batavia City Clerk Roland D. Fisher swore in Cobb as Inspector in Charge. Assistant Police Chief Thomas A. Donahue presented him with his badge of office and introduced him to officers in the department. He replaced Chief Herbert L. Snyder who resigned a day earlier. He immediately toured the building inspecting the cells, rooms, files, offices and courtroom facilities.

Sgt. Cobb established a curriculum for police that covered a 10-week time frame and was mandatory for city police officers to attend. A total of 19 class days were scheduled with topics taught by the FBI, Secret Service, Judge Philip Weiss, Attorney J.Vincent Serve, Attorney Wallace Stakel and state police specialists. Agencies from Genesee, Orleans and Wyoming Counties were offered an opportunity to send representatives to the school.

Classes were given at the Batavia High School cafeteria. Batavia Mayor James J. Mahaney gave those attending a graduation banquet at the conclusion of classes.

Meeting Lieutenant Cobb was a memorable experience. He was striking in appearance and had the quality about him of a man not to be toyed with. Being a Marine Corp veteran, I promptly saluted him, as I had learned in the Marine Corp. Each time the Lieutenant would speak or make an inquiry, I would answer smartly and salute. After several salutes, he told me it was only necessary to salute him in a greeting. He was not a sneaky person giving advance notice if he would be conducting a station inspection. Upon arriving, he would sit in his car for several minutes before entering. He was a man who led from the front as was learned by all at the Rochester riots in 1964. I believe that his strongest quality was that of his support for those under his command. Above all he was family oriented and truly cared for the well being of his men and their families. Right or wrong, if you were truthful with him, he would do everything he could to help you. If you lied to him, you were not a person to be trusted. I honestly believe that his attitude and support for his men is what kept him from being further promoted.

LOOKING OUT FOR HIS MEN
Trooper Richard "Jake" Lathan broke his leg. As most of us know, we didn't make a lot of money in the 60s. The lieutenant went to Lathan's home to see if there was anything he could help with. Unknown to Jake, his wife Gladys said yes, she needed milk, baby food and a few other items. Lieutenant Cobb left and a short time later returned with the shopping list filled. He paid for the items out of pocket refusing re-imbursement.

On another occasion, the wife of a young trooper reported that her husband had confiscated an illegal gun from a truck driver without arresting him. They were having marital problems and she was concerned he might harm her or himself. Lieutenant Cobb went to the residence and instructed the wife to get the gun and put it into a brown paper bag. He then placed the bag in the trunk of his car returning to Batavia where he summoned Sergeant Robert Minekheim. Opening the trunk, he gave the sergeant the bag telling him that he didn't know what was in the bag and didn't want to know, but wanted the sergeant to get rid of it. Minekeim went to one of the many nearby quarries and tossed the bag into the water. Lieutenant Cobb then spoke with the trooper telling him to take a few days off (without being charged leave time) to get things right with his wife. That was the end of the incident. Report? What report!

SERGEANT JOHN J. CHAMBERS - 1930 to 1956

One of the best-known men of Troop "A" retired after 26 years of service and moved to Florida for health reasons. This early retirement was dictated by a rare lung illness. Sgt. John Chambers possessed the rare ability to make a fine record as a law enforcement officer and at the same time make a host of friends. As sergeant in charge of the BCI at Clarence for ten years, he was one of the busiest in the department.

There hadn't been a homicide in Clarence, N.Y. in over 60 years, but in 1950 two murder cases occurred in a period of three months. The killers were brought to justice largely through Chamber's investigative work.

The first case was when a body was found in a water filled ditch some distance from the main road. The body was identified as Mrs. Marion Frisby, who vanished a day earlier from Buffalo, N.Y. Twenty hours later, Chambers and Buffalo detectives arrested Harley Lamar at his Buffalo home. He had admitted that he jumped into the back seat of the Frisby car, as she stopped at an intersection. He kept a rifle to her head forcing her to drive to the lonely spot in Clarence where he attacked her and shot her through the temple. Lamar died in the electric chair.

It took months to catch up with Edward Wolf of Clarence, N.Y. who shot a business associate named Pettingill in the town, then transported his body to Allegany State Park where it was dumped along the roadside. An intense investigation led to Wolf who was arrested when he returned from his honeymoon. He was convicted of manslaughter and sentenced to twenty years at Attica Prison.

At his retirement party held at the Trap and Field Club of Williamsville, he was praised as a policeman who did an outstanding job of protecting the society he served and won the respect and friendship of those who came in contact with him in his official duties or personal life. He went home that night with a happy heart. Chambers died on January 29, 1957 at age 46.

HARRY M. DeHOLLANDER - 1925 to 1962

Harry E. DeHollander was born on July 12, 1900 at Rochester, N.Y. where he attended public school. Enlisting in the US Navy on December 31, 1917, he served aboard the Destroyer USS Balch, an escort vessel that provided security duty for convoys in both the Atlantic and Mediterranean war zones. Harry was honorably discharged on June 4, 1919.

After discharge at age of 18 years and 11 months, he returned to school and worked briefly in local industry. Having been impressed with the US Marines during his navy days, he enlisted in with the Marines in 1922 serving at Parris Island, S.C. where he was promoted to Platoon Sergeant upon graduation from basic training. He was later assigned as a drill instructor until his honorable discharge in 1925.

On August 16, 1925, Harry enlisted in the New York State Police and was assigned at Troop "A", Batavia, N.Y.

Promotions:

Corporal on April 1, 1927

Sergeant on July 1, 1930

Bureau of Criminal Investigation (BCI) on July 31, 1936. Assigned as one of the first troopers in the newly formed investigative unit.

(Promotions to the rank of corporal, sergeant and lieutenant prior to 1936 were earned through deed, valor and investigative ability with most by appointment of the troop commanders. Since 1936, a written examination serves as the primary basis for promotion.)

Lieutenant on February 16, 1947 and assigned to Troop "G". Troy, N.Y.

Inspector on May 16, 1951 and re-assigned to Troop "A" where he supervised all criminal investigations in Western N.Y.

Division Inspector on August 29, 1957 assigned to the Superintendents staff supervising

BCI personnel in "A", "B" & "D" Troops.

Captain February 25, 1960 assigned to Troop "B". Malone, N.Y., as the commanding officer.

Harry as an investigator and a supervisor was instrumental in solving several heinous and high profile crimes in the Steuben County area for nearly 20 years. He earned the respect of the law enforcement community, as well as the citizenry for conducting skilled, persistent and thorough investigations leaving no doubt as to the guilt of a perpetrator that he took into custody.

BATAVIA RADIO STATION WBTA
The station was known for its radio editorials called the "Town Crier". On September 1, 1957 the station broadcast the following commentary:

An old friend took another step up the ladder of success this week, when Harry DeHollander was advanced from Inspector of the Troop A BCI to Staff Inspector in Albany. The area of his new command will include Western New York and we were happy to learn that the inspector will be at least an occasional visitor to his old stamping ground.

A trooper since 1925, Harry DeHollander came up through the ranks earning the rank of lieutenant in 1947 and a transfer to Troop G. He returned to Troop A in 1951 taking command of the BCI unit. To his men, he has been a firm and friendly boss who demanded round the clock performance from his men when a capital crime was under investigation. Working side by side with his staff he held their loyalty and respect and was quick to recognize and give proper credit for a job well done. Congratulations Mr. Dee on a richly deserved promotion and don't forget to drop in and say hello when you're back in the old neighborhood in the new role of staff inspector.

INVESTIGATIONS
On April 10, 1926, he was assigned at the Darien Center outpost. He received instructions to investigate an unattended death at a nearby abandoned farmhouse. Local youths Henry Herr, aged 14 and Raymond Runsing, aged twelve discovered a decomposed male body while playing. DeHollander ruled out any criminal elements determining it to be a natural death. The body had no identification, other than a clothing label from the Liberty Clothing Company, Olean, N.Y. The identity was never determined.

On October 20, 1927, DeHollander and Trooper Walter Robinson confiscated 24 bottles of whiskey and 175 quarts of Canadian ale near Williamsville, N.Y. The occupants fled on foot before the troopers could exit their automobile. The car was reported stolen from Harry Ginsberg, 12 Clifton Avenue, Batavia, N.Y. earlier in the day.

Sheridan, N.Y. farmer Samuel J. Dolce, age 29 was arrested by Investigators Harry DeHollander and William Szymanski on Oct 6, 1937 charged with Arson 2nd degree. Dolce admitted that he set fire to his house and barn in the hopes of collecting on a $2000.00 insurance policy. He had shot his team of horses prior to setting the fire. He lived alone and was employed at the Ludlum Steel Company, Dunkirk, N.Y.

Sergeant DeHollander had investigated a murder in October 1937 at Yates County where Morris B. Close, a Rochester scoutmaster, returning from a visit to Albany was found slain by the roadside and his car missing. Investigative leads and information led DeHollander to Richmond, Virginia where on August 9, 1938, he along with local police took 22 year old Wilfred B. Squires, AKA John Kirkland Howard of Branchport, N.Y. into custody. Confronted with fingerprint evidence, Squires admitted to his true identity and the murder of Close. It was also determined that Squires had killed a Charles Padgett of Aliquippa, Pa. near Kingston City, Missouri whose bullet riddled body was found in a ditch. The Close car was found abandoned near Memphis, Tennessee

During the summer of 1944, Harry and Trooper Frank Easton arrested a man at Friendship, N.Y. for allegedly molesting small boys charging him with Assault 3rd degree. The man had not eaten so they took him to a Friendship diner for lunch. While there, the man fled by climbing out of a bathroom window and hid in a heavily wooded area. When the incident was reported to Albany Headquarters, an extensive manhunt was organized with 20 troopers assigned as well as the Troop "K" bloodhounds being sent. This detail lasted for several days without success. In August 1944, both men were transferred to the uniform force working traffic duty at Athol Springs. This lasted until December 1944, when Harry was re-instated to the BCI and assigned to Westfield, N.Y. Captain J.B. Lynch, Troop "A" commander said the shift was brought about by the shortage of uniform men. He denied that the transfers were punitive, rather only an administrative move to replace older men. The escapee was subsequently arrested in Pennsylvania several weeks later.

In a letter to the editor dated July 27, 1944, W. Bertram Page, former Steuben County Sheriff felt it was the Governor's way of cleaning up the state police and Harry would have to go, because he was appointed under a Democratic Governor.

In January 1955, Superintendent Albin S. Johnson resigned his position creating an opportunity for others to advance. On January 23, 1955, Governor Averill Harriman appointed Francis S. McGarvey, as his replacement. There was a big move to have Inspector Harry DeHollander appointed however it appears that all correspondence supporting his appointment were not sent in a timely manner.

The following are excerpts from correspondence to Major General Harry H. Vaughn from Major Richard J. Smith; US Army dated 18 January 1955.

Inspector DeHollander is one of a handful of Democrats to survive the Dewey purge of the State Police. He was so good, Dewey promoted him. Along with his outstanding ability as an investigator, he possessed administrative skill, sound judgment, tact and discretion. He has the respect of his men and confidence of his superiors. I appreciate your kindness in agreeing to take up the subject personally with Governor Harriman.

In 1961, Harry who had never been sick was taken to the hospital at Malone, N.Y. for a minor medical problem. While there, a nurse errantly administered an anti-biotic. As it turned out, he was allergic to the drug and had a violent reaction. This led to serious heart and coronary problems that required extensive surgery. Harry never recovered enough to return to duty resulting in his unplanned retirement on August 31, 1962.

JOSEPH HEILIG - 1947 to 1953

Joseph Heilig was born at Scranton, Pennsylvania. His family moved to Buffalo, N.Y., where Joe attended and graduated from South Park High School in 1944. He immediately enlisted in the US Navy serving from 1944 to 1946, as a sonar operator working in an anti submarine unit protecting US coastal waters.

On September 16, 1947, Joe was sworn in as a New York State Trooper serving until March 1, 1953. He and fellow recruit Fred Hofmann attended the state police school at Troy, N.Y. for six weeks during November – December 1947.

The following are recollections of Joe's days on the job:

During his four years as a trooper, he was assigned to fifteen different stations with his longest tenure at Franklinville where he worked for almost three years. His first duty station was at Henrietta where he worked with Andy Fisher, Gerald "Bucky" Schusler, Harry Ashe, Donald Girven and Elner Anderson. At Franklinville, his Lieutenant was Richard Barber and Sergeant Harry Ashe. The Troop Commander at the time was Captain Joseph Lynch.

The troop cars were 1946 Ford Sedans that came in various colors with the letters **"STATE POLICE"** stenciled in white above the windshield and side panels of the front doors. Two-way radios had just been introduced and the only way you could transmit on them was to turn the car so it faced a transmitting tower.

The work-week consisted of seven days and five nights of duty. In other words, you worked twenty-four hours a day and were always on call. Troopers received $4.00 a day meal allowance and for miscellaneous expenses.

Sergeant Harry Ashe lost two fingers while helping Trooper Andy Fisher cut wood on Andy's farm. Andy owned several acres in Varysburg, N.Y. where his son, Nick, a retired Border Patrol Officer now resides. While cutting logs on a buzz saw, Harry's hand got two near the blade resulting in the loss of two fingers. He was treated by a local doctor and returned to work the next day. He was forever after identified as "Harry the Hook".

Captain Lynch had no love for Trooper Charlie Schwartz and assigned him to the duty station furthest away from Troop Headquarters and Charlies's home. He was heard to say on more than one occasion that if he could like to send him to work in Pennsylvania, he would.

During a one-day tour of duty, Joe and Trooper Jack Steinmetz made 13 arrests at a migrant labor camp in Genesee County with all committed to jail by the local Justice of the Peace. The Sheriff complained to Captain Lynch that the county could not afford to keep a high number of inmates and wanted him to direct the troopers not to make any more arrests.

Joe recalled being assigned to a roadblock at the intersection of Routes 16 and 39 at Yorkshire Corners and ordered to be on the alert for several wanted men that had just robbed a bank in Erie County. Joe being the diligent officer that he was stayed at his post throughout the day and night until another passing trooper asked what he was doing and told him the roadblock had been canceled about an hour after it was originated. Joe said that there was a benefit to the assignment in that he got to meet all the local residents.

While assigned at Westfield, N.Y., Joe was on patrol near what he thought was Finley Lake. After several hours of patrol, he came across a farmer and inquired as to where he was exactly. Joe was 15 miles into Pennsylvania where he had patrolled the entire day making many new friends.

In September 1948, he was one of the first troopers to respond to the Lena Robinson murder at Scio. The case is fully described under the Murder Caption.

Heilig got the impression that Governor Thomas Dewey wanted a totally political law enforcement system within the state so he could have the ability to control and manipulate them at his pleasure. Keep in mind that the Sheriff of the County is the highest-ranking law enforcement officer and vacancies were political appointments made by the Governor. Due to legislative control, the governor didn't have the ability to manipulate the state police.

Joe regrets resigning from the troopers. He recalled that he had submitted a request for a transfer from Franklinville and it was denied. He thought that if he threatened to quit, he would get the transfer he wanted. Captain Joseph Lynch replied by advising him his resignation letter would be accepted. It was. His salary in 1947 was $1,300.00 and when he resigned in 1953, it was $4,600.00.

He went to work as a truck driver for Jones Trucking Company of Spring City, Pennsylvania that lasted two years. He then was with Buffalo Office of the U.S. Marshall's Service until funding ran out. He served as a Parole Officer for two years before settling into a job until his retirement with the Buffalo Board of Education.

He married Nancy Carey in August 1969 and had two daughters, Linda & Sheila. Joe is one of the most active members in the Niagara Frontier Chapter of the AFNYST.

ALBERT S. KUREK - 1962 to 1985

I was born in March 1939 and grew up in Western New York. I attended Depew Grammar and High School until 1954 before transferring to Buffalo's Kensington High School, when my family moved to the Bailey–Walden section of Buffalo, N.Y. Classmates at Depew that went on to become troopers were Jim Rozanski, Tom McHugh, Ed Rybak, Joe Kupka, Dan Mediak, Jim Kostecki and Patrick Malinowski. Kensington classmates that became troopers were Gerry Raedle, James J. Ryan, Paul Krienheider, Kevin Walsh, Gerry Kalisz, John Kotlarski and Dick Haberer.

I enlisted in the US Marine Corp in January 1957 graduating from boot camp at Parris Island, S.C. I was as a communications specialist with the Third Marine Division at Okinawa. I returned stateside in late 1958 and was assigned to the 2nd Tank Battalion, FMF, Camp Lejeune, N.C. Discharged in January 1960, I immediately found work at the Gould Coupler Company in Depew, N.Y., as a fork truck operator through my father who was employed there. This lasted for several months until a layoff occurred. I then worked at Joy Manufacturing, a new company in Cheektowaga, N.Y. I was eleventh in seniority and was trained as a test lab technician.

During the fall of 1960 and 1961, I played semi-pro football with the then Buffalo Bills as an offensive tackle. We had a great team both years and I looked forward to playing each weekend. Most of the players had been local college or high school standouts. I played service ball in Okinawa while in the Marine Corps. A couple of members tried out for the professional Buffalo Bills and were among the last to be cut. We lost one game in two-years. Masillon, Ohio beat us 21 to19. Gerry Raedle, Gary Stoldt and another high school friend, Danny Buckley were also on the team. We played for the love of the game paying our own way for travel and lodging when playing out of town. Injury would have meant the end of my trooper career, so after joining the state police, my playing days ended.

In February 1962, I was laid off. While at Jaro's Bar, our old gang hangout, (now Salvatore's Italian Garden) in Lancaster, N.Y., I met my high school friend Jim Rozanski. He was in training as a trooper at the SP Academy and provided me with an application. To be honest, I had never heard of the State Troopers until then. Being out of work, I sent the application in and during May 1962, received notification that I had been accepted as a trooper recruit. The first trooper I ever laid eyes on in uniform was Trooper Walter Linden. He was directing traffic at the intersection of North and State Streets, Batavia, N.Y., where physical examinations were being held. My friend Gary Stoldt and I had gone together, however a minor glitch during the physical disqualified Gary. He went on to spend over 40 years as a Police Officer with the Lancaster PD and will retire shortly, as the Department's Chief of Police.

RECRUIT ACADEMY
There was a big push in 1962 to go to a 40 - hour workweek with several hundred troopers hired to accomplish the transition. Recruit training sessions commenced during January, April and June. My acceptance letter directed me to report to Oneonta State Teachers College on June 18, 1962, the location of a temporary academy. I remember traveling there with Larry Francis from Alden, NY. I believe the session was ten weeks in duration. Arriving, we checked in and were given room assignments according to our name in alphabetical order. I don't recall my first roommate, as he quit after a few days and was replaced by Bob Kukla from Long Island. Others in my group were Joe Kwiatek, Bob Hummel, Doug Hedges, Jim Hofmann, Jim Hurley, Jack Hawley, Gary Knight, Elmer Haas, Lenny Jackson, and Tom Kleinhans. Kleinhans was injured in an accident while home and was dropped from our session, but returned at a later date. Each session had two counselors assigned. Our counselors were Warren C. Sargent (Batavia) & John J. McGrath (Malone) who were most knowledgeable and helpful. There were two recruits to a room located at the on-campus dormitories. Meals were provided at the campus cafeteria. We were required to wear suits and ties for class.

Each day started with early morning physical training (exercise & running) followed by a hot shower and breakfast. Then it was off to class from 8:00 AM to 5:00 PM. Classes were an hour long with lunch at mid-day. After dinner, we were required to type out our notes from the class sessions we had during the day. You could hear the distinctive plink; plink of the typewriter keys striking a letter late into the night. The typing was necessary, as all reports at the time had to be type written without error, usually in triplicate using carbon paper. At the end of the week, we were given exams on the materials taught during the week. With weekends off, I was homeward bound every second week. I had my own car and usually traveled back and forth with Joe Kwiatek, Nick Gumhalter and occasionally, Charlie Gibbs. As time passed, we eventually went to a local pistol range where we were required to qualify with the colt pistol and .12-gauge shotgun. Sergeant George Tordy was in charge with Trooper Jim McDermott being one of the firearms instructors. Everyone fired until they qualified with some recruits using the cars headlights late into the night. Somewhere about the eighth week, we were measured and given uniforms. This was a sense of relief, because it meant we had all passed the requirements and had only our final exams to take. I recall many of the recruits wearing the Stetson, then looking into a mirror practicing "mean looks". Finally, it was time to graduate. The graduation ceremony took place at Albany, N.Y. and was highlighted by the presence of Superintendent Cornelius who handed out the Graduation Certificates and Governor Nelson Rockefeller who shook hands with each graduate.

SENIOR TROOPER
After basic training, troopers were assigned to a Senior Trooper for 30 days on the job training or longer if needed. A trooper was in a probationary status for the first year and could be dismissed from the job at any time, if he didn't measure up. My first station was SP Horseheads. The station was an

old two-story house with bedrooms on the second floor. There were two work shifts, 8 AM to 8 PM or 8PM to 8 AM. Sgt. John Reardon was in charge and was from the old school. He had someone come in daily to relieve him on the desk so he could go pay his bills. (This usually meant he was going for a couple of beers) Others I recall were Investigator Winky, Mike Capozzi, Ted Klumpe, Dan P. Kelly, Joe Houston, Bob Baker, Karl Chandler, Bill Myers and Tom Chura. My Senior Trooper was Kenneth A. Epler. He was a tough old bird, by the book and a perfectionist. He was very competitive and absolutely hated being beaten to any kind of accident or investigation by a deputy sheriff. I can recall one instance where he passed a deputy in the center grassy mall of Route 17 to get to an accident first. As it turned out, it was a double fatal car-train accident, my first and it really made my stomach flip. We also were required to attend the autopsy the next morning, also my first. I don't know how I hung in there without getting sick, but I did. Bill Myers was very helpful, as he had just finished his recruit training with Epler as his senior trooper. He gave me a lot of good advise, told me what to expect from my mentor and how to react. Bobby Earl, a black trooper from Buffalo was also a recruit at Horseheads with Tom Chura his senior trooper. Chura never treated Earl, as a fellow trooper and would leave him at the station whenever possible especially during meals. Earl had considered quitting, but I think the many conversations we had convinced him it was only temporary and things would get better after Chura. At the end of my probationary period I was allowed to patrol alone. It was race time at the nearby Watkins Glen with international drivers competing in the car race. Scotland's Jackie Stewart, who I had the pleasure of meeting the next day, won the competition. While driving to the Chemung County Airport, I stopped and summoned Stewart for driving 80 MPH in a 55 MPH zone in the Town of Big Flats. I took him before Judge Gerry Hayward who fined him $100.00. In about November 1962, I was transferred to SP Albion.

SP ALBION
Arriving at SP Albion, I was greeted by Trooper Donald E. Klein, a veteran trooper with a year on the job. Don was the first trooper I worked with at Albion and he introduced me to the many farm labor camps in the area, as well as best places to eat and where the judges lived. Troopers not living locally slept at the barracks and traveled to their homes on their pass days. We worked 60 hours work weeks back then. In January 1963, I got married and resided in an apartment in Lancaster, N.Y. some 40 miles away.

SP ALLEGANY
In about mid February 1963, I was re-assigned to SP Allegany (Olean). Sergeant Eugene Redden was in charge and was genuinely happy to see us new recruits that included Bill Loft, Milford Drake, Bob Hummel and myself. Troopers I worked while there included Vernon Clayson, his brother Michael Clayson, Stewart Hill, Jim Rowley, Gerry Crocker, Dave O'Brien, Merle Van Skiver, Fred Porcello, Gregory Snyder, Larry Austin, Jimmy Johnson, Bill Reynolds, Henry Panus, Gerry Kitchen and Bob McGinty. It was a great station for a new trooper.

Unlike Albion, there weren't any local farm labor camps. There wasn't much investigative work, but when you did get a complaint, you could work it to the end.

A few things recalled were the early morning poker games in the back room at the station. Fred Porcello would initiate the game that started at about 5 or 6 AM and went on until mid morning. Gene Redden being a very tolerant man allowed the games to be played, as long as all necessary work was completed. The work was usually completed by Vernon Clayson who liked to sit the on desk and in reality ran the station for Redden.

On another occasion, Bill Loft fancied himself the top summons writer at the station with 28 traffic arrests for the month. On the last day of the month, Vernon Clayson assigned Loft to desk duty, then went on patrol and wrote 30 traffic tickets for the day.

Our 12-hour duty tours changed weekly, a week of days and a week of nights. While on the night shift, I always worked with Mike Clayson. The shift usually started off with a meeting with his girlfriend (his present wife) for two or three hours. I would sit in the troop car monitoring the radio while he did whatever he was doing. If we happened to get a call on the radio, Mike would cuss and carryon, then jump all over the desk man for sending us on the complaint. After the rendezvous, we would do a little traffic enforcement before heading over to the Great Valley garbage dump where we did firearms training by shooting rats using a spotlight. There was always time for a couple of hours of shuteye before heading over to Route 219 at Bradford Junction. This is the only location that I ever saw the speedometer needle on our 1962 Plymouth Fury go to the maximum reading at 120 MPH and beyond. We estimated our speed at 140 MPH. Route 219 from Bradford Junction to the Pennsylvania state line was straight as an arrow and about eight miles in length. Mike would drive back and forth two or three times a morning just to put mileage on the car. Once in a while, he would bring a guitar on patrol and play it while I drove. He wasn't very good, but he thought he was. One thing for sure, there was never a dull moment when I worked with him.

RETURN TO SP ALBION

In May or June of 1963, I was re-assigned to Albion. I worked with, Bob Gadsby, Ken Murek, Bob Burns, Jim Nashwenter, Jack Hawley, Kenny Kaye, Gordon Mosher, Ted Georgitso and Don Klein. Lieutenant Charlie Cobb was the Zone Commander at Henrietta with BCI Investigators Bob Barrus, Nick Fitzak or Don Smith at SP Clarkson handling Albion cases. Seven of the ten of us at Albion all had hire dates of June 18, 1962. We were all in the same boat so to speak. All of us were newly married with babies at home. Our social life was getting together at one another's home bringing your own snacks and beverage. Once in a while, there was a dollar or two to spare with the guys going to the Club 469 owned by Sam and Butch Burgio. We would play euchre for a draught beer that cost 15 cents.

There was plenty of activity compared to Allegany. During the summer months, hundreds of migrants arrived to work in the farm fields. They couldn't wait until the weekend to start drinking heavily that resulted in some type of altercation where someone was injured. We were called from one labor camp to another on every shift. Two incidents regarding migrants stand out in my mind.

The first was on a Friday evening at the Colony Labor Camp, Sawyer Road, Kent, N.Y. A migrant man had been hospitalized after being attacked with an axe. Another migrant man described by witnesses as "Crazy" was identified as the perpetrator. He was located sitting on a bed in his room with the axe in hand. I took out my .38 caliber revolver and would have shot him, if he made any attempt to attack me. Investigator Donald L. Smith and several troopers from Clarkson arrived as backup. Smith and I holstered our weapons and entered the room and sat on a bed across from the assailant. (Trooper David Corbine had his weapon pointed at the man from outside the room) While talking with him about the assault, he would stutter and close his eyes for a moment. We found an opportune moment during a stutter and jumped him. The axe was taken out of his control and he was ushered out of the room by Trooper Corbine. As they exited, the man reached into his belt and came out with a loaded pistol, but was disarmed and handcuffed by the detail present. (Smith and I were unaware of the gun) Several weeks later, we learned that the man was diagnosed as in a state of complete lunacy and idiocy and was confined to a facility for the criminally insane.

The second incident also on a Friday night was one of the most heinous attacks I had ever observed. Two male migrant men who were roommates fought, when one man called the other man "Gay" and persisted all evening long in making reference to his sexual preference. The gay man finally exploded, took a gallon jug, smashed it and beat the man on the head with the broken neck of the bottle. Over two hundred sutures were required to close the resulting wounds. The perpetrator fled on foot with an all night search for him resulting. Early Saturday morning, Trooper Daniel Geiger traveling along Route 104 observed him hiding in apple orchard and took him into custody. He pled not guilty at arraignment. The disposition was one that I will never forget. Due to the high cost of trial, Orleans County District Attorney Franklin Cropsey decided the most cost effective and speedy disposition was to remove the man from the area. He purchased a one- way bus ticket to the State of Alabama and sent him on his way with a promise never to return to Orleans County.

THE EL RANCHO

A short distance from the station was the El Rancho Restaurant owned and operated by Sam and Kaye Russo and the five Russo kids. If it weren't for the Russo's, many troopers stationed at Albion would have had to resign, because the pay wasn't that great and eating meals out got to be costly. Sam realized the plight of the young troopers and would charge an average of fifty cents a meal whether it was breakfast or dinner. The El Rancho was also a great meeting place.

I first met the very precise and detailed Conservation Officer Charles Robishaw at the El Rancho. A group of us were sitting around a table, when Charlie saw a mouse running along the wall. Removing his .45 caliber pistol from its holster, he verbally calculated the time it would take the mouse to travel to a two-inch space between a refrigerator and freezer against the wall then fired the weapon killing the mouse just as it appeared in the opening. Charlie wasn't wrong too often. He was a good man to have as a friend and was always there when needed. He is still a great friend.

Trooper Ted Georgitso was at the El Rancho seated in a booth against the back wall opposite the front door. The only other person present was the waitress Fran (last name not noted to save embarrassment) who was behind the counter that ran the length of the wall. A car pulled into the parking lot with three dark skinned males exiting. Georgitso immediately announced to Fran that these were the "guys holding up restaurants" and that she was to act normally. He said he was going to shoot them when they walked in the door. Saying this, he took out his duty revolver, placed it on the table covering it with his Stetson. As the men entered, Fran screamed, got on her hands and knees and rapidly crawled on the floor behind the counter to the rear of the restaurant for safety leaving a trail of **"pee"** from wetting herself. This was an example of trooper humor. Fran never forgave Georgitso for embarrassing her in this manner.

The Russo's were stonemasons working with granite for street curbing. Sam worked with the family as needed. While working in his restaurant one evening, a Hispanic migrant worker came in ordering a submarine sandwich. Sam thought he would discourage migrant patronage by making a terrible sandwich. He took everything that was molding or borderline spoiled from the refrigerator and prepared the sandwich. It was made up of green ham, moldy cheese, hairy tuna, brown lettuce and rotten tomatoes with a generous portion of hot sauce between layers. The sandwich was enough to put a healthy man down. Two days later the man returned with several of his friends. Sam thought it was his end, but instead, the man announced that it was the best sandwich he had ever eaten and had come to order several of the same.

Some years later the El Rancho burned to the ground, never to be rebuilt.

In those days, ambulance service was provided by privately owned contractors with little, if any medical training. Ray Severn owned and operated the local service. The first time I met him was on a dark Friday evening at the intersection of Routes 98 and 31A where a fatal accident had taken place. One of the drivers had been partially ejected through the windshield and was decapitated. We searched for the man's head for quite awhile until we heard Severn shout out that he had found it. Looking up, I saw Severn walking along the road carrying the head by the hair. It was quite a grotesque scene.

I would be remiss if I didn't mention Nancy Schurr and Janice Ferris. Both enjoyed socializing with the many troopers that passed through Albion over the years. Combined, they knew more troopers than I did. I recall Bart Stack being assigned at Albion for a short time. He was newly married and couldn't afford to socialize. Wanting him not to be lonely, Janice bought him a teddy bear to sleep with. Years later, inquiries were still made about "Barts Bear". Janice also worked for the gas company and because of her, $25.00 deposits for start up service were waived. That was a lot of money in the early sixties. Here we are some forty plus years later and the troopers still stay in touch with both gals.

I loved working and living in the Albion area and made many lasting friendships. The only problem I had was the medical facilities. Arnold Gregory Hospital could be compared to a first aid station. There seemed to never be a doctor available when needed. I rented an apartment in Albion in late 1963 and resided there with my wife and infant son, Alan. On Thanksgiving Day 1965, I investigated an accident involving two cars that had sideswiped on the Lee Road, Clarendon. One of the cars had a family traveling to relatives for the holiday. Two young boys were injured suffering compound fractures of the arms and legs. Both were taken to Arnold Gregory Hospital for treatment. Some two hours later after cleaning up at the accident scene, I traveled to the hospital to determine injuries for my accident report. Arriving, I saw the two boys lying on stretchers on the hallway floor outside of the emergency room. There was no doctor on duty at the hospital and one could not be located for the emergency. The boys were in severe pain with bones protruding through their skin and were crying endlessly. It was at this point that I made up my mind to request a transfer out of Albion. I wanted better for my family, if they needed medical help. As luck would have it, Dan Geiger was at Clarkson and wanted to come to Albion, Lou Steverson was at Batavia and wanted to go to Clarkson and I wanted to go to Batavia. Lieutenant Cobb told each of to submit the memo request and two days later, the transfer took place.

SP BATAVIA

My first day of work at Batavia was on Friday "C" shift. I worked with Fred Walsh and at the end of the shift we went to "Splashes Tavern" for a few cocktails. We drank a quart of OFC blended whiskey with beer chasers. Fred then insisted we go for breakfast at Texaco Town Diner. (Routes 63 & 20) That was a mistake, as I decorated the inside of Fred's car and wound up sleeping on the couch at his home. We didn't do that to often. I commuted back and forth to Albion until early 1966. We rented an apartment from Ed and Mary Sakaguchi at 525 East Main Street, Batavia, N.Y. and lived there until I built a house in East Pembroke, N.Y. two years later.

SP Batavia Patrol was a transient station. It seems that every trooper assigned to Troop "A" passed through Batavia. The permanent troopers were Tony DiRienz, Harry Crosier, Tom Kennedy, Bob Szymanski, Walter Purtell, Fred Walsh, Raymond Chudoba, Jim Lobur, Dave Schwartz, Len Dayka, Don Cochrane, Bob Hummel, Jim Stephens, Bill Loft and Gerry Kalisz. Genesee County was made up of ten townships with a patrol assigned to each town. Emphasis was on traffic safety, enforcement and public relations. Troopers were encouraged to reside in their patrol areas and become familiar with all aspects of the area. This was quite a switch from the old rules guiding trooper assignments where troopers were constantly being transferred so they wouldn't become too familiar with the local citizens. Under Superintendent Cornelius, troopers were encouraged to take part in community activities where they lived and worked.

Captain John P. Nohlen was the Troop Commander and was a friendly, honest and deeply religious man. As Troop Commander, he was able to convince every available trooper to attend the annual police officers mass and communion breakfast while on duty. Troopers were also allowed to attend Sunday church services while on duty. Nohlen also socialized with the troopers and was a member of the troopers bowling team along with Karl Limner, Howard Smith, Anthony DiRienz, Bob Minekheim, Stanley Sochalec and Gerry Kalisz.

Retired Sergeant Ward Barrows tells of the time Captain Nohlen and he were responding to an accident situation on the west end of Genesee County. Nohlen was driving his big black unmarked Chrysler Sedan with red lights in the grill with Barrows his passenger. As they proceeded through the City of Batavia with lights flashing and siren going full blast, Nohlen would stop at every red traffic signal and wait until it turned green while all the time blasting the siren. Barrows slithered down in the seat as far as he could in an attempt to avoid being seen by motorists that had pulled to the side of the street. Nohlen kept saying **"You Can Never Be Too Careful Sergeant"**. Embarrassing, yes.

Batavia just as any other station in the Division had a variety of criminal, civil and humorous incidents. Here are some of many short recollections of the men I worked with. If they had a nickname, it was probably one dubbed on them by me.

Louis Lang was **"Jitterbug"**. He had a penchant for driving fast and traveling everywhere except where he was supposed to be. When asked for a location check, he would give his location as Alabama; a few minutes later he would be on the opposite end of the county in Bergen. He was everywhere in a short amount of travel time. Sunday mornings were relatively quite so Louis selected this day to take his grandmother for a ride in the troop car. He did this faithfully for several years.

Jim Hofmann was **"Owl"** because of the heavy horned rim glasses he wore on his round shaped face and his natural inquisitive nature.

George A. Berger was **"Sparky"** because of his fascination with the radio handset that he talked on constantly.

Bill Gethoefer was **"Howdy"** because he was tall, slender, red headed and had freckles similar to kids character Howdy Doody.

Henry Haas was **"Horrible Henry"**. He got this nickname during the search of a residence at Corfu, N.Y. He had obtained a search warrant with the property sought being stolen tires. Entering the residence, the lone female occupant threatened to let her German Shepherd dog loose with Haas promising to shoot the dog if she did. He then proceeded to pull drawers from cabinets dumping their contents on the floor. The occupant asked what he was searching for and he said tires. She then went berserk, yelling you can't fit a tire in those drawers and started screaming you're horrible, just horrible. (He really was horrible) No tires were found.

Robert J. Szymanski **"Sleepy Eyes"** commuted daily from Tonawanda, N.Y. along Route 5, a distance of 25 miles one way. During his travel, he averaged recovering a stolen car either abandoned or occupied on a bi-weekly basis.

Harry S. Crosier was **"Digger"**. He worked part time for an undertaker in Bergen, N.Y. Harry transferred to the Troop "E" during its first year in 1967 and was assigned to the Identification Bureau.

Batavia had two troopers that absolutely hated to write traffic tickets, Jake Lathan and Mickey Schrader. On occasion, some of the heavy hitters would take one or two of their summonses and write a non-moving violation for them. Trooper Loft took one of Jake's tickets and arrested a driver for

"Speed not Reasonable or Prudent" that was involved in an accident. A few days later, Jake received a notice for trial on the arrest. Needless to say, Jake never showed up for trial, the case was dismissed and Loft was never given someone else's ticket to write.

On another occasion, an investigation was being conducted into the dumping of hazardous materials at the Byron muck property owned by Darryl Freeman, a local demolition contractor. A large amount of 55-gallon drums were found stored containing toxic materials. Haas decided to walk on top of the barrels, rather than walk around them and fell into one, when the rotted cover came loose. He was stripped of his clothing at the scene and taken to a hospital for treatment and toxic decontamination.

Bill Loft resided at Attica, N.Y. several miles south of Batavia and patrolled the southern part of the county. Without exaggeration, Loft would have a high speed chase at least once a week on Route 98 with the speeder never being caught.

Trooper cars were assigned to two or three troopers and were kept at the stations. Tony DiRienz, when on patrol would not return to the station until he had written at least two traffic tickets for the day. The trooper on the next shift would on occasion wait for up to two or three hours before Tony came in making the patrol car available.

THE "BIG E" RESTAURANT

The Big "E" Restaurant was located a short distance from the barracks on East Main Street. The hard working family of Jack and Frances Bennett along with son Robert and daughter Linda owned and operated the restaurant. Jack baked and cooked homemade donuts, rolls and bread in a converted mobile home trailer at the rear of the restaurant while Frances cooked and managed the eating area. It was a gathering place for all the police agencies in the county. The fact that the Bennett's only charged police half price had a lot to do with the police patronage. They both had a knack of knowing when you were a little short in the pocketbook and would say, " **catch you next time**". I got to be good friends with both of them, as well as son Robert.

Jack always left a key to the back door hidden under an ashtray in the trailer for police. All the local police gathered there for coffee, a donut and a sandwich where we discussed what was happening and who did what in the county. Patrolman Frank Lachnicht would always have a liverwurst and onion sandwich to eat. We would leave payment for what we ate on the cash register as we departed. On one occasion and only once, the trust Jack put in the police was shattered when a city officer that I will only identify as George D. had a family gathering and took a twenty-pound cooked roast of beef that was to be used in the restaurant. When Jack brought it our attention, we did an investigation and forced George to return the beef and politely told him he was no longer welcome at the Big E.

We troopers always had a soft spot for children and kept track of migrant and other families in the area that were needy. On holidays and especially Christmas, we would take up a collection of clothing and toys from our co-workers and friends to distribute to these families. Jack and Frances would without hesitation provide us with several hams, turkeys, bread, rolls and sweets to help make these hard times a joyful remembrance. The reward was in seeing the kids with bright eyes and big smiles on what would have been just another day.

SPORTS

During the 1960sand 1970s, all but a few of the troopers were involved in some type of sporting event. There was a trooper's basketball team comprised of Vern Clayson, Gerry Kalisz, Bud Bradley, Ray Motyka, Bob Hummel, Tom Tucker and Ward Barrows. They played in a tough Batavia City Men's League and were City champions on several occasions.

The Troopers bowling team was made up of Captain John Nohlen, Karl Limner, Howard Smith, Tony Dirienz, Gerry Kalisz, Stan Sochalec, Fred Walsh and Jim Duval. They were also league champs on occasion.

When Vernon Clayson was appointed First Sergeant, new troopers were graded for their athletic abilities before being transferred to their permanent stations. Those that did show athletic ability were assigned at Batavia, Clarence, Allegany or Orchard Park.

Batavia had several slo-pitch softball leagues and troopers always were competitive participants. A team was entered in the Service League during the mid 1960's. Teams in the league were the Elk's, Moose, Legion, Gentner's Tavern, Harvester Hotel and Attica Prison Guards. Our first year uniforms were none existent. Everyone on the team wore black khaki pants and a white tee shirt. That was our uniform. In later years, Batavia Metal Scrapper's, Sterling Homex, Chuck's Sporting Goods and the Primitive Scene nightclub sponsored the trooper's team. Chucks uniforms were very professional and were dark blue and white with red lettering. The Primitive Scene uniforms were yellow with black lettering with everyone looking like a big yellow banana. We had some excellent ball players and would enter police tournaments held in Western New York. We came in second a couple of times, but could never get past a couple of "loaded" out of town teams.

The Thruway Zone four had a team that played in the Buffalo Athletic league and were also quite competitive winning several championships.

Players came and went over the years, but two stuck out in my mind as being the cream of the crop. Gerry Broska was probably the best all around infielder and Ray Motyka the best outfielder that I ever saw play. Broska had it all, speed, lateral movement, a glove like a vacuum cleaner, an accurate throwing arm and live bat. Motyka had deceptive speed. It appeared that he was loping when running to a hit ball. He had the ability to throw you out at home from the far fences and the power to hit the home run ball almost at will.

Those were the good old days. Our wives and children came to the games making it a complete family day. On occasion, we would have a picnic in the park otherwise retire to either Zeno's bar, the Harvester Hotel or East End Hotel for pitchers of beer and soda.

OTHER INCOME

I spent most of my career at Batavia. I had been on the list for promotion to Sergeant on two occasions. In 1969, I had a test score of 85.9, but the list expired with no appointment. I never took another promotional exam and for good reason. It was just as well, as those that got promoted were usually assigned to a troop downstate for two years.

I started attending Genesee Community College (GCC) full time in 1968 on the GI Bill and received aide through the Tuition Assistance Program (TAP) and the Law Enforcement Assistance Program. (LEAP) This provided me with a free education and additional $400.00 a month in financial aid. Bill Gethoefer and I were the first troopers to graduate from GCC in 1971. We earned Associate Degrees in Police Science. I then attended Buffalo State Teachers College earning a Bachelors Degree in Criminal Justice in 1973. This proved to be another windfall for me, as I became a substitute teacher at Pembroke High School for the next five years. Other than an added income, it gave me an opportunity to get to know the kids in the area, as well as their families.

The City of Batavia was going through a period of Urban Renewal during the early 1970s with almost all of the downtown area under demolition. My friend, Eddie Arnold of Arnold Recycling was looking for someone to seek and salvage any valuable metals prior to the buildings demolition. I teamed up with City fire Captain and Batavia Town Justice Charles Barrett and undertook the work of stripping the buildings. We were known by two names, "Sanford and Son" and "Needy and Greedy". No matter what we were called, we earned several hundred dollars a week, each, for our toils. This lasted for about six years. Ed Arnold through whom we were bonded was the beneficiary of our labor.

I truly loved being a trooper and made many lasting friendships both on and off the job. I think I had a good reputation and earned the respect of those I came in contact with. I wasn't particularly keen on arresting people just for the sake of playing a numbers game although it was a big part of our performance evaluation. This may have cost any promotion in the early days. Back in the sixties, we had troopers for each township with my assigned area being Alabama, Oakfield, Pembroke and Darien. Judges Alfred George, Henry Kohlhagen, Stephen Ferry, Ralph Kelsey, John Maha, George Mills and Edward Nanni were top shelf judges and made themselves available at any time of day or night. Each at one time or another told me that there wasn't any question of guilt for any defendant that I arrested and brought before them, it was a question of what the penalty would be. Each knew that if I arrested a person, that person really needed arresting. That was the reputation that I had. I can honestly say that I never slighted anyone because of his or her rank, station in life, color or religion. I always took time to speak with everyone I came in contact with making them feel important, because they were in their own right. Everything has its rewards and these contacts proved invaluable in assisting me when I needed it many years later.

LOADOMETER DUTY
I was assigned to the truck weighing detail three different times for two years at a time. My first partner was Bruce Buttles who had to be the quietest man in the Division. Our daily conversation would be a "morning greeting", "where should we eat today" and "see you tomorrow". It was like he was never there. The scales we used at the time were the heavy 90-pound "goose neck scales" that we carried on a slide out tray in the back of a station wagon. There was a second set of scales in the southern tier that were worked by Roxie Meyers and Bob Becker and a Zone 4 Thruway set operated by Joe Law. We had no quota, but usually would issue about 4 to 6 summons's a day each. There was a lot of construction at the time and overloads were abundant. We tried not to arrest the same driver twice in the same month. As we got to know the drivers, they would stop on their own to get their ticket for the month. We dubbed it the "Once a month club". Fines back then were $100.00. We had an excellent rapport with the drivers and they would return the courtesy by helping us out at incidents or accidents and inquire on the CB radio if we needed any assistance.

My next partner was John Cleary. He was the opposite of Buttles in that we talked about anything and everything. During the winter months, John played in a Thursday night hockey league so he would throw his gear in the back seat and off we went to play hockey. I prayed that he wouldn't get hurt, because I was the senior man and would have to do the explaining. We continued the "Once a month Club" until the implementation of the "Eldec Scales" in 1978. These were mobile electronic platform scales used at a fixed location. The only problem was that truckers were able to take different routes and drive around them. I recall Jim Ceferatti, Jim Lobur, Bob Scott and Gerry Brakefield being assigned to the Eldec team. At some point in late 1978, Gerry Broska, Gerry Brakefield, Jim Ceferatti and I were the roving team. We worked days Monday through Thursday, then would double back at 6 PM Thursday for a night shift. The advantage of working loadometers was that it gave us weekends off.

POLICE BENEVOLENT ASSOCIATION
In 1979, I ran for the elected position of Troop "A" delegate to the PBA. I ran against and beat then long time incumbent Frederick Porcello (Allegany) in a two-man election. I had worked with Fred many years earlier and had a great deal of respect for him. My running had nothing to do with Fred

personally, but was about the direction of the PBA and lack of feedback to the field. Board members had recently arrested PBA President Charles Stuart and had him removed from office. The charges were later dismissed. Fred's aspirations to become the PBA President were nullified with his election loss.

RETIREMENT

During the winter 1984-85, I tore the cartilage in my knee while investigating an accident involving a truck transporting hazardous materials. While at home recovering from knee surgery, the opportunity arose for me to change jobs. At the time, I had served for 23 years and calculated that the difference in retirement pay and staying on the job was about $1.00 an hour. I submitted my retirement papers and was fully retired on July 4, 1985. I took a position with the Department of Defense, as a special investigator conducting security background investigations.

I have no regrets from being a State Trooper, only good thoughts. I always felt that I did an honest days work for an honest days pay. When I first started, I along with everybody else tried to impress our bosses with the hopes of being considered for the BCI. As others got appointed, it was obvious that internal politics came into play. It didn't take too long to wake up to that fact. After several disappointments, I didn't much care about promotion. I came in, worked my shift, did my job and enjoyed being a road trooper. I met many, many people in my twenty-three years on the road that turned into life long relationships. There was no such thing as a routine shift. Every day was a surprise. I always treated everyone with respect and consideration. I felt good about myself at the end of the day. Just being a trooper gave me a feeling of self-satisfaction and pride. I think the important thing is keeping everything in perspective. Being a Trooper is just a job that helps pay your bills. The job does carry a certain amount of responsibility, but remember, when you are retired, you have no more authority that Joe Blow next door.

BERNIECE RUDOLPH SKELTON - 1943 to 1969

Berniece Rudolph Skelton was born at Stafford, N.Y. and attended Leroy High School graduating in 1938. She then attended Geneseo State Teachers College for two years. During her second year, she practice taught but decided against teaching as a career due to a lack of discipline in the students. She married Marvin Skelton on May 31, 1941 and still resides at the Buckley Road, Leroy, N.Y. where she was born.

Her employment with the New York State Police began on May 17, 1943, when she responded to a newspaper ad in the Batavia Daily News. Captain Winfield Robinson came to her home, conducted an interview and hired her immediately. She was the first woman the state police hired as a stenographer assigned to office duties previously conducted by troopers that had been called to active military service. Viola Schwingle Roblee and Edith Schreiner Bloom were hired a short time later. She recalled the troopers being very skeptical of a women's ability to perform their duties, but they proved their worth. She had replaced Clarence Pasto in the BCI unit and always felt that he resented her because of it.

Reporting for work at the trooper's barracks on East Main Street, Batavia, N.Y., her very first assignment was to hand search through thousands of files in an attempt to locate any criminal information on man named Smith. It was a full day's work. Today's computers would have the information in minutes, if not a few seconds.

During her twenty-six years, Berniece worked for many fine men. They included Eugene F. Hoyt, (promoted to Albany) Harry M. DeHollander, Harold L. Kemp, William Lombard, Gerald Schusler,

James D. Russell, Arthur E. Wright and Henry F. Williams. Other bosses at various duties assignments were James Duval and John P. Wilcox who she helped in conducting an inventory of the Troop "A" firearms and ammunition. She also worked with George Wood and Bob Tillman in the BCI, Roy Wullich and Percy Leitner in the Traffic Bureau and many others.

Her memories brought laughter, when she recalled how Inspector John Russell solely on an urge to do so would place a towel on the floor in his office and stand on his head. It made him feel better. William Lombard was her most active boss. He kept her and co-worker Mary Zon buried in reports. He left the troopers to become the Police Chief at Rochester, N.Y.

Life at the barrack's was never routine. There was a staff of highly skilled people that prepared meals for the troopers and civilians, as well as very efficient maintenance people. Emma and Larry Callan were the cooks and prepared excellent meals three times a day. Meals always included many fine homemade pies and desserts. We girls raided the refrigerator and kitchen at breaks in the afternoon and helped ourselves to whatever we wanted. We were never scolded about it so we assumed it was acceptable. Gladys Peio served the meals and did cleaning. She also made handmade doilies and tablecloths in her spare time. There was Mrs. Beatrice O'Grady who I can only describe as jolly and godly. She helped in the kitchen and did cleaning. Her son, Jerome became a trooper and rose through the ranks retiring as a Deputy Superintendent.

Berniece worked with many capable ladies over the years. They included Mary Zon, Mabel Keister, Hazel Monahan Vincent, Beth Acomb, Donna Seaman, Connie Jordan, Faye Pridmore Barone, Dorothy Ring, Mary Nowak, Lana Willard Schlagenhauf, Muriel Willard, Dorothy Manahan, Toni Tabone Bray, Nancy Pfaff Smith, Linda McCabe Beeman, Nancy Quinn, Bernetta McDonald, Linda Keil, Brenda McCoy, Sharlann Walker and several others.

Bernetta McDonald had been injured in an automobile accident at Geneva, N.Y. and Berniece visited her there on many occasions being driven by a BCI member.

Her position in the BCI was very interesting with many crimes solved from the desk. When the BCI men were stationed at the barracks, it seemed crimes were solved via word of mouth with all present contributing a piece of information. When they were later assigned to sectors, she felt that crime solving lost its effective touch.

In 1957, she was stricken with hepatitis and spent almost a year in bed. She was continued on the payroll thanks to her many friends from Albany and Troop "A" that knew how best to handle her sick leave. Norma Bush was hired to take her place for that time.

On a humorous note although not to Berniece, she recalled driving to work in her new car that she was very proud of. At the end of the workday, she got into her car to leave, but it wouldn't move. Everyone was peering from the barracks windows laughing at the spectacle. She was absolutely furious and humiliated, when she found that Sergeant John Long had put the car on blocks making it impossible for her to drive away.

In 1967 just prior to her retirement, Berniece at the request of Captain Arthur E. Wright was assigned the task of establishing the BCI files and acquainting the secretaries at the newly formed Troop E, Canandaigua, N.Y. with proper procedures. Investigator Bob Tillman drove her back and forth for several weeks.

In 1969, Berniece was hospitalized due to a stress related ailment. While there, BCI Captain Henry Williams provided her with an 800 number telephone line so that she might keep in touch with her many friends in the state police family.

Because of her excellent work ethic, Berniece won the respect and admiration of her supervisors and co-workers. She was rewarded many times over with their support when needed in her 26 years with the state police.

She mentions that her co-workers were a very close, friendly group. They celebrated each other's birthdays, anniversaries, retirements and other personal occasions. The girls had a 25th wedding anniversary party for Berniece and Marvin at the Apple Grove in Medina, N.Y. where they presented them with a silver tea set commemorating the occasion.

She retired on August 3, 1969.

Looking back to the time she raided the refrigerator and through the years, she realized that the ladies were accepted although at the time they thought not and through the years proved their worth many times over.

Berniece and Marvin enjoy their retirements and still reside at their Buckley Road home spending winters at Englewood, Florida. She is a social member and avid supporter of the Batavia Chapter of Former NYS Troopers.

HENRY F. WILLIAMS – BCI CAPTAIN - 1952 to 1986

Henry F. Williams was born on May 8, 1930 at Buffalo, N.Y. He attended and graduated from Annunciation High School and Canisius College.

He enlisted in the State Police on April 16, 1952 assigned to Troop "A", Batavia, N.Y. His career was put on hold when he was drafted into the US Army on August 24,1953 where he served in a counter-intelligence unit at Washington D.C. with the title Special Agent .He was discharged on August 1, 1955 returning to duty with the NYS Troopers.

Promotions included:

December 1, 1955 - Assigned to the BCI at Batavia, N.Y.

February 8,1962 - Permanent rank of Corporal

April 5, 1962 - Sergeant in BCI

November 29, 1962 - Senior Investigator

September 29, 1965 - Designated officer in charge of Troop "A" BCI

January 20, 1966, simultaneously promoted to Lieutenant and appointed Captain in the BCI. At age 35, he was the youngest Captain in the Troopers. His promotion also meant a transfer to Division Headquarters where he headed the Special Investigations Unit (SIU) and Organized Crime Task Force (OCTF) until his return to Troop "A" on September 2, 1976.

"Hank", as he preferred to be called, was now back in an environment best suited to him. During his many years in law enforcement, he had developed more close relationships in and out of the law enforcement field than any other person this writer had ever known. His absolute sincere friendliness, trust and warmth showed in the smile he greeted you with. He treated everyone alike, with a person's social status, occupation, skin color and community standing being unimportant to him. He had an uncanny ability to relate to everyone he met. You were a friend until you did something to betray that friendship. This natural demeanor paid huge dividends during the many criminal investigations he conducted. Hank had the ability to glean more useful criminal information by telephone in a day, than an entire law enforcement task force could in a week. Retired Superintendent Thomas Constantine, a close personal friend observed that "Hank had the political skills to bring people together from different factions and different law enforcement agencies and make it work" "No person is irreplaceable, but in the case of Henry Williams, I'm not so sure."

Hank was a supreme politician and commanded respect both inside and outside the Division and while demanding as a supervisor, he projected the image of being a regular guy. He should have become a uniform commander as he thought much larger than any troop commander and his leadership would have engendered a spirit of teamwork.

It was Williams who led the investigation during the Winston Mosely manhunt, the Attica Prison escapee who had brutally murdered Kittie Genovese in New York City surrounded by a crowd of onlookers, the arrest of organized crime boss Stefano Maggadino in 1968 and the 1980 investigation of the .22 caliber killer who was murdering black men.

What everyone will always remember are the TV newscasts during the September 1981, Attica Prison riot, when Hank stood on the front steps of the prison prior to its retaking standing tall and instructed the assault force to be responsible to the man next to him, let no one take your weapon and concluded with a Lord's blessing. After the smoke settled and the body count was totaled, the fingers were all unjustly pointed at Hank as the person responsible for the carnage. He was soon re-assigned to Division Headquarters pushing papers from behind a desk, a measure made to keep him out of the spotlight. Myself and other troopers from Western N.Y. while in Albany, N.Y. would meet Hank for a few light refreshments at days end. Although he loved the State Police dearly, he yearned more than anything to return to duty in Western New York. This was not to be, as Hank died on December 5, 1986 at Albany, N.Y. At the time of his demise, he was the commanding Officer for the BCI Division wide. His wife and six children survive him. Son Mark is a New York State Trooper and son Timothy is an Albany City Police Officer.

VERNON CLAYSON

HOWARD BLANDING

HANK WILLIAMS

EUGENE REDDEN 1941 TO 1967

INV. D.L. SMITH - LT.
CHARLES COBB

ANDY FISHER - JOE HEILIG - 19

STANLY SOCHALEC

BERNIECE
SKELTON

GARY KUBASIAK

BOOK IX — NEW YORK STATE THRUWAY DETAIL

HISTORY

The New York State Thruway Detail originated on June 24, 1954 with the opening of the first section of the super highway. Twenty-nine troopers were assigned under the command of Captain R.V. Annett with Headquarters at the Thruway Division Office, Thompson Road, East Syracuse. These men patrolled the section from Lowell to West Henrietta. On August 1954, a Sergeant and eight troopers were added to the detail when a section of the thruway was opened to Buffalo. At years end, the detail had a compliment of eighty-six men. Two lieutenants, eight sergeants and seventy-six troopers, with eight of the troopers being assigned to the radio-tele-phone network (communications).

The first detail commander of the Buffalo Section was Lieutenant Richard T. Barber.

The Thruway Authority purchased 42 cars for the detail. In early 1955, an additional twenty troopers were assigned to relieve the heavy communications workload and reduce the length of miles patrolled. During 1956, as Thruway sections were opened, patrol vehicles increased from 138 to 169 and five motorcycles. 1956 also brought radar speed enforcement. In 1959, additional segments were opened bringing the total length to 553 miles.

In 1957, the Thruway Detail had 175 radio cars with emergency equipment that included 30 unmarked patrol cars in various colors. Five motorcycles were also assigned for patrol and traffic purposes.

In the early days, the troop cars were fitted with a green light on the left rear fender. This was to allow Sergeants to see the car traveling in an opposite direction. Truckers were told and were convinced that they were used to check the weight of trucks.

Vents were installed in the trunk lids so gasoline cans could be carried in the trunk. Hot-rodders were told they were after burners for fast pursuit.

Cornell University conducted a crash program study wherein Thruway troopers gathered comprehensive information classified in specific detail about injury producing mishaps that were reported on special forms. The program was in effect until 1960 and had an overwhelming influence in the manufacture of safer constructed cars.

On December 14, 1961, the famous "Thruway Detail" became today's Troop "T". In 1962, forty-one troopers were added to Troop "T" to make possible for a forty-hour workweek in 1963 and Troop "T" headquarters was relocated to thruway interchange 23, Albany, N.Y.

THRUWAY MANPOWER
Year	Troopers Assigned
Jun 1954	29
Dec 1954	76
1955	96
1956	142
1957	165
1959	177
1963	217
1973	300
1983	325

WBTA RADIO (BATAVIA, N.Y.) OCTOBER 14, 1956
TOWN CRIER RADIO EDITORIAL

The addition of unmarked police cars to the New York State Thruway patrol seems to be causing concern among automobile drivers who have acquired a real skill as cop-watchers. It should, of course, cause no distress to those who habitually observe the speed limits of 60 MPH for passenger cars and 50 MPH for trucks.

Thus the apprehension over the use of a green sedan or a red convertible as a pursuit car is in the very group that state police want to separate from the total flow of traffic, the habitual speeders.

The Thruway has reduced the incidence of accidents and saved many lives, but the toll can be further cut down by strict enforcement of the speed limits. If you've driven the super highway many times, you are aware of the fact that you can roll along between 55 and 60 and be passed by a good many diesel trucks and at 65 to 70, be outdistanced by passenger cars making speeds up to 90 MPH.

How do they get away with it? Here's the answer we got from a driver who regards himself as an expert in sensing the presence of a police car. They keep a careful watch for the black and white State Police cars as they pass bridges, interchanges, restaurants and other points where cars may be parked. They keep one eye on the road and the other on the rear view mirror. If a pursuing car is gaining on them, they drop down to the pace near the speed limit and maintain a close watch until they can tell whether or not it is a police car.

If these 90 MPH speed demons have to keep a careful eye on every other car on the road, it's very likely that they will give it up as a bad job, particularly after a surprise pinch or two.

The only sensible argument against unmarked cars came from the office of the state police superintendent. The statement that the Trooper is often a friend in need and should be easily identified. There are still plenty of marked cars on the road to be hailed by the motorist in distress.

The unmarked cars are there to do a job that can't be done effectively without them. To create a general respect for speed regulations and most of all strike fear of arrest in the expert cop watchers who stay in line when the black and white car is in view and drive like Indianapolis racers when it isn't.

Maybe it's not the sporting thing to do but at the rate of death and injury on our highways this is no game to be played according to the rules.

Except for the occasional driver who falls asleep at the wheel, it's hard to see how anybody can create a serious accident traveling the Thruway at legal speed. Bare in mind next time you pick up a ticket at a Thruway interchange, cop watching no longer pays rewards.

BUFFALO ZONE WINS SAFETY AWARD

On May 8, 1958, the New York State Police Thruway Detail of the Buffalo Division gained recognition for outstanding traffic safety work for the year 1957 from the Buffalo Courier Express Newspaper. The award, a plaque was the first of its kind won by the Thruway Detail

TROOPER GERALD FORSTER – 1958

Trooper Gerald Forster was assigned to the Buffalo Thruway Detail in 1958. Troopers at the time were required to live in the barracks, but the thruway was an exception. Only one trooper at a time was required to spend a night at the station. There were about fifteen troopers assigned to the Buffalo detail. Troopers were required to patrol at least eight hours a shift and spend four hours in reserve time at the barracks. They had the option to remain on patrol. Each member on the detail had a car assigned to him that they were allowed to take home. A spare car was assigned to each post for use in the event the assigned car was broken down. The detail did not become a troop for some years. His first assignment was a post that covered the "Freeway" from Williamsville to Lackawanna, as well as the Grand Island post. When the Buffalo section of the Niagara portion was opened, Forster was the first trooper to patrol that section. It covered the freeway to Porter Avenue. Prior to public use, troopers were given three days to familiarize themselves with the new section of highway along with its ramps and surrounding areas. There were five members assigned to each post. The posts were from Williamsville to Lackawanna, Lackawanna to Silver Creek and the new Niagara Section that included Grand Island.

ZONE 4 OF TROOP "T"

Zone 4 is responsible for policing the Thruway from the Victor interchange to the Pennsylvania State line at Ripley. It also covers the Niagara section spur through Buffalo and Niagara Falls, N.Y. In 1966, the commanders of the three zone stations were Sergeant C.R. McFadden, West Henrietta, Sergeant R.F. Klein, Buffalo and Sergeant J.E. Farrell, Fredonia. Lieutenant Alexander Gallion was the Zone Commander. Ten troopers were assigned at West Henrietta and Fredonia with twenty-six at Buffalo. The zone had a three-man radar detail; a one-man loadometer detail and a one man warrant detail. Troopers rode single patrol because assistance was readily available from the next post.

THRUWAY TROOPER PROTESTS

During October 1968, Troopers picketed Thruway Headquarters, Albany, N.Y. in protest of the Authorities refusal to improve the troopers radio system. New Jersey police departments, Thruway maintenance vehicles and other agencies used the same frequency making impossible on occasion to communicate during an emergency situation. They also protested the carrying of gasoline in the car for motorists who ran out of it. This directive was dubbed "The Thruway Molotov Cocktail"

The primary job of the thruway trooper is to keep traffic moving ~~smoothly~~.

1963 – 1964 TROOP "T" ZONE 4 PARTIAL ROSTER
Lieutenant – Alexander Gallion

| Sergeants – | G.H. Clune II | R.L. March | J.M. Davidson |
| | | C.R. McFadden | F.C. Hofmann |

Troopers -	J.M. Abate	H.B. Archer	J.P. Balon
	C.J. Coates	J.B. Cornell	S.J. Domagala
	S.L. Domanski	R.B. Earl	R.J. Flis
	G.R.Forster	R.H. Goundry	R. Harlock
	E.C. Hooper	J.A. Kostecki	W.G. Linden
	R.W. Maines	R.P. Miller	W.R. Narby
	B.D. Pagels	R.E. Seidel	J.T. Stofer
	M.E. Thorpe	G.B. Wildridge	N.J. Wolf

PLANE LANDS ON THRUWAY – MAY 31, 1962

An emergency landing on the Thruway near Walden Avenue ended the return trip from Indianapolis for pilot James W. Ryan, 38 of Cheektowaga, N.Y. He told Trooper Gerald Forster that his light planes engine stalled forcing him to make the landing. Other passengers were Patrick Ryan, 12, Lawrence Berg, 40, Joseph A. Klostermann, 52 and Russell Dispenza, 32 all of Cheektowaga. There were no injuries or damage. Ryan was issued a summons for violating the General Business Law.

FLEEING CAR RAMMED

On April 25, 1964, a Thruway patrol was in pursuit of a car traveling at high speed that continued off the super highway into Henrietta with several other agencies now engaged in the chase. The trooper in close pursuit radioed for permission to ram the fleeing car after it nearly struck several children. Permission was granted and the car rammed causing it to strike a tree. Uninjured, the subject exited the car and was taken into custody. A .45 caliber revolver was found in the car. He was later confined to Mattawan State Hospital for Criminally Insane persons.

TROOPER ASSAULTED – OCTOBER 20, 1966

Trooper Gregory B. Wildridge was attempting to place Leonard Knast, 27, Buffalo, N.Y. under arrest for Disorderly Conduct, when the defendant started his automobile and dragged the trooper a half a block. He was convicted of assault before Judge Burke I. Burke, fined $250.00 and given a one year suspended sentence.

BASKET TOOL

On July 1, 1968, Trooper Ronald Junior working the Pembroke Section of the New York State Thruway stopped a car for speeding. During the stop, he noticed a "steel basket tool" on the back seat of the car. He recalled a recent troop memo describing the tool that was used to pry open coin boxes on telephones. He arrested the driver and occupants for possession of burglar's tools. A search of the vehicle produced $1500.00 in nickels, dimes and quarters.

RADAR CALIBRATION – JOE LAW STYLE

Lieutenant Alexander Gallion, Thruway Buffalo was intent on having the radar unit working every day and Trooper Joe Law, the radar operator was intent on working it only now and then. One day, Law in an effort to avoid working the radar unit threw the radar antenna out of the troop car window with the units cables connected. He then proceeded to drag it through the grassy center mall of the thruway and declared it unusable. Law was called in by Gallion to explain the damage. Law simply stated that the unit fell out of the window. It was brought into the station with clumps of sod hanging from the antenna. The lieutenant wanted the unit activated to determine if it would function properly. Law told the Lieutenant that he had no way of calibrating the accuracy unless someone ran down the hall toward the unit. Gallion volunteered and ran from the far end of a long hallway toward the unit. Law reported that it wasn't working, but that might be because there wasn't any metal to reflect the radio signal. He now asked the lieutenant to run toward the unit with a set of keys in his hand shaking them as he ran. Again the lieutenant complied. The station Secretary, Mrs. Dorothy Duscher stood in the doorway of her office shaking her head as she watched the display in the hallway. Oh yes, the radar unit was out of service for quite some time requiring factory repairs.

THRUWAY CRACKDOWN

On June 9, 1972, Lieutenant John C. Ruehl in charge of Zone 4 Thruway-Buffalo issued the following memorandum to Station Commander Robert Klein:

> *A review of V&T activity for SP Buffalo station for the first eight days of June 1972 is nothing less than alarming. In particular June 8 has a stunning 9 V&T arrests for the entire day. This is considered a reflection on every sergeant from SP Buffalo. I will not tolerate such lack of supervision. The first priority will be road supervision. The men that are not producing are to be told in no uncertain terms to get of their ass! This is to be read and initialed by all SP Buffalo sergeants, then returned to me.*

Ruehl noted that strict enforcement of traffic laws resulted in a reduction of highway fatalities. Also cited was the fact that there had been an increase in the number of policemen being slain while on duty and this upswing pointed out only too well the serious nature of police business.

Earlier in the year, Ruehl instructed troopers to step up enforcement of the penal laws involving carrying guns and drugs. He felt there were a few who coasted along and did not do their fair share of enforcement. He promised that any man who refused to do his share and in the process undermined or endangered his fellow trooper would be investigated and if the situation warranted, would be brought up on charges. He further noted that there were too many good people in the zone to let anyone detract from their performance or welfare.

Only a handful of troopers were actively participating in penal law enforcement. As a result, a new performance system was initiated. Troopers were interviewed and counseled at least four times a year by a sergeant. A computer printout was used to rate a trooper's activity and productivity based on the activities of other troopers within the zone.

For one man to dog it while another is working is inexcusable and will not be tolerated.

These get-tough memorandums mysteriously made their way to the local Buffalo newspapers.

(As in any occupation, there are diligent, dedicated employees and there are those that do the bare minimum to get by. This was an attempt by Reuhl's to motivate or intimidate the very few station slugs into doing an honest days work.)

TROOPER BEATEN

In early 1973, Trooper John O'Neill (Henrietta) stopped an eastbound car near the entrance ramp of the Henrietta Thruway interchange for a traffic violation. With red roof lights in use, he approached the stopped car. A second car traveling along with the stopped car stopped abreast of the troop car with four males exiting the car. They immediately started beating Trooper O'Neill knocking him to the ground. They continually punched and kicked at him as he lay on the ground and took his service revolver. A passing South-towns tow truck seeing the red lights of the trooper car thought a service call was required. As he stopped behind the troop car, he observed the assault and immediately radioed for help. He then drove his tow truck at the assailants forcing them to leave in haste. Trooper Frank Best at the Henrietta station a short distance away immediately responded blocking the exit ramp to Henrietta by parking his troop car across the pavement. The first two cars to approach were those involved in the assault. Trooper Best took them into custody at gunpoint. Other troopers rushed to the scene to assist. Trooper O'Neill suffering from rib, chest and internal damage was taken to Strong Memorial Hospital where he was admitted. The assailants were initially taken to the Thruway barracks for questioning. They were then taken to SP Henrietta where Lieutenant Foody led an intensive interview of the suspects. The revolver taken from the trooper was searched for and found hidden under the cushion of a chair at the Thruway barracks apparently hidden there by one of the female passengers. The four male arrestees required medical treatment and were also taken to Strong Hospital for treatment. While guarding one of perpetrators, Trooper Rick Parmenter noticed the attending physician asking questions of the injured defendant and taking notes. The defendant told him that the troopers had beaten him at the station. Sergeant George Zink on location was notified and confronted the doctor. He simply said that the attacked trooper had fought valiantly in self-defense during the assault with the resultant injuries to the defendant. He then took the doctors notes, tore them telling the doctor to tend to his patient and leave the investigation to the troopers. The defendant's were found guilty of Felony Assault.

BEEF CAPER

During the winter of 1973, a tractor-trailer loaded with quarters of frozen beef ran off the Thruway at what is known as the "Rock Cut" at Stafford, N.Y.

The trailer unit had gone over an embankment partially spilling its load on the frozen ground. Although not responding to the scene, the NYS Department of Agriculture and Markets telephonically condemned the entire load, as was procedure with any wreck. The beef was to be discarded at a local dump. Instead, several troopers elected to take some of the undamaged beef quarters for their personal use. Batavia tow truck operator Harmon Houseknecht responding to the scene reported on his truck radio that it wouldn't be too difficult to upright the rig, as the troopers were removing and putting the beef in their troop cars. Thruway maintenance trucks and Lieutenant Gallion near the scene overheard these comments. Gallion traveled immediately to the accident scene initiating an investigation. As a result, he brought charges against eight troopers for larceny of the beef. They were arraigned before Stafford Town Justice Frederick Muskopf. Gallion demanded they be required to post bail or be remanded to the County Jail. Muskopf looking squarely at the Lieutenant asked if he was in his right mind. As a long tenured Justice, he had dealt with the troopers on many occasions and personally felt it was overkill of the situation and for whatever reason, an example was being made of the eight troopers. He released them without bail. The criminal charges were dismissed, but all received 80-day suspensions without pay.

FBI'S TEN MOST WANTED CAPTURED
On April 3, 1974, Buffalo Trooper Joseph Casciano arrested a fugitive and his wife wanted by the FBI for Kidnapping in Roanoke, Virginia. A radio communication had alerted patrols of the possibility the couple were traveling through the area in a green Jaguar automobile. The car, a gray Jaguar was observed going through the Williamsville tollbooth by Casciano. A two-mile chase pursuit ended with the couple being taken into custody at gunpoint. Trooper Robert Hamilton rushed to the scene aiding in the arrest. Unarmed, the fugitives surrendered without incident and were turned over to the FBI at Buffalo. $10,825.00 was found in their possession.

FREDONIA TROOPER OVERPOWERED
During 1974, Trooper Kenneth Olkowski of the Fredonia Thruway barracks was checking on a hitchhiker, when he found a marijuana cigarette. The youth admitted to having more in his knapsack. While opening the knapsack, Olkowski was told not to move and looked up to find a .22 caliber derringer pointed at him. Olkowski was disarmed and ordered to drive to a nearby motel. At the motel, the trooper was ordered into the trunk. As the lid was being closed, a motel guest driving in observed the situation. Olkowski banged on the trunk for attention and instructed the guest on where to find the trunk release switch on the dashboard. A 150-man detail sealed off the area with the hitchhiker captured and gun recovered early the next morning. He was identified as an escapee from a Marine Corp prison in Virginia.

Z/SERGEANT JAMES J. BEERS
Retired Zone Sergeant James J. Beers was assigned to Troop "T" Buffalo, N.Y. in 1975. He provided the following about the Buffalo zone. Eight patrol posts served the Buffalo zone each twenty-one miles in length. Troopers were required to patrol the entire distance, back and forth at least once an hour, eight times a shift, but this proved to be impossible because of arrests, assistance to motorist and meal breaks. Any serious crime or arrest resulted in the case being turned over to the local Troop "A" BCI for further investigation. In the mid 1980s, this changed, when BCI members were assigned to the Thruway. Troopers were required to carry two, one-gallon cans of gasoline and five gallons of water in the vented trunk of their patrol car. This service was stopped after several troopers were burned from radiator steam while assisting motorists and also the potential for a fire or explosion from a rear end collision with the troop car.

TWO-WAY RADIOS
In June of 1976, Sergeant James McDermott, a PBA Delegate filed a grievance relative to the inadequate radio system in use on the Thruway. Thruway radios were hooked into an antiquated system that included maintenance trucks, plows, tollbooths collectors and other personnel. The system was inadequate in meeting the needs of police and did not provide for communicating with cars in adjoining Troop areas. As a result, a new two- way radio system was installed in all 150 Thruway troop cars during April 1978.

TROOPERS INJURED – LATE 1970'S
Troopers Edward Caypless and Michael Mergler were assisting at the scene of a tractor- trailer that had run off the roadway becoming stuck. As they directed traffic around the rear of the tractor unit, one of the drive tires had become overheated and blew out. Both troopers were rendered deaf by the explosion. Caypless received the more severe injury and was ultimately awarded a disability retirement. Mergler was off duty for several weeks eventually returning to duty. He avoided any contact with tractor-trailers, whenever possible.

320

BEYOND THE CALL OF DUTY

Trooper Martin A. Krebs was sent to an accident scene in December 1971 where he found a car with an elderly lady passenger dangling over the edge of a bridge. The car had spun out of control, crashed through a guardrail killing the driver instantly. The car was supported only by a piece of the railing that kept it from falling 30 feet to the concrete below. Recognizing that panic on the surviving passengers part could result in the car being dislodged, Krebs calmly talked with her while getting a rope carried in the troop car. He then had several men hold him by the ankles while he hung over the bridge getting far enough into the wreckage to tie the rope around the woman's waist. He and others then lifter her to safety and comforted her until an ambulance arrived.

During the Blizzard of 1977, Troopers Melvin Thorpe, Bob Sulecki, Alvin Kurdys, Nicholas Parvu and Ron Szymanski, working the Niagara section of the Thruway were told of an injury auto accident. Arriving at the scene, they found a chain reaction accident where a 26-year-old truck driver had sustained a broken leg. An ambulance was able to make it to within ¼ mile of the accident before becoming stuck in five-foot deep snowdrifts. The troopers immobilized the injured truckers leg, then started out carrying him to the hospital. The five troopers alternated carrying the victim and breaking a path in the drifting snow. They finally arrived at Columbus Hospital in downtown Buffalo. The troopers were treated for exposure and Sulecki for frost bitten toes. They returned to duty after treatment.

On the same day, Troopers John R. Bruso and Kenneth L. Chodkowski were instructed to assist a Friendship, N.Y. mother and her ten-week-old baby who were stranded at a Buffalo Thruway toll-booth. The baby needed to be taken to Children's Hospital for treatment on a lifesaving kidney machine. What would normally have been a twenty-minute trip took four hours. The entire section of the Thruway was clogged with stranded trucks and cars with visibility at zero. They made their way onto Buffalo City streets where they were forced to back down many streets and push abandoned vehicles out of their way. They were rewarded with the knowledge they had succeeded where another person wouldn't even give the effort with the child receiving the needed life saving treatment.

THRUWAY – ZONE 4 – BUFFALO, N.Y.
ROSTER – JANUARY 1, 1982

LIEUTENANT –   T.J.Kirwan

SECRETARY –   D.H. Duscher

ZONE SERGEANTS –	L.J. Glascott	R.L. March	R.E. Minekheim	
SERGEANTS - TROOPERS -	J.P. Rozanski	J.J. Beers	R.C. Sulecki	R.W. Miller
	T.P.Anticola	J.F. Bak	R.D. Bernys	
	R.A. Bizub	M.L. Borodzik	J.R. Bruso	
	J.A. Casciano	E.F. Caypless II	K.L. Chodkowski	
	D.L. Denz	A.J. Domagala Jr.	G.E. Dorobiala	
	T.J. Dykas	T.M. Gleason	J.A. Gramza	
	C.S. Hallenbeck III	C.P. Haupt	J.E. Headd	
	G.J. Jakubczak	E.T. Koenig Jr.	M.A. Krebs	
	J.J. Kupka	A.P.Kurdys	G.D. Lata	
	J.R. Loncher	A.W. Maedl	R.W. Maines	
	D.M. May	M.F. Mergler	D.A. Miller	
	R.P. Miller	J. Needham	B.D. Pagels	
	N. Parvu Jr	T.O. Phillips	L.S. Ruberto Jr.	
	E.J. Rybak	R.F. Szczepanski	R.A. Szymanski	
	J.M. Violanti	K.P. Walsh	G.H. Wienckowski	
	G.E. Wood	P.G. Zimmerman		

HENRIETTA SUBSTATION

SERGEANT – J.A. Masco

TROOPERS	F.E. Best	M.W. Borman	F.M. Brown
	W.E. Corrigan	W.Dickinson	P.N. Ernest
	S.R. Jenis	E.A. Lorshnaugh	P.J. Militello
	L.F. Moore		

FREDONIA SUBSTATION

SERGEANT – P.J. Burns

TROOPERS	J.A. Anderson	R.J.Beresniewicz	T.A. Fairbanks
	R.L. Frost	T.A. Reigelman	J.A.Schermerhorn
	J.L.Selig	J.E. Smoczynski	T.E. Sutton
	R.J. Szczerbacki	J.W. Thornton	J.L.Vanzile

PATROLS FOR THE BILLS

A photograph of Trooper Kevin P. Walsh appeared in the May 1, 1985 issue of USA Today. Walsh since 1978 had represented the Buffalo Bills Professional Football Team during the annual drafting of college football players to the pro ranks.

2000 THRUWAY TROOPERS

There are 325 members that make up the State Police Troop "T" that patrol the New York State Thruway System exclusively. Night and day, Troop "T" members do emergency work at the scene of accidents, summon help for thousands of motorists with disabled vehicles and make more than 150,000 arrests each year.

Operating 180 patrol cars, the troopers travel more than 8 million miles a year on thruway assignments. They make approximately 80,000 arrests each year for speeding. Radar teams, low-profile vehicles and aerial speed enforcement efforts supplement regular patrols.

A Thruway communications system provides instantaneous communication 24 hours a day among Thruway Headquarters, tollbooths, and the hundreds of vehicles operated by troopers, administrators, maintenance and emergency service crews and toll personnel.

All communications are centralized at Thruway Authority Headquarters in Albany, N.Y. The communications center is staffed by shifts around the clock with a force of twenty-eight civilian dispatchers, nine senior dispatchers and nine State Police Technical Sergeants. The Authority's Communications Supervisor oversees technical operations.

The entire annual cost for Troop "T" services is approximately $21.5 million per year and is borne by the Thruway Authority. It pays the troopers' salaries and expenses and provides them with patrol cars, uniforms and other necessary equipment.

Trooper David Groblewski – 1961 - Peace Bridge in Background

TWY BUFFALO - 1970S - D. DUSCHEN
R.MINTER- J DORABALA- J.BAK- R.MINIKHEIM-
G.LATA

BOOK X — NEW YORK STATE POLICE SUPERINTENDENTS - 1943 TO 1987

JOHN A. GAFFNEY –THIRD SUPERINTENDENT 1943 TO 1953

John A. Gaffney was born August 28, 1900 in New York City where he attended public school. He served with US Marine Corp during World War I receiving an honorable discharge. He enlisted in the New York State Troopers on January 1, 1923 and was assigned at Hawthorne, N.Y. Gaffney served for two years under the Attorney Generals Office conducting plain-clothes confidential investigations. He was promoted to Corporal in 1926, Sergeant in 1927, 1st Sergeant in 1929, Lieutenant in 1930, Captain in 1937 and Deputy Superintendent in 1943. Governor Thomas E. Dewey appointed John A. Gaffney to be the 3rd Superintendent on December 22, 1943. He served in this position until August 15, 1953 when he retired due to failing health. He then accepted a position with the New York State Thruway Authority as a police consultant. He went to his final patrol on December 14, 1954.

Several organizational changes were made during his tenure. A statewide three way FM radio system was installed making it possible for every patrol car to be in contact with its Troop Headquarters. He relocated the BCI Headquarters from Troy to Albany, N.Y. the Scientific Laboratory from Schenectady to Albany and formed a Central Intelligence Bureau. Gaffney also established a new manual entitled New York State Police Rules and Regulations. The previous guide was the original Colonel Chandler General Order Number 1 from 1917.

ALBIN S. JOHNSON – FOURTH SUPERINTENDENT 1953 TO 1955

Albin S. Johnson was born at Balston Spa, New York on August 16, 1907 and attended Union College in Schenectady, N.Y. He was employed as a semi-pro baseball player until his enlistment in the State Police on July 16,1933. He was first assigned in Troop K. He was promoted to Corporal in 1942, Sergeant in 1944 and First Sergeant in 1947 was promoted to Lieutenant in May 1951. Governor Thomas E. Dewey appointed him Superintendent on August 16, 1953, a position he held until January 1955, when he resigned returning to the rank of Lieutenant. He voluntarily resigned his office to provide the newly elected Governor W. Averill Harriman to have an opportunity to work with his own appointed Superintendent. In 1960, he was promoted to inspector. From May 1951 to August 1953, he served as chief of the State Police Investigators for the State Crime Commission. He retired in 1969 remaining in the Albany area with his wife, Patricia. He died on September 20, 1986.

During his tenure, he obtained a 30% expansion in authorized strength and established the original NYSP Thruway Detail in June 1954, now known as Troop T. He also oversaw the development of the modern straight-legged uniform.

FRANCIS S. McGARVEY – FIFTH SUPERINTENDENT 1955 TO 1961

Francis S. McGarvey was born December 15, 1896 at New York City where he attended parochial and public school. He enlisted in the State Police on July 12, 1917 being an original Camp-man and was assigned at Troop "K". He was promoted to Corporal in 1918, Sergeant in 1919 and Lieutenant in 1923 serving in Troops K and G. He was appointed a District Inspector at Troop "G" in 1935 and Division Inspector in 1936. He served as Troop "B" Commander at Malone. N.Y. from 1939 to April 1943, when he was re-assigned at Troop "C", Sidney replacing Captain Dan Fox who retired.

In 1944, he was promoted to Chief Inspector and on January 23, 1955, appointed Superintendent by Governor Averill Harriman. He was personally acquainted with every man in the Division. Police officer training and continuing education was high among his priorities, as was the providing of the latest tools: high-performance troop cars, modern inter-state teletype system, upgrading blood testing equipment and introduction of SCUBA equipment. He also centralized records & increased division manpower.

He retired on February 9, 1961 at age 64. He was the last of the camp-men still on the job at retirement. He was involved in several high profile cases including the break up of the Jack (Legs) Diamond and the Vincent (Mad Dog) Coll gangs during prohibition. He resided at Collingswood, N.J. where on July 3, 1969, he passed to his final patrol at age 72. His wife, Mabel Post McGarvey and a son, Francis X. McGarvey, survived him.

ARTHUR CORNELIUS JR. – SIXTH SUPERINTENDENT 1961 TO 1967

Born August 2, 1908 in Bayville, New Jersey, Arthur Cornelius Jr. realized at an early age the importance in obtaining a good education. One not to burden his family, he earned extra money by doing menial labor while attending John Marshall College, graduating in 1931. He then attended Mercer Beasley School of Law (now Rutgers University) where he earned a Law Degree in 1934. After graduation, he became a Special Agent with the Federal Bureau of Investigation (FBI) serving from 1935 until his retirement in April 1959. On February 13, 1961, Governor Nelson Rockefeller appointed him to the position of Superintendent of the New York State Police. He was the first superintendent appointed from outside the trooper ranks. During his tenure, he is credited with re-organizing the State Police supervisory personnel. New positions were created, members re-classified, new titles given, new duties assigned and best of all, he fought for and obtained a much needed pay raise for the entire personnel of the Division. Other accomplishments were the initiation of 40-hour workweek from the 60-hour workweek, an increase of personnel from less than 1600 to nearly 3000 troopers and activation of a Troop "E" in Central New York. He also purchased real estate for the formation of Troop "F" and obtained funding of 2.9 million dollars for construction of a Police Academy next to Division Headquarters.

On August 4, 1967, Arthur Cornelius died unexpectedly following major chest surgery. His wife, the former Betty Jane Castle of Detroit, Michigan and two sons, Wayne Alan and Donald Arthur, survived him. He is buried at Memory's Garden, Colonie, New York.

Governor Nelson Rockefeller commented that Arthur Cornelius was one of the truly outstanding public servants in the state. He rendered leadership to the State Police that included its reorganization, a change in concept and standards, an increase in the force, the training of the men and an awareness of the problems society faced.

Cornelius was best described as " One of the best known police officials in the nation and for very good reason; he was one of the best police officials in the nation." He was the model of the police professional in the best sense of the term. Behind his reserved, soft spoken, unfailingly gentlemanly manner was a passion for efficiency and integrity. Any subordinate or criminal who mistook the quiet manner for softness quickly realized the gravity of his error. Under his leadership, the New York State Police was improved in every possible way – in training, manpower, equipment, salaries and working conditions.

It is this writer's opinion that Superintendent Cornelius created the most positive and productive change in the Division of State Police since Colonel Chandler during its inception in 1917.

WILLIAM E. KIRWAN – SEVENTH SUPERINTENDENT 1967 TO 1975

William E. Kirwan was born at New York City on November 7, 1912 joining the State Police on June 15, 1936. He was a graduate of Fordham University in 1933 majoring in Chemistry. He was assigned to the New York State Police Laboratory in 1937 as assistant to Director Dr. Bradley Kirschberg. He was appointed director of the laboratory in 1941 vacated by the death of Dr. Kirschberg, a post he held until 1961, when he was appointed an acting chief inspector. He had been promoted to Captain in 1958. Kirwan was a faculty member of the Albany Medical College where he was an associate in Medico-Legal Pathology, a lecturer in Toxicology and consultant. He lectured on scientific aids in criminal investigations at Purdue University and New York University. As Superintendent, he oversaw the construction of the State Police Academy and its expanded use by various police agencies, introduced women to the force in 1974 and was active in the recruitment of minorities. He re-established an air fleet to serve the state, created new Troops F in 1968 and founded a state Narcotics Unit. He further changed the state's troop car colors from the traditional black and white to the state's colors of blue and gold. Lastly, he obtained authorization for an increase in manpower from 3004 in 1967 to 3,524 and an authorized civilian employment from 377 to 560. He retired on June 25, 1975 residing in Troy with his wife, Josephine. He died on November 24, 1986.

WILLIAM G. CONNELIE – EIGHTH SUPERINTENDENT 1975 TO 1983

William G. Connelie, Assistant Chief Inspector of the New York City Police Department became the eighth Superintendent on July 2, 1975. He held the position until his resignation in July 1983. He was born November 23, 1920 in New York City. The 54-year-old Connelie was a 30-year veteran of the NY City Police Department and resided with his wife Marie in Queens. He was a navigator in the US Army Air Corp during WW II retiring as a Major from the US Army reserve. He was a graduate of John Jay College. The only thing positive during his regime was the appointment by him of competent staff to plan and successfully carry out the security of the 1980 Winter Olympics at Lake Placid, N.Y. The state police were otherwise stagnant during his tenure.

DONALD O. CHESWORTH – NINTH SUPERINTENDENT - 1983 TO 1986

On August 1, 1983, Governor Mario Cuomo appointed 42-year old Donald O. Chesworth Superintendent. He was born on September 15, 1941 in Independence, Missouri. A graduate from Graceland College in 1963, he earned a Law Degree from Yale Law School in 1966. He was a former FBI agent directing organized crime investigations in Monroe County, N.Y. Governor Cuomo's mandate was for Chesworth to change the troopers from a rural road patrol to a top investigative agency. Manpower at the time was made-up of 3,780 troopers and 586 civilian personnel. During his short tenure, he doubled the Organized Crime Task Force from 30 to 75, created a Hazardous Material Unit, initiated a Sobriety Checkpoint Program and a NY State "12 MOST WANTED" list. He re-instituted the mounted patrol unit and developed an auto theft unit, as well as a Print A Kid Program. In November1986, he returned to private law practice in Rochester, N.Y. His leadership revitalized a stagnant organization and provided tools and manpower to fight new age crime.

THOMAS A. CONSTANTINE – TENTH SUPERINTENDENT 1986 TO 1994

Thomas A. Constantine was born on December 23, 1938 in Buffalo, N.Y. enlisting in the State Police on January 2, 1962. He had been employed as an Erie County Deputy Sheriff for two years previous. In 1961, he met Trooper Patrick F. O'Reilly who convinced him to take the state police exam. They became lifelong friends. The rest is history. As a trooper, he was assigned at SP Wrights Corners. In 1966, he was promoted to the rank of Sergeant and assigned to the BCI. In 1971, he was promoted to the rank of Lieutenant and assigned to recruit training at the academy. From 1974 to 1978, he was assigned to the Organized Crime Task Force and promoted to the rank of Captain. He served as the Troop Commander at Troop G from 1978 to 1980 with the rank of Major, when he was appointed staff inspector in charge of employee relations. As Cornelius before him, he was an advocate of education and training. His educational background included graduation from Erie Community College, State University College at Buffalo and Nelson A. Rockefeller College of Public Affairs and Policy. He was appointed Superintendent on January 1987. Innovations during his tenure included:

Statewide Narcotics Control Units
Crime Analysis Unit
Child Abuse Unit
Saturation Speed Enforcement Program
Interpol Liaison Program
DWI Checkpoint
Henry F. Williams Homicide Seminar
1-800-CURB DWI program
Computer Crimes Unit
Consumer Product Tampering Program
On March 11, 1994, President William Clinton appointed Constantine to be administrator of the US Drug Enforcement Agency (DEA) overseeing a force of 7,000 special agents, a post he held until 1999.

In 1999, he became a professor at the Rockefeller College in Albany, N.Y. In May 2000, he accepted an appointment to serve as oversight commissioner of the Independent

Commission on Policing Northern Ireland. He is an active participant in law enforcement circles where his knowledge and innovative ideas are often sought.

BOOK XI — MISCELLANEOUS

Albert S. Kurek - NYSP Retired

HEART AND HOOF BEATS

A crabbed gentleman
Was Shadrach McJunk.
He sneered at the troopers
And called their work bunk.

Said he. Let the sheriff
And the constable do.
The work of these fellows.
By gad! The wars through.

When Shadrack one morning
Awakened from slumber.
He found that some yeggmen
Had got his safes number.

He summoned the constable
Quick as he could.
But got this reply
He's away choppin wood.

He then phoned the sheriff
But learned with dismay.
This guardian of order
Was likewise away.

Now, ------ every trooper
The countryside round.
Leaves word with the central
Where he may be found.

I'll try em, said Shadrack
But wrath filled his soul.
When he learned oe'r the phone
They were out on patrol.

But, two men in gray
Dropped in later to tell.
They'd found all the loot
And, yeggmen as well.

George F. Kenyon
Troop A, 1921

PITY THE POOR TROOPER

If he' neat, He's conceited
If he' careless, He's a bum
If he's pleasant, He's a flirt
If he's brief, He's a grouch
If he hurries, He overlooks things
If he takes his time, He's lazy
If you got pinched, He had in for you
If he passes you, He's easy
If he's energetic, He's trying to make a record
If he's deliberate, He's too slow to make a record
If you strike him, He's a coward
If he strikes you, He's a bully
If he outwits you, He's a sneak
If you see him first, He's a bonehead
If he makes a good catch, He's lucky
If he misses it, He's a chump
If he gets promoted, He's got pull
If he doesn't ---- oh what's the use?

Trooper F.C. Cuddy, Troop T - 1965

ODE TO A TROOPER

A lawman of a special kind
Robust, ready and refined
Takes assignments in his stride
In keeping order he takes pride
Renders service unexcelled
Gets decisive when compelled
Ten foot tall at fairs and fires
Guards at wrecks and fallen wires
When the trains get off the track
He stands by till they get back
A sympathetic friend to all
Ready for to your call.

(James P. Kenny, Rochester, N.Y.- 1967)

McMORROW'S POEM

Danny Escobedo, the celebrated defendant in the 1966 Supreme Court decision restricting police interrogation of criminal suspects was given a prominent place in the office of Erie County, N.Y. Assistant District attorney Michael J. McMorrow. He wrote the following poem bringing "dignity to gangdom" and "status to the hood".

You no longer need a mouthpiece
If you button up your lip
To the golden day a dawning
Sing your praises loud and strong

In this lovely Age of License
Nothing's naughty; Nothing's wrong
Danny-boy, the thing you started
Must constrain the court's in time

Danny boy, you've nobly done it
And you've wrapped it up so good
You brought dignity to Gangdom
You gave status to the hood

Never more will stupid copper
Flash his silly little tin
When he stumbles on a strongbox
Or a load of hijacked gin

Now he's humble, now he's docile
As befits his proper state
Since Earl Warren joined the "Vultures"
And removed the big house gate

Since our rights – at – law are grounded
Let us heist and mug and shoot
Let us use the Black Maria's
To transport our growing loot

All the time we've spent at "show-ups"
Every quizzing! Every tear!
Gladly gone but not forgotten
Through the mist of yesteryear

New horizons beckon onward
For the rapist, yegg or dip
To the logical conclusion
That there just ain't any crime

May you live with love and laughter
You can wager all you're worth
That your gangster pals will bless you
For this heaven here on earth

(Buffalo Courier Express 8/7/66)

DEDICATED TO THE MEMORY OF
CORPORAL A. M. DIFFENDALE

He was taken away in "51
Doing his job as it should be done
Riding patrol o'er hill and dale
Our gallant chum, Al Diffendale.
Ever alert to watch for crime
A regular trooper honest and fine
A task was there and it must be done
No thought of fear in that stout one.

Under the blue of a June day sky
A cattle truck went swiftly by
Young Diff gave chase
And flagged him down
On a rural road outside a rural town.

Without a warning this summer day
A coward's shot took life away
A life God's will has taken back
All honors to the Grey and Black.

We grieve for loved one's left behind.
And know they will God's comfort find
Their adore done waits beyond the pale
All honors to our Diffendale.

(On June 14, 1951, Corporal Arthur Diffendale was shot and killed by cattle rustler Matthew L. Armer near the City of Oneonta, N.Y. Armer was arrested, convicted and sentenced to 60 years imprisonment at Attica State Prison.)

Composed by Corporal Clayton E. Bailey
SP Dryden – 1951

RANK DEFINITION

SUPERINTENDENT
Leaps tall buildings with a single bound
Is more powerful than a locomotive
Is faster than a speeding bullet
Walks on water
Gives policy to God

DEPUTY SUPERINTENDENT
Leaps short buildings with a single bound
Is more powerful than a switch engine
Is just as fast as a speeding bullet
Walks on water if the sea is calm
Talks to God

INSPECTOR
Leaps short buildings with a running start and favorable winds
Is almost as powerful as a switch engine
Is faster than a speeding B-B
Walks on water in indoor swimming pools
Talks with God if memo is approved

MAJOR
Barely clears a quonset hut
Loses tug of war with a locomotive
Can fire a speeding bullet
Swims well
Is occasionally addressed y God

CAPTAIN
Makes high marks when trying to leap tall buildings
Is frequently run over by a locomotive
Can sometimes handle a gun without inflicting self-injury
Dog paddles
Talks to animals

LIEUTENANT
Runs into buildings
Recognizes locomotive two out of three times
Is not issued ammunition
Can stay afloat if properly instructed in use of the Mae West
Talks to walls

SERGEANT
Falls over doorstep when trying to enter building
Says, Look at the choo choo
Wets himself with a water pistol
Plays in mud puddles
Mumbles to himself

TROOPER
Lifts buildings and walks under them
Kicks locomotives off the track
Catches speeding bullets with his teeth and eats them
Freezes water with a single glance
He is God

Author Unknown

YOU MIGHT BE A COP IF:

You have ever restrained someone and it was not a sexual experience.
Your idea of a good time is a robbery at shift change.
You find humor in other people's stupidity.
You refer to your nightstick as your "Dork Slayer".
You believe that "too stupid to live" should be a valid jury verdict.
You have had to put a complainant on hold, while you laugh uncontrollably.
The bigger they are, the harder they fall. Also the harder they punch, kick and choke.
If you park your patrol car in the exact center of the Gobi desert, within 5 minutes someone will pull up and ask for direction.
Glow in the dark sights are just as visible to you as they are to the crook hiding behind you.
The oldest squad car won't be retired. It will be assigned to you.
Flashlight batteries never die in the daylight hours.
Your mouthiest traffic violator will be related to the sheriff.
If the crooks are within pistol range, so are you.
The speed you respond to a fight in progress is inversely proportional to how long you have been an officer.
Perfect 10's only show up to talk when you are busy.
Bulletproof vests might be.
NCIC will be down anytime you see a car listed on a hot sheet.
Your bulletproof vest was supplied by the lowest bidder.
Do unto others, but do it first.
Freebees will only arrive at the station on your days off.
You are ALWAYS downwind from pepper spray.
To err is human, just do it in front of as few people as possible.
Anyone that flirts with you on-duty won't even recognize you off-duty.
The hardest job for a Hostage Negotiator is to negotiate with the crisis committee.
If your patrol car's air is out the suspect will smell worse than a wet dog.
If your raid is going well, you're at the wrong house.
The one time you cuss on the radio, your chief will be listening.

337

You will be decorated for stupidity, and busted for brilliant work.

Field experience is something you don't get until just after you need it.

The only thing more accurate than incoming enemy fire is incoming friendly fire.

You will only talk bad about another officer when they are standing behind you.

After all is said and done, a hell of a lot more is said than done.

You will only get a citizen complaint when your video camera or tape recorder is broken

For every good deed done there is a Lawyer to undo it.

Out of 10 traffic stops, the violator you gave a warning to instead of a cite is the one who file a personnel complaint against you.

After taking a sign language course, you use sign to a deaf driver and citizens call the station to complain about seeing you doing strange things and touching yourself on a traffic stop.

Anyone opting for a foot chase is always carrying at least 20 pounds less than you are. Your time is always less important than the time of the judge and prosecutor.

No good deed goes unpunished.

Just when you get a nice brand new squad car, the first offender you pick up is going to be a drunk that will get sick in the car.

There is a code of silence in law enforcement. Until Internal Affairs, the news media, and lawyers get involved.

(TEXAS POLICE CENTRAL.COM)

DIVISION MANPOWER CHART

YEAR	ACTUAL MANPOWER AT END OF EACH YEAR		
1940 Pre war	900 Troopers		
1944 War years	450 Troopers		
1947	650 Troopers		
1950	759 Troopers		
1955	1254 Troopers		
1958	1407 Troopers		
1961	1719 Troopers	171	Civilians
1962	2379 Troopers	227	Civilians
1966	2822 Troopers		
1969	3271 Troopers	501	Civilians
1974	3524 Troopers	559	
1985	3589 Troopers	726	

BOOK XII — ROSTERS AND CHARTS

TROOP "A" MANPOWER COMPARISON

	1917	1920	1924	1928	1936	1940	1947
CAPTAIN	1	1	1	1	1	1	1
LT. SUPERVISOR	0	0	0	0	1	1	1
LIEUTENANT	1	1	1	1	1	1	1
FIRST SEREGEANT	1	1	1	1	1	1	1
TROOP CLERK	0	1	1	1	1	1	1
DUTY SERGEANT	4	4	7	10	16	16	16
DUTY CORPORAL	4	4	8	11	13	13	13
BLACKSMITH	1	1	1	1	0	0	0
SADDLER	1	1	1	1	0	0	0
PRIVATES	45	45	56	65	75	84	91
TOTAL	58	59	78	95	111	120	127

1947 TROOP "A" ROSTER AND TROOP SHIELD ID NUMBER

TROOP COMMANDER – JOSEPH B. LYNCH
INSPECTOR -   HAROLD L. KEMP
LIEUTENANT -   GRAYFORD R. SMITH
LIEUTENANT -   GERALD T. WOOLSEY
LIEUTENANT -   WILLIAM M. STEVENSON

TROOP "A" SHIELD

NUMBER	NAME	STATION
1	F/SGT. C.E. COBB	BATAVIA
2	T/SGT. G.L. WHITE	BATAVIA
3	SGT. L.C. BENWAY	BATAVIA
4	SGT. O. LAZEROFF	HENRIETTA
5	SGT. D.S. GIRVEN	SILVER CREEK
6	SGT. HARRY ADAMS	GAINES
7	SGT. G.S. WOOD	BATAVIA
8	SGT. V.R. VOIGHT	WAYLAND
9	SGT. S.N. SMITH	ALLEGANY
10	SGT. R.F. WALTER	ATHOL SPRINGS
11	SGT. T.F. MARTIN	WELLSVILLE
12	SGT. J.D. KRICK	
13	SGT. N.H. LIPPERT	
14	SGT. E.L. BROUGHTON	PAINTED POST
15	SGT. H.L. DEBRINE	LEWISTON
16	CPL. R.F. LEMAY	BATAVIA
17	CPL. R.A. GIBSON	CHAUTAUQUA
18	CPL. A.L. RICH	ALLEGANY
19	CPL. C.A. STEPHENS	EAST AVON
20	CPL. E.F. ANDERSON	HENRIETTA
21	CPL. J.J. CHAMBERS	CLARENCE
22	CPL. A.E. NELSON	
23	CPL. H.J. ASHE	
24	CPL. K.E WEIDENBORNER	
25	CPL. A.F. BILY	WELLSVILLE
26	CPL. A.E. WRIGHT	WESTFIELD
27	CPL. A.S. HORTON	DARIEN
28	CPL. C.J. PASTO	BATAVIA
29	TPR. H.M. ELLSWORTH	

30	TPR. F.A. LACHNICHT	BATAVIA
31	TPR. G.J. SCHUSLER	HENRIETTA
32	TPR. HARVEY GREGG	ATHOL SPRINGS
33	TPR. W.A. RIMMER	
34	TPR. K.W. HEMMER	
35	TPR. F.J. DRISCOLL	ATHOL SPRINGS
36	TPR. J.D. KIRWAN	
37	TPR. J.G. McDONALD	BATAVIA
38	TPR. F.A. EASTON	
39	TPR. C.W. JERMY	
40	TPR. J.W. LAWRENCE	
41	TPR. E. KNATT	
43	TPR. G.W. HAMM	
44	TPR. R.C. FITZWATER	EAST AVON
45	TPR. E. REDDEN	NORTH HORNELL
46	TPR. L.A. MELLODY	
47	TPR. T.E. NULTY	
48	TPR. H.E. BOSS	
49	TPR. A.C. FISHER	
50	TPR. J.D. PECK	BLAKELY CORNERS
51	TPR. E.B. WOODWARD	
53	TPR. H.I. MOOSE	
54	TPR. C.L. RICHMOND	
55	TPR. C.L. McCARTNEY	
56	TPR. H.E. KUNOW	
57	TPR. J.D. FENNEL	
58	TPR. J.F. ROWE	WEBSTER
60	TPR. D.J. LIBERA	
61	TPR. M. ANDREWS	BATAVIA
62	TPR. W.E. EBEL	
63	TPR. H.D. SMITH	
64	TPR. G.V. DELANEY	
65	TPR. J.N. SAGE	CLARKSON
66	TPR. R.E. BAILEY	
67	TPR. L.C. NORSEN	
68	TPR. H.F. ELLINGER	
69	TPR. J.H. SHAVER	
70	TPR. C.E. BUKOWSKI	N. TONAWANDA
71	TPR. M.B. GRANT	FRANKLINVILLE
72	TPR. R.A. BRECHT	
73	TPR. J.H. THOMPSON	SILVER CREEK

75	TPR. G.R. COVENY	
77	TPR. M.C. WOOD	
78	TPR. C.A. JORGENSEN	
81	TPR. J.C. MURPHY	
82	TPR. J.S. COLE	
84	TPR. R.F. TILLMAN	
87	TPR. C.L. WATKINS	CASTILE
96	SGT. C.H. LEE	WESTFIELD
97	SGT. M.L. FORT	LEWISTON
107	TPR. C.P. SCHARETT	CLARKSON
109	TPR. J.J. MOULTHROP	
110	TPR. L.D. McCall	
117	SGT. E.J. DOODY	CLARENCE
118	CPL. H.E. HACKETT	CLARKSON
H18	SGT. C.Z. McDONALD	
H19	SGT. P.K. LEITNER	
H20	SGT. J.L. LONG	

TROOP "A" ROSTER SEPTEMBER 1952

Troop Commander – Joseph B. Lynch

ERIE COUNTY

Athol Springs
Lt. F.P. Dwyer
Sgt. N.H. Lippert
Tpr. R.P. Lansill
Tpr. R.G. Dennis
Tpr. J.V. Damiano
Tpr. R.J. Conway
Tpr. D.M. Stahrr
Tpr. H.F. Williams
Tpr. R.T. Powell
BCI
Sgt. R.F. Walter
Cpl. F.J. Driscoll

Blakeley Corners
Sgt. J.D. Peck
Tpr. D.P. Studd

Clarence
Cpl. H.D. Smith
Tpr. E.J. Close
BCI
Sgt. J.J. Chambers

CHAUTAUQUA COUNTY

Westfield
Sgt. C.H. Lee
Tpr. H.M. Ellsworth
Tpr. C.J. Henderson
Tpr. J.T. Allen
Tpr. D.P. Jackson
BCI
Tpr. K.W. Hemmer
Tpr. N.J. Wolf

Silver Creek
Tpr. R.F. Klein
Tpr. M.D. Gavin
BCI
Sgt. K.E. Weidenborner

Chautauqua
Cpl. R.A. Gibson

NIAGARA COUNTY

Lewiston
Sgt. A.S. Horton
Tpr. J.L. Hill
Tpr. R.J. Curry
Tpr. R.V. Spring
Tpr. M.J. Fiordo
Tpr. D.L. Smith
Tpr. C. Schwarzenholzer
Tpr. C.F. Ogledzinski

Newfane
Tpr. E.S. Pawlak
Tpr. F.E. Demler
BCI
Tpr. C.E. Bukowski

GENESEE COUNTY
Batavia
F/Sgt. C.E. Cobb
Cpl. T.E. Nulty
Tpr. J.C. Moochler
Tpr. C.E. Richmond
Darien Center
Tpr. C.L. Watkins
Tpr. C.J. Chwala

BCI
Sgt. G.S. Wood
Sgt. C.J. Pasto
Sgt. E.F. Anderson

LIVINGSTON COUNTY
East Avon
Lt. C.O. Mink
Cpl. Harvey Gregg
Tpr. R.D. Koenig
Tpr. J.W. Lawrence
Tpr. P.H. Beck

Tpr. C.A. Salmon
Tpr. R.E. Minekheim
Tpr. W.E. Frarey
BCI
Sgt. C.A. Stephens

MONROE COUNTY
Henrietta
Sgt. H.E. Hackett
Tpr. E.F. Ver Wiebe
Tpr. T.E. Caulfield
Tpr. W.J. White

Tpr. F.A. Lasher
Tpr. J.H. Keller
BCI
Tpr. M.B. Grant

Clarkson
Sgt. D.S. Girven
Cpl. L.C. Norsen
Tpr. R.W. Hain
Tpr. J.J. Ritter
Tpr. W.F. Peterson

Tpr. E.F. Kwiecen
BCI
Tpr. C.P. Scharett

Webster
Tpr. R.E. Bailey
Tpr. K.J. Hulbert

Orleans County
Albion
Cpl. J.N. Sage
Tpr. L.J. Murphy

STEUBEN COUNTY
Painted Post

Sgt. M.L. Fort

Tpr. C.R. Swarts

Tpr. L.F. Taggart

Tpr. G.R. Coveney

Tpr. E.P. Longhany

BCI

Tpr. J.J. Moulthrop

Wayland

Cpl. J.G. McDonald

Tpr. E.D. Nearing

Tpr. N.E. Minklein

BCI

Cpl. R.C. Fitzwater

North Hornell

Tpr. J.H. Shaver

Tpr. R.E. Powers

ALLEGANY COUNTY
Wellsville

Lt. R.T. Barber

Sgt. H.J. Ashe

Tpr. R.J. Wullich

Tpr. L.D. Mills

Tpr. R.C. Hastings

Tpr. J.C. Murphy

Tpr. V.J. Pleakis

BCI

Tpr. L.D. MacCall

WYOMING COUNTY
Castile

Cpl. F.C. Hoffmann

Tpr. H.A. Dornsife

Tpr. E.J. Fechter

Tpr. A.C. Fisher

Tpr. W.F. Eustice

CATTARAUGUS COUNTY
Allegany

Tpr. D.C. Wasmer

Tpr. R.H. Goundry

Tpr. T.E. Nelson

Tpr. R.P. Slade

Tpr. William Fox

BCI

Cpl. Eugene Redden

Randolph

Tpr. H.E. Kunow

Tpr. C.R. Jackson

Franklinville

Tpr. T.E. Reilly

Tpr. J.P. Heilig

BCI Batavia
Inspector H.M. DeHollander
Tpr. G.F. Brady
Tpr. Montagu Andrews – Fingerprint/Photography

Detached at Albany   Detached at New York City
Cpl. G.J. Schusler   Sgt. A.E. Wright
Tpr. C.L. Macartney

TRAFFIC AND PUBLIC ASSEMBLY

Headqaurters Desk	Sgt. P.K. Leitner	Sgt. C.Z. McDonald
	Tpr. J. Stickney	
Communications	Tpr. J. Rowe	
Sgt. J.E. Long	Tpr. H. I. Moose	
	Tpr. D.C. Wasmer	
Troop Clerk	Tpr. Rigley	
Sgt. R. Brecht	Tpr. Simon	
Tpr. Spielberger	Tpr. J. D. Steinmetz	
Tpr. Polakiewucz	Tpr. J.G. Strunk	

1952 STATE POLICE SALARIES

TROOPER
1st Yr. 2752.80
Maximum 7th Yr. 4270.08

TROOPER BCI
1st Yr. 2370.00
Maximum 7th Yr. 4652.88

CORPORAL
1st Yr. 3987.04
Maximum 6th Yr. 4659.84

CORPORAL BCI
Minimum 4369.84
Maximum 5035.04

TROOP CLERK 4909.05

SERGEANT
& T/SERGEANT 4972.61

BCI SERGEANT
& T/SERGEANT 5347.16

1ST SERGEANT 5541.25

LIEUTENANTS & STAFF SGTS. 6165.50

BCI LIEUTENANT 6540.05

INSPECTOR 6914.60

CAPTAIN 8117.70

TRAFFIC INSPECTOR 6664.90

STAFF INSPECTOR 7659.16

EXECUTIVE OFFICER 8356.05

DEPUTY CHIEF INSPECTOR 8373.07

CHIEF INSPECTOR 9685.13

DEPUTY SUPERINTENDENT 11,335.42

SUPERINTENDENT 15,310.00

CLERKS
1ST Yr. 2180.40
Maximum 6 yrs. 2984.80

STEWARD 3518.40

ASSISTANT STEWARD 2180.40

LABORER 2044.12

(THE ANNUAL SALARIES WERE EFFECTIVE APRIL 1, 1952)

1961 STATE POLICE SALARIES

Superintendent	$27,000.00
1st Deputy Superintendent	17,850.00
Deputy Superintendent	13,815.00
Assistant Superintendent	11,869.00
Chief Inspector	14,425.00
Deputy Chief Inspector	12,755.00
Captain Executive Officer	13,050.00
Captain Troop & Traffic	12,785.00
S/Sgts. & Chief Tech. Sgt.	9,310.00
First Sergeant	9,310.00
Sgts. & Tech. Sgts.	8,545.00
Corporals	6,960.00 to 7,560.00
Troopers	5,200.00 to 7,000.00
Senior Investigator (Sgt)	9,263.00
Investigator (Cpl)	8,467.00
Investigator (Tpr)	7,879.00

With the increase in salary, the per diem allowance was eliminated. Necessary expenses for a trooper compelled to work outside his regular work area would be allowed.

On April 1, 1964, the Westfield and Silver Creek trooper stations were closed with their consolidation at the Fredonia Barracks, 273 East Main St., Fredonia, N.Y. The station under the command of Lieutenant Robert E. Powers was now assigned an additional ten patrol troopers, ten thruway troopers and four BCI men with no disruption of services.

1974 STATE POLICE SALARIES

Training Rate	11,090
At Graduation	11,557
Trooper	12,089
Maximum	13,994
Corporal	14,154
Maximum	15,844
Sergeant	15,363
Maximum	16,213
Z/Sergeant	15,855
Maximum	16,705
F/sergeant	17,408
Maximum	18,258
Investigator	16,119
Maximum	17,028
Senior Investigator	8,384
Maximum	19,292
Lieutenant	20,904
Captain	22,349
Inspectors	23,957
Majors	25,515
Deputy Chief Inspector	26,301
Chief Inspector	30,329
Asst. Deputy Superintendent	27,932
Deputy Superintendent	35,493
First Deputy Superintendent	38,024
Counsel	28,652

1975 TROOP "A" ROSTER

BATAVIA HQ.
TROOP COMMANDER - MAJOR ARNOLD L. BARDOSSI

UNIFORM CAPTAINS

ANTHONY T. MALOVICH	ROBERT F. KILFEATHER	GEORGE R. TORDY

BCI CAPTAIN
FREDERICK J. PENFOLD

BCI LIEUTENANT
RAYMOND P. SLADE

FIRST SERGEANT
VERNON J. CLAYSON

DESK SERGEANT
RICHARD C. HASTINGS

COMMUNICATIONS SERGEANT
GERALD G. LAW

TROOPERS

GERALD M. BROSKA	JOHN J. CICCONE	ROGER GIUSEPPETTI
GEORGE A. HYDER	GERALD M. KALISZ	

CIVILIAN DISPATCHERS

CARL BARONE	HOWARD C. HARTMAN	HOWARD L. BIGHAM
DAVID VESHIA	JOHN P. PRIOLO	JERALD H. SCHLAGENHAUF
JAMES E. LITTLE	MARIE A. FECHNER	NANCY LUDWIG
NANCY BUTLER	ELIZABETH O. BUCKOUT	

BLOODHOUNDS
LEON J. DYWINSKI

TRAFFIC SECTION SERGEANT
WALTER C. PURTELL

TROOP SAFETY OFFICER
DONALD F. KOZLOWSKI

**MOTOR VEHICLE
INSPECTION DETAIL**
SERGEANT WILLIAM F.
STUBBINS

TROOPERS

JOSEPH W. BARRETT	MILFORD J. CLAYSON	DONALD P. DWYER
FRANK E. ENGBLOOM	GERALD J. FENCLAU	RAYMOND M. KRON
MATTHEW R. MESI	DANIEL W. O'BRIEN	SCOTT C. SAUNDERS

**HEADQUARTERS BCI
DETAIL**

JAMES L. DUVAL	JOHN N. BARNHART	DONALD J. MUNCH
LLOYD A. SCHWAB	LEONARD P. BOCHYNSKI	NORMAN J. BIRNER
RICHARD J. CRYAN	FRANK E. DEMLER	RICHARD J. FLIS
GERALD R. FORSTER	DON T. FUHRMAN	AMADOR P. ORTIZ
JOHN D. STEINMETZ	KENNETH J. TROIDL	GERALD C. WEISS

IDENTIFICATION SECTION
RAYMOND H. MOTYKA   THOMAS G. RASH

SPECIAL ASSIGNMENT
RICHARD T. JANORA   JAMES A. YOUNG

**RANGE DETAIL –
FIREARMS INSTRUCTORS**

LEON J. DYWINSKI	NICHOLAS L. GUMHALTER	ROBERT C. HARLOCK
GEORGE A. HYDER	RICHARD T. JANORA	LOUIS P. MACRI
FREDERICK A. PORCELLO	PAUL W. STEVENS	CHARLES VAN EPPS

QUALIFIED SCUBA DIVERS

PAUL D. CAMPANELLA	WILLIAM ERNST	THOMAS J. PALUCH
WILLIAM A. REYNOLDS	MICHAEL T. WRIGHT	

CIVILIAN STAFF

PRINCIPAL CLERK
HAZEL MONAGHAN
DEPUTY PRINCIPAL CLERK
FAYE PRIDMORE

AAMI (TROOP FLEET)
CASTLE B. SMITH   WILLIAM JOYCE

QUARTERMASTER
STANLEY F. SOCHALEC   WARREN C. HOPKINS

BCI STENOGRAPHERS
LANA CUMMINGS   CHERYL SUNDOWN
DOROTHY CHASE   BERNETTA McDONALD   JACKIE FOSTER

IDENTIFICATION CLERK
BARBARA SHEPHERD

TRAFFIC SECRETARIES
TONIE BRAY   MARGARET JONES

RECORDS CLERKS
DONNA SEAMANS   KATHRYN STADING   BRENDA McCOY

**FRONT DESK
RECEPTIONIST**
DOROTHY MANAHAN   MABEL KEISTER

FIRST SERGEANTS OFFICE
LINDA BEEMAN

MAJORS SECRETARIES
DOROTHY RING   NANCY SMITH
MAINTENANCE
LESTER COOPER   VERONICA CHILANO   BERT BRIGGS
RUSSELL CHILANO

ZONE #1 – 5381 MILITARY ROAD, LEWISTON, N.Y. 14092

LIEUTENANT
GEORGE K. ELBEL

ZONE SERGEANTS
GEORGE R. CONVERY   THOMAS C. SMITH   CHARLES R. SWARTS

SERGENTS
GARY D. BUTT   PATRICK F. O'REILLY

TROOPERS
THOMAS M. CAMPBELL   DALE L. COURCY   DOUGLAS A. COWELL
JAMES E. FARRELL   HOWARD F. GABRIEL   ROBERT A. HAMILTON

DAVID W. KENNEDY	GEORGE E. MACK	GORDON J. MASKA
DARL D. McCOY	LAWRENCE McMICKING	WILLIAM V. MINSTERMAN
RODERICK F. O'DONNELL	FRANK J. PANZA	GERALD A. WARREN
EDWARD V. WISNIEWSKI		

BCI MEMBERS

HAROLD L. EICHORST	WILLIAM G. GETHOEFER	EDWARD J. GLUCH
JAMES A. KOSTECKI	MICHAEL G. O'ROURKE	PATRICK J. PETRIE

INTERSTATE 190 & GRAND ISLAND DETAIL

SERGEANT-   JOHN J. DOLPHIN

TROOPERS

DAVID B. CULVERWELL	JOHN E. FECHNER	THOMAS E. GREGSON
JOHN J. KELLY		

WRIGHTS CORNERS – 6424 RIDGE ROAD, LOCKPORT, N.Y. 14094

SERGEANT

JAMES J. KASPRZAK

TROOPERS

ALFRED R. ASTON	LEONARD J. BARON	FRANKLIN J. BRITT
THOMAS E. FLECHSENHAAR	RICHARD W. GUNKLE	DOUGLAS W. HEDGES
JAMES H. KNOTT	RICHARD T. KUREK	GARY J. MAJOR
RONALD R. MALCARNE	RONALD D. MOLZEN	THOMAS J. PALUCH
DONALD F. PRICE	RAYMOND E. SCHILLING	RONALD G. SPINK
ERWIN G. WATT	ROBERT B. WOJEWODA	

RADAR

ROBERT A. BAKER	JAMES R. MITTELSTAEDT

BCI MEMBERS

ROBERT M. BARRUS	RALPH D. FULLER	WILLIAM J. TUMULTY

ALBION – 13968 MILLION-DOLLAR HIGHWAY, ALBION, N.Y. 14411

SERGEANT　　　　　　　　NORMAN R. WRIGHT

TROOPERS

GEORGE R. BERGER	ROBERT J. GADSBY	DANIEL E. GEIGER
ALLAN H. JONES	DONALD E. KLEIN	PAUL F. KULNISZEWSKI
RICHARD W. METZ	KENNETH O. MUREK	JAMES L. NASHWENTER
JOHN H. REUTER	TERRENCE D. RODLAND	

BATAVIA HEADQUARTERS PATROL

SERGEANTS　　　　　　　WARDEN K. BARROWS　　　WILLIAM F. MULRYAN

TROOPERS

BRUCE M. BUTTLES	PHILLIP E. CARROLL	LEONARD F. DAYKA
GEORGE A. GLATT	ROBERT F. HUMMEL	ALBERT S. KUREK
LOUIS J. LANG	RICHARD D. LATHAN	JAMES R. LOBUR
PAUL A. LUKASIEWICZ	DOUGLAS E. RUE	MICHAEL H. SCHRADER
WILLIAM F. SOBOLEWSKI	JAMES R. STEPHENS	LOUIS P. STEVERESON
MICHAEL T. WRIGHT		

RADAR　　　　　　　　　FREDERICK R. WALSH

SCALES　　　　　　　　WILLIAM F. LOFT　　　　　ROBERT C. SCOTT

BCI MEMBERS

DONALD L. SMITH	JOHN W. HERITAGE	THEODORE J. GEORGITSO
HENRY W. HAAS	JAMES R. HOFMANN	THOMAS W. KENNEDY
ORVAL E. SMITH	FREEMAN R. SHAW	WARREN TERRYBERRY

ZONE # 2 – S-3544 SOUTHWESTERN BOULEVARD, ORCHARD PARK, N.Y. 14127

LIEUTENANT   JOSEPH M. ABATE

ZONE SERGEANTS
RAYMOND R. BENSON   KENNETH E. GELLART   STANLEY J. PAQUADECK

SERGEANTS
VICTOR E. BARON   JOSEPH B. KONTRABECKI   LEE A. PATTISON
EDWARD V. QUALEY

TROOPERS
JOHN T. ALLEN   PAUL J. BIGELOW   WILLIAM K. BLACK
ARTHUR R. BUCZKOWSKI   PAUL D. CAMPANELLA   SHANE M. DEVLIN
STEPHEN L. DOMANSKI   ROBERT E. DOSSINGER   ROBERT N. FELDMAN
DAVID J. GROBLEWSKI   NICHOLAS L. GUMHALTER   JAMES E. HALL
PAUL HENNIGAN   WILLIAM J. HUBERT   KENNETH D. KELLOGG
GERALD M. KIRKPATRICK   JOSEPH J. KWIATEK   JOSEPH L. LENIHAN
LOUIS P. MACRI   PATRICK A. MALINOWSKI   JOSEPH C. MULLINS
THOMAS J. SCHULTZ   ALBERT D. SIMMONS   DENNIS L. STEFANIAK
RICHARD E. STEGER   CALVIN J. TRESCH   GREGORY B. WILDRIDGE
PAUL R. WISE

RADAR   EUGENE J. DOMZALSKI   JEROME A. HUBERT

SCALES   ROBERT J. FISHER   RICHARD C. WARD

BCI DETAIL
NORMAN E. MINKLEIN   WILLIAM J. COOLEY   ROBERT B. EARL
GEORGE E. KARALUS   RICHARD C. LEWANDOWSKI   RICHARD B. OLMA
STANLEY F. PAWELEK   MICHAEL J. POLEON   JACOB D. WILLIAMS

CLARENCE – 10189 MAIN STREET, CLARENCE, N.Y. 14031

SERGEANTS

KEVIN J. ENSER	RICHARD F. HENDRICKS	ROBERT J. SZYMANSKI
LEO A. KLISZAK		

TROOPERS

GEORGE A. BERGER	THOMAS BLAJSZCZAK	THOMAS A. BOWMAN
JEROME R. BRAKEFIELD	GEORGE W. BROWN	DAVID D. DOMON
WILLIAM ERNST	THOMAS J. FULTON	CHARLES C. GIBBS
RONALD L. HADSALL	ERIC W. HAMMERSCHMIDT	ROBERT C. HARLOCK
ROBERT F. KELLY	RICHARD G. SCHILLING	ARTHUR L. TAGGART
JAMES E. WILSON	WILLIAM J. WOODS	

INTERSTATE 290 & KENSINGTON EXPRESSWAY PATROL

PHILIP E. ATTEA	ANTHONY J. BIANCHI	JAMES A. CEFERATTI
WALTER H. HERBAR	TTHOMAS J. KENNY	DENNIS C. SULLIVAN

BCI MEMBERS

EUGENE J. FECHTER	MILTON C. BARTLETT	HARRY C. LOGAN
RICHARD F. MANNS	GEORGE McCOLLUM	DEWEY E. ROHL
JOHN B. RUSSELL		

WARSAW – ROUTE 19 & BUFFALO, ROAD, WARSAW, N.Y 14569

SERGEANT   BART J. STACK

TROOPERS

WILLIAM H. CRANSTON	LARRY P. FRANCIS	DENNIS G. GARRY
WATSON D. HARTWAY	MARTIN F. HOCKEY	JOHN G. HOLLANDER
PAUL R. MAKSON	DOUGLAS G. MILLER	GARY F. WILKERSON
FRANK E. ZDINSKI		

ZONE # 3 – ROUTE 394, FALCONER, N.Y. 14733

LIEUTENANT   RONALD A. BUTTERFIELD

ZONE SERGEANTS
HERBERT E. JOHNSON   PETER M. NIELSEN   ALBERT S. WHALEY

SERGEANTS   GARY W. KNIGHT   DAVID L. SNYDER

TROOPERS
GAIL C. BENTLEY   ERTIS J. BRADLEY   TIMOTHY E. CHASE
BRIAN L. CHENEY   DANIEL J. CONLAN   DANIEL J. DELMONTE
JOHN C. MEYERS   JOHN M. MURRAY   REINOLD H. NELSON
DONALD O. NORDINE   PETER ROUGHEAD   GARY W. ROWE
JAMES E. SMOCZYNSKI   CHARLES W. VAN EPPS   JACK L. VAN ZILE

RADAR   JEFFREY R. GUSTAFSON   RICHARD E. STEINBACH

ROUTE # 17 EXPRESSWAY DETAIL
ROBERT C. BECKER   THOMAS M. MATECKI

BCI DETAIL
ROBERT E. BURNS   DAVIL L. CARR   JOHN B. CORNELL
JAMES V. BURNS   PHILIP F. TRAPANI

FREDONIA – 10274 ROUTE #60, FREDONIA, N.Y. 14063

SERGEANTS

PAUL D. HARRINGTON	RAYNER J. CURRY	ARTHUR F. PUROL

TROOPERS

DAVID J. BAKER	JOHN P. BALON	DONALD W. BLUMAN
ELMER J. HAAS JR.	ALBERT M. HAPPELL	HARRY B. KOWAL
CLIFFORD C. LEE	JOHN E. LONG	JAMES W. MacCUBBIN
DANIEL F. McNAMARA	PETER B. MEYER	JACK A. MILLER
THOMAS J. O'BRIEN	KENNETH W. OLKOWSKI	DAVID M. SKRETNY
KENNETH F. SNYDER	TERRY E. SUTTON	DONALD P. TEFFT
LEON M. WINKOWSKI		

SCALES

	HERBERT B. ARCHER	RONALD J. KUCINSKI

BCI DETAIL

JOHN W. ANNA	THOMAS L. BUCK	TERRENCE D. FIEGL
LEONARD R. KWILOS	RICHARD K. LEROY	REGINALD P. PERRY

ZONE # 4 – ROUTE 17 & MILLER ROAD, WELLSVILLE, N.Y. 14895

LIEUTENANT   DOUGLAS O. PARR

ZONE SERGEANTS
FAY W. SCOTT   RICHARD E. HABERER   MERLE VAN SKIVER

SERGEANTS
LARRY J. GLASCOTT   ELTON B. INGALLS   JAN R. KETCHUM

TROOPERS
VICTOR E. BARON   DALE S. BUTTS   PHILIP M. CARLSON
PATRICK J. CONNELLY   JOHN J. COSGROVE   ROBERT L. ENOS
RICHARD L. FISHER   PAUL J. GONSKA   CLIFFORD E. GOOCH
JOHN E. HAYES   NOEL HERBERGER   GEORGE W. KNIGHT
ERNEST T. KOENIG   ROXIE G. MEYERS   DENNIS G. VESPUCCI

RADAR   ROBERT A. NITSCHE   PAUL W. STEVENS

SPECIAL POST # 31
STEWART S. MILLS   MICHAEL W. SCHROEDER   ALBERT J. TUTTLE

BCI DETAIL
CLARE R. JACKSON   ALLEN J. EMERSON   VINCENT L. EVANS
WILLIAM K. GOETSCHIUS   CHARLES J. McCOLE   DAVID M. O'BRIEN

ALLEGANY – 3224 WEST STATE ROAD, ALLEGANY, N.Y. 14706

SERGEANTS   RONALD W. MILLER   V. JOSEPH PLEAKIS

TROOPERS
EUGENE B. ADAMS   LAWRENCE L. AUSTIN   ROBERT G. BUBBS
DAVID C. GEE   HAROLD D. HATCH   STEWART E. HILL
JAMES B. JOHNSON   ROBERT E. JOHNSON   EDWARD G. KNOX
ROBERT E. MENTER   PATRICK E. MOONEY   JOHN M. POCKALNY
FREDERICK A. PORCELLO   WILLIAM A. REYNOLDS   JAMES E. ROWLEY
GREGORY R. SNYDER

BCI DETAIL
JOHN T. STOFER   ROBERT W. BROWNING   HENRY J. PANUS
ROBERT McGINTY

FRANKLINVILLE – NORTH MAIN STREET, FRANKLINVILLE, N.Y. 14737

SERGEANT   CHESTER J. CHWALA

TROOPERS
DOUGAL L. KEAR   CARL L. KLEIN   ALBERT P. LORENZ
BURTON C. MUSICK   RAYMOND J. O'BRIEN   RICHARD J. ROGERS
FRANK C. RYAN   NELSON R. WAITE

ARREST STATISTICS

YEAR	TRAFFIC ARRESTS	CRIMINAL ARRESTS	MILES PATROLLED
1945	44,858	4,690	9,049,143
1950	59,536	6,563	13,652,055
1955	101,356	3,935	27,806,962
1960	186,707	3,484	35,185,731
1965	432,701	19,003	47,472,150
1970	510,234	45,576	54,905,385
1975	554,278	64,573	58,179,141
1980	674,945	48,792	58,224,063
1984	650,857	61,582	62,867,517

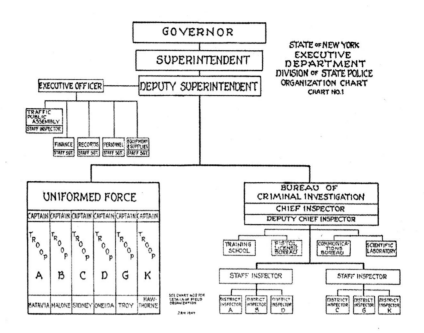

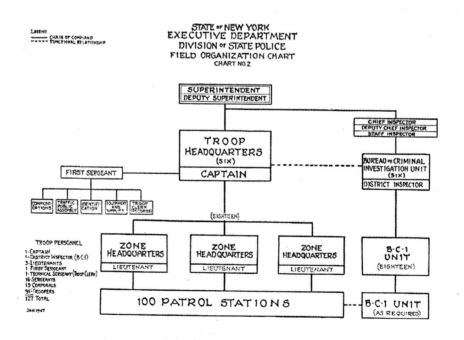

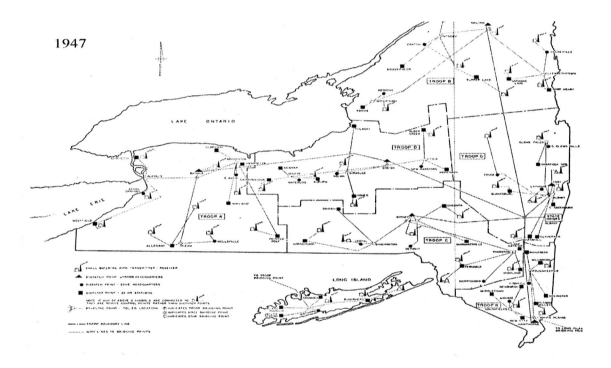

EXECUTIVE DEPARTMENT
DIVISION OF STATE POLICE
DIVISION HEADQUARTERS
ALBANY, NEW YORK

GENERAL ORDERS   May 19, 1955
M-18

Subject: Service Record Rating.

To: All Members of the Division.

1.   Effective June 1, 1955 and to remain in force until the
Rules and Regulations are ammended. Each man shall be rated on a
basis of actual performance of duty in accordance with his personnel
record. The rating shall be 20-80, each year of service represents
one point, up to a maximum of twenty points, eighty points represents
actual performance of duty which has not suffered any demerits during
a two year period. Each personnel rating shall begin at date of appointment or when promotional examination is taken and continue to
date for next examination for designated rank,

2.   Demerits are penalities for infractions detrimental to the
Division and shall not exceed more than five demerits for any single
infraction. Five demerits shall equal one point. Demerits may be in-
curred in greater weight through the Superintendent where charges are
filed against a member along with other disciplinary action. Any
member may appeal to the Superintendent in writing for a review of his
demerits where justification warrants. The Superintendent may designate an Officer of the Staff to represent him in such a review.
Service rating shall carry 50% weight, written examination 50% weight.

3.   Penalities for demerits may be applied for the following:
1- Disobedience to orders   11- Unfounded criticism of officials
2- Discourtesy   12- Failure to respond to duty
3- Uncleanliness   13- Disrespect to superiors
4- Profanity   14- Circulating erroneous reports
5- Improper wearing of uniform   15- Lack of punctuality
6- Negligent wearing of uniform   16- Refusing to accept
7- Negligent care of uniform   responsibility
8- Negligent smoking in uniform   17- Intoxication
9- Negligent report writing   18- Failure to carry badge
10- Unfounded criticism of   19- Failure to keep revolver clean
    superiors   20- Making false entry in blotter

4.   Demerits may be given for improper operation of
installations:
1- Failure to light sign
2- Failure to keep quarters clean and orderly
3- Failure to keep blotter in order
4- Failure to keep teletype and telephone messages in order
5- Failure to keep radio records in order

Service Record Rating   -2-   May 19, 1955

6- Failure to keep station equipment in order
7- Failure to safe guard firearms
8- Failure to safe guard evidence
9- Failure to keep prisoners under surveillance
10- Failure to send reports as required
11- Misuse of telephone
12- Misuse of teletype machines
13- Misuse of radio equipment
14- Permitting lascivious pictures in station
15- Keeping dogs or other animals at station
16- Failure to keep Division-Troop Orders in proper form

5.   Demerits may be given for improper use of motor equipment:
1- Unnecessary speed
2- Reckless driving
3- Failure to keep car clean
4- Failure to check motor parts
5- Failure to check body parts
6- Failure to check car equipment
7- Failure to use chains in slippery weather
8- Failure to report damage to car
9- Failure to have authorized emergency equipment in car
10- Failure to set hand brake or leave car in gear when parked
11- Carrying materials other than equipment
12- Carrying dogs in car
13- Unnecessary parking of cars in dangerous places
14- Using car for unofficial purposes

6.   For efficient application of the demerit system, certain
responsibilities must rest upon the shoulders of Officers through frequent inspection and observation; to wit: it shall be the duty of each
Zone Lieutenant to inspect each station in his zone frequently, and
enforce all regulations pertaining to the orderly operation of same.
He shall inspect each man's equipment, condition of firearms, handcuffs
complete, shield, and make note of serial number of each, at least
once each month. He may recommend demerits if condition warrants, by
submitting a report to the Troop Commander, advising member of such
infraction and causing an entry on same to be made in the blotter.
Each Lieutenant shall be responsible for all uniform personnel assigned
to his zone. In the event of any failure to enforce and conform with
such rules, he shall be considered derelict in his duty and suffer the
reduction in seniority as may be prescribed by the Superintendent.

7.   Merits may be given for outstanding performance of duty,
which will be evaluated by a Board of Officers assigned by the
Superintendent. Such merits will be rated as five merits for each
instance; except when unusual circumstances indicate that a greater
number of merits should be considered by the Superintendent. Merits
may be used to waive demerits if personnel record so indicates.

8.   District Inspectors of the Bureau of Criminal Investigation
will make frequent inspections, but not be confined to any definite

Service Record Rating   -3-   May 19, 1955

periods, but when duty may be so adjusted. They will be responsible for the enforcement and conformity of such rules applicable to members of the Bureau, and suffer penalty for failure to enforce same and subject to such action as the Superintendent may prescribe.

9.   Troop Commanders shall receive reports from Lieutenants and Inspectors recommending demerits and shall decide the weight of penalty to justify the action. It is expected that Troop Commanders shall inspect each station in their troop territory at least twice a month and observe personnel, inspect installation equipment and motor equipment. Troop Commanders may impose demerits when such infractions come under their observation and shall notify the personnel concerned in writing. Troop Commanders who fail to enforce and conform with such rules may be considered derelict in their duty and may suffer reduction in seniority as may be prescribed by the Superintendent.

10.   This order cancels and supersedes "GENERAL ORDERS M-3", dated February 17, 1955.

Francis S. McGarvey
Francis S. McGarvey,
Superintendent

21 April 1960

#	TITLE	NAME	DATE APPTD.	DATE LIEUT.	DATE DIST. INSP.	DATE CAPT.	DATE STAFF INSP.	DATE DEP. CH. INSP.	DATE CHIEF INSP.
1	Dep Supt 7/15/44	GM Searle	8/1/22	7/1/29			(7/1/30) (Dep Insp) 6/1/36	6/19/36	
2	Ch Insp	MF Dillon	6/16/23	6/15/36			6/1/47	1/31/57 (Act. Troop Comm. G 11/1/47 - 9/10/48)	8/29/57
3	Dep Insp	DF Glasheen	3/1/29	8/1/43		8/1/45		8/29/57	
4	Captain	CO Mink	7/1/34	10/1/51		2/26/59			
5	Captain	RV Annett	12/16/29			4/1/56	5/15/42		
6	Captain	GW Ashley	4/16/32	11/1/53		3/26/59			
7	Staff Insp	JJ Quinn	7/1/24		7/15/44		1/37/57		
8	Staff Insp	JW Sayers	6/1/33		10/1/51		7/17/58		
9	Staff Insp	RE Denman	6/15/36	8/1/53	8/16/54		2/25/60		
10	Captain	JP Ronan	6/16/21	5/1/33		7/15/44			
11	Captain	HT Muller	8/1/31		7/1/42	12/16/44			
12	Captain	CA Lawson	3/1/27	2/15/47	(9/15/44) (Prov.) 2/15/47	7/1/54			
13	Captain	JJ Lawson	5/1/29	(1/1/45) (Prov.) 1/1/49	5/1/51	11/16/55	2/1/55		
14	Captain	JA Steeley	12/16/25	1/1/45		1/1/49 & 8/29/57	11/16/55		
15	Captain	HM DeHollander	8/15/25	2/15/47	5/16/51	2/25/60	8/29/57		
16	Dist Insp	RJ McDowell	5/16/21	12/1/45	2/15/47				
17	Dist Insp	JC Dwyer	1/16/30	(8/16/45 Prov.) 3/16/51	7/17/58				
18	Dist Insp	WF Driscoll	7/1/36	5/1/51	2/1/55				
19	Dist Insp	HJ Sanderson	10/1/24	9/1/44	1/31/57				
20	Dist Insp	JW Russell	5/16/27	10/1/47	8/29/57				
21	Dist Insp	AS Johnson	7/16/33	5/16/51	2/25/60 (Supt. from 8/16/53 to 1/24/55)				
22	Lieutenant	CP Curtin	5/16/28	8/15/43 (2/1/47) (Reduced from Capt)		6/16/45	1/1/45		
23	Lieutenant	JA Murphy	6/1/21	2/1/44					
24	Lieutenant	EM Galvin	5/16/36	4/16/43					
25	Lieutenant	FP Dwyer	7/16/28	11/16/51					
26	Lieutenant	FA Nolan	7/16/36	11/16/51					
27	Lieutenant	C Wichmann	7/1/36	8/16/53					
28	Lieutenant	HA Scoville	7/1/31	11/1/53					
29	Lieutenant	JP Nohlen	7/15/36	11/1/53					
30	Lieutenant	HJ Berglund	7/16/31	11/1/53					
31	Lieutenant	CE Cobb	7/1/32	11/1/53					
32	Lieutenant	JJ Micklas	7/1/36	9/1/54					
33	Lieutenant	RE Sweeney	7/1/40	9/1/54					
34	Lieutenant	JC Smith	7/1/31	9/16/54					
35	Lieutenant	FJ Murphy	8/16/39	11/1/54					
36	Lieutenant	DF Roche	7/1/41	12/1/55					
37	Lieutenant	KE Weidenborner	7/1/36	12/1/55					
38	Lieutenant	LC Viehl	7/1/40	11/18/56					
39	Lieutenant	JH Smith	7/1/36	1/31/57					
40	Lieutenant	WC Keeley	7/15/36	7/4/57					
41	Lieutenant	MJ Hynes	7/1/40	7/18/57					
42	Lieutenant	AJ Robson	8/1/36	8/1/57					
43	Lieutenant	HE Blaisdell	7/15/36	8/29/57					
44	Lieutenant	WJ Sjoblom	3/16/46	7/17/58					
45	Lieutenant	WR Spelman	8/16/39	11/6/58					
46	Lieutenant	JJ Coyne	6/1/41	2/26/59					
47	Lieutenant	TH Denlea	5/16/47	4/9/59					
48	Lieutenant	HJ Ashe	6/15/36	8/13/59					
49	Lieutenant	DM McGranaghan	6/15/36	10/22/59					
50	Lieutenant	JC Miller	7/15/40	2/25/60					
51	Lieutenant	TF Darby	6/15/36	4/21/60					

PERS. 30   3-26-62

NEW YORK STATE POLICE
ALBANY

QUALIFICATIONS FOR POSITION OF TROOPER
SALARY RANGE $5200 – $7000

ALL APPLICANTS MUST POSSESS THE FOLLOWING QUALIFICATIONS:

(1) UNITED STATES CITIZENSHIP.

(2) MALE BETWEEN THE AGES OF 21 AND 29 YEARS (*candidates must have reached their 21st birthday and must not have passed their 29th birthday on the effective date of appointment. Candidates who have not passed their 20th birthday at the time of filing their application will not be permitted to participate in the examination*).

(3) HEIGHT NOT LESS THAN 5'-8'' MEASURED IN BARE FEET.

(4) WEIGHT IN PROPORTION TO GENERAL BUILD (*candidates will be rejected if overweight or underweight*). MINIMUM WEIGHT 145 – MAXIMUM 216.

(5) FREE FROM ANY PHYSICAL DEFECTS WHICH WOULD BE A HANDICAP IN THE USE OF FIREARMS OR SELF DEFENSE; NO MISSING LIMBS.

(6) PHYSICALLY STRONG, WELL PROPORTIONED, CAPABLE OF ENGAGING AND QUALIFIED TO ENGAGE IN STRENUOUS PHYSICAL EXERTION.

(7) NO DISEASE OF MOUTH OR TONGUE.

(8) CANDIDATE MUST HAVE A MINIMUM OF 16 NATURAL PERMANENT TEETH OF WHICH A MINIMUM OF 8 MUST BE IN EACH DENTAL ARCH. ALL MISSING TEETH WHICH CAUSE UNSIGHTLY SPACES OR SIGNIFICANTLY REDUCE MASTICATORY OR INCISAL EFFICIENCY MUST BE REPLACED BY BRIDGES OR PARTIAL DENTURES WHICH ARE WELL DESIGNED AND IN GOOD CONDITION AT THE TIME OF THE EXAMINATION. TEETH MUST BE FREE OF ANY UNCORRECTED DENTAL CARIES.

(9) NORMAL HEARING.

(10) EYESIGHT: NORMAL COLOR PERCEPTION AND DEPTH PERCEPTION; VISUAL ACUITY NOT LESS THAN 20/40 IN WEAKEST EYE CORRECTED TO 20/20 IN EACH EYE.

(11) GOOD MORAL CHARACTER AND HABITS AND GOOD CREDIT RECORD.

(12) MENTAL ALERTNESS AND SOUNDNESS OF MIND.

(13) MINIMUM EDUCATIONAL QUALIFICATION: GRADUATION FROM A SENIOR HIGH SCHOOL. NEW YORK STATE HIGH SCHOOL EQUIVALENCY DIPLOMA WILL BE ACCEPTED. *No other equivalency diploma will be accepted.*

(14) POSSESS CURRENT VALID LICENSE TO OPERATE A MOTOR VEHICLE (*candidate must obtain New York State License to be eligible for appointment*).

(15) NEVER CONVICTED ON ANY CRIMINAL CHARGE.

PERSONS NOT POSSESSING ALL OF THESE QUALIFICATIONS WILL NOT BE CONSIDERED AND SHOULD NOT FILE APPLICATIONS.

THIS APPLICATION MUST BE FILLED OUT IN INK OR TYPED, *IN DUPLICATE* AND SIGNED IN THE APPLICANT'S OWN HANDWRITING AND FORWARDED TO SUPERINTENDENT, NEW YORK STATE POLICE, 162 WASHINGTON AVENUE, ALBANY, NEW YORK. *Receipt of this application will not be acknowl_edged but those qualified will be notified to report for examination at a later date.*

- -

NOTE — The written examination will be held April 28, 1962 at the following locations: Albany – Bay Shore – Binghamton – Buffalo – Elmira – Glens Falls – Middletown – Olean New York City – Plattsburgh – Poughkeepsie – Rochester – Syracuse – Utica – Watertown

INDICATE BY CIRCLING ONE LOCATION WHERE YOU DESIRE TO TAKE THE EXAMINATION. RETURN THIS PORTION OF THE SHEET WITH YOUR COMPLETED APPLICATION.

★ **HEADQUARTERS**

Connecting all Departments
162 Washington Ave., Albany............518 HO 5-4721
★ State Police Scientific Laboratory
    8 Nolan Rd., Albany 5................518 HE 8-3578

Troop A

★ Headquarters, Batavia...............716 FI 3-2200	
Substations:	
★ Athol Springs.........................716 NA 7-2311	
East Aurora.............................716 NL 2-1611	
★ Clarence.............................716 RL 9-6831	
Grand Island ....(Buffalo) 716 RR 3-4511	
★ Westfield............................716 FA 6-3031	
Silver Creek..........................716 YE 4-2552	
★ Lewiston ....(Niagara Falls) 716 BU 5-9611	
★ Wrights Corners ......(Lockport) 716 434-5588	
★ Wellsville ....Wellsville 1000	
Belfast ....Belfast 10	
★ Allegany...................(Olean) 716 373-2550	
★ Falconer............................716 JA 4-7189	
Franklinville ....Franklinville 5872	
★ Avon................................716 WA 6-3248	
Castile...............................716 HY 3-5130	
★ Painted Post........................607 XN 2-3101	
Wayland...............................716 PA 8-3832	
★ Clarkson............................716 NE 7-5311	
★ Henrietta ....(Rochester) 716 BR 1-4646	
★ Webster.............................716 TR 2-1988	
Albion................................716 LT 9-5963	
Chautauqua 2352	
★ Bath 607 776-2191	
★ Hornell 607 324-3995	

**Troop Organization
1966-70**

■ **Troop Hdqts.**
● **Zone**

BIBLIOGRAPHY

REFERENCE:
NEWYORK STATE POLICE ANNUAL REPORTS
NEW YORK STATE POLICE – 80TH ANNIVERSARY
HISTORY OF THE NEW YORK STATE POLICE
INSIDE DETECTIVE MAGAZINE – JULY 1965
MASTERDETECTIVE MAGAZINE – JUNE 1961
REAL DETECTIVE MAGAZINE - #102, 1969
TROOPER MAGAZINES - VARIED

NEWSPAPERS
BATAVIA DAILY NEWS
BUFFALO COURIER EXPRESS
BUFFALO EVENING NEWS
DUNKIRK EVENING OBSERVER
OLEAN TIMES UNION
ROCHESTER DEMOCRAT & CHRONICLE
WELLSVILLE DAILY REPORTER

PUBLIC LIBRARIES:
BATAVIA RICHMOND LIBRARY
MEDINA PUBLIC LIBRARY
OLEAN PUBLIC LIBRARY

COUNTY CLERK'S OFFICE'S
ALLEGANY COUNTY
GENESEE COUNTY
ORLEANS COUNTY

PERSONAL INTERVIEWS:
JAMES BEERS – NYSP RETIRED
JOSEPH CASCIANO – NYSP RETIRED
JOSEPH CHRISTIAN – NYSP RETIRED
PETER DETOY – NYSP RETIRED
EUGENE FECHTER – NYSP RETIRED
DOUGLAS HEDGES – NYSP RETIRED
JOSEPH HEILIG – FORMER MEMBER NYSP
GARY HORTON, GENESEE COUNTY PUBLIC DEFENDER
GEORGE MILLS – NYSP RETIRED
DONALD MUNCH – NYSP RETIRED
THOMAS PHILIPS – NYSP RETIRED
ROBERT STODDARD- FORMER NYSP
FRANK STROLLO – NYS CORRECTIONS RETIRED
KENNETH TROIDL – NYSP RETIRED

ABOUT THE AUTHOR

Albert S. Kurek has spent 40 years in law enforcement. He served in the United States Marine Corp from 1957 to 1960, the New York State Police from 1962 to 1985 and as a Special Agent with the Defense Security Service from 1985 to 2002. A lifelong resident of Western New York, he is a graduate of Genesee Community college and the State University College at Buffalo, New York.

He enlisted in the State Police on June 18, 1962 attending the state police school held at Oneonta, New York during that summer. He was assigned to SP Horseheads where the very capable Trooper Kenneth Epler provided his on the job training. During the next three years, he was assigned at SP Albion, SP Allegany and again at Albion. In 1965, he requested and was transferred to SP Batavia patrol where he remained until 1980, when he was detailed to the first Hazmat detail and re-assigned to SP Clarence. While at Batavia, he worked two duty tours on the Loadometer Detail and was elected to the PBA, as the Troop "A" delegate in 1979. He served as the PBA Vice President under President John Canfield until his retirement in 1985. An avid New York Trooper history buff, he maintains a mini-museum at his home with several one of a kind item's. He also has in excess of 100 albums containing trooper photo and newspaper articles.

Printed in the United States
61197LVS00002B/79-306